# James Jesus Angleton

# James Jesus Angleton,

## THE CIA, AND THE CRAFT OF COUNTERINTELLIGENCE

MICHAEL HOLZMAN

UNIVERSITY OF MASSACHUSETTS PRESS Amherst

Printed in the United States of America

LC 2008003106
ISBN 978-1-55849-650-7 (paper), 649-1 (library cloth)

Designed by Richard Hendel
Set in Adobe Minion and Meta Book by dix!
Printed and bound by Thomson-Shore, Inc.

Library of Congress Cataloging-in-Publication Data

Holzman, Michael Howard, 1946–
James Jesus Angleton, the CIA, and the craft of
counterintelligence / Michael Holzman.
p. cm.
Includes bibliographical references and index.
ISBN 978-1-55859-650-7 (pbk. : alk. paper)—
ISBN 978-1-55849-649-1 (library cloth : alk. paper)
1. Angleton, James, 1917–1987. 2. United States. Central
Intelligence Agency—20th century. 3. United States.
Central Intelligence
JK468.16H65 2008
327.12730092—dc22
2008003106

British Library Cataloguing in Publication data
are available.

*For Jane*

# Contents

# Preface

> *What I shall write now follows a different plan, supplementing the previous formal chronicle with a disclosure of what really happened.*
> *Procopius,* Secret History

What really happened in his time, according to Procopius, was that the Empire had been taken over by demons who wished to inflict as much misery as possible on the human race. There are those who would argue, similarly, that the official and public history of the United States during the Cold War conceals a secret history of "what really happened," a history which could be documented from files kept in the basement of the Central Intelligence Agency. Some believe that this, too, is a story about demons; others believe that it is a story about honorable men. "The history of the CIA is the secret history of the Cold War," wrote Thomas Powers in *The Man Who Kept the Secrets: Richard Helms and the CIA*. "So it wasn't just himself and the CIA which Helms was protecting when he kept the secrets. It was the stability of a quarter-century of political arrangements, the notion of a Free World, a 'history' of American response to 'aggression,' a stark contrast of American 'morality' with Communist 'expedience,' an illusion of American rectitude unclouded by reality. The true history is not the antithesis of the child's history; it is not all crime, greed, and imperial reaching. But the true history is a long way from what we tell ourselves on the Fourth of July" (344).

Powers assumes that the "true" history is the secret history, which is tantamount to assuming that public, official histories are not "true," that official histories are told from the viewpoint of official entities and therefore serve the purposes of those entities. In some cases, indeed, official histories make claims that are demonstrably untrue about specific events. In many cases they are filled with accounts of bureaucratic activities while containing little about the causes and consequences of those official actions. For these reasons Powers is right: as long as official histories are written for official purposes, we will need secret histories—not that the latter, any more than the former, reveal "what really happened," but because they can sometimes tell us what *else* happened and add something to our understanding of the motivations of individuals, as well as the reasons of state, that contributed to the events of the time. Or, in the case of this study, the events of our time.

The child's history is what is taught in the schools. Its truth (or, if we shy away from such words, its accuracy) is important, as the accumulation of what is taught in school, and in universities, shapes the consciousness of those who in their turn will contribute to the shaping of society itself. The Jesuits famously claimed that they would answer for the lives of the children whom they had educated. And it was said that the battle of Waterloo was won on the fields of Eton. These are received ideas; they seem natural enough. Perhaps that is because they are true. Perhaps that is because they are part of our own ideological formation.

How are we to know? We might try what passes for an experiment in the historical sciences: to devise a narrative about an exemplary case, to see if it coheres. In order to do so, we will need to identify a system of education that is fairly singular, and some sort of accessible *subsequent* life that we can examine to determine if it was a *consequent* life. Are those educated by Jesuits, who become, say, diplomats or military officers, given to making decisions in such a way as to make their Jesuitical training obvious? Are their decisions different from those made by people who were formed by different educational systems? We could look through old yearbooks from some Loyola High School, then trace the lives of graduates with official careers. Or, to add a certain density to the experiment, we could look in other places.

For example, there was the school of the New Criticism at Yale, beginning in the 1930s. Its catchphrases—moral center, unity, close reading, ambiguity—are part of the heritage of intellectual life in this country, and, through a certain cousinship of ideas (or ideology), that of Britain. Given the "moral" power of the New Criticism, we might be able to test the theory that education can be intellectually formative, in a strong sense, by looking at the career of someone who was educated in the ways of New Criticism—and who did not pursue a career in English departments, but undertook some other line of work, one that had direct effects on the world.

Having moved from the Jesuits to the New Critics as the generators of our ideological influences, where, then, should we look for public effects? The secret world of the Central Intelligence Agency seems an appropriate choice. That world was strongly tied to a relatively small number of educational institutions, Yale being one of the most important. (See Bourdieu, *The Field of Cultural Production*, 124.)

This study began with such considerations, with thoughts about the economic justification for the comparatively large investments in such courses as freshman English classes (and "daily themes"), and with the common impulse to make some sense of one's own times and experiences. As one historian of another aspect of these matters puts it, "If a theory of education was to be a theory of government in the making, the application of abstract principles acquired in schooling was indispensable in order that they not merely remained a 'mixed mass of ideas' floating in the mind, but were selectively acted upon by the learner in his response to the demands of state" (Viswanathan, *Masks of Conquest*, 90).

And so this study has come to rest on the singular career of James Angleton, chief of the Counterintelligence Staff of the Central Intelligence Agency from 1954 to 1976, with the argument that sufficient attention to such a singularity might be more broadly illuminating. Robin Winks first called attention to Angleton as a figure at the intersection of the New Criticism and counterintelligence and was followed in this by William H. Epstein, who argued that the New Criticism was the source of "those modes of analysis that came to be associated with anti-communist counter-intelligence." Specifically, Epstein claimed, "Angleton's approach to counter-intelligence can be characterized, almost in his own language, as 'the practical criticism of ambiguity,' a phrase derived from the titles of two of the most influential texts of formalist criticism, Richards' *Practical Criticism* and Empson's *Seven Types of Ambiguity*" ("Counter-Intelligence," 83). This study follows the lead of Winks and Epstein and seeks to establish the study of secret intelligence as a realm of the history of ideas, crossing what Pierre Bourdieu called the "most disputed frontier of all," that which "separates the field of cultural production and the field of power" (43).

Research involving the Central Intelligence Agency has particular limitations and has by now established a certain tradition. There are materials that have been released by the Central Intelligence Agency and other governmental institutions. There are materials that are released in response to Freedom of Information Act appeals. There are interviews with named and unnamed sources. There is conventional archival research and readings of previous work in the field. Much of this is as unreliable as and more often intentionally misleading than sources in other branches of historical study. When picking up a new book about the CIA, one finds oneself asking: Who is the ventriloquist? Which of the interviewees has used the opportunity to "play" the interviewer? Thus it has been with some ambivalence that I have imposed upon the generosity of former CIA officials who have been willing to talk, write, or communicate via e-mail about James Angleton. None have spoken on condition of anonymity. Members of the Committee and its staff have spoken with me about the work of the Church Committee. Carole Minor, then at the Center for Intelligence Studies, was helpful in locating some documents, and equally helpful in informing me that other documents could not yet be released. Concerning other primary sources, I have had some pleasant days working in the archives at the New York

Public Library, Yale, Harvard, Stanford, Princeton, and the National Security Archive at George Washington University, and found the invisible archivists at the headquarters of the Federal Bureau of Investigation perhaps more helpful than they realized. The overwhelming riches of the National Archives have supplemented the others. Concerning secondary sources, there is an enormous literature on the CIA and its predecessor, the Office of Strategic Services. I have benefited from this, as is evident in the citations. There have been two biographies of James Angleton, one by Tom Mangold, the other by David Martin, both focusing on the so-called Molehunt; there is also the book of that name by David Wise. There is a nearly book-length chapter devoted to Angleton in Robin Winks's *Cloaks and Gowns*, particularly valuable for the Yale background. I have found it useful to check these against one another and against other, more specialized studies, such as Timothy Naftali's and Edward Epstein's, as well as against primary sources.

Many friends and colleagues have read and commented on parts of the manuscript at various stages of its production, principally Lois Feuer, Terence Hawkes, Steven Lavine, Lewis Lapham, Gerald and Evangeline Monroe, Christopher Norris, Susan Plum, and someone who wishes to remain anonymous. They have my thanks and apologies. Jane MacKillop has read the entire manuscript many times, patiently providing criticism, support, and encouragement. Finally, I would like to thank the extraordinarily patient editorial staff at the University of Massachusetts Press: Clark Dougan, Carol Betsch, and, in particular, Mary Bellino.

# James Jesus Angleton

# 1

## The Players Are Introduced

Senator Frank Church chaired hearings in 1975 concerning "Governmental Operations with Respect to Intelligence Activities." Great public trials—or their close equivalent, congressional hearings such as those of the Church Committee—are a characteristic activity of public life in the United States. The scene of these affairs is theatrical. They are entertainments, mechanisms for incremental change, sometimes educational morality plays. They both instruct and delight. The hearings take place in the heavily ornamented, high-ceilinged rooms of the Capitol, Roman eagles and gilded Corinthian orders striking the note of Shakespearean historical tragedy. The senators in their dark suits and starched white collars, seated at the back of the stage in a raised and heavily carved row of seats, look down across a considerable space at the low, green baize-covered, insubstantial table behind which the witnesses are placed, facing their interrogators from folding chairs. Young aides come and go through secret doors behind the senators, carrying notes, kneeling to whisper in senatorial ears, as the senatorial eyes continue to stare forward, toward the witnesses, or, perhaps, over the heads of the witnesses, to the audience and the cameras at the back of the chamber.

One of the most striking witnesses to come before the Church Committee was a tall, stooped man, then in his mid-fifties, dressed in a dark bespoke Savile Row suit, his large glasses both calling attention to his eyes and concealing them. This was James Angleton, as often as not referred to as "the legendary spymaster, James Jesus Angleton," with a certain emphasis on that second given name, a name unusual in the United States, although common enough in Mexico. Angleton was Mexican American, but as it was not the custom in his time to note such matters in the circles in which he moved, the name was usually mispronounced, if pronounced at all, and simply added a certain increment to the mystery. He had, it was said, read all letters passing between the Soviet bloc and the United States for a generation. He had, it was said, violated the founding charter of the Central Intelligence Agency by overseeing the infiltration of antiwar groups in the United States in the 1960s and 1970s. It was said that he had helped found the Mossad, the Israeli secret service. It was said that he had helped rig the Italian elections in 1948; infiltrated the Vatican; funded the non-Communist European trade unions; stolen the text of Khrushchev's secret denunciation of Stalin; been a friend of Kim Philby; kept the CIA free of any American Philbys—and, according to some, had nearly destroyed the Agency in order to do so.

The opening exchange between Angleton and a member of the committee, Senator Walter Mondale, had a bantering quality:

SENATOR MONDALE: Now, you are an attorney?
MR. ANGLETON: No, I am not, sir.
SENATOR MONDALE: Well, that might be an asset.
MR. ANGLETON: That is my cover, Senator.[1]

We might give this innocuous exchange something of a closer reading. Angleton was not an attorney, but he had attended Harvard Law School. He was very familiar with assets of various kinds, that being a term of art in the intelligence community, but, of course, not-being-an-attorney is not an asset in that sense; it is, as Angleton corrects Mondale, a cover, as was the banter. At the end of his career, Angleton appears on the public stage for the first time, and marks that appearance with a telling rhetorical signature: ambiguity.

The atmosphere of the times was one of high ethical concern. The Vietnam War was finally over; the Watergate hearings had done much to vindicate the system of government that the war and the Nixon administration had seemed to call into question. A series of revelations concerning CIA covert activities had appeared in the same newspapers that had uncovered Watergate, often over the same bylines. It had seemed natural, in those times, for Senator Church to comment on the hearings in this fashion: "Twenty-five years ago, this country had a matchless moral position from which it exercised immense leadership and influence in the world. Anything the United States stood for was automatically endorsed by three quarters of the governments of the world. Now we have had 25 years of manipulation by methods that were plainly copied from the KGB: coercion, false propaganda, bribery, abduction, attempted assassination, and where are we at the end of that 25 years?"[2]

The issue, for Church, was, he said, one of ethics, or morals. As with many Americans before him, Senator Church believed that there had been a time when American public life had been carried on at a level different from, and ethically superior to, that of other nations, and for that reason those other nations, as Gentiles should, had recognized our leadership. So had President Wilson believed; so, before him, had some of the generation of Henry James, and so some of each generation back to that of John Winthrop. And then, the story goes, after this long period of high virtue, we had been corrupted by

Europeans, and, like the heroine of a James novel, adopted their styles, and lost both their respect and our own. It was a compelling story. It was a story with all the marks of truth: unity, seriousness, timelessness, densely allusive to the masterpieces of the Western tradition. It was a story that Angleton himself might have told, might have heard in Rapallo from his first mentor, Ezra Pound. That it was a story that existed entirely on the plane of myth—or ideology—was of little moment under the circumstances. Myths, ideologies, are not unreal; they have their effects, as they have their uses.

Another senator asked Angleton, who until a few months earlier had been chief of the Counterintelligence Staff of the CIA, to define his specialty.

> SENATOR MORGAN: [W]ould you again draw the distinction between counterintelligence and intelligence gathering?
>
> MR. ANGLETON: In the ultimate, they are about the same thing. Counterintelligence is more or less all of the programs of which the distillate is counterespionage. In other words, the sum total of counterintelligence activity includes dossiers, identification of individuals, travel control and a whole series of other dossier items. It forms the counterintelligence base. From that can be developed a product which is counterespionage, the dealing in confrontation with other intelligence services: as a rule, dealing with their aggressive aspects, whether it be subversion, whether it be espionage, and in certain instances in the world of double agents, dealing with their counterintelligence.[3]

A bit later another senator tried his hand at a definition, only to be corrected:

> SENATOR BAKER: [C]ounterintelligence was to protect our intelligence resources?
>
> MR. ANGLETON: It was to penetrate and frustrate the espionage and subversion from outside.[4]

Counterintelligence is the activity of gathering intelligence so as to confront, penetrate, and frustrate other intelligence agencies, "and in certain instances . . . [deal] with their counterintelligence." It is, as Angleton had famously quoted T. S. Eliot, a wilderness of mirrors. It is where Angleton had lived since 1943.

Like Senator Church, Angleton believed in a theory of decline in the virtue of the nation, but he identified that virtue, not with prestige alone, but with political, if not military, power: "When I left the Army, as many of us did, " Angleton replied, "I believed that we were in the dawn of a millennium. When I look at the map today and the weakness of power of this country, that is what shocks me."[5] Angleton had left the Army in 1947 as head of counterintelligence in Italy for the Office of Strategic Services (OSS). Looking at the map then, he would have seen Europe, Japan, and China in ruins, Britain bankrupt, the Soviet Union triumphant but devastated. Only the United States was untouched by war, wealthy, in sole possession of the overwhelming power of the atomic bomb. The millennium, of which this imperium was the dawn, was delayed by the onset of "a secret war that has continued since World War II"[6] between the United States and not just the Soviet Union but the entire "Communist bloc" of states.

> I think that as far as the bloc is concerned, you have a unified approach to the United States as the main enemy. They are bound together by ideological ties. There has been a process of de-Stalinization which was concluded in 1959, which reconciled vast differences, and which in essence was a return to Leninism. There was enunciated the policy of the main enemy, and the main enemy was the United States . . .
>
> The nature of the threat rests within some thousands of pages of interrogation of very-high-level Soviet and bloc intelligence officers who were, in turn, very close in their activities to the political guidance of the Central Committees. And this cohesiveness dates from the period of 1959, when the intelligence services were changed from being the protectors or the preservers of the cult of personality of Stalin, and reverted back again to the days of Duchinsky and the revolution and Lenin, where every intelligence operation has a political objective.
>
> And it ties together with the entire philosophy—and I do not base this on reading information available at the corner drugstore; this comes from the interrogation of individuals who were in the system and had positions of high responsibility in intelligence—and the underpinning of those regimes are their intelligence and security services.[7]

Angleton's interpretations of his time, as he stated them to the senatorial committee, were in the first instance ideological. He was not an analyst of political history like Kennan or Kissinger. He looked at the world around him, and saw it as the scene of ideological (rather than political or military) struggle. Angleton took an ideology to be something like the New Critical idea of a poem: "unified" and "cohesive," a set of ideas powerful enough to determine events—and seeing a single ideology prevailing from the Pacific to the Adriatic, he concluded that that entire vast territory was united in that "secret war" against the United States. There was no real Sino-Soviet split; even Tito's independence was suspect. Angleton's position in this regard has been ridiculed. There was obviously a Sino-Soviet split; Tito's was obviously a different system than that of the Soviet Union. But Angleton was not a fantasist; like Lenin, he believed in the preponderance of ideology. If two groups share the same ideology, they are in some deep sense the same.

Operationally, Angleton believed that the only reliable sources of information concerning "the bloc" were to be obtained from the intelligence and security services of those countries, that is, from defectors. From which it would follow that, when the Soviets wanted reliable information about the United States, the place they would look would be the CIA. And it would follow that the penetration of the CIA would logically be the highest priority of the Soviet intelligence services. The person in charge of frustrating such attempted penetrations, in this scenario, Angleton's scenario, would have particularly awesome responsibilities. From 1954 to 1975 that person was James Angleton. The secret war was indeed a "looking glass" for the various intelligence services involved, each gazing at the other and finding its own image; hence, it is hardly surprising that the history of the CIA might be described as "25 years of manipulation by methods that were plainly copied from the KGB: coercion, false propaganda, bribery, abduction, attempted assassination," except that the modeling worked both ways, and both had drawn on a figure first delineated by Britain, the progenitor of the Great Game.

There is much evidence that during the Vietnam War the basic guarantees of the Bill of Rights essential for a free political system—freedom of speech, freedom of assembly, freedom of the press—were suspended for all those actually or potentially opposed to the government's policy. Similarly, those guarantees were also suspended for those actively engaged in the effort to extend civil liberties to African Americans. For some people, those thought by governmental agencies to be leaders of the antiwar and civil rights activities, the basic rights of economic and physical security, including freedom from the threat of bodily harm, were also violated, and preparations were made for imprisonments in concentration camps on the scale of the incarceration of ethnic Japanese during the Second World War. As it is difficult to argue that freedom of speech, say, exists if it is only allowed for those who agree with the government, it must be said that during this period these rights were not suspended only for individuals, but were in fact suspended for the country as a whole, as surely as they would have been if the Congress had voted the Executive wartime emergency powers on the scale of those given Lincoln, Wilson, Roosevelt, and the second President Bush. That in fact no such vote was held would indicate that the actions of the government during this period were illegal—unconstitutional. There had been, in effect, what the Peruvians call an "auto-coup": the government itself overthrowing the rule of law. And yet, it was not perceived as such at the time, and it is not generally now seen in that way. School textbooks do not refer to the "Johnson and Nixon dictatorships"; there were few trials of government officials for their actions; few of the laws and executive orders of the time were rescinded on the basis of the illegal activities of the day. The persecutions of the 1960s and 1970s revealed, as did the persecutions supported by the Truman and Eisenhower administrations misleadingly known as McCarthyism, that relatively few Americans live political lives, and fewer, beyond those, care whether it is possible to do so. Those persecutions (and those of the first years of the twenty-first century) also demonstrated that Americans are content to have the basic human rights of their neighbors violated, up to and including the point of officially instigated, if not officially executed, murder, so long as those whose rights are violated and whose lives are disrupted—or ended—can be portrayed as "other" in some way and the role of the government hidden.

And, finally, there is implication in all this of the American university system, which, as in the 1950s, presented an appearance of opposition to the persecutors while in many cases acting as their agents. The cruder aspects of this complicity included the use of police by university officials against the young people in their care; improper firings of faculty at the instigation of the government; and the corruption of the hiring and promotion system, by which it became accepted as "normal" to consider the subject and methods of a scholar's research and teaching against ideological criteria. Thousands of university officials—teachers and administrators—acted for the secret intelligence services of the state as recruiters, advisors, and informants. Entire fields were reoriented toward subjects and methods of use to the state through the steady deployment of budgetary, hiring, and promotion policies, which, at first effected in one or a few universities, soon affected most. This corruption of the educational system was one product of the Cold War—perhaps not the most important, viewed objectively, but sufficiently important for those who believe that the nature of society itself is continuously created by the experience of its young people in schools and universities. At one point there are children learning a child's version of history from their teachers, undergraduates learning specific forms of thought from their professors; at another point there are, as Senator Church put it, "25 years of manipulation by methods that were plainly copied from the KGB: coercion, false propaganda, bribery, abduction, attempted assassination." The points are connected; one thing follows from the other.

# 2

# Yale English

*Jan. 14, 1939*
*Dear Mr. Angleton*
*I was so pleased to hear from you. I am very glad you have started writing on your own and I am sure I wish you a long and happy literary life.*
*John Powys*

In 1939, an unusually worldly Yale sophomore published two poems in a new campus magazine:

*Pianola à 2 francs*

Pousse un bouton
salaud,
seulement un jeton
de deux francs,
une salée pour cinq,
écoute ça salaud ?
C'est oripeauswing-
musique
sensuel mouvement.
Vois-tu ces hanches
en poire,
balançantes?
Allant retournant
une tournée, une tournée
tapant et battant
duvet-lèvres
flouchantonnant
si doucereux sente . . .
Salaud, c'est toi
qui l'a fait,
toi et ton
sale petit jeton.

*Caresse primordiale*

Trait de pinceau
esquissé en vermeil,
deux pétales muets,
cherchant,
ouvrent à trouver
les siens
intimes
en flammettes . . .
ce fruit
de la connaissance,
elle chuchote
doucement,
c'est très bon
n'est-ce pas?

Which could be translated as:

*The player piano costs two francs*

Push a button,
bastard,
just a two-franc token—
a set for five.
Are you listening, bastard?
It's tinsel swing
music—
a sensual movement.
Do you see these hips?
Pear-shaped
balances
Going and coming
turn and turn again
tapping and hitting
feather-lips
crooning
so sweet, feel it
Bastard, you've done it
you and your
dirty little token.

*Primordial Caress*

A trace of the paintbrush
sketched in filigree,
two mute petals,
looking,
opening to find
their
intimates
in small flames . . .
This fruit
of knowledge,
she whispers
sweetly,
It is very good,
isn't it?

The poet, James Angleton, was the son of James Hugh Angleton, known as Hugh Angleton, an adventurer who alternated between careers in business and in the military. The elder Angleton had taken part in Pershing's expedition into Mexico in pursuit of Pancho Villa, during which he met and married Carmen Mercedes Moreno of Nogales, in the northern Mexican state of Sonora. The border between the United States and Mexico in that region was, and is, famously permeable. Their son returned to the area throughout his life, marrying into a wealthy Tucson family, the d'Autremonts, which, among other things, allowed him to maintain contact with his mother's relatives a few miles across the desert in Nogales.

Cicely d'Autremont Angleton said of her husband's maternal grandmother, "She was a woman with great dignity, an individualist with a strong personality, who would not let anyone boss her around. She was a saintly woman, all her family loved her. She lived in poverty, but she never cared. She was very bright, but had no formal education. Her intellect was along intuitive and emotional lines . . . Jim was like her. He learned his patience from her, together with a strong fatalism, a Mexican Indian trait, which held that you cannot change destiny, and that you accept hardship. Jim's mother was very smart, too. She had no schooling, but she had this incredible family trait of good intuition. Jim got this from her, too. This came from the Latin side."[1] Cicely Angleton was sketching her husband's character in this account of his mother and her family—intelligent, intuitive, fatalistic, "an individualist with a strong personality." She points to matters that seemed important to her in retrospect: the family's poverty, its ethnic identification as "Mexican Indian," questions of education.

Early in 1917, after the Pershing interlude, Hugh Angleton took his wife home to Idaho, where he began a career with the National Cash Register Company. Hugh and Carmen Angleton had four children in Idaho: James Jesus, almost immediately (December 9, 1917); Hugh Rolla two years later; then Carmen and Dolores. From an early twenty-first-century point of view there is hardly anything more American than to be the child of Carmen Moreno of Nogales and Hugh Angleton of Boise, and there is nothing surprising in Cicely Angleton's comment in the 1980s that "Jim was a Chicano, and I loved him for it. I never saw anyone as Mexican as he was. He was a Latino, an Apache; he was a gut fighter."[2] But at the beginning of the twentieth century these matters were looked at differently. During his Idaho childhood, James Angleton had some experience of local prejudices. In later life he never used his middle name.

Hugh Angleton had begun his business career in a Horatio Alger vein. There are stories of muleback cash register deliveries to isolated frontier towns, and—with the boom and the modernization of the 1920s—a gradual rise through the National Cash Register Company ranks, first to sales manager and then to a vice presidency for international operations in Dayton (ca. 1927).[3] In 1933 he went to Italy to inspect the NCR operations there, liked what he saw, and—in lieu of a promotion—bought the Italian franchise from the company, moving his family to Milan in December 1933, when their eldest son was sixteen. There they lived on the Corso Venezia in the Art Nouveau Palazzo Castiglioni. Hugh Angleton became president of the American Chamber of Commerce in Italy, the center of a network of connections between U.S. and Italian business, on the one hand, and the Italian and U.S. governments on the other. It was a very long way from Sonora and Boise to the palazzo on the Corso Venezia and all that went with it: the vacations in the Haute-Savoie; the Masonic friendships with the important people of the Fascist zenith; the diplomatic friendship of the American ambassador, William Phillips; and the Rotary business connections with corporate peers from other American multinationals, including IBM's Thomas Watson.[4] This was all very familiar: the Masons, Rotary, the Chamber of Commerce—a continuation of Main Street in Dayton; on the other hand, Milan is not in Ohio. Hugh Angleton traveled widely in France and

Central Europe, met with the German and American naval attachés in Rome, and generally kept track of matters at the boundary between politics and business. The tall, busy, athletic, extroverted, quintessentially American father; the polyglot close-knit family around the Mexican mother in the palazzo; the comings and goings of those years (business trips, vacations, Boy Scout Jamborees in Hungary and Scotland) formed a background to James Angleton's early life markedly unlike that of many of his contemporaries.[5]

The Angleton boys were sent to England for their schooling, where "the course of studies in English public schools was designed to foster those leadership qualities required of a governing elite: independent thinking, a strong sense of personal identity, and an ability to make decisions on one's own authority. Making men leaders also meant that they had to be marked off from the rest of society."[6] For James Angleton this process began at Chartridge Hill House in Buckinghamshire, then continued at Malvern College in Worcestershire, from 1933 to 1936, where he would have been able to contemplate the ruins of the priory and add some French and German to his mother's Mexican Spanish and his father's business Italian.[7] The English public schools have had their own versions of provincialism, but by this time Angleton was collecting environments; no matter how limited each might have seemed in itself, as experiences they summed into a considerable cosmopolitanism for a young man. One of his biographers thought that "Angleton's British period gave him moral focus, and also influenced his appearance and style. He absorbed Old World courtesy and the quiet good manners never deserted him . . . He certainly adopted conservative clothing like a uniform. In hottest Israel or deepest Australian outback, Angleton remained in collar, tie, and dark business suit. He normally bought two or three English-cut suits from his tailor every year, demanding only the best material, one hundred percent wool, worsted cashmere, or mohair."[8] Layers of personality: Mexico, Idaho, Ohio, Italy, England.

It could have been at Malvern that Angleton encountered *Gerontion*, the poem Reed Whittemore read at Angleton's funeral nearly half a century later. Stripped of the closet drama of "Madame de Tornqist, in the dark room," and "Hakagawa, bowing among the Titians," the lines can be read as the reflections of a mind that had gone to school with Donne, forced inward by the self-examinations of a secularized Puritanism, examinations in which one can never award oneself full marks, can only hope for undeserving forgiveness (after such knowledge). As such, they would appeal to young men of the generation that thought of the World War as belonging, like the civilization it had destroyed, to their fathers—and would continue to appeal, taking on completely other meanings, as that generation found itself in a fifty years war, one fought, as Angleton so often emphasized, in an Eliotonian wilderness of mirrors. Ten more years in Dayton before a move to England might have produced the expatriate consciousness of another Eliot or Pound, but the effect of an adolescence in Europe appeared to have made Angleton somehow more unselfconsciously American, part of a generation that would see itself not so much at school with European culture as the heir, and then natural possessor, of that culture.

Angleton appeared at Yale in 1937 in the costume of a young Englishman, with, for a few years, something of that accent, before Boise resurfaced. Multilingual, well-traveled, with this extraordinarily dense background, he lived in New Haven as if the purpose of that old evangelical college was to support poetry and poets. (The campus was at that moment, in the midst of the Depression, the raw construction site of the world's largest group of buildings in the Gothic style—1930s New Haven Gothic.) The role he played was familiar enough in other settings, that played by Ford and Pound and Eliot himself in certain moods—the impresario, the agent, of verse. It was only the location that was a bit odd, and the youth of this agent of the muses. (But Lincoln Kirstein was doing much the same thing up at Harvard with *Hound and Horn.*) Angleton had a gift for making himself known to those interested in his interests, which might have been a result of observing his father's construction of commercial-political networks in Italy. His friend Whittemore said, "I saw him as a great salesman and publishing entrepreneur. He got the salesmanship from his father. He was good at playing up to people to win favor. He took pictures of Pound and Cummings. This was a form of flattery."[9] It was an effective form of flattery. Some of the photographs were published in *Time*. In any case, the attentions of this handsome and intelligent young man with his exotic background was itself a form of flattery. The roles were traditional, comfortable, for all concerned.[10]

Almost immediately upon his arrival in the United States, Angleton was in correspondence with the poets who interested him; for example, William Carlos Williams, who commented on one of the poems quoted above, "The small portrait is very french Figaro Figaro Figaro Figaro Figaro. I enjoy it and see no harm in it. I do them in like manner from time to time and believe the exercise is good—it makes the mind nimble, trains in condensation, pitter patter and sharp vision."[11]

Angleton's French poems were published in a luxe college literary magazine, *Vif*, which called itself a "Revue Francaise Inter-Universitaire." The sixteen pages of vol. 1, no. 1 (Février 1939) included "Les Modes de Vassar," an article by E. Reed Whittemore, *fils*, reproductions of works by Legér, and so forth. The masthead informed the readers (who doubtless already knew this) that it was a joint production of Yale, Vassar, and Mount Holyoke students, with a staff that included as "Redacteur en Chef" James J. Angleton, whose "Note du redacteur en chef" read as follows: "*Vif* is new. It is a magazine issued without any pretensions, to serve as the connecting link and as a stimulant between those at American universities who love the French language. We summon the goodwill of some readers, for we guarantee against too severe criticism, and we call for the collaboration of others, for we have confidence in these studies and these sensitive articles, agreeable and interesting."[12] This inaugural issue included congratulatory letters to *Vif* from, among others, William C. Bullitt, then, as U.S. Ambassador to France, otherwise occupied with putting in place an intelligence network against the coming war. Poetry and Yale, and the worlds of high politics and secret intelligence exemplified by Ambassador Bullitt, are lines that intersected, however faintly, for Angleton as early as that first issue of *Vif.*

One might argue, more generally, that these matters—art and education and the varieties of the active life—are always continuous, both within themselves and with one another. Looking with sufficient care at any of them will eventually lead the observer to the others. This is hardly a novel thought. For example, it is a commonplace that not only what but the way in which people are taught to think in school *matters*, and may affect their actions in the world long after they have left school. Or, to quote something written about the same time as Angleton's poems and Bullitt's letter, there is a "close relationship of educational theory and political theory. One would indeed be surprised to find the educational system and the political system of any country in complete disaccord"[13] One would, indeed, contend that such a division for any length of time is impossible. Eliot went on to argue in *The Idea of a Christian Society* that "a nation's system of education is much more important than its system of government; only a proper system of education can unify the active and the contemplative life, action and speculation, politics and the arts." On the other hand he warned that, in the less than ideal world of the 1930s, "the next step to be taken by the clericalism of secularism, is the inculcation of the political principles approved by the party in power,"[14] a step which Eliot presumably found objectionable, but which was taken, as a matter of course, by his academic disciples on both sides of the Atlantic, as was the tradition.

Yale occupied a highly specific position in American life in the early twentieth century. It was not as patrician or as cosmopolitan as Harvard, nor was it as provincial and class-bound as Princeton.[15] (Allen Dulles, Angleton's great patron, did well academically at Princeton; Kennan, the theoretician and sometime puppet master of the Cold War, did not, but neither seems to have been much affected by their undergraduate studies.)[16] Yale in those years was large enough to contain more than one world: that of the secret societies, that of a lingering clerical tradition, that of scholars of a donnish cut respected, in their way, even by the more social or athletic Yale men. Of course the balance among these factors changed as the century went on. While the New Haven life at the beginning of the century of as significant a figure as W. Averell Harriman could be narrated at length without reference to courses or professors, William F. Buckley's mid-century memoir, as critical as it is, reads as something of an annotated course catalogue. Even before the great transformation occasioned by the GI Bill and the arrival of de facto federal funding, and women, Yale served students from a range of backgrounds; serving them, to be sure, then as now, differently. It may not be too much to say that Harriman's Yale, for example, like his Groton, was *employed* by the Harriman family to deliver certain results—in the manner of a tennis coach they might have employed—results known in advance, through methods basically known, through methods transparent to Harriman and his family. And then Yale, for a generation or two, produced for Harriman and his ilk a succession of young men who implemented his vision of the American Century. Dean Acheson, the son of an Episcopal bishop, had entered Yale from Groton in 1911, and became part of a Yale that included Cole Porter and Archibald MacLeish. There were other young men whom Yale made useful for Harriman; perhaps the last was the brilliant Richard Bissell, whose once shining career was to run into the sands at the Bay of Pigs.

The public world in which Angleton lived, the world of the Second World War and its successor (or continuation), the Cold War, was formed by men of Harriman's generation and class and run by their lawyers, men like Acheson and the Dulles brothers. Harriman could hardly be said to have had a world view. He dealt directly with the facts of the robber-baron capitalism that was his father's legacy, and, when he was faced with a novelty like Soviet Russia, dealt with her leaders in the way that he would deal with a rival railroad owner or banker, in terms of deals to be negotiated, bond issues to be floated, material to be transported. His lawyers constructed theories appropriate to what needed to be accomplished as they drew up contracts or floated stock issues: theories supportive of investments at Baku, or in the Urals after the Russian Revolution; internationalist, Wilsonian theories supportive of German bonds into the 1930s.[17] These lawyerly constructs shaded into political platforms when politics impinged on bonds, or when the lawyers themselves moved from Wall Street into the State Department for a term. But one could not say that their thought was theory-driven. The theories, such as they were, were often enough simply useful rhetoric. Even the theories of one of the most seemingly ideological of Harriman's lawyers, John Foster Dulles—with his apocalyptic pronouncements about "rolling back Communism"—were easily set aside, as in 1956 at the Austrian border with an insurgent Hungary left to the attention of Soviet tank columns rolling *forward* unchallenged, Radio Free Europe promising wonders.

The younger products of Yale—Angleton, Richard Bissell—took their education and the view of the world it constituted more seriously.

In 1937, Angleton found an intense world of scholarship and poetry at Yale which, if it had existed in their time, seems to have been unknown to and without interest for the hard men of Angleton's father's generation.[18] Angleton and his classmates, in impressionable late adolescence, had entered one of the more powerful mind factories of the century, that of the New Criticism. The New Critics, who had just swept into New Haven from Louisiana State University, Sewanee, Kenyon, and Vanderbilt, had three pillars to their system: a canon of poetry in English, basically drawn (rather oddly, it must now be said) from the seventeenth and twentieth centuries; a method for the study of that poetry; and a view of the world not far from T. S. Eliot's own famous royalism, classicism, and Catholicism. (Or, in certain ways, identical with it: William Wimsatt, for example, was later to assert that the reason for studying poetry is to draw closer to the Mystery of the Incarnation.) Maynard Mack's undergraduate seminars were laboratories for young literary scientists in the I. A. Richards and William Empson modes, intensely reading seventeenth- and twentieth-century poems and decrypting them with their universal key, *Understanding Poetry* by Brooks and Warren.[19] This tradition of reading ultimately derives from classical philology and its transposition to English literary studies in the early twentieth century.[20] Be that as it may, by the 1920s that history, if ever known, was forgotten, and it was I. A. Richards, at Cambridge, who popularized it as a "scientific" literary criticism. It was perhaps for that reason that he attracted a mathematics undergraduate, William Empson.

Richards famously told the story that as he was lecturing on rhetorical tropes, and happening to mention ambiguity, he had casually suggested that there was more than one type, perhaps three or four, to be approached a few days later by Empson, who suggested that there were seven. Like any good tutor not knowing what else to say to a brilliant student, Richards told the young mathematician to write a paper on the subject. The resulting book, *Seven Types of Ambiguity*, is an unusually pure example of scientific criticism in the Linnaean mode. Empson began his argument with this statement of purpose: "I propose to use the word [ambiguity] in an extended sense, and shall think relevant to my subject any verbal nuance, however slight, which gives room for alternative reactions to the same piece of language." (In the first edition, the last phrase read: "adds some nuance to the direct statement of prose.") Given this definition, Empson finds that "in a sufficiently extended sense any prose statement could be called ambiguous."[21] One pictures Empson in his room in that gray, still-medieval Cambridge of Wittgenstein and Keynes, taking out a piece of paper and writing at the top that mathematician's proposition from which the remainder of the argument will be deduced: "Thus a word may have several distinct meanings; several meanings connected with one another; several meanings which need one another to complete their meaning; or several meanings which unite together so that the word means one relation or one process. This is a scale which might be followed continuously. 'Ambiguity' itself can mean an indecision as to what you mean, an intention to mean several things, a probability that one or other or both of two things has been meant, and the fact that a statement has several meanings."[22]

A few years later, undergraduates at Yale reading Empson's book in their newly built faux–Cambridge Gothic rooms would remember of this careful exposition, if nothing else, "the fact that a statement has several meanings." Empson was forced to leave Cambridge for the possibly unique offense, in that context, of excessive heterosexuality, eventually making his way to China (which was attracting English intellectuals in those years, first as advisors, like Bertrand Russell, to the local intelligentsia in search of alternatives to Confucianism, then as observers of Mao's solution to that problem). Empson participated in the Long March, and continued, as we shall see, via lectures and drinking parties in New Haven, to a career that seemed somehow not quite what was to be expected, ending in a "burrow" in Sheffield, alcoholism, and a knighthood.

Empson's peculiar achievement was to find a way of talking about poetry which was at once exemplary of the commitment to literature that he found essential in a critic (his most damning phrase about a colleague was that he "didn't have a craving for literature"), exact, teachable, and seemingly quite detached from the political quarrels of the day. *Seven Types of Ambiguity* is a compelling book. Years after reading it, the flavor of the writing remains: the confident tone, the impression of an exact thesis and an irrefutable argument, and the implicit conviction that ambiguity is a significant—perhaps the significant—fact of language.

While Angleton and his college friends were reading Empson, they were also immersed in the teachings of the American New Critics, which soon would be codified in *Understanding Poetry*. This was an overtly programmatic work, proclaiming as error the prevailing orthodoxy "that all students of literature should be regarded as historians." "More important still, and much more fruitful than the problems of origins and development, are those of content and significance. What is the human matter, what the artistic value of the work? . . . [T]he student of literature . . . must be instructed, partly at least, in the mysteries of the art."[23] Brooks and Warren sought so to instruct students; sought to inculcate a sense of sacramental mystery and craft to replace the lost secular clericalism of the philologist. In addition to its function as an anthology, *Understanding*

*Poetry* was a casebook, an introduction to a methodology of reading. To this end, Brooks and Warren prefaced it with an enormously influential "Letter to the Teacher."

> The editors of the present book hold that a satisfactory method of teaching poetry should embody the following principles:
> 1. Emphasis should be kept on the poem as a poem.
> 2. The treatment should be concrete and inductive.
> 3. *A poem should always be treated as an organic system of relationships, and the poetic quality should never be understood as inhering in one or more factors taken in isolation.*[24] (Emphasis added.)

The New Criticism was not content to be merely another way of looking at poetry. Its claims were total. On the basis of an emphatic rejection of a prevailing literary historical orthodoxy (and, here and there, a lingering impressionism), and, of course, in opposition to the fashionable Marxism of the day, it proposed a "scientific" method complete with enumerated steps to be taken by the investigator. For the New Critics, "the" poem is a poem because it has a poetic quality, something that cannot be isolated in one part or another—it is not verse, nor is it imagery—but inheres in the poem as a whole. Only when the student has the whole picture can he make sense of any particular factor, and once given the whole picture, the merest fragment makes sense, is meaningful, is imbued with the quality of the whole. The dynamism of the New Criticism, as with Loyola's system, was in its method: if sufficiently practiced at an impressionable moment, it had ambitions to form the mind itself. The New Criticism was a powerful method not merely for the analysis of poetry, but as a function of a unified world view applicable to all manner of things. It was not a value-free method. On the contrary, its proponents would argue vigorously that it was a method deeply rooted in a particular set of values; a method, in the final analysis, for promulgating those values.

It was understood that the poems studied would be unified, each "a whole," characterized by technical matters—verse, imagery—but crucially identified *as poetry* by something else, intuitively recognizable, so that given the merest fragment the whole is discernible. That quality was strongly associated with what the New Critics (and their British cousins) would call the "moral," a term that in the first half of the twentieth century retained some of its Victorian connotations of unquestionable approbation and centrality. It will be recalled that just before Angleton went to Yale, T. S. Eliot had issued some rather uncompromising statements to the effect that the fate of Western civilization itself depended on moral issues that easily resolved themselves, for him, into Christian doctrine, which in turn meant the Established Church, with the emphasis on the Establishment: the manifestation of state power as a system of belief. It was not for nothing that Eliot pointed to Dante, the poet of Scholasticism and Empire, as what a later critic at Yale might have termed the strongest of poets.[25] The coherence, the unity, of poems and of poetry was centrally important to critics of the generation of Angleton's teachers, important, not least of all as pointing to what they might call a higher coherence, a higher unity: that of Christian dogma. From Eliot's point of view in the late 1930s, liberalism and the totalitarianisms of the right or of the left were equivalent paganisms. His idea of a Christian society included only a limited degree of tolerance, because "a positive culture must have a positive set of values, and the dissentients must remain marginal, tending to make only marginal contributions."[26] We are here in a mental world similar to that of medieval Catholicism, with its carefully circumscribed tolerance of groups—each with a specific, placed, group identity, rights, and duties. Later, as dogmas faded, that higher coherence became a matter of belief, eventually, perhaps, a matter of nostalgia, but the imprint of this mental world remains: its sharp divisions between the correct and the erroneous; its penchant for carrying matters to the extreme; its blurring of the line between a fierce rhetoric and legal (or illegal) action in support of its beliefs; its readiness to stigmatize groups or individuals as threats to the community and outlaws.

Words have consequences. Choose, now: poetry and Christianity or pagan barbarianism. This was clear enough to anyone who, like the young James Angleton, read the daily newspapers through a sensibility formed in Mussolini's Milan.

In the United States, the slope was less slippery than that down which Eliot—and Pound—slid in Europe, perhaps because of the reversal of class identifications between the high and low churches, perhaps because of the then still lingering power of the Enlightenment in the U.S. Constitution and public life. It is difficult to imagine even Eliot himself publishing *The Idea of a Christian Society*, in the first instance, in the United States, and perhaps not insignificant that he did not wish it published in the United States at all. The early New Critics presented their students with a range of messages for poetry, from Wimsatt's Incarnation to a secularized "moral vision" they were able to find in a surprising variety of literary works, from those of Renaissance poets to those of Victorian novelists. But there *was* a kind of nonnegotiable final analysis to the New Critical methodology Angleton encountered at Yale. It lay in exactly that moral vision which, according to his teachers, was to be found everywhere in poetry, trailing after it remnants of late-Christian glory, which could be generalized into a conviction that, read with sufficient care, all texts, no matter how thoroughly encoded, would yield at least two messages: the overt meaning and the hidden meaning; the latter, inherent in some larger pattern, visible only to the elect.

The New Criticism presented itself as a methodology, as scientific, in a sense, and this is how it was received by generations of students, first at elite institutions like Yale, then all through American higher education. Absorbed in the fascinating techniques of New Critical close readings, unwilling to relinquish skills so hard-won, its students had little time to question their charismatic professors' discrediting of alternative methods, such as the previously dominant historical approaches. The exception that makes the rule in this case is the great school of eighteenth-century literary studies that flourished at Yale simultaneously with the New Criticism.[27] The serried rows of the monumental editions of Boswell and Pope marked the limits of exploration in that literary world, presenting an alternative if anything more removed from the social world of the day than was the New Criticism. At first a rich man's hobby, then virtually an industry, the production of editions of conservative poets and biographers played no role in opening the mental world of New Haven to influences beyond those marked out for study by the New Critics. Its professors constituted the loyal opposition, respected but powerless in New Haven, later active but hardly more influential in the Office of National Estimates at Langley. None of this was disturbing for undergraduates like James Angleton. Children of successful businessmen or heirs of more significant wealth, the interests and stance of their teachers were familiar from table talk at home. No one was sent to Yale in the 1930s in order to be radicalized.

Out of class—and he was usually out of class—Angleton and his lifelong friend Reed Whittemore turned from *Vif* to produce *Furioso*, a venture that would continue under Whittemore's editorship into the 1950s. *Furioso* was remarkably important for a student publication, according to at least one observer, "one of the major literary periodical voices of its era, as important as the *Sewanee Review* or the *Kenyon Review* or the *Partisan Review*."[28] The files of *Furioso* allow us to follow Angleton, month by month, from early 1939 until he left Yale for Harvard in 1941.[29] It is, for the most part, a correspondence to, rather than with, Angleton, as we do not have much of his side of the exchange in those files. Nonetheless, it allows us to gradually build up a portrait of the future chief of Counterintelligence as a young editor. It is worth quoting extensively from these letters for our purposes, for soon enough there would be no more public record of Angleton's thought, voice, and actions, until he resurfaced in Senator Church's hearing chamber at the end of his career.

Just two weeks after William Carlos Williams's letter in praise of Angleton's *Vif* poems, Archibald MacLeish wrote from his Harvard University office, where he was then curator of the Lucius W. Nieman Fellowships.

> March 23, 1939.
> Dear Mr. Angleton:
> Thank you for your letter and particularly for your criticism of "Air Raid" which I read with great interest and great pleasure.
> I wish the two of you could arrange some time to run up to Farmington and give me a chance to ask you some questions . . . it would be nice to see you and talk about Mr. Pound and various other matters.

A few years later, MacLeish, as Librarian of Congress, helped Wild Bill Donovan set up the OSS. And a few years after that, he was central to the efforts, first to have Pound put in Saint Elizabeth's, rather than tried for treason—as mad, not culpable—then to have him released: a national treasure, if mad.

Running both in the *Furioso* editorial files and parallel to them is a correspondence between Angleton and E. E. Cummings which was to continue for two decades, gradually extending to include Angleton's wife, Cicely d'Autremont, and her family, as well as Marion Morehouse Cummings. The exchange as we have it begins with this letter from Cummings:

> May 31, 1939
> Dear Angleton—
> in certainly printing a certain poem, you and your confrere have paid me one deep compliment, and I heartily thank you both
> am not a "critic"—I hope—am a learner or impossibly someone who loves (which cannot be measured) what couldn't and will not be measured.
> Most people are amorous of misunderstanding: tell them "I can't tell you" and they bark "so I'm lousy, eh?" But I can tell you "your magazine cover's the best I've seen" and improbably you won't mew "he thinks the contents stink".
> enclosed—everything your correspondent has to say about my pictures; should be very glad indeed to have you quote it.[30]

That first summer of the European war, while Angleton visited his family in Italy, he wrote (in August) to Cummings:

> Dear E.E.
> . . . If a bomb or the food doen't [*sic*] lay me low I am going to see Ezra next week. The old boy has got plenty on his balls and every time

I get the least bit worried he lifts me up to the point that I feel like murdering professors, or at least cutting off their dung-dragging beards. However . . . however . . . however.

Milan has been very pleasant and there is nothing to do which means that I read one novel and dream about the next issue of Furioso . . .

I guess that the crapwriters in America have been telling you that Italy wants war. Frankly I have never seen any country that wants peace so much as do the Italians. They damn well won't fight and a friend of mine who has just been called tells me that after a week he and a thousand others haven't even received uniforms . . . The boats are not treading anymore and I may have to stay over here longer. Maybe the crapwriters are right. For security . . . no address . . . no signature just a goddamn lousy american who is getting the wind up and who is going to buy a nice little goggled gas-mask to-morrow . . .

as ever the furious man with a sister who smoked your cigarettes and drank your brandy.[31]

The letter to Cummings hints at a settled routine in Milan, too comfortable and familiar to be worthy of comment, although the concern with security may have had something to do with the U.S. intelligence role that Angleton's father was beginning to play.

While in Milan, Angleton wrote to T. S. Eliot, offering to bring out an Italian edition of his poems. (It seems reasonable to assume that this project emerged from Angleton's talks with Pound.) Eliot's response to Angleton's proposal was sent to New Haven: "I should of course be very glad to see a volume of my verse translated into Italian . . . If you wish to pursue your design, I should say that the first step was to assure yourself of an Italian publisher, and get him to communicate with Faber & Faber, who hold the rights in my work."[32] Angleton introduced himself to Eliot by way of an offer to do him a favor, that favorite favor of poets, publication. They were to remain friends at least through the war. It is useful in many fields to have a talent for cultivating one's elders.

Angleton returned to a university seemingly oblivious to events in Europe. His future colleague, Cord Meyer, remembered that when Meyer himself had arrived at Yale "in the fall of 1939, war had been declared in Europe, and the march of German armies across that continent reverberated like approaching thunder." And yet, "to an extraordinary extent, the university preserved its academic calm and usual ways."[33] Angleton, less studious than Meyer, took classes but did not take them very seriously unless they had to do with the new poetry or the New Criticism or Italian. For the most part he worked at *Furioso* and at his own poems. He lived, as many undergraduates lived, in a nocturnal welter of papers and cigarettes, habits he kept throughout his life. Early that fall, William Carlos Williams sent *Furioso* an article commenting on Pound, and sent Angleton a reading of Angleton's own love poetry.

> Dear Angleton:
>
> You are quite right, what I have said about the semi-divine Ezra had better be modified . . . He is, as I meant to imply in my article, a poet. I greatly admire your defense of him. It does you credit . . . The fragments of a poem which you send are hard to judge, I know they pick up bits of Sappho and name them as great but—anyhow I want to see more. Don't mistake me, I like the rich color and the intensity (a bit nostalgic) of the feeling—but I'd rather see more before judging. I wonder if you weren't the poet in love—more poet than lover. So far I don't feel any despair even the despair of the hedonist who can't get enough. Oh well, I'm probably just envious of your youth, your presumed ability and the plowing you did. Them things aint frequent.[34]

This may refer to "Caresse Primordial" or poems like it. The following month Angleton wrote to Cummings to bring to the poet's notice Angleton's sister Carmen, whom he was initiating into the new literary world, and to mention that the Yale Library had given him a hundred dollars to produce a bibliography on Pound.[35] Carmen Angleton eventually followed her brother onto the editorial staff of *Furioso*. Their close lifelong relationship supported a strong connection between Angleton and a postwar trans-Atlantic café society that eventually included literary figures like Mary McCarthy and Hannah Arendt.[36]

In Europe, toward the end of 1939, Britain and France, having finally declared war on Germany, stood by while Poland was overrun and were planning an invasion of the USSR via Norway, Sweden, and Finland. But in New Haven, the poets continued to need publishers, and both publishers and poets had their reading to do and their parties to attend. We find John Peale Bishop referring to "Your [Angleton's] account of your pleasant, bottle-emptying week-end with Eberhart and Empson."[37] Cummings remained in touch with Pound, despite the war, and shared some of Pound's political views.[38] Early in the new year, Richard Eberhart reported on more Empson socializing: "Jan. 12 [1940] 5 pm Empson time . . . Dear Jim . . . Went to a Chinese dinner on Emp's last night, with the IARs, Ted Spencer, a beautiful Chinese girl, etc." We then hear from Empson himself, expressing gratitude for Angleton's help with lectures and drinking binges at Yale; with this letter the war begins to make itself known.

The White House
Fulford, York
Feb. 19
My dear Angleton,

. . . Thank you very much for running me about as you did; I enjoyed it very much and realise it may be very valuable to me . . . I had about an hour's grilling from the customs for cheating the mails by carrying suspicious letters but certainly your package . . . It made a good end to all the police grillings on frontiers of the trip, in the blackout and the deep snow; they were so cold that in the end they took my word for it (at Liverpool that I wasnt a spy) . . . You with your restless appetite for organising things might be able to tell me of an American publisher who would be interested in [an American edition of *Ambiguity*] . . . Dont run yourself about into a nervous wreck, my dear Angleton, my own nerves are much more placid since I got home.

Yours very gratefully,
W Empson[39]

A "restless appetite for organising things" would be a good caption for a portrait of the young Angleton.

Neither spies nor censors surfaced in *Furioso*'s second issue, which included a "Review of Modern Poetry and the Tradition" by Cleanth Brooks and, by Andrews Wanning, "A Primer for Modern Poetry" in which Wanning ventured that "we hear a lot these days about the modern critical revolution; but we hear few definitions. I will risk offering a simple one: the essence of that revolt lies in the discovery that it is possible and proper for a poet to mean two differing, or even opposing things at the same time,"[40] an Empson-style thought that Angleton no doubt read, and may have noted. Angleton himself appeared in this issue as an advertiser, describing himself as a "frantic bibliographer" in search of "obscure" works or manuscripts of Ezra Pound; this, following his commission for a bibliography of Pound from the Yale Library.[41] The word "frantic" was characteristic of the young Angleton, despite Empson's advice.

With the new year William Carlos Williams had changed his salutations from "Angleton" to "Jim."

Feb. 29, 1940
Dear Jim:

. . . I admire your courage and persistence in continuing to publish Furioso. I hope you will continue with it, making it more and more furious, if possible, as you go along. It was the name of the thing that first attracted my attention to it. I do not think you have quite lived up to your name.

> You ought to be, you and your generation, furious at the mess of things my generation has left in your collective laps. But you do not rave, as youth should, you are still too polite.

Angleton was furious enough when writing to Cummings.

> Dear E.E.
>
> Back to New Haven and a hell of a lot of trouble, Thomas ain't got nutting on me.[42] I have a bad cold but it's nothing to the headache that charles henri ford is. He writes do this, do that. He tells his pal Tyler to send us everything. A whole drawerful of rejected stuff from Furioso to Ford's pals. (Tyler, Anderson etc). For Gawd's sakes the guys got more brass than I have and I can't do a damn thing about it. It's a bloody business and I just wonder when my nerves are going to break and I'm going to run right out of this damn house and grab a feather-lipped soft-crooner by his knotted neck and digslash my razor right through every swollen vein. A bloody business this ford gang.
>
> Anyway I've got insomnia . . .
>
> Jeem angel ton[43]

The signature was, perhaps, a phonetic rendering of his mother's pronunciation of his name. ("Feather-lipped" provides the translation of "duvet-lèvres" from the cafe poem in *Vif.*) The tone of Angleton's *Furioso* letters is consistently energetic, occasionally violent (sometimes in a positive sense, sometimes negative). It is not the careful precision of Eliot; it is not what one might expect from an academic or a bureaucrat. It is what one would expect from a young man on the fringes of the great world of literature, but with only a marginal, indeterminate place within it.

A couple of months later, Angleton was thinking more about the wider world and had apparently confided his apprehension about the effects of the coming war on his family's business interests to Eberhart, who replied, "The threat to your family standing if Italy enters the war I take philosophically. I have lived through much . . . I lived through loss of family fortune—I know what it means. But one must be strong, one must fight, and one must be philosophic. And Youth is its own boon, it keeps off Evil for a while."[44] Easy enough, as the joke goes, for Eberhart to take *Angleton*'s family troubles philosophically. But if Angleton was suddenly financially insecure—and if he was, after all, only an undergraduate with nothing like the Laughlin steel fortune behind him—in a couple of years he had made a position for himself, even if at the margin, in the transatlantic literary world. He was a friend of Pound, one of the many drinking companions of Empson, a frequent correspondent of Cummings and Williams. All these famous poets took this young man very seriously. It seemed natural enough, for example, that the projected Italian edition of his poems should continue to interest Eliot: "I am of course altogether agreeable in principle to your suggestion of a volume or volumes of Italian translation of my work . . . I should think that Eugenio Montale might be good for the poetry, if he knows enough English."[45] An Italian translation of Eliot by Montale would have been a remarkable volume. Eliot appears to have seen Angleton as a replacement for, say, Ford Madox Ford, or an alternative to James Laughlin of Harvard and his *New Directions*: someone eager to create publication opportunities, someone a bit like Eliot himself at his desk at Faber and Faber; something of an equal.

Angleton's efforts on behalf of poets he admired—always much older men—is also reflected in a letter from Empson sent a few days later: "It is very kind of you to be still thinking about getting me a job in America, and I hope to work there some time after the war, but I don't think I could, or would want to, go till then . . . [T]his is the proper place for an Englishman to be at present."[46] "This" being in the middle of the Battle of Britain. Empson was an iconic figure, worshipped by his students, a kind of alcoholic saint of literature (anxious, in a postscript to these remarks, not to have them published, as being easy to interpret at that juncture as critical of Auden and Isherwood). Empson's was a particularly fine form of English patriotism, the patriotism of "Little England." In Rapallo, however, the first of Angleton's famous friends, Ezra Pound, was sliding toward treason.

> A six lire stamp on one Upim (Woolworth wop) envelope brings one letter from Rapallo . . . "If the American people STILL want Lipmann and Shittery Thompson and cant yet print me/then they better go die . . . something is diseased in the nation; and no therapy will save them. All of which you can discuss with cummings and Slocum." I don't know if you would be interested in this as you seem to agree with MacLiesh's policies concerning anti-Hitler ejaculation and then you join in with the boys to write a letter to Life though you did not reveal to me the candid interior of the cummings' mind. Anyway, I have received a couple of letters from Ezra and he seems to be active and bitter. He has a habit of enlarging on his journalistic Inferno and placing more people there: a helluva lot of people have fallen through the hole of his outhouse.
>
> . . . Best regards to Mrs. Cummings.
>
> Jim Angleton[47]

Angleton's socio-poetic networking secured another node in his web of transatlantic connections when *Furioso* printed a poem by Marianne Moore.

She wrote, "It is generous of you to offer to send copies of the last number for me to friends, and I should be grateful if one could be sent to H.D.: Mrs. H. D. Aldington, 49 Lowndes Square, S.W.1 London, ENGLAND."[48] The address is interesting enough to warrant some explication. The poet known as H.D. (Hilda Doolittle) had been engaged to Ezra Pound before they both went to England, where she married Richard Aldington and was close to D. H. Lawrence. She was also a friend, and would become a closer friend, of Norman Pearson, a Yale professor who was beginning to take an interest in Angleton. At the time of Moore's letter, H.D. was living with Bryher, the daughter of an English publishing and shipping magnate, Sir John Ellerman, in Lowndes Square, where Bryher maintained something of a salon.[49] Bryher's memoirs tell us much about their lives on the literal and figurative margins of Bloomsbury. In a year or two that life would include Pearson. Soon afterward, Pearson's generosity would have it include his various protégés.

Pearson's academic career was unremarkable, at first glance. A closer look shows various gaudy aspects. For one, he had virtually an alternative, if not primary, academic specialty: that of the professor well known in literary circles—someone making himself useful to poets, in particular, to the point that, for example, he eventually came to hold the copyrights on the later books of H.D. He began these activities during the early 1930s, while still a student, and continued them to the end of his life, working on anthologies with Auden (and said to be the addressee of a famous obscene poem), socializing with everyone from the Sitwells to Gertrude Stein, writing introductions and letters of introduction, finding publishers, arranging lectures and readings. It is a recognizable quasi-academic role, facilitated, perhaps, by the prestige of Yale, by Pearson's personal and family connections, by the intensity of his interest in the poetry of his generation and that immediately preceding.[50] It was not unlike the life Angleton was then building at Yale. By the early 1940s Pearson, although still merely an instructor, was well on his way to a respectable academic career of a more common sort: delivering papers to the Modern Language Association and the English Institute, publishing here and there, conducting a wide correspondence with colleagues at other universities, a correspondence which is notable for the trouble he took for others: writing to Colorado and Iowa, for example, recommending Auden for a teaching position.[51] He was a frequent recommender (and frequently recommended). He was sufficiently involved with the academic life of Yale to help in an effort in the period of the run-up to the Second World War to maintain funding for the teaching of the liberal arts there.

Shortly thereafter he took up a third career: he was to become one of the more significant American spymasters, and mentor of generations of American intelligence professionals, based first in London, later, in New Haven. It was Pearson, as it happened, not Pound, who was to stand godfather to Angleton's career.

Angleton's letters in 1940 become if anything more frantic, reflecting the tensions of the coming war and his peculiar position: caught between two or three languages, half attached to Italy, half to New Haven, with the complication of Pound on both sides.

> Dear E.E.,
>
> Thanks for the swell letter . . . I feel wonderful. I! I! I have finally resolved a curse on both their houses. No speeka da Engleesh etc. No I am beginning to feel that Ezra had plenty on the ball when he wrote the cantos [*sic*]. It's terrible but I am looking for some sort of myth, something that will bring things all around to a solution; whatever the damn language is that they will make me speak I'll jabber it if they'll only let me fish ever so often. Then everything will be puddle-wonderful and when you squeeze the udders of experience they will give forth sweet milk . . . Anyway I'm happy and in love and everything else and you are the only person worth telling . . . Excuse exuberance, nasty habit of mine besides exaggeration . . . Empson asked me to say hello to you and Mrs . . . He is answering Lord Haw Haw on the B.B.C. . . . Dreadful bit of trash is Wyndy Lewis' 'America I presume,' New Book . . .
> Jim Angleton
>
> Coherent review of New Cantos in next issue![52]

"I am looking for some sort of myth, something that will bring things all around to a solution." Those looking for a myth usually find one. It might be said that Angleton was to find one in the Cold War itself. The language remark is also telling. There are few references to Angleton's languages in the literature about him. Some of his colleagues mention his "restaurant French"; none seemed aware of his abilities in Italian or Spanish. And yet the *Vif* poems testify to more than the ability to decipher a menu, and it would be surprising if fifteen years or more of occasional residence in Italy were not to have an effect, and more surprising if his mother's Spanish had been completely lost on him. It is likely that the linguistic complexities of his early life had a strong influence on his identity, just as the accompanying national influences—Mexico, Idaho, Italy, England—also must have created an accompanying complexity. That is not something that he would have discussed at Langley.

*Furioso* published many of the contemporary poets anthologized in *Understanding Poetry*, including Cummings and MacLeish as well as Pound. Eberhart wrote about this aspect of the magazine's policy in October 1940: "Furioso's main merit, to date, I suggest, stems from your sort of genius for rounding up the partially or fully knowns: they still also need print, in one sense more so than the total unknowns."[53] If this was the strategy pursued by Whittemore and Angleton, it was clever enough. It is one thing to be the undergraduate publisher of other undergraduates, quite another to accumulate a supply of credit chits from the "partially or fully knowns" of the day.

However, this phase of Angleton's life was coming to a close. In June 1941 Angleton graduated from Yale, in the lowest quarter of his class.[54] No credit was given for *Furioso*. But if his academic standing bothered him, he had other matters on his mind. Soon after graduation he tried to join the Army. Cummings wrote to Pound that "Jim Angleton has been seemingly got hold of by an intelligent prof [Pearson?] & apparently begins to realise that comp mil ser might give the former a respite from poisonal responsibility . . . maybe he's developing?"[55] But Angleton's health was never good—all his life he had periodic bouts with tuberculosis—and his sister's health was reaching a crisis.

Dear Cummings,

You must forget this long silence of mine and put it down to over indulgence. My sister had a bad time of it for three months and I have been somewhat upset. It seems that for a number of years she has been seeing visions and hearing voices. [T]hese short trances finally developed into something much more serious. At the end it appears that she would pretend that she was ill just so that she could obey some voice and hallucinate for weeks in the infirmary. She succeeded in fooling the medicos by placing her thermometer on a hot-water bottle and faking a high temperature. It took them three weeks to discover that she was suicidal and since that time she has been in the Penn. hospital taking insulin and electric shock. It was a terrible experience to take her there and to see her trying to come out of a trance but void of any power of speech. However it has been a great joy as they have stopped her treatments to-day and she is really on the road to sanity. This is not only to excuse my silence but to tell you how much she enjoyed your contribution to Furioso. I was afraid lest she believe I was trying to give her something not suited to her. Instead it gave her much pleasure and she said that many times she thought herself to be Joan, that she could understand the voices and the uncharted countries of her mind; apparently a world which began with beautiful thoughts and myths but became so horrible that she could only obey these guardian voices and become desperate. In a way then a great deal of her cure is attributed to your "Speech" for it interested her. I don't know if you've ever seen anyone who lives a kind of death. Nothing interests them. They connive to deceive you. They have no love for parent or friend, they are completely imprisoned within their mind. That's the way Carmen was but your poetry did reach her and make her seek out beyond and I thank you . . .

I miss seeing you and Marion . . . If luck is with me I shall be in Harvard next year. Reed has gone into the army and I have been rejected as a weakling, but with few regrets . . .
Jim Angleton[56]

Angleton had been seeking a myth that would bring coherence to his life. His sister had found myths that did anything but that. Carmen Angleton, daughter of Carmen Moreno of Nogales and Hugh Angleton of Boise, living in Milan, then Philadelphia, had a difficult balancing act to perform. So did her brother.

In spite of his grades, Angleton had applied to Harvard Law School. The application was rejected. He then asked Norman Pearson for a recommendation, which Pearson supplied. There is a draft letter to Harvard on Angleton's behalf among the Pearson papers. (Written on the reverse of a piece of hospital stationery. Pearson was often in hospital with a tubercular hip and its complications.) Here is how Angleton, a young man about to leave Yale, struck a perceptive tutor:

> Angleton is a young man of great, and on occasion, not always practical enthusiasms. While a student at Yale he has edited and published *Furioso*, a magazine of verse whose quality as an undergraduate magazine has been surpassed only by Harvard's own *Hound & Horn* of some years ago. Its duties have unquestionably interfered with the routine of his classroom work in a manner which, mathematically speaking, has been considerably to the disadvantage of his grades. Yet *Furioso* has been in every way a *fine* magazine. If it were possible to grade it on undergraduate academic scales he would have received, I feel sure, a mark of 100. The magazine is a demonstration of industry, shrewdness, and common sense. It represents the solution of infinite problems. All of these solutions are demonstrations of qualities which go into the making of a first-rate lawyer, quite as much as the demonstration of a high grade into the routine classroom memorization of textbooks in, let us say, anthropology, hygiene, English, or the like. They are recommendation beyond the scope of the report card, and they ought equally to be taken into consideration.
>
> I have known Angleton for several years in an academic way, despite the fact that he has taken no classes from me. I can say quite flatly that he is one of the few undergraduates who has made their mark on Yale.[57]

Harvard relented and Angleton, settling into the life of a Cambridge law student, sent Pearson a note of appreciation.

Dear Norm
Thanks for the generous letter. I am sweating away and am trying to do my best. Will write when I can . . .
Yours,
Jim[58]

While Angleton was at Harvard both he and his father were interviewed by the FBI, which was collecting information about Pound, whose radio broadcasts from Rome were leading to a treason indictment.[59] During his interview, Hugh Angleton denied knowing much about Pound, whom he said he thought was indeed guilty of treason. The FBI report of the interview with the elder Angleton depicts a father not overly protective of his son.

> [Hugh Angleton] stated that he had heard from other persons that POUND is considered to be a noted poet and writer and that his son, [James Angleton] presently a student at the Harvard University Law School, Cambridge, Massachusetts, had been quite impressed by subject and by his writings and in 1937 had made a special visit to Rapallo in order to meet POUND and to talk with him. He also stated that . . . he had discussed POUND with his son on a number of occasions and that his son was still very friendly toward the subject and his political theories.[60]

Angleton later gave E. E. and Marion Cummings a comic account of the FBI visit that followed his father's referral.

> [O]ne F.B.I. agent came to my study in Cambridge. Tell me all he says. Sir, I replied. Firstly I can rely upon my Constitutional rights and tell you nothing or I can deceive you or I can tell you all; but if I tell you all it will take a long time. Tell all, he mutters. Therefore I tell him all: I take him from 1913 through all of Ezra's poetry—through the books of Cantos explaining and declaiming. He writes in one notebook and then in several. I don't talk of Fascism or Jews—I talk of Jefferson and Social Credit, The New English Weekly, and America I love you. Thank you Mr. Angleton, he says, and looks hopelessly at his notebooks. I only wanted to give you both sides of the picture, I said. Poets are funny and art's a strange thing he replied and left.[61]

The FBI's account of the interview with James Angleton has also survived. It is more lengthy than his, but not quite as detailed as might have been expected.

According to this report the young law student admired Pound's poetry, agreed with his political theories, but found the latter distorted by Pound's prejudices against Jews and International Bankers, thought the radio broadcasts that were the grounds for the treason indictment incoherent, and agreed both to testify and to name names. It was a well-balanced performance: loyal to his friend, yet helpful to the authorities.

Although Angleton had gone to Harvard Law School in preparation for a business career, for some he was still that romantic figure, the poet in the garret. A Vassar girl found herself in his Cambridge apartment one day in 1941:

> There was nothing in the room except a large reproduction of El Greco's *View of Toledo*. It showed a huge unearthly green sky. Jim was standing underneath the picture. If anything went together, it was him and the picture. I fell madly in love at first sight. I'd never met anyone like him in my life. He was so charismatic. It was as if the lightning in the picture had suddenly struck me. He had an El Greco face. It was extraordinary.[62]

Half a century later she published a poem about the scene:

> *First Sight*
>
> One rainy day on Brattle Street my weekend date
> walked me up three flights of narrow stairs
> to meet his college room-mate.
> At the long end of a barely finished room
> How do? the young Chicano said politely
> melting from El Greco's stormy painting of Toledo
> before he disappeared again.
> I fell right through the creaky floor-boards,
> through damp roses wired to the sidewalk,
> past St. Theresa's plaster statue in the garden.
> Beware, she warned, of hollow cheeks
> and auras sketched in lightning.
> That bounced me up again.
> Hello I said or didn't say.[63]

Angleton, abandoning the law, entered the Army on March 19, 1943. He and Cicely d'Autremont were engaged in April and married July 17, 1943. Cicely d'Autremont was wealthy, very intelligent, and knew what—and who—she wanted. In any case, short engagements were common under the circumstances.[64]

Battle Creek, Mich.
Aug. 26, 1943
Dear E.E. and Marion—

Sir & Madam, an old soldier remembers you with news of consequence. I was married here in Battle Creek to a lovely girl Cicely d'Autremont who lives in Tucson Arizona . . . [T]he Army snaffled me; sent me to Seattle Washington (Fort Lawton) then banged me into the Military Government School for Enlisted Men here at Fort Custor. I graduated a few days ago. While waiting in line for furlough papers and subsequent transportation to Seattle, they received a telephone call "Hold Angleton." I am held awaiting anxiously my fate—fine or superfine.

However—I am enjoying a belated honeymoon—gold bricking as no soldier ever gold bricked before. My wife's eyes hold my immortality. So who am I to fear the lion's mouth, the Jap's quick judo—death by flies—tinfish and water . . .

Best—as ever—
Jim[65]

Cicely d'Autremont's parents were leading citizens of Tucson, with a considerable fortune that derived from Duluth mining and lumber interests, and local Tucson investments that included the city's second-best hotel. Her father, a banker, served in the Arizona state legislature; her mother was active in the community, occupied with charitable work among the African American and Mexican American people there. The family's way of life included trout and bass fishing in private streams along the Canadian border, visits to New York, vacations on Cape Cod. The aura of independent means noticed by observers of Angleton in later life—the English bespoke suits, the Mercedes, the private streams and the Tucson "mansion"—was based in part on the wealth of his wife's family.

Before disappearing into the war, Angleton took care to introduce the rest of his new family to E. E. and Marion Morehouse Cummings:

150 E 50th
New York City
Dec. 20, 1943
Dear ee and Marion,

This is just a short farewell note before my 'taking off' . . . My father, da Major, is with the 5th Army and has ordered 36 corn-cob pipes. It seems that his supply of tobacco has run out and he finds that a low grade of dung plus Italian shag is obtainable at the front. I hope to see him soon with a brks-bag full . . . I do not question why. I only march (a little out of step) where da grapes of rath are brewed; listening to a number of officers inform me on the gratness of this an that and the porcine ways and mechanics of killing or be killed . . . Carmen is going to run FURIOSO during the next months. I hope to take care of the London end and sell subscriptions and bleed people of the ills . . . If my mother-in-law asks you to visit her for your health be assured she means just that. Your time will be your own and the desert, the colors, the good dry air, the horses, the Mexican fruits etc etc will also be yours. She is a wonderful woman who has done much good in this world.

As ever,

Jim Angleton[66]

The connection between the Cummingses and Helen d'Autremont lasted until the end of Mrs. d'Autremont's life. They exchanged letters and visits, saw one another from time to time in Tucson or the Northeast. James and Cicely Angleton remained part of this friendship, visiting and corresponding with the Cummingses until first E. E., then Marion Morehouse Cummings, died in the early 1960s.

These personal letters, occasionally businesslike, occasionally frantic, give us, as in an epistolary novel, a sketch of a character, a version of the young Angleton: a poet and publisher of poets, the protégé of Maynard Mack and Norman Pearson, the friend of Pound and Cummings, a minor Modernist figure. He valued poetry, or a certain kind of poetry, and a certain approach to it. He had won the respect of some of the best-known poets of his time, and that of those of his professors who shared his interests.[67] Was he influenced by the New Criticism? How could he not have been? It was an approach to reading that he transferred to other texts, a guide that he trusted as he wandered far from New Haven, far, seemingly, from poetry itself.

# 3 OSS

If today you walk down Duke Street or St. James's from Piccadilly toward Pall Mall, you enter a London of art dealers, banks, and men's clothing shops. There are paintings by Raphael on sale, if you would like to buy one, or you might wish to have a pair of shoes made for five hundred pounds; you could look into Christie's to see what sort of antiques are on offer this week, or strike out west to the Ritz for lunch before an afternoon of shopping at Harrods. It is a world where middle-aged Englishmen wearing butcher-striped Turnbull & Asser shirts and double-vented suits shout across tea tables at their wives about the lack of decent food in the Seychelles, while their daughters and someone else's sons (or someone else's daughters) meet at Quaglino's or Green's, and the streets are filled with limousines carrying Gulf harems: a gilded hijab frame, kohl eyes, black chadors over iridescent couture. Fifty years ago these cobbled streets were the center of the secret war.

The headquarters of the British Secret Intelligence Service were across the Park, in Broadway, behind New Scotland Yard, midway between Buckingham Palace and the Houses of Parliament. We can listen to someone who was there describe its physical arrangements and those in St. James's: "Broadway was a dingy building, a warren of wooden partitions and frosted glass windows. It had eight floors served by an ancient lift . . . It was a short walk from Broadway Buildings across St. James's Park to the wartime headquarters of MI5 in St. James's Street. But the difference in style was considerable. Even the entrance compared favourably with the dingy hall at Broadway, and the first good impression was confirmed upstairs. The offices looked like offices; so far as I know, there were none of the makeshift rabbit hutches that disfigured so much of Broadway. The officers sat at desks uncluttered by dog-eared paper. At most, half-a-dozen neat files, each nicely indexed and cross-indexed, would be awaiting treatment."[1]

In 1943, Section V (counterespionage) of MI6 moved to offices on Ryder Street. "We were two minutes from MI5 and fifteen from Broadway. If we came to work early, we could look down from our windows and see Quaglino's offloading its horrible garbage from the night before . . . When Section V moved into its Ryder Street premises, Norman Pearson and his colleagues had taken office-space, with Cowgill's backing, in the same building."[2]

That voice belonged to H. A. R. (Kim) Philby, who worked at the time for SIS, formerly MI6, the British foreign intelligence service. MI5 is the designation of British domestic intelligence. Pearson, of Yale University, James Angleton's mentor, had moved from New Haven to work in X-2, the counterintelligence department of the Office of Strategic Services, a new American intelligence agency headed by William "Wild Bill" Donovan, a Wall Street lawyer and First World War hero. These are some of the organizations and people that would form James Angleton's world during the Second World War.

Kim Philby is as readable a guide as any—better than most in some ways—to the bureaucratic intricacies of the British Secret Intelligence Service during the war. In *My Silent War*, a book that he wrote in cooperation with his colleagues in the Soviet intelligence service, he tells us that "SIS is the only British service authorised to collect secret information from foreign countries by illegal means . . ."

> The basis of SIS activity is the network of agents, almost always of foreign nationality. These agents work, directly or indirectly, under the control of an SIS office, known as a "station," housed in a British Embassy and thus protected from the action of local authorities by diplomatic convention . . . Information collected by agents finds its way, directly or by devious means, to the local SIS station responsible for their recruitment in the first place. There it is given a preliminary assessment, for value and accuracy, by SIS officers disguised as diplomats. If considered of interest, the information is transmitted, with appropriate comment, to London headquarters. Transmission is normally by foreign service communications, radio or diplomatic bag, according to the degree of urgency.[3]

That is how *both* services that employed Philby worked in the field. It was the model followed by the Americans when setting up their services, and, generally, by the services of other countries. The system is reasonable, not unlike that followed by news agencies or financial information services in the period before computerization allowed more centralization of information processing. It is essentially a paper and, as we would now say, a text-based system. Reports were gathered from agents (who, as likely as not, had based them on reports from other services or had invented them out of whole cloth to meet the needs of the market), elaborated, endorsed, collated, passed on in great sheaves. Once harvested in the field, these reports and their accompanying commentaries were sent on to the central processing unit, which was also an administrative center.

> The structure of headquarters in London was based on a division of responsibility for the production and assessment of intelligence. Those who produced the stuff should submit their wares to independent scrutiny before the finished article was sent to government departments. In accordance with this principle, headquarters was divided into two groups of sections, known respectively as "G" Sections and Circulating Sections. The "G" Sections administered overseas stations, and supervised their operations . . . Circulating Sections assessed the intelligence received, and passed it on to interested government departments; they would then pass back to the "G" Sections the judgments of those departments, together with their own. The Circulating Sections were divided, not regionally, but according to subject matter.[4]

The logic behind this system was that field staff, combining administrative, operational, and analytical roles, would be able to annotate and contextualize information gathered by their agents. Its weakness was that the field staff may have only local knowledge and may be self-limiting as interpreters because of their multiple roles: they may identify with one agent, dislike a second; they may be manipulated by a third. They may also be over-worked, needing to spend much time during regular office hours on their "cover" assignments as visa officers or press attachés, and needing to attend to the social obligations of the diplomatic life after hours. Back in London (Washington, Paris, Moscow, Berlin), regional administrators would have wider knowledge, fewer extraneous responsibilities, and less emotional involvement with agents (whose identity was usually at least nominally concealed from them). They would be able to enrich the analysis, but they too had administrative responsibilities and a definitionally regional outlook. Thus the Circulating Sections, which would be thought of as purely analytic and critical, were able to call on outside expertise and able to place the processed material resulting from these previous steps with "customers" who might benefit from it. Of course, those in the Circulating Sections were far removed from the field, lacked an intuitive feel for the situation, were uninvolved with the lives and fortunes of agents, and so forth. The strengths and weaknesses of each group—those in the field, the Governing Sections, and the Circulating Sections—were meant to fit together in such a way as to wring the final gasp of meaning from each item of information gathered by agents in the field. On the other hand, human nature being what it is, the whole dynamic was unstable: differences of interpretation becoming differences of opinion, which in turn fuelled power struggles.

Then there were Mr. Philby and his friends, operating at a tangent to the entire ensemble. According to Philby,

> Section V, to which I found myself attached, was in a peculiar position, in more than one respect. In name, it was a Circulating Section and its subject matter counter-espionage. But, whereas the other Circulating Sections dealt with regular government departments, such as the Foreign Office, the Admiralty and the rest, whose knowledge of secret operations was marginal, Section V's main "customer" was itself a secret organization: MI5 . . . [Cowgill, head of Section V, had] specialist officers of his own attached to overseas stations. Nominally, such officers came under the general administration and control of the "G" sections; but most of the latter were far too busy to pay them any attention, and their day-to-day instructions emanated direct from Section V . . . The general effect of this arrangement was that Section V, though still a Circulating Section in name, acquired some of the functions of a "G" Section. It became a hybrid, regarded with a degree of suspicious incomprehension by the rest of SIS. The position suited Cowgill well. It enabled him to claim that counter-espionage was an esoteric art, calling for wisdom not revealed to the common run of intelligence officers.[5]

Some held that James Angleton was to follow Cowgill in this claim, as well as in the structure of his organization, the Counterintelligence Staff of the CIA, modeled, it would seem, on Section V of MI6.

Georg Simmel, in his essay called "The Adventurer," argued that an adventure exists outside the time of everyday life, and, writing in his university study at the end of the nineteenth century, held that when we think of an adventure we first think of something erotic. But there is another kind of adventure, with another kind of allure, and that is the adventure of war. For some young people the intensity of that experience is literally formative. It exists outside of time, persisting as a set of images underlying the remainder of life, setting the terms of that life, its limits, its expectations. Years later, after the war is over, talking quietly in a Georgetown restaurant or a Roman café (a London club, the bar in the American Colony Hotel), thoughts still flow in the old channels, those scoured by war, the rest of life having been somehow dull, monochromatic, fundamentally uninteresting.

One might hazard the proposition that institutions are susceptible in the same way, some succumbing to that old siren song: falling in love with war. Human institutions, even intelligence organizations, are, after all, only groups of people.[6] The war-infatuated youth of American intelligence organizations was spent abroad—as if in response to a *donnée* of Henry James. It was spent, crucially, in those bomb-scarred and blacked-out streets near St. James's Park, where men like Angleton studied under two masters: one local, clubby, knowing, deceptively friendly and civilized; the other Celan's "master from Germany."

Among those British secret service officers who took their American counterparts in charge was Malcolm Muggeridge, who was famously to describe the arrival of his American colleagues: "Ah, those first OSS arrivals in London! How well I remember them arriving like *jeunes filles en fleur* straight from a finishing school, all fresh and innocent, to start work in our frowsty old intelligence brothel. All too soon they were ravished and corrupted, becoming indistinguishable from seasoned pros who had been in the game for a quarter of a century or more."[7] The English intelligence brothel was a rather large, rather complex enterprise, something like that Parisian establishment supported and enjoyed by Charlus, with separate chambers catering to various tastes. The public areas were kept sufficiently innocuous so as not to frighten visiting American graduates. Further on, further on *in*, there were peculiarly English complexities, culminating in Turing's anguish after Bletchley Park, and finally, oddly enough, in a Washington, D.C., caught between imperial moments, where one humid morning-after in the early 1950s two spies shared a bed and a bottle of champagne. And, of course, in the cellars, the Continental contribution, which would reemerge in all its horror much later, far from Europe.

The Great Game was much further along when the Americans arrived than Muggeridge's quarter of a century. But, for our purposes, the Great Game was, and remained, Kipling's: the struggle of Britain with Russia for imperial domination, which continued until that final senile spasm, fittingly enough, at Suez. Much of the prewar staff of the British Secret Intelligence establishment had seen service in the Indian police force and continued to pass back and forth between London and the colonies well into the 1950s. In this tradition, "Communism" was simply another term for Russian imperialism—not that it looked that way at the time. At the time, the tradition of running secret warfare operations against the Russians was expressed as pious anti-Communism: "[T]hroughout the 1920s and early 1930s, until the rise of Hitler showed that the threat to Britain could come from the extreme Right as well as the extreme Left, the communists became SIS's main preoccupation. It devoted the largest single part of its budget to Russia—in 1920 it spent £20,000 on agents in Helsinki to cover North Russia alone; this should be compared with the £2,000 it spent in Berlin. It sent its best officers—fluent Russian-speakers with long experience of the country and its people, capable of passing as Soviet citizens—to Moscow and Petrograd with virtually a free hand to establish networks of agents, finance counter-revolutionaries, and to do all in their power to crush the communist menace in its infancy."[8] Most of those networks, much of that treasure, was absorbed by the Trust, Lenin's extraordinarily successful Potemkin counterrevolutionary organization. Angleton would say, "If you want to understand Soviet deception, you have to go back to the Trust. It is the prototype."[9]

"The Trust," *Trest*, was the cover name of a Soviet disinformation and active measures effort which operated for six years in the early and mid-1920s. It was chiefly concerned with the leading White Russian émigré organizations: the Berlin-based Supreme Monarchist Council (the VMS) and the Paris-based Russian Combined Services Union (the ROVS), which was led by General Aleksandr Kutepov. Toward the end of 1921 a Soviet secret intelligence officer, Aleksandr Yakushev, first "revealed" to the VMS representative in Reval (now Tallinn, Estonia) that there was a powerful anti-Soviet underground that wanted to cooperate with the émigré organizations. The following year the Trust made contact with the ROVS in Warsaw. To add to the bona fides of the effort, General Nikolai Potapov, a former Czarist officer, traveled to meetings with the VMS and ROVS, purporting to represent the vast organization of the Trust while in fact working for Soviet secret intelligence. People believe what they want to believe. Soon enough, Yakushev, Potapov, and their associates were fully informed about the "order of battle" of the émigré organizations inside and outside the Soviet borders. Among other accomplishments, they lured the self-styled British "master spy" Sidney Reilly to the Soviet Union, and his death.[10] Stalin replicated the Trust in Poland after the Second World War. The Trust became Angleton's Rosetta Stone for the interpretation of Soviet affairs. Later still, as farce, Hoover built his own Trust within the dry shell of the American Communist Party.[11]

Part of the story of secret intelligence in the twentieth century is the play between the continuity of Great Game bear-baiting and the discontinuities produced by the eruptions of Germany onto the playing field: each time, the British secret intelligence services turning with reluctance from their engagement with Russia to meet the German challenge. The English ruling class had thought of itself in imperial terms for a century or two; the center of the Empire was India; the sole threat to British dominion in India (so it was thought, when little thought was given to the Indians themselves) was from Russia. For men of the British governing class who came of age in the period before the Russian Revolution, Germany was a distraction, its demands perhaps negotiable. And, for that matter, for most purposes they felt that the Russian Revolution itself was also a distraction, an ideological disguise taken on by the old foe. Communism for them, as an ideology, despite moments of hysteria in the press, was not so much a threat as an opportunity to build new and stronger alliances against Russia, to weaken the Labour and Congress parties with purges of activists. Hence, perhaps, the lack of much interest in "positive vetting" ("Are you now or have you ever been . . .") of members of the intelligence establishment in

Britain until the mid-1940s.[12] A gentleman's beliefs were his own business: that had been settled with the Catholic Emancipation Acts. It did not occur to anyone in Whitehall that a gentleman's beliefs might be sufficiently unorthodox and deeply held as to affect his actions. There was quite enough to keep the relatively small intelligence establishments of the time between the wars busy, raiding Soviet trade missions and keeping track of members of the Communist Party of Great Britain. When the Germans began to be perceived as the principal enemy in those quiet streets around St. James's Park (in 1936? 1940?), the secret world turned briefly from its fascination with Russia, and militarized.

Despite the interests of its practitioners and the romance clinging to its memory, the secret war was only a small part of World War II. Compared to the war screaming from the headlines—the great battles on the Eastern Front, the epic in the Pacific, the endless, equivocal violence in China—it involved few people, consumed little treasure. Parts of it were routine housekeeping in service of that greater war. Everyone who came to Britain from Germany and its allies was interned, prisoners were questioned, beaches were mapped, two and two were endlessly summed . . . and the results, as often as not, disbelieved or disregarded. But at least twice the secret war was crucial. In the matter of cryptography, the secrets called ULTRA in Europe and those revealed by "Magic" in the Pacific allowed the Allies to read the mail of the Axis powers, and this changed the course of the war at sea, profoundly affected that on the land.

Some of these effects on the land war were, for the British, inadvertent. In the winter of 1942–43, John Cairncross, a Treasury official also reporting to the KGB, was assigned to the decoding works at Bletchley Park. That place has often been described. Here is one of those descriptions: "Bletchley Park, some fifty miles north of London near the main road and railway to the northwest . . . was one of those large and rather ornate houses of red brick with timbered gables in the prosperous late Victorian style, probably built by one of the wealthy owners of the many brickworks which abound in this rich clay area. There must have been twenty or more rooms in the house, which was a long two-story building, entered through a pretentious porch. There were spacious green lawns with the regulation cedar trees, a croquet lawn and a ha-ha, a sunken boundary fence that was invisible from the house and gave the idea of unbroken space . . . Bletchley was only a small town. It was not beautiful; five miles away was Woburn Park and Abbey where the Duke of Bedford lived."[13] In this telling, not particularly accurate, description, the great houses of the nobility serve as orientation points—geographical, social, aesthetic—to the vulgarities of the owners of brickworks and the routine of war.

The British government filled the ugly rooms and then the uglier temporary buildings ("huts") at Bletchley, crowding the grounds of the mansion with mathematicians and linguists and clerical workers of various kinds. After the First World War, in order to facilitate the encoding and decoding of commercial communications, a German firm developed a machine with keys like those of a typewriter and an interior fitted with wheels and wires and levers, such that each time a key was struck, a different signal was sent. The resulting message was meant to be an enigma to unauthorized readers, and Enigma became the name by which the machine and its products were known. Between the time of its invention and the beginning of the Second World War the Enigma machine had been improved in various ways—and bought in large quantities by the German military and government. Those wishing to read German military and governmental communications therefore began projects that would enable them to decode intercepted messages that had been encoded with the Enigma machines. First the Poles, then the French worked on this problem, until they were no longer free to do so. Hence, Bletchley Park, where heroically captured Enigma machines were analyzed and turned inside out, as it were, by Alan Turing and others. These new machines, which assisted in the decoding of the Enigma intercepts, led to the theoretical and architectural basis for modern computers.

The British secret intelligence community established a program to share information with the American cousins in the Office of Strategic Services (OSS). On the British side, there was no unanimity of opinion concerning overfunded new agencies of a foreign power moving in at the very center of their intelligence services. As Rhodri Jeffreys-Jones put it, "Some British individuals were reluctant to give too much help to a nation that was ready to supplant their own country on the world stage and that was ideologically opposed to the British Empire. Nevertheless, the British did hand over some cryptanalytic 'golden eggs,' did supply ancillary services, and did train a number of Americans."[14] They had little choice. The sheer amount of work to be done in cryptanalysis, as in other aspects of the war, required American help—and the Americans were not going to allow themselves to be simply used by the British in this war, as many felt they had been in the previous war, as cannon fodder to fill the depleted ranks of their supposed betters in the Old World.

This was the background for the decision of the British Wireless Board in July 1942 to ask General Eisenhower and Admiral Stark for one American officer each from the U.S. Army and Navy to be "appointed by them for approving information connected with the American forces."[15] The Wireless Board controlled ULTRA, that "superior source" that was the supreme prize in the world of Allied secret intelligence. The American army officer sent over for this assignment was Norman Holmes Pearson, whom his superiors thought would look to the British to be an American version of their Oxbridge-connected traditions of Bloomsbury on the one hand and SIS on the other; an American "don" recruiting students into an American SIS.[16] The organization Pearson represented was not the Army per se, but the new OSS, under General William Donovan.[17] The invitation to Pearson was not simply a manifestation of cousinly friendship. The "British were apprehensive about the vast counterespionage responsibilities the upcoming invasion promised." They needed help.

> In return for OSS men and materials, the British now proposed to throw open their legendary ISOS London archives, that worldwide register of suspects, those precious card catalogues. Furthermore, OSS counterintelligence specialists were authorized to "study and summarize British decodes of any [Axis] intelligence message," including raw Abwehr decrypts . . . With this single breakthrough the OSS was made. One declassified OSS after-action study states: "Here was a field in which OSS would have otherwise been unable to participate effectively at all. The British provided files, sources for information, operating techniques, trained assistance and facilities which proved indispensable. It would have taken OSS perhaps decades to gain by itself the experience reached in only two years of British tutelage, and to build up the extensive files it was able to copy from British sources."[18]

Donovan established a counterespionage branch of OSS, X-2, to formalize the liaison with MI6 in June 1943. (Two months after Pearson's arrival in London—the paperwork was running a bit behind the war.) His General Order Number 13 (revised, issued June 19, 1943, effective June 15, 1943) listed the functions of this Counter-Espionage Branch as:

> To collect from every authorized source appropriate intelligence data concerning espionage and subversive activities of the enemy . . . To analyze and process such intelligence in order to take appropriate action thereon, and to exchange such intelligence with appropriate authorized agencies . . . To institute such measures as may be necessary to protect the operational security of OSS, and to prevent the penetration of our espionage and other secret activities . . . To cooperate with the counter-intelligence agencies of the United States and our Allies, and afford them timely information of enemy attempts at penetration or subversive action from areas in which X-2 is authorized to operate . . . To prepare secret lists of subversive personalities in foreign areas for the theater commanders and such other governmental agencies as the Director may prescribe . . . *The X-2 Branch shall maintain its own separate liaison and separate channels of communica-*

> *tions within existing OSS facilities* . . . The X-2 Branch shall establish and maintain its own files and records.[19] (Emphasis added.)

After the war, separate liaisons and separate communications were to be the Grail of Angleton's Counterintelligence Staff at CIA.

By the early summer of 1943, Pearson, three other American officers, and four secretaries were working with Felix Cowgill in the offices of MI6, Section V. Pearson's MI6 office, 22-A, was near that of Kim Philby. Cowgill and Pearson got along well, as Pearson would have made it his business to ensure.[20] Part of Pearson's strategy for making friends with his British counterparts was to utilize the services of the dining rooms at the Connaught and Prunier's. Those liaison meals were a common feature of OSS life in wartime London: "'Almost immediately on my arrival in London,' remembers OSS veteran Lyman Kirkpatrick, Jr., 'I found myself plunged into a series of lunches that would last from 1 P.M. through a good part of the afternoon, and dinners that lasted well past midnight. Our European friends were formidable consumers of alcoholic beverages, with apparently little effect, and I always wondered whether they also put in the same long office hours that we did.' The entire routine was quite a 'strain on the liver.'"[21] (Wartime practices became habits in the postwar world. Cold War Washington was submerged in alcohol: two or three martinis before lunch, wine with it, highballs while dressing for dinner, another martini or two, then dinner with more wine and cognac afterwards. These habits lingered from wartime adventures.)

When Pearson was not dining with British Secret Intelligence, he was having tea with the Sitwells at the Ritz, just up the block, or with Bryher and H.D. at Lowndes Square. In Bryher's *The Days of Mars, A Memoir* we catch a glimpse of Pearson in wartime London: "What I called the 'Lowndes Group' [after her residence at 49 Lowndes Square, SW1] had begun to form round H.D., before I arrived from Switzerland. Besides Hilda, her daughter Perdita and myself, there was Norman Pearson directly he arrived from America in April 1943, the Sitwells, the Hendersons, the Dobsons, Robert Herring, George Plank, Mr. Baylis, Philip Frere and Mrs. Ash . . . What we should have done without Norman Pearson I do not know. Hilda had met him in New York but my friendship with him began only after he landed in England in 1943. He rescued Perdita from a dreary job in the country to do far more interesting work in London and, after its liberation, in Paris, and kept up our spirits during that final difficult year when we were too exhausted to care whether or not we survived until the peace."[22] The "dreary job in the country" involved working with the code breakers at Bletchley Park, which Perdita called "Tapeworm Manor," a rather daring reference to the tapes of the decoding machinery.

As another example of Pearson's helpfulness, Bryher cites an occasion when, in 1944, "Norman Pearson returned towards the end of January, after an absence in Spain and Portugal, bearing two bananas, two oranges and a pineapple."[23] We might recall the great banana orgy scene near the beginning of *Gravity's Rainbow*, the shortages, and the comparative wealth of the Americans in London in order to appreciate those bananas and that pineapple, which Bryher describes as being ceremoniously divided among the elect of the Lowndes Group and consumed with religious gratitude.

The atmosphere of wartime London is also recalled by such archival ephemera as this OSS notice, dated February 25, 1943: "Every traveler as soon as he reaches London should go to No. 3 Grosvenor Square and apply for a membership card to the No. 3 Grosvenor Square Club. There are no fees to belong to this club. The atmosphere is very congenial, the bar good, and the food—considering the local situation—pretty fair and the prices reasonable."[24] The "local situation" was one of severe rationing and nightly bombing.

Perdita, H.D.'s daughter, was first Pearson's own secretary, and then that of his assistant James Angleton. She described her new job in a letter to Bryher and H.D., her adopted and natural mothers, who were, somewhat confusingly, one would think, lovers addressed collectively as "Kitten."

> 29, Ovington St.
> Tuesday
> Dearest Kitten,
>
> Thank you so much for this morning's letter, which was most morale-supporting—just at a moment when my morale did need a tremendous lot of support. All is well that ends well, as they say, and all has ended well . . . The work is interesting I think, or rather, will be, when I've sorted it out; at the moment it is so involved and so hectic, full of strange documents, everything as involved at [*sic*] it could be. But all very pleasant and fun, and the girls of which I am the latest are a very snapped up, decorative bunch. It seems to be even more hush-hush than the previous phase of my career, which is a great bore, as I should so like to tell the world. However, it IS fun . . . What fun that little Cafe des Allies is. I've had several of my meals there these last few days, and at lunch to-day, they turned on the Free French news bulletin for the benefit of some Frog customers, which gave it a delightfully Vevey kind of atmosphere. I can see it will become as great a stand by in our lives as La Speranza.[25]

Morale was good in the OSS. They were fighting a just war against a clearly defined enemy. They had comic theme songs:

*PAEN, POZZUOLI*

(To be sung to the tune of "Solomon Levy")
We are the boys and girls who work for OSS, alas!
You wonder what we do? Well you can—Oh, well, let it pass.
Our right hands even never know just what our left hands do,
But we know what always happens—all but who in hell pays who . . .
The present simply bores us stiff; the future is our goal!
and 'though we never play an ace we've several in the hole!
We soften up the hardest facts (roll flat, then whitewash some),
And with our cocky cutters *stamp the shape of things to come.*[26]
(Emphasis added.)

There are three copies of this among Pearson's papers. This may be an indication of authorship. On the other hand, he may simply have liked it. As three-quarters of a century later we experience the slow growth of a STASI-like mentality among Pearson's successors, we can only wonder at the innocence of those days and the accuracy of the prediction that secret intelligence agencies would stamp the shape of things to come.

During the period when Pearson was setting up shop in London, Angleton was being shipped first to the West coast and then to Michigan. The call to "hold Angleton" had come from a friendly conspiracy involving his father, James Murphy (head of X-2), and Pearson, in response to Angleton's own selection of OSS over the Judge Advocate General's office.[27] Murphy wrote an expediting memorandum in September 1943: "I would greatly appreciate it if you could get provisional security for Corporal James Angleton, in order that he may commence OSS school on Monday. His father is with this branch, and was with OSS previously . . . In addition young Angleton is very well known to Norman Pearson, who recommended him to me before I left London."[28]

Max Corvo has given an account of his experience of the field course, which may have been similar to Angleton's. "The training program at the SO camp was mostly physical, and it was conceived to test endurance and courage. Long marches were the order of the day; running the obstacle course was another exercise; and night compass runs through the woods were staged to inculcate a sense of direction-finding and map reading . . . The course on explosives . . . taught not only the formula of successful destruction, but also on discipline and inner control. The trainees were expected to ignite a stick of dynamite and walk with the stick, place it in the middle of a field, and walk (not run) coolly away, timing themselves so that they could be out of harm's way by the time the explosion occurred."[29] Describing Richard Helms's experience at a similar OSS training course, Thomas Powers commented that the purpose behind such training was that it "put a man in the right frame of mind, it gave him a bearing of confidence, and it let him know the nature of the business in which he was engaged, which, office routine at one end, was treason, betrayal, and violence at the other." [30]

Angleton did well at the OSS training schools and made a strong impression at the camp.[31] "I considered him extremely brilliant but a little strange," said a fellow trainee. "I met a lot of important Americans from Donovan on down, but Angleton was the personality which impressed me most. He made a terrific impression. A very exceptional man. He had something more. He had a strange genius I would say—full of impossible ideas, colossal ideas." [32] Angleton's performance both at the OSS schools and in the training course also impressed Murphy, who sent him off to London to assist Pearson at X-2.

Part of the work of X-2 was barely distinguishable from military police duties. "Whenever somebody trusted the wrong friend, or blurted out too much in an unfamiliar bed, or lost a shipment of bullion, it was the X-2 team which squeezed the truth to the surface." [33] There were other less routine responsibilities, but that which really mattered in London, that which gave OSS its margin of survival in the ceaseless bureaucratic battles of wartime Washington, was access to ULTRA, the product of Bletchley's decoding operations—and ULTRA's application in the Double Cross system.[34] The Double Cross system was the centerpiece of the English counterespionage effort. It succeeded in the nearly unbelievable feat of turning *all* German espionage agents in Britain into agents of the British Empire—at the crisis, so confusing the response of the German armed forces to Normandy that Eisenhower was able to open the second front,[35] this the raison d'être of Double Cross, the goal and ultimately the reward of the entire effort. In the mind of the Germans it added an entire army group to the Allied order of battle before Normandy, which was a feat at least equal to the Red Army's ULTRA-informed triumph at Kursk the previous year (ULTRA provided by a KGB spy). It could be argued that the success of the offensives on both fronts was thus ultimately traceable to ULTRA and its manifestation in the operations of Double Cross.[36]

The activities of Double Cross proper were coordinated by an interagency group (it was a bureaucratic war) which should have been designated by two crosses, "++," but, due to a deficiency in the design of English typewriters at the time, or so goes the story, was written "XX" instead. This mistyped double cross then read as twenty, hence the Twenty Committee, which in turn gave rise to the American designation X-2 for the U.S. counterespionage group.[37] The British Twenty Committee, created in January 1941, was a subcommittee of the Wireless Board, composed of the directors of intelligence reinforced by others.[38] As Sir John Masterman schematically put it, the Twenty Committee existed:

1. To control the enemy system, or as much of it as we could get our hands on.
2. To catch fresh spies when they appeared.
3. To gain knowledge of the personalities and methods of the German Service.
4. To obtain information about the code and cypher work of the German Service.
5. To get evidence of enemy plans and intentions from the questions asked by them.
6. To influence enemy plans by the answers sent to the enemy.
7. To deceive the enemy about our plans and intentions.[39]

This seven-point program may be taken as that of any secret intelligence service wishing to be successful. As we have seen, this one was very successful. It was, in fact, dangerously, *perfectly* successful, casting a halo over counterespionage, setting an impossible standard for later efforts—and giving rise to the not unreasonable suspicion that if, incredibly enough, all German agents in the Second World War had actually been double-agents, controlled by the British, how was any Cold War service to be sure that the same had not been done to them? Perhaps it was a bad lesson, that dreamtime of total control. After Double Cross, for counterintelligence officers that idea lingered for a generation: everything we think we know may be sheer manipulation, betrayal.

The care and feeding, the "housekeeping," for German double agents in England that Angleton learned in Ryder Street was a model of thoroughness. A "turned" agent would be provided with two guards, a radio operator, a house and housekeeper. His wallet would be stuffed with an identity card (in some plausible name) and the essential ration book and clothing coupons. There were "businesses" on obscure streets where visitors could be interviewed and their comments recorded.[40] In addition to these groundlings, housing, and paperwork, the system required a surprising number of MI5 officers: case officers, who dealt with the housekeeping, guard, and communications duty and officers who dealt with reports and messages sent and received, questions, and instructions, and another who followed up on what was learned from the agents.[41] Say nine men and women to support each agent. Of these, the most important was the case officer, the archetype of the intelligence professional. Years later Norman Holmes Pearson underlined a lesson from the wartime experiences of case officers: "It cannot be too strongly insisted . . . that the most profitable cases were those in which the case officer had introduced himself most completely into the skin of the agent."[42]

Each profession has its formative field work. As an anthropologist's first tribe or neighborhood is to his or her professional formation (ever after, many anthropologists refer to "my" tribe, village, tenement), so the experience of "running" an agent defines the case officer, the intelligence professional. They frequently (always?) in later life ask the question of whether a particular person is being run by someone, and if so, by whom. They tend to regard the world as being divided between the runners and the run. Their ultimate three o'clock in the morning terror is that they themselves are unwittingly being run. Only a naïf, in that wilderness, believes in the innocence of strangers, colleagues, or, if they have such things, friends. For their American students, the British were the great masters of this arcana. As Pearson put it: "These were the ecologists of double agency: everything [like the parts of a poem] was interrelated, everything must be kept in balance."[43]

The success of the XX Committee led to an elaborate problem in filing and cross-indexing. "As the number of agents grew, the volume of information contained in the messages grew also to a truly formidable size, and it was highly important that all this information should be carefully indexed and readily available for reference, since the messages of any one agent at any time had to be consistent with the messages sent by him at an earlier date . . . and not wholly inconsistent with the messages of other agents."[44] The heart of the operation became an ever-growing card file, a catalogue not of books, but of people: a virtual library of subversion. Its replication would be one of Pearson's great claims for OSS's war record. Peter Wright described the Registry as it was ten years after the war: "There were three basic categories in the Registry," he wrote:

> The first category was Personnel Files, or PF's, which were buff-colored files arranged in alphabetical order. There were about two million PFs when I joined the Service in 1955 . . . Then there were subject files, or organizational files, such as for the Communist Party of Great Britain. Subject files very often ran into several volumes and were elaborately cross-referenced with the PFs. The final main category was the duck-egg-blue List File. This generally comprised material gathered during a particular case which could not easily be placed within either of the two previous categories. There were also Y-Boxes. These were a means of separating particularly sensitive files from general access. For instance, all suspected spies were Y-Boxed, as were most defectors . . . Files were located by using the card

> indexes . . . The concourse of the Registry was always busy with trolleys transporting files from the Registry shelves to special lifts. The trolleys ran on tracks so that files could be shifted at great speed up to the case officers working on the floors above—F Branch on the first floor, E Branch on the second, D on the third and fourth, and A Branch on the fifth. The Registry employed enormous numbers of girls to maintain efficient delivery of files within the building, as well as the massive task of sorting, checking, and filing the incoming material. In [MI5 director until 1940 Vernon] Kell's day the Registry Queens, as they were known, were recruited either from the aristocracy or from the families of MI5 officers. Kell had a simple belief that this was the best vetting of all.[45]

"I was asked about him, and I said I knew his people," Colonel Valentine of MI6 commented, which sufficed as vetting for Kim Philby.[46] During the war the Registry had been housed in Blenheim Palace, a suitable home for squads of aristocratic clerks.

The American theorist of "strategic intelligence" Sherman Kent underlined the importance of such files: "Acquiring knowledge of personalities is one of the most important jobs of an intelligence organization. The ideal biographical file would have tens of thousands of names in it, and against each name a very wide variety of data. There must be a wide range of data because there are so many pertinent questions always being asked about people. What sort of man is he? What are his political and economic views? What are all his names and when was he born? Can he speak English? Who are his intimates? What are his weaknesses? How long is he likely to hold his present standing? Where was he in 1937? Etc."[47]

One of the great achievements of OSS was to duplicate, and expand upon, the British Registry. By the end of the war the American registry included approximately 400,000 names of America's suspected enemies, domestic and foreign.[48] It became one of Angleton's special interests.

Double Cross was an *English* triumph. The Americans were observers and students. Their achievements were *as* observers and students gradually acquiring the expertise necessary to replace their teachers in the Great Game.

It was to play these roles that Angleton sailed from New York on December 28, 1943, to take up work with Double Cross under Pearson. This was early in America's war (if after Midway), but well into the final phase for Europe. The office Angleton shared with H.D.'s daughter Perdita, 23-B, was next to Pearson's in the Ryder Street MI6 establishment. Perdita remembered Angleton appearing late one afternoon—then, after only a cursory hello as he entered, "doors and drawers and files were flung open, and he was into everything; pulling, leafing, thumbing."[49] Given conditions in London, his own nocturnal habits, and work that for the first time in his life absorbed all his attention, it was none too surprising that Angleton moved an army cot into that cramped Ryder Street office.[50] It was, in any case, a good address.

The tide of war, as the phrase goes, had turned. But the Americans still had much to learn, and in London James Angleton finally became a good student: "London was Angleton's professional matrix."[51] Among his new colleagues he found Kim Philby, now an occasional briefing officer for the Americans, Pearson's frequent lunch companion.[52] "Philby 'gave a one- to one-and-a-half-hour talk on the subject of turning agents—double agents,' one of the Americans recalled. 'I do remember being very impressed. He really knew what he was doing.'"[53] Philby and Angleton may have become friends in London; Philby may have felt he had a mentoring relationship with Angleton; Angleton may have shared that feeling.[54] These matters are impossible to disentangle at this distance. Later, all the parties concerned had too much at stake to be trustworthy witnesses.

By February 1944, X-2 London had a staff of seventy-five. Angleton was then in his mid-twenties, a newly minted second lieutenant, chief of the Italian Desk for the European Theater of Operations at X-2, with the not obviously applicable experience of four years of promoting and studying poetry at Yale and a year or so of legal studies at Harvard (and behind those Malvern, Milan, Dayton, Boise, Tucson/Nogales). An oddity of his official position was that among the reports he received were those from his father, now Lt. Colonel Angleton, who from late 1943 through the first half of 1944 represented X-2 in its discussions with Marshal Pietro Badoglio.[55]

There are various descriptions of Angleton's London routine. Here is one: "When free he would visit with T. S. Eliot, write poetry in his office or, wearing a coat and hunched over his fire, produce reports that were, he said, too urgent to wait, so that one of the secretaries would have to remain behind after hours to type them, making her way down through his always complex manuscript, in which there were footnotes, and notes to notes, and marginalia, and sheets decorated with commands, 'To X,' and 'Over,' and 'Insert B here.' No one was surprised when one day a typist came up with one of his poems, stuck in the middle of a report."[56] From time to time Angleton would exercise the prerogative of an American officer and seek relief from Army rations at Quaglino's or the Connaught Hotel.[57] And at least once he attempted to reconnect with his *Furioso* network. There is a reference to Angleton at this time in a letter from Empson to I. A. Richards. Empson writes that Angleton had "turned up" at the BBC, where Empson was working, "very mysteriously." Empson took him to a pub, naturally enough, "to meet the BBC Features and Drama side, who mocked at him rather, and he disappeared equally mysterious but I thought maybe in a huff . . . He was in mufti." And then: "Give him my best wishes if you see him," implying that Angleton might be renewing his literary connections in wartime Britain.[58]

However, he must have decided very soon after his arrival in London that, of the two careers his mentor Norman Pearson had on offer, the poetic-academic and that of counterintelligence, it was the latter that would become his lifelong study. If a student of these matters begins (not with the early Elizabethan dramatists and the French Symbolist poets but) from the shining example of the Double Cross system, the lesson is obvious. "The key [to counterintelligence,] he concluded from close analysis of ULTRA's application in MI6 operations, was penetration—a conviction reinforced by his future experiences on the ground as OSS chief in Italy . . . It became a central axiom of Angleton's theory that penetration was essential to achieve the manipulation necessary to deceive an enemy by forcing him into an unreal world . . . His experience in wartime Britain taught him how vulnerable even the most supposedly secure counterintelligence service is to clandestine penetration."[59]

Angleton had first been taught close reading by American masters: Pearson's colleagues at Yale, chiefly Maynard Mack. The war would teach him to read all over again. It taught him to read secrets. It also taught him to look for secrets to read. "Angleton became fascinated by the refinements of counter-espionage, where the original penetration was turned back on to the enemy. The game required not merely traditional skills and patience, but dispassionate intellect to identify unnoticed German successes and constant analysis to protect against deception. [He] explored the Byzantine possibilities open to the counterintelligence practitioner for exploiting his vulnerable opponents and sowing discord and confusion."[60] All this was the fruit of his study in Ryder Street.

While Angleton was learning his trade in London the war in Europe entered its final phase. The first months of the new year were spent in preparation for the Normandy invasion (with that very significant help from Double Cross), while Italy was conquered, one museum and cultural monument at a time; Rome finally welcoming another wave of northern invaders in June as British MPs encamped at the foot of the Spanish Steps, American officers replaced Germans on the arms of local working girls. Summer brought the liberation of France and the destruction of Warsaw; fall the last German victory at the Rhine, the liberation of Greece, the deportation to concentration camps of the last major European Jewish population, that of Hungary. By the end of 1944 the frontiers of the Thousand Year Reich were reduced to those of the old Holy Roman Empire: Germany, Austria, some of Northern Italy. The atmosphere in London was one of incipient triumph, tempered by the constant bombardment by the V-1 jet missiles and then by the V-2 rockets. Much of official London had been destroyed, as was more of the East End and large swaths of other English cities.[61] Many of Angleton's English friends lived in conditions of great deprivation, having lost homes and relatives—33,000 English civilians were killed in the war—the rich suffering a devastating decline in living conditions. The platforms of the Tube were filled with Henry Moore's sleepers each night; the windows of the clubs along Pall Mall were smashed; even Parliamentarians huddled over Neolithic fires at the very center of Imperial Whitehall. Bryher's writings of the period reflect this, raging against the incompetence of the authorities, the shortages, and the degrading regulations nearly as much as at the Germans themselves.

Angleton's new wife was understandably concerned about how her husband was faring under these circumstances. She wrote to Pearson in July 1944, asking for his care in loco parentis.

> Dear Mr. Pearson:
>
> . . . Because of your personal interest in Jim I asked you . . . if you would occasionally keep an eye out for Jim and see that he is not careless during these rocket bomb raids. Please do not tell Jim, but I must confess the worry is nerve-wracking. He does not tell me, probably because of his fear of censorship, what I wish most to know: if he is sleeping in air raid shelters, eating & working in them; if he is careful about staying away from movies, restaurants, etc. Is it too great an imposition to ask you if sometime, when you are not too busy, you would be kind enough to write me a few lines, telling me about those things? Being so much out of touch with him is very hard, and I would be more than grateful for any kind of reassurance you can give me. The exacting role of the Heroic War-Wife is something I fear I can never learn.[62]

The next month their first child was born: James Charles (Charles, neither Hugh nor Jesus). Cicely Angleton wrote Pearson again in October, rather wistfully asking him, as her husband's boss, to send Angleton on vacation.

> Dear Mr. Pearson:
>
> Because you were kind enough to write me before about Jim, and because you have known him for such a long time, I hope you will not mind this second letter about him. From what his father and friends have told me, and from what he himself hints at once in a while I gather he is working much too hard. May I put in a very earnest request?—namely that you give him a good boot in the direction of Northern England and vacation? I realize that he is a very difficult person to boot when he has his

mind on something else, but I really think it necessary for him to let up a little. He admitted in a letter yesterday that he is mentally very tired and for Jim to admit such a thing is a sure sign he needs a little rest. I would appreciate your help so much. In this case I fear that a word to the wise is not sufficient; he needs a good push—to a place where he can have nothing more on his mind, for a while, than the stupendous progress of his wonderful little son James.

I repeat, I would be more than grateful for any assistance you can give me in this conspiracy.

Very sincerely,

Cicely d'Autremont Angleton[63]

No vacation was forthcoming from this proposed benevolent conspiracy.

Angleton was living in his office, matching the information from ULTRA with reports from Italy, beginning to establish his reputation. "If 'Philby was the most gifted of the British,' as one intelligence officer said, 'Angleton was the most gifted of the Americans.' A fellow X-2 officer said that 'Jim was a very respected American among our British counterparts. He was probably more on a basis of equality with his British counterparts than anybody.'"[64] Sometime in 1944 he received a unique confidence from the head of British secret intelligence: "'We've been penetrated by the communists,' Menzies told Angleton in 1944, mindful of MI5 reports, 'and they're on the inside, but we don't know exactly how.'"[65] Perhaps Menzies also shared this confidence with Angleton's colleague, Kim Philby.

Angleton seems to have seen Perdita, his London secretary, during a quick visit to Paris, as he can be glimpsed in the margins of her correspondence:

Monday [Paris, March 1945]

My pets,

Just in haste—Norman is lurking behind the paneling waiting to carry this off to you . . . We're still terribly busy and working very hard . . . Things have been quite gay, because all the Chiefs gathered over the week-end for one of those jamborees when they hold endless meetings and drink and smoke and talk incessantly and achieve nothing whatsoever—however, they think they do, and it seems to raise their morale. Norman of course was here, and my friend Ezra from Italy, who went back after lunch and said he would ring you up tonight, though he is so erratic, I doubt whether he'll get himself organized before next week. But if a strange voice did ring up saying it was Lt. Angleton and had seen me—that was him.

Apparently Perdita's pet name for James Angleton was taken from Angleton's favorite poet, her mother's one-time lover. This was rather daring, at that moment, when Pound himself was on his way to what seemed then to be a certain treason conviction.

Perdita's letters give a lively sense of life in the clerical ranks of OSS. In July 1945 she wrote H.D. and Bryher from the Rhineland:

> Sunday 29th July
>
> Darlings . . . Life here has been the same giddy whirl. The usual thing—champagne, and Senior Officers fighting for one's company. I've acquired a rather devastating new Colonel whom I secretly call Heathcliffe and one of these days I know I will to his face. Immensely tall, with a rugged profile and great shaggy eyebrows; not a brain in his head—but quite a nice sort of background for a girl on the dance floor. Then there was a dance at the 825th Tank Destroyers new club (they wear a most intriguing patch on their shoulders, a furious black pussy cat mangling a tank in its jaws) on a very, very hot night; they transported their dance floor to the bottom of the garden, with a long, long strip of carpet right down the lawn all in the midst of terrific Rhineland hillery [*sic*] and a full moon, and they had one of the best GI swing bands I have ever heard with a treacly crooner who sobbed into the microphone practically non-stop and brought down the whole place. We girls went in civilian clothes, which really was heaven, after eight solid weeks dragging the same old blanket of a GI skirt around day and evening; oh so wonderful being a girl again, I can't tell you. We brought out all our most lurid scent, and pinned flowers in our hair and wore our highest heels—strictly illegal, I may say, and to get there we had to camouflage ourselves in our trench coats, those nice stout waterproof ones, you remember—which we meticulously wrapped ourselves in (on the hottest night of the year) and went creeping out to our jeeps in the blazing sunshine, feeling desperately criminal . . . Last night we had an OSS party down at the club—which turned out to be extremely gay. I had a very good time (civilian clothes again) with four escorts, my favorites at that, who remained glued at my side throughout, and whenever one of them took me to dance, the other three huddled together in a solid conclave, one holding my handbag, the other my drink, and the other my cigarette; that sort of thing really does wonders for one's Inferiority Complex . . . Also went to the Eagle night club . . . very modern and snappy, on New York lines, and has a displaced Belgian band, and a displaced Belgian cabaret show—a troupe of middle-aged chorus girls doing a middle-aged tap dance in tarnished sequins.[66]

There is rather obviously a movie to be made of these memoirs: *The Jitterbug Spy*, perhaps. Angleton had written in a similar style when at Yale and Harvard. Cicely Angleton did also, and continued to do so all her life, in letters and in poems written with the ease of letters. There may be letters in sealed archives from James Angleton's OSS and CIA years that displayed the personality of the *Vif* poems to friends. Or it could be that, as with Perdita herself, time and responsibility did their work, and the id-propelled vivacity of youth was transformed, in his case, into the mask of command. As Angleton commented much later, in a different context, concealing a vivid public personality may have been simply one more of the sacrifices he made for the West, or his vision of it.

# 4 Italy Eavesdropping on the Pope

The Centro Storico, the old center of Rome, is interestingly dominated, if you happen to be an artillery officer, by the heights of the Borghese Gardens and the Ludovisi district at the top of the Spanish Steps. The Ludovisi district was created in the late nineteenth century from a Prince Ludovisi's then-suburban estate. Its main avenue, the Via Vittorio Veneto, is today one of Europe's centers of consumption, restaurants and shops (always referred to as "elegant") alternating their offerings to the wealthy tourist, who, as often as not, finds lodging there of a style similar to that which can be found in London at Claridge's or the Connaught. As with the similar streets between Piccadilly and Pall Mall, here too can be found traces of the secret war. The Palazzo Margherita, where the Veneto makes a ninety-degree turn, houses the American Embassy, and there are still American government offices nearby on the Via Sicilia. The Via Archemede is on the other side of the Borghese Gardens: Broadway to the Via Sicilia's St. James's.

Tracing Angleton's career in Rome during the years immediately after the end of the Second World War, when he worked from offices in those streets, is an archeological endeavor. These shards at the bottom of the trench, for example, speak of the closing months of the war, when all of Italy was a complex transportation system—carrying Axis dignitaries and their looted gold through Allied lines to refuge in South America; carrying Jews from the camps to Palestine. The next layer, protected by what was until recently an impenetrable covering of official secrecy, contains shards inscribed with the origins of the Cold War.

In November 1944, when Pearson became chief of X-2 for all Europe, Angleton was transferred to Italy as commander of SCI Unit Z.[1] SCI units were joint British/American outfits placed in each theater of the war, with special communications and clearances, receiving ULTRA messages and carefully dispensing the information contained in them in such a manner as not to indicate from whence it came. The SCI units in Italy reported to the London head of MI6 counterintelligence, Kim Philby. Angleton's access to ULTRA in Italy gave him an enormous advantage as he went about his business, officially described as "the extermination of the German intelligence system so as to make it impossible for that system to continue or be resurrected in any organized form."

Angleton had spent much of his youth in Italy, that prewar Italy dreaming of grandeur and degradation. Going to Italy from London was a kind of homecoming, even if the great palace at Caserta, outside devastated Naples, and then those offices near the ancient center of desperate Rome, were far from his father's Milanese palazzo. It must have been comforting for Angleton to once more hear the language, walk pavements past Roman manhole covers stamped "SPQR," eat and drink something like the meals and wines he had remembered evenings at Quaglino's. He was to stay in Italy as long as possible and often returned there, not least as, after the war, his parents and sisters once more made their homes in Milan and Rome.

There is an unfriendly portrait of Angleton from those first weeks in Italy. An American Army officer, James Milano, had met Angleton "by chance in the bar of the Allied Headquarters . . . Milano had not been impressed. The man was clearly a highly competent intelligence officer, but Milano had thought him a self-satisfied snob."[2] Perhaps Angleton was busy that day, laying down his networks. Perhaps he and Milano simply did not hit it off. Angleton was many things, but not self-satisfied; possibly, however, what an American would call a snob.

When Angleton had arrived in Italy in 1945, the situation was customarily complicated. The wider context of the war had left the peninsula divided between the Allies in the south and the Germans in the north, each supporting their favored Italian government. The German zone was contested by the partisans, who were in turn divided in many ways, chiefly between those many who were Communists and those comparatively few who were not. The Allied zone was also somewhat contested, in this case between the British and the Americans: Churchill wanted Italy for his chain of revived Mediterranean monarchies; the Americans were not at all enthusiastic about that project.[3] These divisions played out in the secret world as a conflict between OSS and the British Services, an aspect of the history of OSS in Italy that has been documented in a remarkable account by Max Corvo, an Italian-American from Middletown, Connecticut, whose father had been an anti-Fascist activist in Sicily, forced into exile by Mussolini in the 1920s. According to Corvo, the "British policy was to treat Italy as a private preserve. Their field officers expected Italy to become a zone of exclusive British influence once the war came to an end. But SI [OSS Secret Intelligence] Italy had other ideas. We wanted the Italians to make up their own minds about the future. We envisioned a postwar Italy that would stand side by side with the United States in the international alignment which would undoubtedly take place after the war."[4] The Italians were assisted in making up their own minds to stand side by side with the United States in a variety of ways. Italian Military Intelligence and similar organizations, for example, were subordinated to their American equivalents.[5] And, as we shall see, the United States offered some help with the formation of governments and the determination of elections. OSS itself had organizational difficulties in Italy, conflicts between Corvo's Italian-American legion, on the one hand, and U.S. Military Intelligence, on the other, problems that were exacerbated perhaps by ethnic prejudices and certainly by emerging U.S. domestic political issues.[6]

Elements of OSS had entered into liaison activities with the Communist partisans with some enthusiasm.[7] At first they had Donovan's support in this, or at least they thought they had.[8] Times and war aims changed. It became less acceptable in Washington to have OSS officers in Italy (or elsewhere) who were openly sympathetic with local Communists.[9] The resulting personnel realignments were read in the field as purges. Some people were discouraged by this. These actions were accompanied by a complicated series of organizational and command changes. In London it was felt that the atmosphere was still "murky." Hence the younger Angleton's dispatch to Rome, which was well received. "When Angleton first arrived in Italy, the administrative head of all OSS counterespionage in that country cabled the X-2 office in London: 'Air much clearer.'"[10] Corvo was also pleased: "Gradually, as the OSS buildup in Italy developed and more X-2 personnel became available, we started security clearances for our prospective agents through X-2 . . . When Lieutenant Jim Angleton was transferred from Britain to Italy in charge of X-2, he broached the idea of some cooperative undertakings. I was gratified by his intense interest in the work."[11] What was that work? Not so different from that of a student of the New Critics at Yale: a matter of reading carefully, something for which Angleton had been particularly well trained.

OSS's role in Italy for the remainder of the war consisted of SI's support for the partisans in the north (the area under German occupation) and counterespionage in the remainder of the country. Angleton was principally responsible for the latter.[12] He was able to operate more or less as a free agent,[13] moving into rooms in Rome and living there the nocturnal life he had begun in New Haven and continued in London.[14] Of course, this pattern was more customary in Italy. "At the SSU (Strategic Services Unit) offices . . . Angleton's would always be the lone light burning in the middle of the night. 'I caught him one night,' an SSU officer recalled. 'He had all these goddamn poetry books out.'" The women working in his office were less disturbed by the ways of their dashing young counterintelligence officer. They "found this enigmatic wraith somewhat attractive." Romantically enough, Angleton thought that like Keats before him he would die in Rome of tuberculosis. "Every day he was complaining he was dying of TB," one of the SSU men said. "He had a premonition that within three years he'd be dead."[15] It was not a pose. Angleton did in fact have tuberculosis and would spend time after the war in hospital to treat it. And those scarred lungs would eventually fail him.

As experts in the personnel and methods of the enemy, Angleton's X-2 officers assisted the larger and more numerous units of the U.S. Army's Counterintelligence Corps in locating and neutralizing German and Italian Fascist agents. Angleton was in a position to direct aspects of the Army's security program because of his access to ULTRA and the instruction he had received in London in the arts of doubling and controlling enemy agents, skills that Army counterintelligence officers did not have. When the Army picked up an agent, one of Angleton's X-2 staff was called in to assess the agent's potential as a double agent. If the results of the review were affirmative, X-2 assumed responsibility for the agent.[16]

X-2 was still an extension of British secret intelligence, with its "superior source" from signals intelligence. From one point of view ULTRA was tantamount to an intrusion of late-twentieth-century information technology into the 1940s, similar, in this way, to the success of the Germans with rocket science, or to that final trump card, the American atomic bomb. Angleton and his colleagues appeared to be carefully collating POW interrogations and the like to assemble materials that could be used as a basis for the understanding of the situation in the field. While they were in fact doing that, they were, more importantly, using these materials as cover for the information handed to them by British ULTRA. Concealing the junction was of the highest importance and not at all a simple matter. It is for this reason that, in the first few months of 1945, Angleton invented the "Key"—"an easy-to-revise compendium of information about the various German and Fascist Italian intelligence services that could be shown to officers not indoctrinated into ULTRA. The trick was to comb POW interrogations for corroboration of facts first learned from ULTRA. Once a detail had been found in a less sensitive place—a SECRET interrogation report instead of a TOP SECRET ULTRA decrypt—it could be disseminated."[17] This quasi-academic exercise may have been the origin of Angleton's practice, attested to in most accounts of his CIA years, of dropping mysterious allegations into a conversation, then, when questioned, dismissing his interlocutors with the statement that they were not cleared to know his sources. In Italy, at least, this had been a simple statement of fact.[18]

The tasks at hand for Angleton were in a sense routine, centered on liaison activities with U.S. and Allied intelligence services, interrogations of line-crossing German agents, meetings with colleagues and officers of other services, the writing of reports. There, what was called his legend became elaborated. "Angleton haunted the streets of Rome, infiltrating political parties, hiring agents, drinking with officers of the Italian Secret Service, and sitting up all night in his . . . office reading agents' reports." This was not an individual endeavor. OSS, like the CIA after it, was an instrument, occasionally a weapon, in the hands of its masters. "Angleton and his men pursued US policy in Italy. In a nutshell, this was to fund and dominate the re-launched Italian Intelligence services; to undermine the British, who had plans to restore the Italian monarchy; and to bribe or browbeat Italians into voting for 'centrist' parties and against Communists."[19] File after file in the National Archives is filled with the flimsy copies of reports received, reviewed, and sent on by Angleton's unit. Many of them take the form of short narratives describing the line-crossers, their original stories, the modifications produced during questioning, and occasional ironic evaluations. There are local situation reports, personality lists, historical studies; reports on the developing situation in Yugoslavia and the efforts by Tito's secret intelligence service to support the Italian Communists; reports on the surviving Italian Fascist organizations; reports on looted art, relations with the Italian intelligence services, interviews with prostitutes, reports on currency matters, clippings from newspapers; reports on dealings with the Vatican.

The overall impression is of Angleton sitting at the center of a great web of agents, a trusted, knowledgeable, highly professional officer (although often dressed in mufti: those famous Savile Row suits). It is easy to visualize him in the Via Sicilia or the Via Archemede, flipping through papers, annotating them in his small, neat, hand, writing summaries, pursuing the paper craft of counterintelligence. "Whenever you went to Rome to meet with Angleton, you found him propped up behind his desk facing you through two big stacks of papers . . . You would sit on a sofa across from the desk and he would peer at you through this valley of papers."[20] This image is repeated in accounts of visits to Angleton's Washington offices during the Cold War.

Counterintelligence is lived by those involved as a series of files, each with its peculiarly untrustworthy narrative. Angleton's career in wartime Italy can be epitomized by three such cases: Princess Pignatelli, SALTY, and the VESSEL affair.

The case of the Princess Pignatelli was a piquant example of the indeterminacy of counterespionage work. In spring 1944, Maria Pignatelli, who had been a client of Donovan's law office before the war, journeyed from German-occupied Rome through the Allied lines to Naples, where she contacted OSS, offering to become an informant. She had relatives who were intimates of Mussolini's rump government in Northern Italy, which possibly made her attractive to OSS. On the other hand, the British Secret Intelligence Service was suspicious of the princess and within a few weeks had arrested her Naples contacts, shooting one to death as he tried to escape. In mid-May, Allen Dulles, then in Berne, was given a copy of a message sent by the German ambassador in Rome to Foreign Minister von Ribbentrop, announcing that "the Italian princess, Maria Pignatelli . . . fled from her home in Naples . . . to Rome, in the disguise of a midwife with . . . papers which she had bought." Pignatelli met with Field Marshal Kesselring in Rome, then went north to meet with Mussolini, then returned through Allied lines to Naples. She was said by the German ambassador to be helping to set up sabotage networks in Allied-occupied areas of Italy. Acting on this intercepted intelligence, OSS had her arrested when she next passed through the front lines. She naturally enough claimed innocence when interrogated by OSS. Angleton did not believe her, writing, "Though the name Pignatelli has been the subject of considerable controversy . . . recent information . . . reveals that Princess Pignatelli in fact did come through the lines on behalf of [a double agent] and revealed considerable information to [Franz] Land of the GIS [German Intelligence Service], General [Artur] Maeltzer, and proceeded on to Mussolini and [Francesco] Barracu [undersecretary in Mussolini's Fascist government]." This would seem to have been sufficient for the firing squad. The princess, however, with her good connections on all sides, played out the clock until the armistice removed her from the jurisdiction of Allied intelligence forces.[21]

Until August 1945 most of Angleton's operations in Italy were, like this case, the extension of a program of military security: battle lines and the borders of various zones of control were crossed by individuals in either direction, the bona fides of those individuals were examined by intelligence and counterintelligence experts. Interrogations led to reports, which gave rise to more reports and further interrogations. The flimsy carbon copies were placed in manila folders, the folders in filing drawers. Those files today can be requested at the National Archives, the reports read. What do they mean? As usual, there are contradictory readings, like those derived from the Pignatelli story. In general, such readings seemed to prove to counterintelligence specialists, close readers like Angleton, that agents should be treated as guilty unless proven innocent. (But who can be *proven* innocent?) This was a lesson he learned by heart, took to heart. Angleton was always surprised by the surprise of others at his systematic suspicions. How else should a counterintelligence officer view the world? With trust in the purity of the motives of all the Princess Pignatellis he encountered?

The Pignatelli case led to a favorable outcome for Angleton in the everlasting bureaucratic struggle between intelligence and counterintelligence imperatives: the then head of X-2, James Murphy, "had been recommending to Donovan that no agent be employed by the OSS in any part of the world who had not first been cleared by X-2."[22] The Pignatelli case confirmed this: Corvo and his colleagues in Secret Intelligence from that moment had to have Angleton's approval for their initiatives, a measure of control that he would seek to establish—with varying degrees of success—in later years in the CIA.

Angleton followed the custom of his Double Cross mentors of calling groups of agents by related names. A circuit of his sources called Rose, Pansy, Briar, and Bloom wandered around Rome, entering houses, stealing documents, recruiting the mistresses of foreign diplomats, and reaching up to Milan while it was still under German occupation to identify sites of interest to the Allied armies. Others in Angleton's employ recovered caches of Fascist documents—and such perhaps more attractive accumulations as the royal treasury of Ethiopia.[23]

An aspect of Angleton's work in Italy which would continue into his CIA career was his involvement in and reliance on liaison arrangements with other intelligence services.[24] In Rome he laid the basis for his eventual triumph in the 1960s: the general alliance of Western counterintelligence services. He had established strong relationships with British secret intelligence while in London and continued these in Italy, in spite of the difficulties encountered by OSS SI. In Italy he did well with the French, as he had in London, and pioneered a relationship with the nascent Israeli units.[25] From the time of his arrival in Rome, he in practice controlled some of the Italian services. Angleton's relationship with the Italian services can be epitomized, for better and for worse, by two cases with naval titles, one called SALTY, the other VESSEL.

The SALTY activities bridged World War II and the Cold War. OSS forces in Italy had worked closely with Italian naval saboteurs organized into the OSS Marine Unit. Capitano di Fregata Carlo Resio approached Angleton in November 1944 with two offers: radio operators to assist in penetration work behind German lines in the north of Italy; and that the OSS Marine Unit use the Italian GAMMA school for frogmen at Taranto as a basis for the creation of a U.S. sabotage group to be used in the Pacific.[26] Angleton, deciding that it was worth running the risk of infiltration in order to strengthen X-2 relations with the Italian intelligence services, used these offers as the basis for general cooperation. He gave Resio himself the code name SALTY, and, beginning in January 1945, received from him a series of reports useful for counterespionage operations. The reports concerned both remaining Fascist activists and Soviet-supported Communist plans. X-2 headquarters found the latter irrelevant to the war effort, writing Angleton in February 1945 that "We would further like to know from you whether you feel that all of this information actually ties in with German activities, either in the present or along the lines of future operations. Without an explanatory tie-in and evaluation, much of this information seems to be rather meaningless."[27] SALTY, in Washington's view, was a premature anti-Communist. In Berne, Allen Dulles was moving toward his perhaps Himmler-inspired negotiations to secure a German surrender in northern Italy, making the Soviets increasingly uneasy. The SALTY reports, like those Dulles was forwarding from his source ("George Wood") in the German Foreign Office, were inopportune under these circumstances.[28] Angleton, unlike Dulles, dropped the issue, but he continued to work with Resio and to broaden his relationship with the Italian intelligence services.[29]

The notorious VESSEL affair dated back to Corvo's work in 1944.[30] Corvo suggested in August of that year "that we undertake a project that would immediately start the collection of intelligence material on Japan. This intelligence material was available in the form of studies and reports of the SIM files in Rome and in the offices of various companies that had done business in the Far East."[31] It must have seemed terribly clever to develop a source in Rome that would yield information about intrigues in Tokyo. Here again, the prize sought was a negotiated peace settlement. If there were factions within the Japanese government that wanted an early peace (as Dulles, among others, believed that there were such factions in Berlin), then the first step toward supporting them would be to identify the interested parties. It was a gamble. The reports could be disinformation and, in any case, the entire effort ran counter to explicit Allied policy: unconditional surrender. Nonetheless, in the fall of 1944 Corvo's associate Vincent Scamporino formed a group to gather information about Japan and in December the group "was assigned the difficult task of using Vatican connections to bring the war in the Far East to a quick finish . . . the operators from [the Italian SI and Reports Board] section established close ties at the highest levels of the Vatican secretariat . . . This 'penetration' made it possible to get a close look at the various diplomatic chanceries in the world"[32]

At this point matters become more than customarily murky. Reports from Scamporino's source "at the highest levels of the Vatican" were plausible and extraordinarily detailed. Donovan was particularly interested in Vatican matters and possibly had his own relationship with Vatican intelligence: from 1941 he funded, among other things, a Catholic intelligence service called Pro Deo.[33] When he began to receive what seemed to be genuine papal documents—including agendas and minutes of meetings—he was grateful to have this opening to reports from a secret intelligence service with worldwide contacts, particularly valuable for insights into events in Tokyo. He passed the materials directly to the president, pleased, as the ability of OSS to deliver information at this level was a major coup. On the other hand, he was running some risk in passing "raw" intelligence to the highest policy levels, but it was a risk he was perhaps only too willing to run, as a move in the rivalry between OSS and the other U.S. intelligence services preparatory to the expected foundation of a postwar unified intelligence agency.

The reports included such seemingly authoritative accounts as the following: "On 10 January [1945] the Japanese Emperor attended a secret council meeting during which someone dared to speak about peace feelers. The Emperor was informed that certain Japanese individuals have been attempting to interest [the Pope] in mediating the Pacific War. The Emperor did not express any disapproval of these efforts . . . Someone at the meeting declared that such activities might be a useful preparation for a time more opportune than the present. The Council was skeptical of mediation possibilities, evidently believing that only force of arms would settle the conflict."[34] This was fairly dazzling. Brigadier General John Magruder, director of OSS intelligence services, soon sent an appreciation to OSS in Rome: "VESSEL material is greatly valued. It constitutes a unique line into Japan. You will appreciate that definitive checks are difficult to elicit in high places. However, we know the President is interested in the material as is State."[35] But in February the situation began to unravel. A number of the VESSEL reports were found to be false and a consensus developed in Washington that they were disinformation, perhaps meant to influence the deliberations getting underway at Yalta. When Angleton compared notes with Scamporino they found their respective places on VESSEL's distribution list and soon discovered the names of the other customers: the Soviet, British, and French news agencies; the American, Argentine, British, and Polish embassies; during the German occupation, various German and Japanese newspapers; the British intelligence services.[36] It had been a good business, but now it was coming to an end.

OSS SI canceled their subscription to the VESSEL material. However, Angleton continued his, at five hundred dollars per month, in an attempt to identify VESSEL's source and perhaps use him, as Angleton had been taught by Double Cross, as a U.S. agent. This was the characteristic counterintelligence strategy Angleton would follow throughout his career. Also characteristically, the operators, OSS SI in this case, disagreed, not wishing to play a supporting role in what was now a counterintelligence operation. More puzzlingly, Angleton seemed to continue to believe that the material itself might have value, establishing direct contact with the source, Vigilio Scattolini, and maintaining it through 1946, continuing to accept the VESSEL reports and sharing them with the American Embassy in Rome. This was a mistake. "Ultimately, a CIA postmortem on the case concluded that Scattolini's reports had contributed to 'informing, misinforming and thoroughly confusing those individuals responsible for analyzing Vatican foreign policy during the period involved.'"[37]

Others have taken a darker view of Angleton's role in the VESSEL affair: William E. Gowen, then a special agent with the U.S. Army's Counter Intelligence Corps in Rome, thought that Angleton had fabricated the entire VESSEL file: "According to Gowen, Angleton had coerced Scattolini and his assistant, Setaccioli, into translating the Italian-language versions of the fake Vessel material under threat of execution as alleged German spies . . . The originals of the Vatican messages were actually written in English by Angleton personally . . . Angleton first in the OSS, then in the CIG and finally in the CIA produced hundreds of completely false reports for more than three years, while stationed in Rome." According to John Loftus and Mark Aarons, "To its credit, the CIA admitted that its Rome X-2 files are bogus. The [National] Archives placed a warning notice on the JVX file so that future historians will not be misled."[38] That the VESSEL reports have been judged by the National Archives to have been bogus does not, of course, prove that they were composed by Angleton himself.

As the best student of the VESSEL affair, Timothy Naftali, sums it up, "In his use of ULTRA material and the other products of liaison and penetration operations, Angleton demonstrated a firm grasp of the principles of effective counterespionage. He knew both how to make use of the intelligence that he had and how to develop new sources. Throughout, his objective was to extend his coverage of foreign activities likely to affect U.S. interests. This implied an exacting definition of counterespionage, which obliged the field officer to monitor all foreign intelligence-gathering in strategic areas and to control every possible channel through which an adversary might acquire American secrets . . . This sureness of touch had its negative side. It nourished a self-confidence that occasionally led Angleton astray. The VESSEL debacle showed that Angleton could relax his principles if he became personally involved in a case."[39]

The manner of proceeding that Angleton had learned in London and Rome was one to which he remained loyal for the next thirty years. It was often fruitful. When it was not, it could lead to spectacular mistakes. VESSEL was a forerunner of the central case of Angleton's final phase, the Golitsyn affair, which some observers believed also had led to "informing, misinforming and thoroughly confusing those individuals responsible for analyzing" foreign policy during the period involved.

The Princess Pignatelli affair illustrates the ordinary day-to-day business of counterintelligence: Here is a person offering her services as an agent. What are her bona fides? Is she our agent or theirs—or both? What are the risks involved? The benefits? SALTY gave Angleton experience running an agent-in-place in a "friendly" service. And VESSEL showed his willingness to play for high stakes on a broader stage. With these cases and others Italy provided Angleton with a good practicum for his advanced counterintelligence studies. It also may have given him a brief refresher, or reminder, of earlier studies of a different kind. Angleton's duty station in Italy brought him home not only to the familiar ground of his own family's activities, but in close proximity with his mentor, Ezra Pound.

In April 1945, Pound, who had been indicted for treason for his propaganda broadcasts during the war, surrendered to American military police in Rapallo. They sent him to Genoa, where he was arrested by a Sergeant Pierce, a member of Army counterintelligence. Pierce happened to be an intellectual with interests in contemporary poetry. (Of course, H.D. had said that every American sergeant wrote poetry.) He recognized Pound, who was on the Army's most wanted list, and acting on orders from the Attorney General placed him in high security detention and under a suicide watch. "We took him on the third floor of the building where there was a special room—very small—but it had no windows."

> It had a thick wooden door and it turned out we had to have a peep hole cut in that door so that we could observe him; you know, the suicide watch thing, so on and so forth. All there was in that room at that time was a cot, nothing else. There were no toilet facilities and we had to march him down the hall every time he needed to go . . . the next day, one of the guards had liberated somewhere what the Italians call *cecciole de caca* . . . a night bucket, you know. So that's what we put into the room. And every time you go down the hall with Ezra Pound, he had to carry it. We weren't being cruel to him, but I wasn't going to carry it. None of the guards were going to carry it and so, the greatest poet of the century was walking down the hall with this bucket.

Pound was interrogated in Genoa for two and a half weeks. "When he would talk about the Left Bank crowd in Paris; Hemingway, Gertrude Stein, James Joyce, Eliot—anyway, his spirits increased and he took to pacing up and down that little room."

> That's what I remember best because that's when he began to let his mind speak out about what he really believed in. And what he really believed in was Mussolini and fascism and that 80 Jews controlled the entire world finances, they started all wars for their benefit. Roosevelt—his real name had not been Roosevelt. Rosenfeld was his name. He would go on for a long, long time about this business of economics, the gold standard, social credit . . . and then it was all the fault of the Jews. He was so viciously

intolerant that it didn't make sense until you realized that he really meant it. He wasn't just talking. In one of his broadcasts, he had said "100 Yids should be shot for every Fascist soldier that falls." That's on the record. That's recorded.[40]

Pound was then taken from Genoa to Pisa and imprisoned "in the Cage" in a prisoner of war camp.[41] His life there became the material for his final Cantos, among the most beautiful of the series.

so light is the urging, so ordered the dark petals of iron
we who have passed over Lethe.[42]

What can be said about the paradox of a great poet who was also a criminal? His jailer in Genoa, Sergeant Pierce, said, "When the chips went down, he chose one side, which was the side we were fighting, which was killing a lot of us. He was against us. He tried to help Mussolini and Hitler. Of course he was a great poet, but it's like saying somebody is a great basketball player so he can get away with murder or something."

David Martin claims in his *Wilderness of Mirrors* that Angleton visited Pound in Genoa, but offers no proof for his assertion.[43] If Angleton did make such a visit, as a ranking intelligence officer, there would not necessarily have been a record. There is, among the papers of Rome X-2 in the National Archives, an interrogation report concerning Pound written when he was first taken into U.S. Army custody, but it is unsigned. On balance, some of Angleton's colleagues think it rather more likely than not that Angleton did make such a final visit to his old master. Much later, during the Vietnam War, the Angletons went on a pilgrimage to Pound's Cathar country. Cicely Angleton was to write in her dissertation on what she referred to as the Church's twelfth-century "counter-insurgency" campaign.

Pound's case remains somewhat mysterious. He was treated very harshly, at first, sent back to the United States expecting to be hanged, then through the efforts of many of the contributors to *Furioso*, consigned to a mental hospital, awarded the first Bollingen Prize for poetry, and finally released to return to Rapallo.[44] Other Axis broadcasters, lacking friends in such high quarters, did not get off so lightly.

As time went on, and not much time at that, Fascism lost its threatening aspect, becoming—as doctrine—more and more difficult to distinguish from the ideologies of the victors, until, finally it was only the anti-Semitic component that remained as powerfully self-condemning as ever. Hence Pound's efforts to appear to distance himself from that, while leaving the remainder of his convictions in place. The paradoxes of Modernism in poetry reach their extreme in Pound. It is not that we have trouble with poetry that expresses a repellent set of ideas—if so, how could we read any of the classics that exalt power?—but it is that in *The Cantos* the ideas are frequently so filled with inhuman vitriol as to dissolve the poetry itself. Which brings to mind not only Pound's colleague Wyndham Lewis, but also Lawrence, Celine, certain poems by Eliot and Yeats. (Just as, in the earlier of Eliot's model periods, Swift's poetry and that of certain Elizabethans similarly limit our pleasure in the verse through the ugliness of their matter.) This is not simply a question of aesthetics. As Pound himself pointed out, "The one thing you should not do is to suppose that when something is wrong with the arts, it is wrong with the arts only. When a given hormone defects, it will defect throughout the system."[45] Or, as Eliot more memorably put it,

> I that was near your heart was removed therefrom
> To lose beauty in terror, terror in inquisition.

Angleton's career in the period 1945 to 1948 was both part and formative of the processes that transformed the dynamic world of the Second World War into its static Cold War successor. At the highest international political level there were rapid and massive changes, a reversal of alliances that began from the moment it became clear that the Allies were defeating the Axis regimes. Within the United States, wartime tolerance of Communists and Communist sympathizers gave way to the beginnings of McCarthyism. In the world of secret intelligence, the Office of Strategic Services failed in its bid to become a postwar intelligence agency, was dissolved and then almost immediately rebuilt through a bewildering series of holding organizations, a process that culminated with the founding of the Central Intelligence Agency and the national security state itself. Throughout the first part of this period of transformation Angleton remained at his post in Rome. His was one of the success stories of the transition: he had found his métier, and was fortunate enough to be not so highly placed as to be purged with the OSS leadership, but sufficiently important to be protected during the demobilization. (In contrast, say, to Norman Holmes Pearson, who sought a leadership role in postwar intelligence, but in the end had to settle for Yale and a dual career as a founder of American Studies and a talent-spotter for the Central Intelligence Agency. Or perhaps those were the same thing.)[46]

Angleton's institutional context had been determined first by his association with Yale and then, briefly, Harvard, and finally, through the intervention of mentors and family members, OSS. OSS made him a military man—and, to an extent, like so many young men who spent their formative years in uniform, his viewpoint remained at a certain level military. He was accustomed to the chain of command and to seeing the world in terms of allies and enemies. He identified with his Service, the nascent intelligence corps, and followed its birth pangs in the immediate postwar period with anxious attention. The character of the postwar American intelligence establishment was also formed during those years, which saw its first covert action success: the Italian election of 1948 (an electoral coup, as it were) in which Angleton played a pivotal role.

It was during this period that James Angleton first connected with the man who was to replace Pearson as his mentor. Allen Dulles, making his way home with his wife from his wartime post in Switzerland, traveled down to Rome through the territory only recently relinquished by the German generals with whom he had negotiated Operation Sunrise.[47] Dulles's biographer tells us that "both Allen and Clover [Dulles] found Angleton immensely attractive and pleasant company; their friendship—personal and professional—endured for the rest of their lives."[48] (And beyond, as it was Angleton who composed the eulogy at Dulles's funeral and carried his ashes out of the church afterward.) Angleton made himself at home in the Dulleses' suite in the Hotel Hassler. There, he and Dulles spoke of "their common perception of the Red challenge, and of the drastic sub-rosa measures required to meet it including the recruitment of influential Italian agents, without over-scrupulous concern for past Fascist affiliations."[49] Quite the contrary, as a matter of fact: the only stronger surety of anti-Communism than "past Fascist affiliations" being past Communist affiliations, like those of the trade unionist Jay Lovestone, if repudiated with sufficient energy and publicity.

A few months later, what had been whispered in staff meetings of the OSS and murmured over drinks at the Hotel Hassler was broadcast to the world. On January 5, 1946, President Truman, making one of several declarations of the Cold War, said that "the Russians will soon be put in their places. The U.S. will take the lead in running the world in the way that the world ought to run."[50] The Soviet response was as might have been expected. The next month Stalin said that a renewed conflict between capitalism and Communism was inevitable, which in turn encouraged American hitherto premature anti-Communists. Soon J. Edgar Hoover "began to bombard the White House with indications that the Soviets were planning war. In February he told Truman he had heard from American Communist sources that Communist uprisings were scheduled in France within six weeks, the start of an advance that would place 'Soviet troops on the Atlantic Coast and on the Mediterranean.'"[51] In August, General Vandenberg, second Director of Central Intelligence, sent a "Memorandum for the President" stating that "Soviet propaganda against the U.S. and U.K. has reached the highest pitch of violence since Stalin's February speech and follows a line which might be interpreted as preparing the Russian people for Soviet military action."[52]

The world seemed to be moving from one phase of the Apocalypse to another in the late 1940s. The Red Army was said to be taking up advanced positions across Europe; the Communist parties in Italy and France assuming that share in the government that had preceded coups in Eastern Europe; Mao moving east from Yenan to occupy Beijing; American generals predicting the outbreak of World War III every few months. The Western intelligence agencies were already forming the alliances necessary to implement those policies which were to become known under Kennan's rubric of containment: "[T]he ABCA military agreement [was] reached in Quebec in 1946. This committed Britain to four-power military links with America, Australia and Canada . . . When British Army officers and Intelligence men, thirty years later, spent as much time in joint meetings with the officers of a foreign power as considering how best to serve their elected government, this agreement was at the root of the relationship . . . It was the first unacknowledged alliance of the Cold War."[53]

Meanwhile, J. Edgar Hoover, unwilling to rely on his powers of persuasion with the new president, resumed his campaign to convince the public at large that the only hope for freedom was to declare war on Communism at home, if not abroad, with a return to the activities of the Palmer period: mass arrests, deportations, internments.[54] This was part of a domestic anti-Communist offensive of which Hoover was the legitimate, and legitimizing, front. His allies were arrayed to his right.[55] There was, then, a certain order of battle among anti-Communists. It began with Averell Harriman and his peers, those whose names are now most frequently associated with large-scale private philanthropy. From Harriman, we move to the ever-changing holders of the great offices of the State, and Harriman's employees, his lawyers, managers, bankers, and assistants, when he was, from time to time, a government official himself. All these were internationalists, more or less Wilsonian opponents of a system of ideas and power that, if implemented in places where they had investments, threatened them with direct financial harm. Beyond them were the isolationist anti-Communists, the churchmen, the anti-Semites, the simple opportunists, for whom anti-Communism was a crusade or a flag of convenience. And, at first to one side, there were those, like James Angleton, believers in a militarized anti-Communism, not so much as an ideology as a way of life.

Half a century on it is perplexing to review these matters. On the one hand we have the nightmare of a Stalinist Soviet Union, the Gulag state, and on the other we have a West which in the name of freedom was enlisting the surviving elements of fascism in a worldwide struggle for power, with the domestic consequence of a political system that seemed in the next few years (as again sixty years on) to honor civil liberties only so long as they were not exercised. There was Sartre, of course, who, in full knowledge of the Gulag, refused to abdicate his freedom. But, to paraphrase Stalin, how many divisions had *Les Temps modernes*?

Angleton's career in Italy uniquely bridged the transition from the anti-Axis alliance to the Atlantic anti-Comintern struggle, a transition which was accompanied by the demise of the OSS and the creation of its CIA successor. As most of his peers and future mentors closed up shop with the end of the war, Angleton continued to work in Rome, shifting smoothly from interrogations of German agents crossing the front lines to "psychological warfare" activities directed against the Soviet-supported Italian Communist Party.

Following the pattern he had established in London, Angleton in postwar Italy concentrated on the erotics of counterespionage: liaison and penetration. These were not independent activities. "The sources of counterespionage information available to Angleton interacted constantly to produce a better picture of the adversary. Some hitherto obscure reference in an intercepted message might begin to make some sense, for instance, when compared to an interrogation report gained from an Allied service."[56] This was a skill he had acquired at Yale, honed in London. By "the end of 1946, Angleton, or those directly responsible to him, had amassed over 50 informants and had penetrated 7 foreign intelligence services, including Tito's OTSEK ZASCITA NARODA (OZNA), the French Service de Documentation Extérieure et de Contre-Espionage (SDECE), and the Italian Naval Intelligence Service, the Servizio Informazione Segreta (SIS)."[57] Later, these avenues into other intelligence services were to become of crucial importance to Angleton as chief of the Counterintelligence Staff of the CIA, but already in 1946 Angleton was receiving liaison reports from the British, various Italian intelligence agencies, that of the Vatican, and that of the ambiguous Croatians, fresh from their role as eager Nazi collaborators. Angleton was, in particular, "coordinating many matters with the Vatican's sophisticated intelligence apparatus," sharing, for example, "the confidences of the Secretary of the Croatian Cofraternity of Saint Jerome in Rome, Dr. Krunoslav Draganovic . . . Draganovic facilitated the American services in Italy (a $1,400 payoff was standard) by providing safe houses across his syndicate of Rat Lines. Along Draganovic's underground railway the Jewish Agency regularly smuggled its coordinators in and out of Soviet 'denied areas' . . . Angleton never drifted far from what was boiling in the camps."[58] (Draganovic concluded a long career as an anti-Communist functionary and U.S. intelligence asset by retiring in 1967 to the then still-Communist Yugoslavian province of Croatia. This raised questions in some minds as to how many employers he had during the Cold War.)[59]

In these activities Angleton was following a policy of "long-range counterespionage," seeking to lay the foundations for a postwar effort to track the intelligence operations of all the governmental and quasi-governmental actors in his theater. As "military commitments are gradually discharged," he wrote, "there is a sharp increase in the number of long-term espionage suspects which is accompanying the transitional phase to normalcy."[60] We might pause over that sample of Angleton's mid-1940s official prose style, and this:

> Dear Norm[an Pearson],
>
> For a number of weeks I haven't found a moment to write a personal letter to you. There was always the chance that it would go into the wrong hands and then, until Roger arrived, I didn't know what had happened to you . . . I was pleased with your info and glad that you haven't forgotten me . . . Anyway please destroy this letter as I can only blow off steam to you. I'm still angry with you for having tipped glasses with every field-station except Rome . . . It's not very pleasant news to hear about the changes. I always liked this outfit because of the people in it. There was always the feeling that the linen would be washed among ourselves because we were or are damned good friends underneath the cold memos and hot cables. I feel that's the only way you can keep a service going. It's for that reason that I sincerely hope there will be a deus ex machina saving the situation which really means saving the personnel. I'm sorry to hear that Bob left and I am more than sorry to hear of your decision. I hope you will reconsider Norm because in spite of the differences we've still got the biggest hump before us . . . People don't learn this business unless they take it by slow absorption and there are many of the best that just lack the proper kinds of filters . . .
>
> I'll send the books soonest. All the best from
>
> Jim
>
> P.S. Please destroy!

"Furious," irreverent "Jeem angle ton" has vanished. Two years of war, of the drafting and reading of reports, of increasing responsibilities, had forged a new style: when personal, subdued, semi-formal, pessimistic; when official, redolent of the vocabulary and syntax of bureaucracy. During this period of the end of one war and preparations for the next, James Angleton continued to work in Rome, winding up the one, and working toward the first American victories of the second.

Angleton's Second World War lasted almost exactly two years. He had gone to London as a specialist in contemporary literature, as a law student perhaps intending to go into his father's office machine business. At the end of the war he was in charge of X-2 for all of Italy and was, quite possibly, America's most accomplished counterintelligence expert. War would also give Angleton a new persona: remote, mysterious, omniscient; a new mask modeled on faces he had met in Ryder Street. These would stay in place, in public, for the rest of his life.

The cost of Angleton's professional success during this period was personal: nearly intolerable strains on a marriage that came to exist in name only, as the separation from his wife Cicely extended to multiples of the amount of time they had spent together. (It was during this period that Cicely Angleton wrote to the Cummingses that "I have sort of forgotten what he looks like.") Angleton, who had left the United States in 1943, shortly after marrying Cicely d'Autremont, saw her again for the first time in November 1945, when he stopped in New York City for two days on the way to OSS headquarters in Washington for a two-week consultation. Their reunion was not a success. As Cicely Angleton saw it, "We just didn't know each other anymore. Jim was wishing we were not married, but he was too nice to say it. He thought the situation was hopeless. He was all caught up in his career. We had both changed. It was typical of a war marriage. It was exactly what his father had warned us about in 1943 . . . Jim no longer cared about our relationship, he just wanted to get back to Italy—back to the life he knew and loved. He didn't want a family. The marriage seemed to be annihilated then and there."[61]

Nonetheless, like millions of others, the Angletons bought a house in the suburbs (Alexandria, Virginia), but then, unlike others, went off in opposite directions, James Angleton back to Rome and Cicely Angleton to her family's compound in Tucson, from which on March 16, 1946, she wrote to E. E. and Marion Morehouse Cummings: "Mrs. Angleton broods over a huge tome entitled 'divorce charges' and decides the best reason is because she has made him so unhappy, in the meantime quietly & continually flogging herself with a leather thong."[62] The Angletons were only in some ways typical of their generation. She was better educated, her family considerably wealthier than most; he was intent on building a career far from either Wall or Main Street. In other ways, however, they were swept along with the era: even Angletons and d'Autremonts find that their choices are only among the limited number on offer in their time. For example, the next month Cicely Angleton decided, as was the fashion, that it would be best for her to try to "adjust" to the situation, seeing a psychiatrist recommended by Marion and E. E. Cummings.[63] On the one hand there were psychiatrists to help her to "understand," and therefore presumably accept, her husband's behavior. On the other hand, she portrayed herself as reading "Griselda, in Chaucer," in order to become patient with her lot—an older therapeutic tradition.

A few months later, Cicely Angleton was still living at her parents' house: "Tucson Aug. 1946 . . . No word from James. Sent him the d[ivorce] papers and he refuses to sign."[64] And then: "No divorce yet. Jim suddenly doesn't want it, the poor little darling, I have sort of forgotten what he looks like, but he's still a poor little darling. Anyway, for a while after that startling piece of news I became all custard pie, of course, but now it's hardening petit by petit. It's tiresome being married to someone who keeps saying he's confused for five years. He may come back in a few months. Yes, I could get a divorce without his consent but should I ever get married again, he would quash it. It's all in the GI Bill of Rights, but I think it's unfair."[65] In July 1947 there occurs, in passing, one of the few political comments of the Angleton/Cummings correspondence, when Cicely writes, "It was so good to have your letter . . . When [the Cummingses] feel creaky and ancient . . . Russia will kiss the other cheek and everyone knows that can never be . . . We are all blazing hot and it's a wonderful excuse why I am not divorcing Jim. It's simply too hot to do anything except to take naps and make wills and other charming pastimes."[66] Later in the year she wryly charts the space to which women were being restricted in the postwar world and continues her semi-humorous account of her marital tribulations.

> 10 Oct. 1947, Tucson
>
> At the moment I am going to business school and am learning typing and shorthand. There is a wonderful buxom blond in my class, a Fielding kind of person, and I was complaining one day about the lack of jobs for women, and she said, between loud reports of chewing gum, "Kid, whattya expect? There ain't nothin' for a girl except bein' a secretary, bein' in the dime store, or jerkin' sodas. Now which are you goin' to do?"

Cicely Angleton, with her Vassar degree, was no doubt adequately educated for business school in Tucson or the secretarial work for which it was intended to prepare her. She was less prepared for the course of events in the United States, which, paralleling those in Europe, were closing down the political and social space achieved in the 1920s and 1930s for dissent and a public life for women. Faced with the gathering militarization of American foreign policy, women, even those as privileged as Cicely d'Autremont Angleton had few choices beyond "bein' a secretary, bein' in the dime store, or jerkin' sodas"—or becoming "homemakers," mothers, and patients of such as the Cummingses' friend, the Dr. Wittels of this world.

These domestic dynamics of everyday life had their analogues in the public sphere. Just as Yale prepared its students for careers as members of the governing classes, who would later inform Yale as to the services expected of it for the next generation, very soon the techniques of "adjustment" used by American psychiatrists to reconcile women like Cicely Angleton to their reduced place in the world would be projected abroad as panaceas for groups who might otherwise decide that they wanted, say, higher wages or a choice of their political system. In the America of the late 1940s, as wives went into therapy, some of their husbands went into the practice of what was termed psychological warfare. Among these was James Angleton, who had by then once more left his wife to plunge "back to the life he knew and loved" in Rome: the secret world of counterintelligence.

# 5 Coup d'État

For most Americans the fires and mushroom clouds over Hiroshima and Nagasaki meant the end of war. The troopships reversed course in mid-voyage to Tokyo Bay; sailors pushed airplanes into the South China Sea and the victorious aircraft carriers set their course for Hawaii; the troops marched from their hometown victory parades to college campuses suddenly forced open to unprecedented numbers—and types—of students by the GI Bill. Even Yale filled with students too battle-hardened and too poor to be absorbed by the old system of casual study and serious socializing. In Washington the managers of the war turned their attention to demobilization and the dismantling of the great machine that had brought victory, while their civilian colleagues destroyed the now suspect New Deal agencies. Factory managers thanked the women who had produced the tanks that had helped win the war and sent them home to have babies, while returning men went into the factories to make Fords and Frigidaires—and after work went home to the new suburbs, their wives, and their new babies. Madison Avenue turned from marketing war bonds to marketing the ensuing deluge of consumer goods, and the lights on Wall Street burned late as brigadiers-turned-bankers toiled to dispose of the floods of money that were the fruits of victory—as devastated Europe shivered and starved in the dark.

Sometime four or five years earlier the capital of the world had moved from Whitehall to Washington, but the move still seemed temporary, as if at any moment peace would truly come and Washington would return to its southern slumbers. There was, it is true, a double line of great office buildings marching on either side of the Mall from the Washington Monument to the Capitol, most of a classical style uniform with the late-Imperial offices that form the core of London; some decorated with the squared columns and eagles common to what now appears to have been the international style of state power, as ubiquitous in Berlin and Rome as Washington and Paris. And the bridges across the Potomac were solid enough, guarded by heroic figures in the best Socialist Realist manner, a gilded celebration of equine and human buttocks and pectorals. But, slightly to one side of the tremendous force field extending from Old State across the bridge to the still new Pentagon in Arlington—the dipole of the emerging Cold War—the Mall itself was littered with flimsy temporary buildings. Those near the reflecting pool housed what was left of the OSS, which with increasing urgency was being converted into a new agency, Donovan's dream, a Central Intelligence Agency with both intelligence coordination and intelligence procurement functions.[1] Blanketed with the alternating rain, snow, and ice storms of the Washington winter, the dank heat of endless Foggy Bottom summers, the future was stirring fitfully in those insecure spaces.

That Washington dominated the world as no power had since the Rome of the Caesars or the Chung-tu of the Great Khans was evident to everyone except, perhaps, a few men in the Policy Planning Staff of the State Department, their colleagues commuting between New York and Washington, and scattered remnants of the OSS in Washington, Berlin, and Rome, busy with the next war. Staring out over the ramparts on the Potomac, they thought the world looked grim. The Red Army had not matched the demobilization of its allies; Communist unions controlled the factories and docks of France and Italy; Communist parties were bidding for power from Prague to Paris, and even Britain had a Socialist government. Matters seemed particularly grave in Italy, where the Communist Party had acquired immense prestige and something like majority support, not to mention military experience. Italian democracy seemed fragile and, from Washington's point of view, untrustworthy. Some people, it was thought in Washington, were not to be trusted with democracy. It was a sentiment that would gain currency there with the Cold War. Eventually it applied even at home.

Back in Rome, Angleton had learned through his penetration agent, SAILOR, who still held a key position in Italian military intelligence, that early in 1946 elements in the Italian military command were beginning to lean toward the United States among the competitors for the favor of the emerging Italian government. "Intending to mount a serious campaign, Angleton asked [Washington] to be forewarned by cable of any government speech seemingly favorable to Italy that he could use to convince the Italian intelligence services that 'their loyal collaboration with our service works to better their dubious position at the peace table.'"[2] Angleton's objective, it should be noted, was "loyal collaboration with our service"—in other words, the subordination of the Italian secret intelligence agencies to the American. Already at this relatively early date Angleton's analysis of geopolitical matters was radically focused on the relationships among secret intelligence services. In the 1940s, when he said "Italy" he meant the Italian secret intelligence services, as in the 1960s and 1970s, when he said "Soviet Russia" or "China" he meant the Soviet or the Chinese secret intelligence services. Later, denying a Sino-Soviet split in the 1970s, for Angleton, was in the first instance a denial of a split between the Chinese and Soviet intelligence services. True enough, perhaps, as far as it went.

The situation in Italy between the fall of Mussolini and the election of 1948 was chaotic. The losers were quickly identified: first of all the Fascists, of course, hung from lampposts, paunches splayed across the front pages of newspapers. And, a bit later, the king and his party, who had moved too late and too timidly for the British to rescue them. The winners were the two great international movements: the Church and the Communist Party. For two or three years their struggle remained in the balance, tilting now in favor of the one, now of the other. Palmiro Togliatti, the surviving leader of the Italian Communist Party, back from Moscow, was successively justice minister and minister without portfolio in the Badoglio government, then vice-premier to Alcide De Gasperi as prime minister. There were those in the Italian Communist Party, partisans and union leaders, who wished to—and in some cases did—try for power with the guns they had used against the Fascists and Germans. Togliatti, convinced this would bring bloody reprisals from the American Army, disarmed his comrades and, supplied with funds from the East, tried to best De Gasperi in national elections. De Gasperi was a Vienna-educated Tyrolese who had spent the 1930s and the war years as a Papal librarian, inventing Christian Democracy behind those mellow walls as the Vatican struggled first to keep the Pope out of German internship, then to stop the Red Army at the historic divide between the Orthodox and Catholic lands. At the end of the war the Vatican rescued the odious Croatian government, smuggling those and other mass murderers down to Rome and on to Buenos Aires, then, financed by its American daughter church, the American Federation of Labor, and the U.S. secret intelligence services, it succeeded in constructing an electoral victory for De Gasperi in 1948 that blocked the Communists from national power and corrupted Italian politics for half a century.

Angleton had waded into these marshes in the classic military counterintelligence role of interrogator of prisoners and civilians caught crossing military lines; establishing liaison relationships with the Italian secret intelligence services and the Vatican's specialists; finally joining with Jay Lovestone—onetime leader of the Communist Party of the United States, "foreign minister" and bagman of the American Federation of Labor—to facilitate the construction of a network of anti-Communist trade unions in Europe west of the Elbe.

The situation in Italy was worrisome for U.S. postwar planners. Their problem was to find a way to unify the parties of the center-right and center-left before the Communist Party could come to power. Matters appeared to approach a crisis when, in the June 1946 elections, Italians voted out the monarchy and gave a majority of the Constituent Assembly to the Left.[3] To make matters worse from Angleton's point of view, that autumn the Communists and Socialists renewed their wartime alliance. In the November elections the Christian Democratic vote declined while that of the Communists increased. A decision was taken in Washington to support the Christian Democrats and to attempt to split the Socialists.[4] Ted Morgan has traced such "splitting" tactics back to Stalin and Lenin himself, which gave their application in this instance a nice irony: Italian Communism was to be fought by American ex-Communists using methods imported from Moscow. The key figure in this strategy was the extraordinary Jay Lovestone, soon to become one of Angleton's closest friends.

Prominent anti-Communists like Lovestone began their careers, presumably, with a belief about society—that it might be improved—a belief shared by many people in the middle decades of the twentieth century. Lovestone and his friends differed from most in moving to action, joining those in their own and other countries who shared their beliefs about human betterment and, perhaps, their propensity for conspiracy. Falling into conflict over control of the groups they had formed as instruments for effecting their beliefs, they struggled first with their co-conspirators, then, naturally enough, with their own former beliefs, eventually allying themselves with the enemies of their former allies, new friends who held beliefs antithetical to those with which activists such as Lovestone and his old friends had begun their public lives. Struggles that had begun *within* the Communist Party became struggles *against* the Communist Party, so that, for example, at the critical point of the Depression, Lovestone was asked by the head of the United Auto Workers to help "purge" Communists from its executive board.[5] It followed that when a Free Trade Union Committee was created by the American Federation of Labor in 1944, Lovestone was the natural choice to be the committee's executive secretary. His associate, Irving Brown, moved to Europe as the Free Trade Union Committee's representative on the ground, organizing anti-Communist efforts on the docks and in factories in France, Italy, and elsewhere. Millions of labor dollars flowed into the creation and support of anti-Communist unions in Europe and Latin America, much of that effort, and those dollars, directed by Lovestone.[6]

After World War II, Lovestone helped form a sort of anti-Comintern, as if some former ally of Luther or Calvin had become a Jesuit. (Was it Koestler who said that the final battle of the Cold War would be between the Communists and the ex-Communists?) Burton Hersh tells us that Angleton thought Lovestone "One of the only really great men of the labor movement, a discerning student of international politics, and custodian over 'the finest archives that ever existed on the Communist Party.' Jim Angleton had recognized in Lovestone a peer in clandestinity, a fellow adept of 'many covers, many passports,' perfectly positioned to expedite liaison between the CIA and George Meany over at the AFL."[7]

What would be called the "Lovestone Empire" flourished throughout the early Cold War, establishing relationships and funding patterns that were put at the service of the CIA; making its archives available; teaching the Agency such skills as the proper way to split labor unions and political parties. The Lovestone archives were an important dowry for the anti-Communist trade unionists as they moved closer to the CIA. It had been just such archives, the reader will recall, that had formed an essential part of the earlier attraction between the British secret intelligence services and the OSS. Files have always been catnip for American secret intelligence.

To return to the prototype of such efforts, Lovestone observed that if in 1947–48 he could split the Italian Socialists, then their right wing would vote with the American-supported Christian Democrats, creating a new center, while their left wing could be discredited by being portrayed as an instrument of the Communists. Using networks previously set up by Lovestone and Irving Brown, in 1947 both the AFL and the U.S. government began to pour money into the right wing of the Socialist Party.[8] While Lovestone and Brown labored behind the scenes for James Angleton and his associates to create new political alignments in Italy, center stage, the Italian prime minister, De Gasperi, managed in ten days in Washington and New York in January 1947 to obtain a $100 million Export-Import Bank loan.[9] This was when $100 million was real money. On May 5, 1947, the American ambassador met with De Gasperi and told him that he would have "strong American support" if he would remove the Communists from his governing coalition.[10] Following this hint, De Gasperi suddenly resigned on May 12, 1947, forcing the dissolution of the coalition government, forming the required minority Christian Democratic government on May 31. American approval of the success of this exercise in Lovestonite splitting tactics, recognition of the new government, followed two days later.

The already rapid pace of American intervention in Italy was accelerated by Secretary of State George C. Marshall's speech at Harvard on June 5—timed at least in part to influence developments in Italy—outlining what would become known as the Marshall Plan. The Marshall Plan was rejected by the Soviet Union in July (much to the relief of its designers). Some weeks later, William Donovan, now presumably just another Wall Street lawyer returned from war, had a word with the new secretary of defense, James Forrestal, on the steps of Columbia University's library. Like the Italian Communists, the "French Communists, he said, were buying up copies of literature that might embarrass them, purchasing printing presses, 'and carrying on all these activities which characterize a psychological warfare operation' . . . the United States had no effective official counter to this activity . . . The American Federation of Labor was already assisting the anti-Communist component of the French labor movement. According to Donovan, the knowledge that this assistance came from an American source boosted the morale of the anti-Communist French workers. On the other hand, such assistance was neither enough nor appropriate in its provenance." Later, Donovan wrote Forrestal, "I am sure you would think it unwise to let this pass beyond your control."[11]

How much was AFL funding for European unions ever "beyond the control" of the U.S. government? When was the AFL an independent actor? When did it cease to be one? Certainly by 1947, or 1948 at the latest, the AFL had become another "stop" in something like Frank Wisner's "mighty Wurlitzer" of governmental psychological warfare. Of course, by then the CIA was itself, in some sense, an instrument of the ancient anti-Communism of the AFL. Which way do the currents run in these matters? Both ways.[12]

On September 7, 1947 (after the international governing and political classes had returned variously from their Cape, shore, and beach holidays), Togliatti, in a speech which was taken either as a threat of civil war or as a warning to those who might start one, claimed to control a force of thirty thousand armed men. Meanwhile, the U.S. Congress had created the Department of Defense, the National Security Council, and the Central Intelligence Agency—the administrative infrastructure for the Cold War. The new secretary of defense, Forrestal, immediately gave weapons from Allied stockpiles in Germany to supporters of the Christian Democrats: Fascist veterans, among others. On September 24, Kennan's State Department Planning Staff issued a civil war scenario for Italy. Kennan said that the Italian government should "outlaw [the] Communist Party and take strong action against it before elections. Communists would presumably reply with civil war, which would give us grounds for reoccupation [of the] Foggia fields or any other facilities we might wish. This would admittedly result in much violence and probably a military division of Italy; but we are getting close to the deadline and I think it might well be preferable to a bloodless election victory, unopposed by ourselves, which would give the Communists the entire peninsula at one coup and send waves of panic to all surrounding areas."[13] Civil war with foreign intervention was, in Kennan's opinion, preferable to the "bloodless victory" he expected in a fair election by a group the United States opposed.[14] Kennan's recommendations for activity in Italy fell between containment and what later would be called "rollback": covert action perhaps best placed in the containment column; military occupation, which would likely have brought confrontation with Tito, more along the lines of the liberationists.

The new National Security Council issued NSC 1/1 on November 14, 1947:

"The Position of the United States with Respect to Italy," which stated that "the United States should make full use of its political, economic and if necessary, military power in such manner as may be found most effective to assist in preventing Italy from falling under the domination of the USSR either through external armed attack or through Soviet-dominated Communist movements within Italy, so long as the legally elected government of Italy evidences a determination to oppose such Communist aggression." That last clause was a nice concession to international legality. Not that the U.S. government was taking any chances with the nature of "the legally elected government of Italy."

NSC 1/1 was as close as anything to a formal, if secret, declaration of the beginning of the Cold War. The form that struggle was to take was indicated when NSC 1/2 ordered a campaign to counter "Communist propaganda in Italy by an effective US information program and by all other practicable means." Later in the month the situation in Italy, from the point of view of the National Security Council, took another turn for the worse. The State Department reported that the Italian Communist Party had begun a violent campaign against the Right and the police, calling wildcat strikes, attacking police stations and prisons, wrecking the headquarters of the right-wing parties, finally mounting a general strike in Milan and seizing control of the prefecture on November 28.[15] The American Embassy in Rome requested a troop build-up in Libya in anticipation of an Italian government call for intervention.[16] Washington disagreed, thinking it sufficient to send in more surplus supplies from Germany, this time for the Italian armed forces; after some hesitation on the part of the Italian government, this was done.[17] The United States had the means at hand to project a threat of direct military action, as it still had occupying troops in Italy. The American government decided to suspend withdrawal of those troops if Communists seized control of all or part of Italy prior to the agreed end of the Occupation on December 15, 1947. In the event, the Communists did not move and U.S. troops were withdrawn from Italy on December 14. They were to be replaced with what was called "psychological warfare," a term James Miller tells us "had taken hold in military circles in World War II, when General Eisenhower had established and used a psychological warfare board" on the British model. "It referred to covert operations that boosted the morale of friends or undermined the morale of enemies. In the context of European politics in the late 1940s it meant, for example, the issuance of unattributed publications, false attribution, forgery, and the secret subsidization of publications . . . [I]n December 1947 . . . National Security Council directive number 4/A put the CIA in charge of covert 'psychological' operations, with the State Department supplying policy guidance."[18]

It is somewhat surprising to learn that bribery and fixing elections were "psychological" activities, less surprising that literature, art, and music also fell under this rubric. But for the National Security Council and the CIA all these were considered useful and legitimate weapons in a conflict that was believed to be, in the first analysis, as it were, ideological.

General Eisenhower, upping the ante, "recommended that a list of potential Italian agents be prepared and passed on to the Central Intelligence Agency . . . for possible use in covert operations in Italy."[19] This was, to borrow Richard Helms's phrase about his own commission in relation to Chile thirty years later, the equivalent of handing James Angleton a marshal's baton to tuck into his knapsack. The problem was how at once to intervene and to conceal that intervention. The methods chosen were "private donations," union funding, conventional overt U.S. governmental support, and covert action. According to Burton Hersh, "When Jim Angleton got word out that Communists in Italy were buying up all the newsprint in the country toward the end of 1947, and Forrestal panicked because there seemed no loose cash anywhere around the government with which to blanket radio time or bribe the traditional middlemen, Allen [Dulles] pitched in without a qualm. A collection plate circulated among the Morris chairs of the Links and Brook clubs, and within days one of Angleton's Special Procedures people in Rome was turning over millions of lire in a satchel to a well-dressed intermediary inside the Hotel Hassler."[20]

This is a pretty story. Unfortunately, it is only partially true, if that. Perhaps there was an Episcopalian collection plate circulated among the leather armchairs of Princeton-in-New York. But those were not the funds that made the difference. Angleton and his colleagues had a variety of other, larger sources. Among other things, the Rome Embassy itself was gearing up for direct action.

> A memorandum prepared by Dr. Henry J. Tasca, member of Embassy Rome staff (Treasury) transmitted December 27, 1947, recommended countermeasures to policies and tactics of the Italian Communist Party identified by the Embassy. Among the countermeasures he recommended are: A) dissemination of information regarding democratic processes; B) provision of direct aid to selected political parties; C) counterintelligence and penetration of communist organizations to corrode and sabotage the party from within; F) encouragement of non communist labor movements; G) support for democratic movements prepared to engage communists should violence result, including selection and training of energetic young leaders for use in electoral campaigns, civil war, or partisan activity in the event of a new world war. Many of Tasca's recommendations were evident in subsequent US statements of policy, overt action plans, and covert activities.[21]

• • •

In the midst of all this, toward the end of the year, Angleton was finally transferred from Rome to Washington, to the new civilian secret intelligence organization, where he could better coordinate the flow of governmental support for Italian matters. Cicely Angleton wrote to the Cummingses with the domestic repercussions of this news.

> 10 Oct. 1947, Tucson
>
> Jim is coming home next month and oh crisis crisis. Well well, he will be a brave man and will earn all my respect if he can face mother, who will be sitting in the front hall nursing a shot gun. It is going to be very strange, and he certainly will be bored; well, in ten years from now it won't matter.[22]

It was not only her mother who did not approve of James Angleton's treatment of his wife. Her sister Ann asked the Cummingses, "How are we all going to break the witches spell that hangs over Cicely? I despair."[23] And then, answering a letter of condolence on the death of her father, Cicely Angleton wrote to the Cummingses with a collage of Cold War political and psychological metaphors: "I was very happy to have your letter about father, because you said exactly what mother and I feel about him . . . Mother is fine. She has a guilt complex about having a swimming pool and so is trying out her own Truman doctrine on little boys in the neighborhood who don't have them and tribes of them come each day and retaliate in good Stalin fashion by taking over the whole place."[24] E. E. Cummings replied with a letter about Isak Dinesen, rather than Stalin, with a closing gentle statement of admiration (and perhaps a plea) for Angleton: "And what a miracle of momentous complexity is The Poet!"[25]

James Angleton, when he finally returned to Washington, did so to join the Central Intelligence Group, one of the successor organizations of the OSS, on December 20, 1947. Angleton was moving against the tide in this choice of careers, as most of those of his generation who had served in the war were intent on peace and business. His father, "da Major," tried to persuade him to join the family business in Italy, arguing that real men made money, but Angleton was convinced that secret intelligence was to be his business: spending rather than getting. In any case, Cicely Angleton did not want to live in Italy and James Angleton had finally decided that he did not want a divorce. Therefore—and thereafter—Cicely Angleton kept house in the Virginia suburbs for her husband and their children, while James Angleton continued to attend to the fate of the West.

The overt funding for Italian Christian Democracy came, let us say, from collection plates in America's Eastern Establishment club-land. Behind that was the Lovestone empire of anti-Communist labor organizations, and now behind *that* was the Central Intelligence Group, which was so sufficiently well-supplied with dollars that the other sources were useful chiefly as screens, conduits, and supplements.[26] (When Angleton used AFL channels to send to Italy fifty times the amount the unions had available, it might be said that the AFL's foreign operations had become, in effect, Central Intelligence fronts.) The agency with which Angleton increasingly identified himself was evolving, from a relatively weak coordinating group caught between the military intelligence units and the FBI, into the primary vehicle for the president's prosecution of the Cold War.

One of the more exotic rumors abroad at that time held that the U.S. government had supplied large sums in "black currency" to the Catholic Church in Italy. This "black currency," if indeed it ever existed, was said to come "from captured Nazi German assets, including money and gold that the Nazis had looted from the Jews."[27] Not that sources mattered. Other funds came from the American taxpayers via concealed accounts, and yet others from European taxpayers in the form of Marshall Plan counterpart funds, which financed U.S. covert operations in Europe. It is said that ten million dollars went to Italian operations from another Marshall Plan source, the Economic Stabilization Fund.[28] This is still something of a mystery. One story goes that "the CIA's station chief in Rome cabled [CIA director Admiral Roscoe] Hillenkoetter that the key to success was money: at least $10 million. [A day's worth of De Gasperi's Washington efforts the previous year.] Without any further question this amount became the benchmark figure for all subsequent planning."[29] William Corson commented:

> In order to maintain "plausible denial" and avoid the danger of letting the Bureau of the Budget know about the operation if the president's confidential funds were used, it was considered necessary to get the money from another source . . . The source finally selected was the Economic Stabilization Fund . . . [which] was operated and controlled under the discretionary authority of the Secretary of the Treasury, who could spend its funds without reporting the details of those transactions to Congress . . . John W. Snyder, then Secretary of the Treasury, was discreetly approached by Forrestal and Hillenkoetter . . . $10 million *in cash* was withdrawn from the Economic Stabilization Fund, after which it was laundered through individual bank accounts whose owners in turn "donated" the funds to a variety of front organizations which either bought Italian lira or transmitted the funds directly to the CIA's secret assets and front organizations in Italy.[30]

The pattern of initial private initiatives, publicly known, and later CIA initiatives, closely held, was to appear in many situations during the Cold War.

In Rome, on January 21, 1948, and then again on the 29th, Ambassador Dunn "warned Washington that all signs pointed to a massive victory for the Left."[31] A U.S. position paper dated February 10 noted that the Italian government was "'under strong and persistent Communist attack aimed ultimately at the creation of a Communist dictatorship subservient to Moscow. The political position of the Communist party is stronger in Italy than in any other country outside the Soviet orbit. This strength stems primarily from the prevailing economic distress . . . ' The paper reiterated earlier recommendations that US armed forces not participate in a civil war but should continue to hint at the threat of force."[32] On February 16 the Central Intelligence Agency issued ORE 47/1, "The Current Situation in Italy," predicting that the "present Government will continue without radical change until the national elections in April, the outcome of which will be influenced by the results of US interim aid and the prospect for the ERP [the Marshall Plan]."

> It appears that neither the Communist-led bloc nor the Christian Democrats will gain a clear-cut majority and that the moderate Left will probably do poorly. As a result, the rightist parties will hold the balance of power . . . Having failed to win dominance through the elections, the Communists are expected to launch a campaign of general strikes or even to attempt armed insurrection should the Kremlin find such extreme measures necessary . . . In the event of a Communist uprising, the Italian Government's armed forces would be capable of maintaining internal security provided: (1) the current reorganization had achieved an integrated defense system; (2) additional modern equipment had been secured; and (3) the Communists had not received appreciable outside aid. The armed forces are incapable of offensive and could fight only a limited defensive war . . . The Communists are believed to possess the military capacity of gaining temporary control of North Italy. If they receive material assistance from Yugoslavia and/or France, the Government will require foreign aid to regain control of the area.[33]

On February 25 came the coup in Prague. On March 5, General Lucius Clay, U.S. commander in Germany, acting on information from the ex-Nazi Soviet expert General Reinhard Gehlen, issued his famous, intemperate, and unsubstantiated cable predicting that war with the Soviet Union "may come with dramatic suddenness."[34] Clay's cable adding to the sense of crisis, on March 8 NSC 1/3 authorized covert funding of the Italian Socialist Labor Party and the Christian Democrats by the CIA's Office of Special Projects, with Angleton coordinating the effort from Washington.[35]

As the CIA's Ray Cline later wrote, "CIA got the job of passing money and giving the technical help needed to get out the vote and win the election . . . These covert action programs in Italy were viewed simply as part of diplomatic and military policy. George Kennan . . . [who] took an active role in support of all aspects of implementing the Italian policy . . . cabled: 'As far as Europe is concerned, Italy is obviously the key point. If Communists were to win election there our whole position in the Mediterranean, and possibly in Western Europe as well, would probably be undermined.'"[36]

The European Recovery Act, announced at the beginning of the Italian crises as a long-term structure for U.S. involvement in European politics—and immediately as a way of preventing Communist electoral victories in France and Italy—was signed on April 2, 1948. President Truman, at the same time, in violation of international agreements, authorized covert shipments of arms to right-wing groups in Italy.[37] Funds were transferred not only by, but also, as we have seen, through labor unions, and through such groups as Common Cause of New York City, which had connections with the liberationist emigrant community in the city.[38] Swiss banks offered their services, as was customary, for more direct transfers.

In addition to American dollars, Italy was flooded with American movies stressing the prosperity of the United States. To sharpen the contrast between war-devastated Russia and golden America, "Hollywood . . . printed extra copies of *Ninotchka*, Greta Garbo's 1939 satire on Soviet life, and made special arrangements to show the movie in Italian theaters."[39] A "letters to Italy" campaign was launched by Generoso Pope, publisher of the right-wing *Il Progresso Italo-Americano*. Sample form letters were distributed, sound trucks circulated in Italian neighborhoods in the United States, urging the inhabitants to include instructions to vote for the Christian Democrats with their CARE packages.[40] Finally, on April 18, all these efforts came to fruition when the Christian Democrats won an unexpected 48.5 percent of the total vote (and an absolute majority in parliament), up from about two-thirds of that a few months earlier (and a February CIA prediction of 35 percent).[41] The U.S. government was quite sure where the responsibility lay for this victory: the National Security Council "granted the CIA a blanket authorization for covert operations" as a reward.[42]

The Italian campaign was the coming-out party for the CIA and set the precedent for a generation of covert action programs. In addition, "Two developments of far-reaching importance . . . took place during this election campaign," according to Christopher Simpson, author of *Blowback*. "First, U.S. security agencies successfully tested a series of propaganda and political manipulation techniques that were later to come into widespread use around the world, including inside the United States itself. Secondly, the CIA established much deeper and broader ties with the hierarchy of the Roman Catholic Church in Rome than had previously been the case. This not only had a powerful impact on the Italian political scene but also . . . laid the foundation for the Agency's relationship with Intermarium, an influential Catholic lay organization made up primarily of Eastern European exiles that operated under the protection of the Vatican."[43]

In retrospect, this first victory of the Cold War may have been too complete. According to James Miller, "By taking off the gloves in Italy, the United States had embarked on a perilous new policy."[44] It was a policy that was secretly continued in Italy itself throughout the Cold War: "All in all, between 1948 and 1975, over $75 million was spent by the CIA on Italian elections,"[45] part of a worldwide program of secret and illicit support for the system of Christian Democrat parties and their analogues, like the particularly corrupt Japanese Liberal Party, as well as titular Socialist parties in Italy and elsewhere—in order, it was said, to strengthen democratic institutions (and to balance Soviet support for local Communist parties). When the subsidies stopped, the entire Italian political system collapsed. As was said in another context, the United States had destroyed nascent Italian democracy in order to save it.

The key operative of this Italian campaign, James Angleton, was then just thirty years old. He had spent three years in Rome, maturing from the brilliant student of espionage—whom men as different as Pearson and Philby were eager to claim as their protégé—into a master of the game in his own right. Educated at Yale, indoctrinated into the secret world in London, hardened in Rome, later to be betrayed by Philby: each of these experiences was formative of Angleton's complex character. It is no wonder that E. E. Cummings exclaimed, "And what a miracle of momentous complexity is The Poet!"

A secret intelligence agency collects, analyzes, and distributes information. None of this activity would need to be secret if all the necessary information were legally obtainable. But ever since the spectacular demonstrations by Harvard and Yale professors at the beginning of the Second World War, that by far the better part of the information desired about a government and its military could be obtained from open sources, it has been understood that some information (nominally ten percent) could not be obtained in this way. Hence the need for a secret intelligence organization. The point of secret intelligence as such, as William Johnson and others have pointed out, is that some of its methods are illegal.

The early CIA's Office of Special Operations (OSO), built on the Strategic

Services Unit (the operational remnant of OSS), had responsibility for "procurement," that is, for the illegal acquisition of information. The mission of OSO was "the conduct . . . of all organized Federal espionage and counterespionage operations outside the United States and its possessions for the collection of foreign intelligence information required for the national security. Such espionage and counterespionage operations may involve semi-overt and semi-covert activities for the full performance of the mission." The Office of Special Operations was also to be responsible "for the security of operational materials and methods" (that is, counterintelligence) and "for the collection, processing, and distribution of foreign counterespionage intelligence information."[46] Foreign Division M was headed by Angleton's friend Richard Helms, who had responsibility for both intelligence and counterintelligence activities in Central Europe.[47] Counterespionage, or Staff C (all that remained of X-2), was in the hands of an ex-FBI agent, William Harvey, a bloated alcoholic with the manners of a comically corrupt cop in a Raymond Chandler thriller.[48]

Opinions are divided about Harvey's role in the CIA and his relationship with the FBI. One story runs that he had fallen into disfavor with Hoover and had taken refuge in the new Agency. Other views are more subtle. They claim that J. Edgar Hoover had "acted to place FBI agents with extensive experience in this area of intelligence within the OSO." In any case, "At the time of Harvey's shift [from FBI to CIA], the OSO top job was very much up in the air. The conflicts and the lack of anyone with clear stature in the intelligence community provided Harvey with an opportunity to take over the OSO leadership, but to do so he needed to gain some allies (in addition to Hoover) and to get rid of some internal competition. His first and perhaps best ally was James J. Angleton, Jr. [*sic*], who at the time was the keeper of the X-2 flame . . . With Harvey in his corner, Angleton moved up to take over the counterespionage responsibility from Colonel Richard Hawes, and in the course of this perturbation acquired the further responsibility for liaison with the FBI on matters dealing with what would later become the Israeli intelligence service."[49]

Something like that. The "Special Procedures" group of the Office of Special Operations (boxes within boxes on the organization chart) was described in a March 22, 1948, memorandum as responsible for covert operations. "The primary objectives of such operations will be: (1) to undermine the strength of foreign instrumentalities, whether governments, organizations or individuals, which are engaged in activities inimical to the United States; and, (2) to support U.S. foreign policy by influencing foreign public opinion in a direction favorable to the attainment of U.S. objectives."[50] It was through the Special Procedures Group that Angleton had worked to influence the Italian elections in 1948.

Kim Philby wrote a colorful, if customarily untrustworthy, account of Angleton's position in the CIA in those days:

> The driving force of OSO at the time was Jim Angleton, who had formerly served in London and had earned my respect by openly rejecting the Anglo-mania that disfigured the young face of OSO. We formed the habit of lunching once a week at Harvey's where he demonstrated regularly that overwork was not his only vice. He was one of the thinnest men I have ever met, and one of the biggest eaters. Lucky Jim! After a year of keeping up with Angleton, I took the advice of an elderly lady friend and went on a diet . . . Our close association was, I am sure, inspired by genuine friendliness on both sides. But we both had ulterior motives. Angleton wanted to place the burden of exchanges between CIA and SIS on the CIA office in London—which was about ten times as big as mine. By doing so, he could exert the maximum pressure on SIS's headquarters while minimising SIS intrusions into his own. As an exercise in nationalism, that was fair enough. By cultivating me to the full, he could better keep me under wraps . . . Although our discussions ranged over the whole world, they usually ended, if they did not begin, with France and Germany. The Americans had an obsessive fear of communism in France, and I was astonished by the way in which Angleton devoured reams of French newspaper material daily . . . Angleton had fewer fears about Germany. That country concerned him chiefly as a base of operations against the Soviet Union and the socialist states of Eastern Europe.[51]

Angleton's liaison activities, which were central to his concept of secret intelligence, included, besides the British and Commonwealth services, three others that were to be career-long special interests: the intelligence services of Italy, Israel, and Germany. He had the advantage of a family "station," as it were, in Rome, where after the war his father maintained the Villa Angleton as a center of expatriate cafe society, with interesting connections to the Vatican: Pope Paul VI was said to be "close to James Angleton." When the future pope was archbishop in Milan,

> the prelate needed only to hint that Catholic Action could benefit from a squadron of sound trucks, and they were all but loaded on the next eastbound freighter . . . Following Angleton's contacts in, OSO operatives were able to infiltrate and ultimately pretty much co-opt the Italian security services. "This was an Angleton-Rocca thing," a participant observes. "We had officers working right in with every branch of Italian intelligence—naval, air force—and the relationships were extremely close . . . Then on

the sensitive side you went further. You were able to get very senior officers in the service to focus on what *we* wanted done unbeknownst to their bosses." Of course, "You have to see that they're happy. Their motivation is high, they want to work with you, deep down, but at the same time you want to have an element of control . . . You're not only offering gifts but you're saying, Geez, you're trying to put that son of yours through college, and it's a little rough, and we'd be delighted to assist you . . . I don't think that's venality. I think that's good common intelligence sense." . . . Most vital were "important liaison services that we could guide and direct and have influence on," one professional emphasizes, "to see that they worked on the *Soviet* target, dammit, and didn't get involved in a lot of their routine crap, you know, even though their bosses might not necessarily agree . . . To duplicate it, we would have had to have a station of a couple of hundred people [rather than sixty]."[52]

CIA relations with then-Cardinal Montini went further than the provision of sound trucks. A long-term investment was made, for example, in orphanages. The cardinal had a particular interest in orphanages, for which he sought and received assistance from the Agency. The Agency thought that "if such institutions were adequately supported, many young people would be able to live well there and so would not one day fall into Communist hands."[53]

Eventually, between secret intelligence service liaisons, sound trucks, purchased elections, and even orphanages, the CIA managed to turn the Italian intelligence services into what amounted to (or seemed to the CIA to be) a set of client organizations. Italian consulates in the Soviet Bloc furnished information about rail junctions and military bases; Italian businessmen provided information through the Legal Traveler program.[54]

During and immediately after the war, perhaps through Angleton's good offices, the Italian secret intelligence services began to work with the Israeli services, a relationship which they were to maintain. These contacts preceded the establishment of the Israeli state, building on what had been a more overt presence at the end of the war, when the Palestine Brigade moved up the peninsula and eventually over the Alps into Austria. (One former OSS officer remembers the terror and astonishment of the Austrian villagers as a line of trucks decorated with Stars of David rolled by in 1945.) In Washington, in 1948, as the British pulled out of Palestine, "Israeli affairs were being handled by the same Middle East Division of the CIA that dealt with Arab matters. As Arab and Jew were at each other's throat in Palestine, loyalties soon became strained. A State Department employee was found passing classified material to the Israeli embassy and a Jewish woman working for the Middle East Division caused a panic by asking for a transfer on grounds of divided loyalties."[55] In later years Angleton would simply assume that the loyalties of all American Jews might be similarly divided between their allegiance to America and their interest in the survival of Israel.

Angleton was one of a very small number of intelligence professionals choosing to remain in U.S. government service in the late 1940s. As such, he had responsibility for professionalizing the new Agency's operations. According to William Hood, "After the passage of the 1947 legislation establishing the CIA there was much to be done formalizing procedures for the most routine activities—relations with other government offices, the Civil Service, Department of State, the Department of Defense, the FBI, the Bureau of the Budget—and in the process, to protect the equities and independence of an agency the likes of which had never before existed in Washington . . . [Angleton was] active in establishing and codifying liaison procedures and practices, agent clearance procedures, operational reporting requirements, and other practices and disciplines that are now taken for granted within the CIA."[56]

Angleton was laying the foundation of a secret intelligence establishment on what were already classic lines. We are told that his work also involved "maintaining 3 by 5 cards in the registry on those diplomats who, because of their possible collaboration with the Nazis or other problems in the past, were potential candidates for recruitment. To do this job, he maintained close relations with top officers in French, Italian, and West German intelligence." In other words, he was responsible for an all-important Registry on the British model, for liaison with the French, Italian, and West German intelligence services, and he was one of the founders of the CIA's Soviet Division.[57] In May 1949 he was made head of Staff A of OSO in charge of the collection of foreign intelligence, which included liaison with the CIA's counterpart organizations abroad. "Since the CIA still relied heavily on the British, French, Germans, and other 'partners' to do much of the recruitments and covert actions in postwar Europe, these so-called liaisons were the very mechanism through which the CIA organized the secret war against the Soviet Union."[58] The CIA was dependent for most of its foreign intelligence on such liaison relationships until the 1960s. Angleton's expertise in the area, and his continuing contacts, were vital to his influence in the Agency.[59]

Amidst all this, Angleton's return to the United States had brought about a gradual improvement in his marriage. In April, 1948, for example, Cicely Angleton had written to Marion Cummings from Tucson that "Jim is home and things are much better. He is less confused, more relaxed and more on an even keel, and not so tormented. At present he is in Mayo's having a slight operation . . . he'll be out of there soon and then will return here to recuperate and thence to Washington and the terrible grind. At least the Italian elections went off all right which ought to relieve some of the pressure off both Jim and the Pope."[60] Three weeks later, Cicely Angleton's mother, Helen d'Autremont, wrote to Marion Cummings, filling in some details.

> Jim has been here for several months (early January) but recently had to make a trip to Rochester for an operation on hemorrhoids—That was miserable but he is back after four weeks in Rochester—feeling like a new man—much more relaxed—and better in every way. Cicely has been under great strain—hardly knew what to do. Jim realized while on this last trip—just what his behavior had been and he has suffered from the realization. He has many problems—can he meet them. [*sic*] Cicely feels protective but does not want to always hold that position. IF you could see them I feel you would both have much help for us—But we cannot always discuss this with long suffering friends . . . Cicely & Jim go to Washington June 5. He has a job for 1 year with the State Department.[61]

This letter calls for some unpicking. Mrs. D'Autremont's chronology has Angleton going to Tucson immediately after his arrival in the United States—and she and her daughter agree that he spent the month of April at the Mayo Clinic in Rochester, Minnesota. William Johnson, who had known James Angleton at Yale and in 1948 was teaching at Carleton College with Reed Whittemore—part of a group that was continuing to edit *Furioso*—dates his own recruitment to the CIA from a visit Angleton paid to him at Carleton at this time. It is possible that Angleton was able to remain in communication with Washington, and hence, Italy, through a CIA training facility or the Air Force base near Tucson, or by other means, or that he did not go to Minnesota until after the Italian elections, and that Mrs. D'Autremont's placing of Angleton "here" in Tucson did not exclude time spent in Washington—as opposed to Italy.[62] And, of course, his "job for 1 year with the State Department" was to be a job for nearly thirty years with the CIA.

In the summer of 1948, while the Angleton-D'Autremont family vacationed on Cape Cod, James and Cicely Angleton's marriage continued to be in question. On July 22, Helen D'Autremont wrote to Marion Cummings that "Cicely spent a while with us on Cape Cod and took [their son] Jamie back with her. She is not yet certain. I value your opinion—it comes back to me all the time. Jim is not down to fundamentals but he is trying to make the marriage real. He realizes his dependence on Cicely and Jamie but that is, I suppose, of no great value." Marion Morehouse and E. E. Cummings had originally been James Angleton's friends. These letters show us how after the war the inner circle of that friendship was formed by Cicely Angleton, Helen D'Autremont, and

Marion Cummings, all trying to decide what to do about the Angleton marriage. (E. E. Cummings seems to have been for the most part a silent recipient of correspondence.) Mrs. D'Autremont, whose political and social opinions were quite liberal—unlike those of the Cummingses—had herself at this point begun to sympathize with the anti-Communism that would culminate a few years later in McCarthyism: "I think back on your realization of Communist activities three years ago and I should think you might well be pretty complacent about your judgments and their present vindications" in the hearings of the House Un-American Activities Committee that summer.[63] In September, looking back on the summer, Mrs. D'Autremont is slightly more sanguine concerning her daughter's marriage: "As for Cicely, she came to the Cape twice, once with Jim. She is really grateful for your point of view as she is still puzzling it out. Jim's brother, Hugh, is to be married the eleventh, in Chicago & she will be at the wedding. Maybe Jim will be there, too, but cannot be sure yet . . . We have had a good summer—a mixture of generations both here and in Truro that we have all enjoyed . . . Also our re-reading 'Four Quartets' with deepest interest."[64]

A document written a few months later gives us a rare glimpse of how James Angleton saw his marriage. In his will, dated military style 1.22.49, he gives everything to Cicely except for certain personal gifts. His fishing tackle is to go to his son, "in order that he might have some small inclination to follow this sport," which was a passion for both James and Cicely Angleton. Small gifts were to go to twenty-five OSS and CIA colleagues, including Allen Dulles, Richard Helms, Angleton's deputy Raymond Rocca, and Norman Pearson; "a bottle of good spirits" each to Pound, Cummings, and "other poet friends from *Furioso* days." The will further states:

> To my family, my ever loving and most tolerant mother who has achieved the state of grace; to my father who has some of my faults, but to whom I owe more than I can say . . . there is nothing left to give except my love and whatever spirit may still remain to repay in those ways which are in no way helped by material things. To my wife, whom I have loved beyond my own life, it is not possible to express the intense joy of living with you during times when matters were difficult to resolve—not because there wasn't a will to do so, but that hubris and vanity destroy the outgiving of love. You have brought me those things which make Death's other kingdom more lonely, and the tragedy of dying will always be that there was never enough time or enough life to overcome the shortcomings of myself, and love as I know I've always loved you—without the pride and the vanity . . .

Concluding with this formula: "You who believe or half believe, I can say this now, that I do believe in the spirit of Christ and the life everlasting, and in this turbulent social system which struggles sometimes blindly to preserve the right to freedom and expression of the spirit. In the name of Jesus Christ I leave you."[65]

The references to Dulles, Helms, and Rocca place Angleton in the world of secret intelligence of that time: Dulles his senior; Helms his contemporary; and Rocca his assistant. This constellation would remain stable until Dulles's death, after which Angleton, Helms, and Rocca would continue to maintain their mutual loyalties.

The prose style of this document is classical, more carefully written and mature than any other writing by Angleton that has survived, full of Eliotonian echoes ("Death's other kingdom," "You who believe or half believe"); the statement of love for Cicely Angleton is enormously moving, particularly in the context of the difficulties in their marriage—obliquely alluded to—at that time. It expresses a religious spirit not found elsewhere in Angleton's writing and unknown even to colleagues who knew him, or thought they knew him, very well. Equally striking is the mention of Pound, then held in a mental hospital in lieu of prison or worse for treason. It was not only at Cambridge that personal loyalty could take precedence over reasons of state.

Although Angleton's intelligence service was continuous from the time he joined the OSS, bureaucratically his status was not regularized within the Central Intelligence Agency until he formally joined it in the summer of 1949. (The Central Intelligence Agency Act of 1949 was passed at the end of June.) Angleton's Personal History Statement, submitted July 18, 1949, with his pro forma application to the CIA, has been preserved in the files of the Federal Bureau of Investigation. It lists his "present address" as 601 South Lea Street in Alexandria, Virginia, and his "permanent address" as c/o Southern Arizona Bank, Tucson, Arizona, the address used by his wife's family.[66] According to these documents he was then thirty-one years old, six foot one, weighing 150 pounds, a "build" he called "medium" but which one would think on the thin side for that height. Under the sections for information about relatives, in addition to that for Cicely Angleton there are listings for a son, James Charles ("Jamie," age 4½), and for Angleton's father, mother, brother, and sisters. His parents were living at Via Adolfo Cancani 10 in Rome, where James Hugh Angleton was serving, once more, as president of the U.S. Chamber of Commerce for Italy. Angleton's younger brother Hugh, whose age was given by Angleton as "27 (?)," was "presently visiting family in Italy." Carmen Mercedes Hauser, age "26 (?)," recorded as "presently travelling in Europe with husband," had married a journalist, Ernest Hauser (whose residence Angleton gave as "Travels extensively—Often at Hotel Scribe, Paris, France"). At the time Angleton filled out the questionnaire he listed his other sister, Dolores Magdalena Angleton (age 17), as living with her parents. The information about Carmen is the most detailed, an indication of how close they were and remained.

Angleton gave as his five character references ("who know you intimately") John Sweeney, Curator, Poetry Room, Widener Library, Harvard University; Andrewes Manning, of Harvard University; James Murphy (formerly of OSS, then in law practice in Washington); S. C. Allyn, a colleague of Hugh Angleton at National Cash Register in Dayton, Ohio; and E. Reed Whittemore, then teaching at Carleton College. His five additional references ("persons who know you socially in the United States") were Norman Holmes Pearson, Yale University; F. S. C. Northrop, Yale University; Hubert Will, of the Pope & Ballard Law Office in Chicago; Culver S. Ladd, of Silver Springs, Maryland; and John Merritt Fisher, whose address Angleton gave as "Albee Bldg., Washington, D.C." Out of these ten references, five were associated with Angleton's *Furioso* years, two with his time in OSS (counting Pearson in both categories).

Under the heading "Financial Background," Angleton said that he was not "entirely dependent on" his salary, giving as sources of other income "Idaho Ranch, family sources and securities." Not being dependent on his CIA salary was important in the social world of the CIA. It would become more important when Allan Dulles became DCI, as Dulles thought social standing a prime indicator of suitability for leadership. (The dependence on his salary of Richard Helms, for example, was counted against him by those who were concerned with such matters.) Angleton listed his "Clubs, Societies and Other Organizations" as "Chi Delta Theta (Yale Literary Society)," 1940–41; Signet Society, Harvard University, 1941–42 (?); Pow-Wow and Scott Clubs, Harvard Law School ("Law Debate Societies"), 1941–43; Old Malvernian Society, Malvern, England, "'Old Boys Club,' 1937—? Probably still a member"; "Italian Language Society (?)," Yale, 1938–41, and Boy Scouts of America, "1930 (?)—1938 (?). (Attended two world Jamborees while in Europe which more or less kept me in good standing locally)"; and Mory's (a dining club), Yale University, 1938–41. Under "Foreign Languages," Angleton listed Italian (Speak—"Fluent"; Read—"Fair"; Write—"Fair"); French (Speak—"Fair"; Read—"Fair"; Write—"Fair"); and German (Speak—"Slight"; no claims for reading and writing). The questionnaire inquired as to whether the applicant had "any qualifications as a result of training or experience, which might fit you for a particular position." Angleton's reply was "Extensive travel and residence in Western Europe; education & background; *writing and analytical criticism which tend toward the intelligence field.*" (Emphasis added.) And in response to a question about the use of intoxicants, he said, "yes . . . moderately."

Taken as a careful presentation of self, the answers Angleton gave stressed his education, particularly its literary aspects. It is a self-portrait of a gentleman: not entirely dependent on his salary, in touch with his cosmopolitan family (if not quite sure of the ages of all his siblings), socially active in the past but at the moment without memberships in any organizations, except the probable continuing honorary connection with the Boy Scouts. As was routine, the CIA passed Angleton's application to the FBI for positive vetting (not then a practice in the British secret intelligence services). In a memorandum dated August 22, 1949, J. Edgar Hoover (probably only notionally) sent it on to the Washington Field Office of the Bureau "to conduct a thorough, discreet investigation concerning the character, reputation, patriotism and loyalty" of the applicant.

A search of the Bureau's central files threw up the old reports on the treason investigation of Ezra Pound ("James was instrumental in having Pound lecture for a club at Harvard during the Spring term of 1939"), causing the Washington office to note that "all offices should be alert to develop any foreign tendencies or sympathies on the part of applicant." The Butte, Montana, office of the FBI found Angleton's birth certificate in Boise, verifying his parentage and noting that "former friends and business associates of family furnished nothing derogatory. Family left Boise about 1925 while Applicant a youngster, and loyalty and patriotism unquestioned." The agents conducted three interviews in Boise. One of the interview reports commented that "the family enjoyed a splendid reputation and that its loyalty and patriotism was of the highest order."

The Phoenix office questioned the Tucson police and the local credit bureau without success, but found a person willing to testify that the D'Autremonts were regarded "as being of excellent reputations and character." The New Haven office interviewed Angleton's old professors, who dealt with the Pound matter: "Both stated that applicant's association with Pound did not mean that he subscribed to Pound's ideas. Neither criticized applicant in any way." The Chicago office, perhaps quoting Hubert Will, reported that their informant "Stated he considered ANGLETON to be a person of good character, reputable associates, and loyal to the United States; that he knew of no subversive foreign tendencies or sympathies on part of ANGLETON; that he would recommend ANGLETON very highly for position of trust." An informant of the Cincinnati office said "that the entire ANGLETON family can be trusted to the limit with any confidential information." The San Diego and Los Angeles offices confused James Angleton with someone wanted for causing damage to the icebreaker *Northwind* in 1944. This took some effort to unravel. An informant in Minneapolis reported that as he had known Angleton to be an officer in Rome, and that Angleton "operated entirely in civilian clothes . . . he . . . believed that applicant was an officer in the O.S.S." As this informant was probably Reed

Whittemore, Angleton's Yale roommate and co-editor of *Furioso*, this was probably something of a joke. Angleton's neighbors all reported that they thought he was a "100 percent American" about whom nothing derogatory was known. The investigation was completed in September 1949.

As we have seen, the Angletons' marriage had stabilized in 1949, James and Cicely Angleton living together in the Washington suburbs and soon beginning to enlarge their family.[67] There were, however, from time to time work-related occasions for irritation. At the end of the year (November 22) Cicely wrote to Marion Cummings: "You are probably surprised at the Tucson postmark. Jim is cavorting around Europe having a wonderful time in Greece, Paris, Italy. Really! the hush hush men deserve little pity, and this isn't even considered a vacation. If seeing the Parthenon and contemplating the Erechtheum isn't a vacation heaven help us and let's all get into the government."[68] By late 1949, then, Angleton was taking an active part in the Truman administration's intervention in Greece and tending to his liaison activities in France and Italy, while having time for a bit of sightseeing. It was enough to cause some irritation for a well-educated woman left behind to tend the children.

Ben Bradlee has vividly described the Washington milieu the Angletons entered at the end of the 1940s:

> Socially, our crowd consisted of young couples, around thirty years old, with young kids, being raised without help by their mothers, and without many financial resources. The Janneys—Mary and Wistar, who worked for the CIA; the Winships—Liebe and Tom, who worked for Senator Lev Saltonstall of Massachusetts; Sue and Nick Nikoloric, who worked for Abe Fortas's law firm; Scotty and Jack Lanahan—she was F. Scott Fitzgerald's daughter, and he, too, was a lawyer; Tony and Steuart Pittman, another lawyer. The men were mostly working at the lower levels of government, journalism, or law. We ate with each other at night, bringing the babies and one dish, or one gallon of Almaden Mountain Red or White at three bucks a gallon. We all had interesting jobs, or thought we did. We were all involved one way or another with the events taking place in the sleepy southern town that World War II had made the capital of the free world, to quote Phil Graham. We had a confidence in ourselves and in each other that seems to have disappeared a half century later. We knew we were going to make a difference, and have a good time doing it.[69]

The leaders of the early CIA were well-educated men. Many were lawyers, some had advanced degrees in history, some, like James Angleton, had been thoroughly schooled in the New Criticism.[70] Faced with new challenges, men like Angleton naturally enough considered those challenges through the lenses of their education. Insofar as this was the case, the New Criticism and its analogues in the training of historians were influential in the view that the early CIA took of the world. One aspect of that world view was to value culture and the arts as central, not ancillary.

As it happened, the Communist leaders also were, as often as not, well-educated men, some with a wide European culture. When they set about asserting their claims, they did not only count on the divisions of the Red Army and the votes of the Communist-dominated French trade union movement, the Confédération Générale du Travail (CGT); they sought to mobilize the European intelligentsia on behalf of the Communist initiatives of the 1940s and early 1950s. The United States and Britain responded with their own cultural offensives. The conflict between the United States and the Soviet Union in the early Cold War years, therefore, was played out partially as an arms race, partially as a struggle for "the mind of Europe." The field of battle for the latter was located in the first instance in Paris, the capital of Western culture for much of the modern period. An aspect of the strategy of the Communists was to claim Paris for the Left. The reply of the CIA was to counter that claim by the assertion that the center of Western civilization had followed military and economic power to a new home on the western shores of the North Atlantic as exemplified by the new Abstract Expressionism.[71]

Connections between secret intelligence and the arts are intricate. The practice of close reading taught by the New Critics was seen in a favorable light, for example, as an item on a job application. Nonpolitical painting such as Abstract Expressionism could be lavishly supported under the heading of psychological warfare, at a time when "political" was taken to mean only the politics of the Left. "Old boy" relationships were another strand: given the limited group from which managers of governmental and nongovernmental enterprises were at that time drawn, there would naturally be many interconnections. Thomas Braden, for instance, had been placed at the head of the Museum of Modern Art by Nelson Rockefeller before the latter found him a more appropriate position directing cultural aspects of psychological warfare in the CIA.

But that natural effect is to be as ironically construed as that end of ideology promulgated by Schlesinger's *Vital Center*. Just as the end of ideology was simply another ideology, so the coincidence of a self-perpetuating elite moving among those in positions of power in the CIA, the State Department, the foundations, and the universities was also less than a chance situation. If Angleton's career is the lens through which these arrangements are viewed, it can be seen that beyond the literal, financial, level, he was intellectually connected with these seemingly arcane matters by his own experiences with *Furioso*, which had published modernist art as well as poetry, and by the continuing interest that he and his family took in intellectual and cultural matters.[72] His sister, Carmen Angleton, became a notable figure in transatlantic intellectual circles, specifically those gathered about the Congress for Cultural Freedom, its conferences and magazines. She was close to Nicola Chiaromonte, editor of the Congress for Cultural Freedom's Italian publication *Tempo Presente*. Her postwar Roman home was a resting place for liberal anti-Communist figures when they were in Italy, and she introduced some to her brother. The Congress for Cultural Freedom, in its turn, was, of course, funded by the CIA. Although Angleton did not have line responsibility for these activities, he was close to those who did, such as Thomas Braden and Cord Meyer. Angleton continued his cultural interests throughout his CIA career, maintaining connections with poets, especially his college roommate Reed Whittemore, reading widely, sharing pilgrimages to European cultural sites with his wife. Hence his fascination for those who believe such matters are important.

On the other hand, Angleton devoted most of his life to other pursuits, those we might characterize as a new Great Game: the struggle over the future of Europe. Part of that struggle, to be sure, was cultural; part amounted to what we now call low-intensity warfare, usually covert; part was the everyday business of counterintelligence.

# 6

## Friends, Lovers, and Spies

Much of Angleton's career was entwined with that of his London colleague Kim Philby, now best known as one of the Cambridge spies. Where at Yale the secret society of Skull and Bones had been the incubator of establishment financial and political figures, at Cambridge the no less secretive Apostles had produced philosophers, poets, and aesthetes. For much of the first half of the twentieth century the Apostles were dominated intellectually by John Maynard Keynes, who, with Lytton Strachey, had made it a tight world of male intellect and homosexuality. The thrills of secrecy, the assumption of superiority, the unquestioned loyalty to fellow Apostles fostered in the society were summed up by E. M. Forster's saying that he would have preferred betraying his country to betraying a friend, a dictum that was acted upon more literally than he would have supposed by the next generation. Guy Burgess and Anthony Blunt were typical, recognizable types of the Apostles of their time, Blunt perhaps more than Burgess, as the intensity of the political interests of the latter would have seemed extreme to someone like Strachey. (Although even Strachey had been political enough during the First World War, something of a leader in the pacifism of the time and place.)[1]

If many Apostles had been, almost as a matter of course, pacifists during the First World War, they were equally naturally of the Left in the 1930s. In Britain in the late 1930s, "the young saw their country as being governed by a clique of men, as incompetent as they were misguided, who were determined to put the interests of their class, their inherited wealth, their way of life before the interests of humanity, justice or indeed of Britain itself."[2] Once the Apostles became politicized, it did not take a genius in Moscow (or in Comintern Paris) to recognize that there was much to be gained by attending to these privileged young men. According to Noel Annan, "it was part of communist tactics to capture groups and societies," and he notes that "of the thirty-one members elected to the society between 1927 and 1939, fifteen were communist or *marxisant*."[3]

Those who would become known as the Cambridge spies were not members of the Communist Party of Great Britain, nor were they employees, in the strict sense, of the Soviet intelligence agencies. As with similar networks in Germany,

France, and elsewhere in Europe (and America), they were idealists who were recruited by Communist sympathizers or members of the British Communist Party for activities "against the fascists" or "for peace." Key figures in the English story were Maurice Dobb and James Klugmann. Dobb, a famous Cambridge scholar, and Klugmann, an open member of the Party in Cambridge, acted as talent-spotters for the Soviets much as Strachey had acted as a talent-spotter for the Apostles. The art of the Comintern recruiters was to find likely young men and steer them away from overt Popular Front politics and membership in the Party toward underground work and long-term penetration of the Establishment. Dobb, say, would suggest that they join one of the popular political-touristic journeys to Moscow, where they would receive special treatment and the advice that they could best serve the interests of "world peace" by publicly renouncing the Party and concentrating on their studies. On their return they would declare their disillusionment with Russia and join the Anglo-German Fellowship, like Guy Burgess and Kim Philby, or the Foreign Office, like Donald Maclean. (In contrast, the Rupert Brooke of their generation, John Cornford, was a charismatic recruiter for the Party itself, and with Vanessa Bell's son Julian a very public Red hero-martyr of the Spanish Civil War.)

Guy Burgess, whom Yuri Modin, the final KGB "controller" of the Cambridge Five, judged to be their leader, has been the subject of much more or less accurate vilification in the histories of the time. It is said that he was an alcoholic, which was true; and an aggressive homosexual, which was also true; arrogant and habitually dirty, true also, if only typical of his generation and class. However, the sum of these descriptions, if taken at their profoundly negative face value, makes it something of a puzzle that Burgess held responsible positions in the English Establishment between 1938 and 1951 and had the friendship of so many of its luminaries. He worked for the secret intelligence agencies, for the BBC, and for the Foreign Office. He was a friend of men like Harold Nicolson, W. H. Auden, and Stephen Spender. He was associated with Nicolson's chief, Minister of Information Duff Cooper, who for a time during the Second World War was responsible for the Security Service.[4] Burgess had access to Churchill. Graham Greene, novelist and intelligence officer, counted himself as a friend to the end. There was something more there than the buffoon recalled later by people who had good reason, of course, to distance themselves from him after 1951. Stupid undergraduates did not become Apostles. (And, for that matter, neither homosexuality nor personal uncleanliness nor alcoholism was seen as disqualifying in others at the center of the Westminster and Oxbridge villages.)

If we are to understand the Cambridge spies, we cannot begin by blinding ourselves to Burgess's abilities and his charm, for those he wished to charm.

These were considerable, if somewhat specialized, assets. On the one hand he prided himself on the speed of his seductions, the technique of which seems to have been a homosexual variation on Frank Harris's sudden lunges on the drawing room sofa. On the other hand, he was as quick to apply a practical intelligence to the intricate problems of international politics and finance. Modin illustrates the latter with an account of Burgess's first success for the Comintern, a prewar effort to demonstrate his value to the British secret intelligence system. In 1938, "British counter-espionage had concocted a scheme to divide the Zionists into warring camps . . . I believe the plan was to create an effective opposition to Chaim Weizmann, the Zionist leader . . . Guy [Burgess] began [to put this policy into effect for MI6] by working on Victor Rothschild . . . [who] brought his own influence to bear on his father, Lord Rothschild. He managed to discredit Weizmann so comprehensively that Lord Rothschild actually launched a short-lived Zionist opposition movement."[5]

Burgess had good contacts with the Rothschilds. He had been a friend of Victor Rothschild's at Cambridge, and afterward worked as an investment advisor to Lady Rothschild, doing well for her, it was said, or being paid by her for redundant advice as a favor to her son, it was said by others. As usual, it was probably something of each, Lady Rothschild finding the handsome, aristocratic young friend of her son charming and, it seems, good enough at what she asked him to do. The connections with Victor Rothschild remain tantalizing. It would have been too good a thing if he had been one of the Five: a Jew and a Rothschild at that. And yet, although there were many whispers, few dared accuse Rothschild, even when the molehunters discovered that Rothschild's wife had once shared a flat with Burgess and Blunt. Cleared, as much as anyone was ever cleared by the spycatchers, Victor Rothschild eventually became the overseer of British intelligence, the unseen presence behind that secret world. So close were the keepers and the seekers of secrets.

Burgess's Soviet controller thought that his relationship with Rothschild was just one example of how "Burgess was particularly brilliant at establishing unusual contacts with people in every walk of life. As the years passed, his principal value for the KGB shifted from his ability to recruit first-class agents to his knack for gathering information without making his source aware that he was being interrogated."[6] These sources varied from Rothschilds to the rough trade working class men passed around in Burgess's circle. Referring to Blunt in what was probably a slip for Burgess, Noel Annan writes that he "was a master of manipulating other people and had an eye for any discretion that could be used to disarm a potential enemy. He also had an eye for those in government circles whose loyalty to the Homintern he could rely on—such as

Harold Nicolson, a man who had no truck with communism but who did not hesitate to correspond with Guy Burgess after he had fled to Moscow. Nicolson saw that as an act of loyalty to the in-group and to the ideal of friendship in defiance of the Establishment. The Soviet agents who recruited the spies knew, as good marxists, that social structures and institutions give protection to those who were to lead double lives and nowhere more so than in England where the clubs of public school, Oxford and Cambridge colleges, the small top civil service grade, the scientific community and, not least, the homosexual fraternity interlinked."[7]

It was "Soviet agents," urbane, Paris-based stalwarts of the Comintern, not Russian bureaucrats, who recruited the Cambridge spies. Indeed, those recruited were a mystery to the Moscow bureaucrats who received their reports. At the highest levels of the Kremlin's secret intelligence services they were suspicious. At the lowest level—that of the translators preparing the material for the analysts—they were dazzled. "In the summer of 1944," Yuri Modin wrote, "most of my time was taken up by the batches of photographic negatives that filtered in from London . . . All of our thirty-odd agents in London were directed to work on a single given subject; they would then send in whatever they could find, which was subsequently analyzed. Gradually, by comparing each agent's contribution, we were able to establish a kind of hierarchy among them. Five names stood out from the rest, of men who quickly showed themselves to be the most valuable spies."[8] (It is worth noting, given the hyperventilating that has gone on over the identity of the "Fifth Man," that Modin casually refers to "thirty-odd agents in London.")

Over the years Modin developed a case of collective hero worship for his favorite five mysterious agents. His regard for them was heightened when, in 1944, the five declined offers of life pensions from the KGB, saying that it was sufficient that they had played a role in "fighting Fascism and promoting world revolution." Burgess's letter declining a pension included the statement, "I cannot see how any self-respecting individual could live in my country and not work for the Party."[9] Such sentiments were common in Burgess's class at that time. Even that stalwart of the anti-Communist Left, George Orwell, felt similarly in the late 1930s: "I do not see how one can oppose Fascism except by working for the overthrow of capitalism, starting, of course, in one's own country. If one collaborates with a capitalist-imperialist government in a struggle 'against Fascism,' i.e. against a rival imperialism, one is simply letting Fascism in by the back door."[10] Of course later Orwell felt differently, naming names when the time came to do so.

Maclean, like Burgess, has been the object of misinformation in the standard accounts of the time. He has been portrayed as a negligible minor clerk in the Foreign Office. This was not the case. The son of a cabinet minister, he went from Cambridge into the Foreign Office, where, for a decade or more, he had a shining career. However, his entry into the diplomatic service was not without incident. At his interview, he found that his "communist past at Cambridge was known and he was asked about it. He replied that he had held such views and had not entirely shaken them off. The candour of his reply impressed the board. So did his appearance. He was not unlike Rupert Brooke, as moody as he was handsome."[11] (Not everyone agreed that he was handsome. Burgess, who had the opportunity to satisfy his curiosity in the matter when they were at Cambridge, found Maclean, or later said he had found him, physically unattractive: "*all* that white flesh," which sounds sincere enough.) Maclean was to become First Secretary in the British Embassy in Washington during the final phases of the Second World War, then head of the American section of the Foreign Office during the initial stages of the Cold War.[12] These were critical positions, part of the course of honors that might have led to the leadership of the Foreign Office itself. An alcoholic, perhaps, but not a minor clerk.

Donald Maclean was in Washington from 1944 to 1948 in a leading position in the British Embassy. All communications between London and Washington went through his hands, and those of interest were forwarded to Moscow. His value to Stalin only increased when he "was assigned a top-secret mission to co-ordinate the American Manhattan Project . . . with the British Tube Alloys project. Tube Alloys had been launched in the summer of 1941 by the scientific consultative committee chaired by Lord Hankey, whose secretary at the time was John Cairncross, yet another Soviet agent. It is no overstatement to say that [because of Maclean] the KGB was able to follow the political evolution of the Western atomic programme from its genesis right through to the first test detonation near Alamogordo, New Mexico."[13] Maclean's next assignment was to Cairo, a vital post for the British at the time. There, the tensions of the war years had their belated effect. After a series of scandalous alcoholic binges leading up to a nervous breakdown, he was sent home on half pay for six months, then, all forgiven, made head of the Foreign Office's American section. He remained useful to both of his employers in that position, for example as co-director of the secretariat for joint British, American, and Canadian nuclear policy.[14]

Anthony Blunt, the brilliant art historian, had been recruited by Burgess, then moved by Burgess's influence into MI5, where he was given responsibility for keeping track of Soviet diplomats in London, and immediately showed what someone with his access could do for Moscow. As Modin explained, "The first specific mission the British gave Blunt was to examine the way their services went about watching and following people . . . Blunt's report enabled us to adapt our methods to those of our adversary . . . from then on we were quickly able to establish which of our Soviet diplomats were being watched, when, how and by whom. Thereafter it was a simple matter to hoodwink the British without their suspecting anything."[15] Later, when MI5 was trying to keep Burgess and Maclean under surveillance, there were repeated mysterious problems. It is not surprising. But this was just one of Blunt's services to Moscow Center. Again according to Modin, during World War II "the Soviet Embassy in London was always informed well in advance of any actions against us contemplated by British counter-espionage. We knew exactly which aides at the embassy interested [S]IS, and when and how they would be approached by our opposite numbers. We had the names of all those who the British believed could be persuaded to defect . . . We were also fully aware of every detail of the work being done by British counter-espionage against the British Communist Party. We knew the whereabouts of their bugs, the identities of their *agents provocateurs*, who their agents were and what information they were providing."[16]

At the crisis, when Burgess and Maclean went missing, it was to Blunt that Dick White, head of MI5, turned for help and advice. And who better? Dick White said of Blunt (but of course it goes for Philby and the others as well) that "He was a very nice and civilized man and I enjoyed talking to him." Later, he felt differently, writing, as Angleton might have, "You cannot imagine how it feels to be betrayed by someone you have worked side by side with unless you have been through it yourself."[17] In view of this and earlier achievements, it is not surprising that "Blunt was several times congratulated by the KGB . . . for the brilliance of his work: notably when he sent us a detailed operating chart of the British counter-espionage services and a full list of its agents abroad."[18] However, for all that, there were those in Soviet secret intelligence who did not believe the information they were receiving from their English agents, who they thought were playing a double game. In the end it was a close call. They could as easily have been cut off by their handlers—as they may have been, from time to time—or, like so many others, they could have been lured to Moscow and murdered, precisely because they were idealists.

Which brings us to Kim Philby, who would haunt Angleton's professional life, as if a doppelgänger summoned from some Muscovite hell at each crucial moment of the Cold War. Philby's legend, in both senses of the word, is almost impenetrable. The son of a man who in his own life summed up the Great Game, given his emblematic nickname as if by a Gypsy fortune-teller, "Kim" Philby was sent by Dobb to the heroic Red Vienna of the 1930s, recruited to the clandestine world and married there by a passionate Austrian Jewish Communist, then busily covered his trail by writing fascist journalism from Madrid.

Philby was brought into the British secret intelligence service in 1940 by

Burgess, then serving in an SIS school for spies(!). As he tells the story in his autobiographical confection, *My Silent War*, Philby was still a journalist in 1940,working for the *Times*, accredited to the Headquarters of the British Army in France. Evacuated to London, seeking to avoid conscription and seeking a position useful to the Comintern, he first attempted to join the Government Code and Cypher School at Bletchley Park, then he had an interview "near St. James's Park station," home neighborhood of British secret intelligence, with a Miss Marjorie Maxse, who spoke vaguely of interesting employment and invited him back for a second interview, where he found himself being jointly interviewed by Miss Maxse and Guy Burgess, "whom," he comments drolly, "I knew well."[19] After being told to report for duty with the Secret Intelligence Service, in the same office that then employed Burgess, "I decided that it was my duty to profit from the experiences of the only secret service man of my acquaintance. So I spent the weekend drinking with Guy Burgess"—one of a long series of such weekends. Philby was assigned to Section D, specializing in foreign sabotage operations.[20] Burgess then came up with the idea for a training school for underground work, and soon enough—in Philby's fairytale mode of storytelling—it came to pass, and they both went to work there. (Another member of the team was Tomas Harris, also recommended by Burgess "as a sort of glorified house-keeper, largely because he and his wife were inspired cooks."[21] And perhaps because Harris himself might have been one of Burgess's fellows of variable allegiance.)

At the end of the summer Philby and Burgess were transferred to the headquarters of the Special Operations Executive (famously commissioned by Churchill "to set Europe ablaze") at 64 Baker Street, from which Burgess was dismissed into the Ministry of Information, leaving Philby to pursue his own career in British Secret Intelligence.[22] At first Philby wrote lectures on the technique of propaganda, fitting work for an ex-journalist. When the Germans invaded the Soviet Union, Philby "decided" to find more active work, and once again turned to a friend, this time the aforementioned cook, Tomas Harris, who was by then in the Iberian section of MI5. (Harris, when not cooking or otherwise engaged, was an art dealer, specializing in Spanish painting, Goya in particular.) Harris found him a job in the counterpart organization, MI6, and by September, 1941 Philby was working in Section V of MI6, which "was responsible for the collection of counter-espionage information from foreign countries by illegal means," as part of its Iberian section.[23] Modin claims that as early as 1941, "thanks to Kim Philby, we possessed a nearly complete list of British agents operating throughout the world."[24] The Soviets were convinced that the British, on the other hand, were operating in the dark, as the archives of the British espionage and counter-espionage services were stored in London's

Wormwood Scrubs Prison, which burned early in the war.[25] There were copies of most of these files, but they were not, in any case, utilized effectively.[26]

When the Allies invaded North Africa, Philby had that area added to his responsibilities, followed by Italy, where he helped form the Special Counter-Intelligence (SCI) Units.[27] (It was to one of these units, as we have seen, that Angleton was at first to belong in Italy as X-2's representative and from which all else followed. Thus Angleton was in this sense as well, Philby's protégé at an early stage of his career.) In September 1943 Section V moved to offices in Ryder Street, where X-2 was also housed, around the corner from MI5 in St. James's, and about that time Philby became deputy head of the Section. Finally, after a successful intrigue, toward the end of the war, Philby became head of both Section V (with Graham Greene as his deputy) and Section IX, the latter responsible for actions against the Soviet Union.[28] In retrospect it was, all in all, rather breathtaking.

James Angleton and Kim Philby, who had been in and out of one another's offices in Ryder Street, reconnected in Rome in the summer of 1945 during what was subsequently known as the Volkov Affair. Constantin Volkov was a Soviet diplomat in Istanbul who made the mistake of attempting to defect to the British. The paperwork landed on Philby's desk in London (he was in charge of counterespionage for MI6 by then), who graciously undertook to travel out to Istanbul himself to handle the matter. He took his time. When he finally arrived in Istanbul the Soviet embassy claimed to know nothing of any Volkov (there were stories of a mysterious aircraft arriving from Russia, a heavily bandaged figure on a stretcher pulled aboard). It was most unfortunate. There was nothing for Philby to do but go back home. "Philby returned empty-handed to London. But he stopped off briefly in Rome to touch base with James Angleton . . . Angleton expressed sympathy that so promising a case had been lost, and put Philby on the London plane after a drinking session."[29] (The Angletons were always pleased to offer hospitality in their Roman territory. In the 1960s Carmen Angleton would operate a virtual bed and breakfast establishment for the New York intelligentsia from her apartment there.)

The war had ended with a barrage of honors, demobilizations, and rearrangements of careers. Angleton, for example, received the Légion d'Honneur for his wartime work with the French,[30] while his mentor Norman Holmes Pearson received an array of honors from his own government and others. Kim Philby was made a member of the Order of the British Empire and, like Angleton, stayed in the Game, in Philby's case as head of an anti-Soviet counterintelligence section of MI6[31] (the British equivalent of Aldrich Ames's position a generation later).

Many people had reason to be pleased by this. Modin, for one, commented that when "Philby was made overall controller of MI6's secret agents in the Soviet Union . . . [h]e was also in charge of recruiting spies and mounting sabotage operations against Communist parties in the USSR and elsewhere . . . [w]e knew in advance about every operation that took place by air, land or sea, even in mountainous and inaccessible regions."[32] Burgess also continued to be valuable to the Soviets. In 1946 he became private secretary to Hector McNeil, the second most important official in the Foreign Office, which gave him virtually unlimited access to Britain's foreign policy process. He forwarded to Moscow, for example, the documents concerning Britain's position for the Big Four foreign ministers' conference in Paris in 1946, and that in Moscow the following year.[33] American secret intelligence found Soviet knowledge of these matters puzzling, suspecting spies in Berlin, unwitting of the secret communications lines between London and Moscow.

On the other hand, Blunt was demobilized by British secret intelligence—and demobilized himself from Soviet secret intelligence at war's end. The Soviets were willing enough to let him go. Unlike Burgess and Philby, he had a career to look after, and tastes and talents that in civilian life would not lead naturally to access to information of use to Moscow. Nonetheless, his war work was appreciated. Quoting Modin again, "Blunt had done sterling work for us during the war. Without the slightest risk of exaggeration I can affirm that over the years he supplied us with literally thousands of documents. He had helped change the course of the war, and his work unquestionably spared the lives of tens of thousands of Soviet soldiers."[34]

Burgess, Blunt, Philby, and Maclean were at the heart of the British intelligence and foreign policy establishment for nearly a decade. Thanks to them, for most of that time what was known in London was almost immediately known in Moscow. Their positioning at the nerve centers of the Anglo-American alliance was no secret to the counterespionage specialists of the American and British governments, but only one of those officials understood the deeper significance of those assignments, and that, of course, was Philby himself. For the others, for Angleton, for example, they seemed loyal and capable allies. Philby was more than that for Angleton, who considered him to be a friend.

This was the basic configuration of counterintelligence in the early days of the Cold War, the arrangement of personalities that would shape its structure and dynamics until the mid-1970s. The story of Philby, Maclean, Burgess, and their colleagues and friends forms a central theme of the master-narrative of the Cold War. The theme of "betrayal" has seemed and still seems to explain much about the conflict between what was later to be called the Evil Empire and the American-led alliance, "the West." If the ideology of "the Vital Center" was self-evidently superior to that of "Soviet Russia," the stalemate that lasted for a generation could only be attributed to betrayal, and here was a set of appropriate villains, false friends, comrades from wartime London, the privileged children of the owners' class in England, just the sort that needed no vetting: Communists, homosexuals, and spies. (Actually, only Burgess was all of these. Philby and Maclean were Communists and spies, but not very often homosexual. Blunt was a spy and a homosexual, but apparently only a Marxist, not a Communist.) Here was a perfect explanation for the West's failures in the secret world.

And in a way, of course, it was, while being at the same time an explanation for its successes.

The first armed covert action of the Cold War, the Albanian affair, began toward the end of 1948. The idea came from the British Foreign Office, which saw the Balkans as part of its rapidly shrinking sphere of influence. In November 1948 the "Cold War sub-committee" of the "Russia Committee," chaired by Gladwyn Jebb of the Foreign Office, decided "to liberate the countries within the Soviet orbit by any means short of war." Air Marshal Arthur Tedder, for his part, wished to "overthrow of the Soviet regime itself, within five years. The plan was to set about 'promoting civil discontent, internal confusion and possible strife in the satellite countries.' Stalin would then be worn out garrisoning his satellites."[35] Albania was then, as now, the poorest country in Europe, and its Communist regime seemingly had not yet settled in. Bordering on a Greece virtually occupied by the British and the Americans, and a Yugoslavia now declaring itself to be hostile to the Soviet Union, with a long coastline easily accessible from Italy, far from the main bases of the Red Army, it seemed a perfect target of opportunity. "Roll-back" would begin there.

All the British lacked was the money to do something about it. As usual, the Americans had the money. According to a contemporary memorandum from the Finance Office of the Office of Policy Coordination (OPC, then a covert action bureaucratic rival of the CIA headed by OSS veteran Frank Wisner), "Reference is made to the various *general and specific agreements* between ECA and CIA, wherein certain portions of the 5% Counterpart funds of ECA are made available to CIA for the purpose of furthering the Marshall Plan by [one word blacked out—"covertly"?] combating Communist elements in participating countries . . . We are advised that disbursements have been made for specific purposes, such as the purchase of a newspaper for a labor group, the underwriting of a peace conference, direct propaganda and other miscellaneous activities. In addition, we are now informed it is now proposed to use small portions of these funds for . . . entertainment and developmental expenses incurred in dealing with principals of foreign political and labor groups."[36] Thus the covert manipulation of foreign governments and public opinion manifests as an accountant's procedural report.

In March 1949, Gladwyn Jebb and Lord Jellicoe arrived in Washington for a three-day meeting on Albania with Robert Joyce of the State Department and Frank Wisner. The group decided to attempt to "detach Albania from the orbit."[37] Angleton, working from the Office of Special Operations in the CIA, and not one of Wisner's "Fizz Kids," as Wisner's aide Carmel Offie called them, was not asked to advise the Wisner's group, and was, in any case, then and later opposed to most covert operations. (In his view they made too much noise and endangered agents engaged in the collection of intelligence.) On the other hand, even at that date, Angleton had a few agents-in-place scattered about in remote regions like Albania, reporting on local conditions.[38]

"Wisner inevitably found himself, Dick Stilwell recalls, mostly 'trying to get the CIA to avoid withholding support.' Part of the justification for mounting such a sideshow was to relieve Tito. But Angleton—and Joyce as well—remained skeptical of Tito's intentions, and went along with Lindsay's shipments of weapons to the Yugoslavs in hopes that, estranged from the Russians, Tito's regime might collapse and usher King Peter back onto his throne."[39] Ignoring Angleton, Wisner reached his agreements with Jebb and Jellicoe, visiting London to confirm the operation.[40] As a result of those meetings a Special Policy Committee was formed in Washington for joint oversight of the Albanian effort. It consisted of Joyce from the State Department; Wisner's representative, Frank Lindsay; Jellicoe, who was the British Embassy representative; and, for SIS, Kim Philby.[41] According to Philby, the vast American airbase at Wheelus Field in Libya was used as the supply base for the operation. Although OPC had a base at Bari, Italy (Max Corvo's old stamping ground), OPC and SIS chose Malta as a training site, security at Bari perhaps being considered somewhat lacking. And then, there was the romance of a Mediterranean island: "Whenever we want to subvert any place," Philby claimed Wisner told him, "we find that the British own an island within easy reach."[42] About thirty Albanians willing to be trained as parachutists and small boat crews were found in the refugee camps. A Mr. Smiley (!) of the British Special Operations Executive and Michael Burke, formerly of OSS and Warner Brothers, handled the Albanians.

After training by the British in Malta, the "first squad of nine men waded ashore" on October 2, 1949, "off Albania's Karaburun Peninsula, where goat tracks wove across the mountains and into the interior. Several succumbed to ambushes at once: the Albanian military waited. Slipping through security cordons, a handful of the guerrillas crept into their home town, Nivica. They handed out reading matter and exhorted their incredulous relatives to form into resistance groups, after which the United States and Britain would smuggle in gold and radios. But nobody promised anything; after several embittering weeks four of the nine were lucky to pick their way across the northern Greek border and report to the British on Corfu . . . Theirs was the fortunate expedition. Successive parties crawled ashore; tribesmen—even relatives—remained so inscrutable the infiltrators were terrified of spending their nights in the villages. Few made it back."[43]

Encouraged by this, the Special Policy Committee decided on a second try, even though Angleton reported that one of his men in Otranto had observed the departure of the Albanians, and even though both he and the members of the Special Policy Committee thought that there had been leaks from the Albanian refugee community in Rome. To deal with these problems, when the next two hundred fifty Albanians were recruited they were taken for training to a camp outside Heidelberg. In September a group was "inserted" by land from Greece, and in November, some of them returned, reporting another failure. Therefore, another group were sent in by boat, with equal luck. "The day the *Stormie Seas* put out of port early in October 1949, a 'flurry of telegrams' reached Angleton in Washington from supporters throughout the Italian services. In 'great glee' Angleton summoned McCargar to his office and spread before the project director the array of operational details to which *he* was privy already. What must the Communists know? 'His motive was ostensibly to warn me as a colleague,' McCargar was quoted afterward, 'But I imagine that he was also anxious to show off his own omniscience to us OPC newcomers.'"[44]

After the failure of this phase of the operation, McCargar, the OPC coordinator, was promoted and replaced by a Mr. Gratian Yatsevich. (Presumably Mr. Smiley remained with the project.) Having tried the sea and land, the next attempt was by air; Polish pilots dropping the Albanians from DC3s. That route failed, also, most of the parachutists being immediately rounded up, killed, or, what amounted to the same thing, sent to prison. Failure only led to an increase in funding, as was the custom, and eventually sixty more Albanians were dropped onto their homeland, a few making their way back to Greece. All in all, perhaps two hundred Albanians were killed or captured in this way. The reprisals cost nearly a thousand additional lives. It is a nice calculation as to whether responsibility lay with Philby, who claimed credit, but is not always to be believed, or to the culture of carelessness with the lives of others that was taking hold at Wisner's OPC.[45] Phillip Knightley's summary seems reasonable: "Philby told the Russian intelligence service about the operation in principle. Moscow told Tirana. The Albanian security service then penetrated the Albanian émigré organizations—if they had not already done so—and one or more of these penetration agents managed to be selected for the CIA-SIS operation. Once infiltrated into Albania he handed over his team to the Albanian security authorities who then forced the team's radio operator to work for them. From that moment, Albanian security would have controlled the whole operation and could have played a 'radio game' in order to lure the rest of the CIA-SIS teams to their doom . . . The Albanian exiles were dupes, sent to make a noise, to show that the CIA was active in the fight against communism."[46]

OPC's Albanian operation set a pattern that the CIA was to follow until, and beyond, the Bay of Pigs. As for Angleton, "What was remembered about the Albanian fiasco was that Angleton was against it."[47]

At about the same time as the Albanian fiasco was playing itself out Angleton became responsible for liaison with the nascent German counterintelligence office: the Gehlen Organization, a most unusual affair. Reinhard Gehlen was a major in the German Army when the war started and in 1942 became head of the General Staff's intelligence unit for the invasion of the Soviet Union, Foreign Armies East. As a lieutenant colonel stationed at the General Staff headquarters, he from time to time briefed Hitler—as it happened, first on the progress of the German armies, then on that of the Soviet Union's. At the end of 1944 he became a brigadier general. His group ran agent networks behind the lines of the Red Army, conducted "black propaganda" activities, helped organize prisoners of war into "patriotic" anti-Soviet units of the German Army. The most famous of these was the Russian Liberation Army, under the command of the former Red Army general A. A. Vlasov.

Gehlen, then, was the German General Staff's expert on the Soviet military and Soviet nationalities affairs. Foreign Armies East worked closely with the Abwehr (Gehlen was an admirer of Admiral Canaris), had sources in the British Military Mission in Moscow, and benefited from the ability of the Germans to read American message traffic. There were also useful contacts with MI6. In the closing months of the Second World War, according to Gehlen's memoirs, "the British MI6 . . . supplied us a copy of Mr. Churchill's political intelligence appreciation of February 1945 . . . I saw that Churchill's analysis viewed our position far too favorably in the East . . . I now believe MI6 supplied this document to us so that we might enable them to warn the British cabinet how exaggerated was the British estimate of our ability to withstand the Russian onslaught in the East."[48] If Gehlen is to be believed, MI6 was attempting to manipulate its government in a similar fashion to that attempted by Dulles with his Operation Sunrise.

Once it became clear to Gehlen that the Germans were going to lose the war he formulated a plan not merely to personally survive, but to bring his unit intact through the Gotterdämmerung of the Third Reich and into the postwar world. The extent to which he succeeded in this can be illustrated by the postwar career of one of his lieutenants, Major Heinz Danko Herre, who was

Gehlen's operations officer early in 1943 and then worked on the Vlasov project. After the war he became Gehlen's personal assistant, head of the evaluation section from 1953 until 1958, when he became chief of operational intelligence procurement. In May 1964, Herre became the West German Federal Intelligence Service's representative in Washington. He eventually retired with the rank of brigadier general.[49] There was war, defeat, and change in regime, but Gehlen's men, like the Vicar of Bray, prospered without interruption.

According to Gehlen, early in 1945 "my staff and I anticipated that the need to defend the West would sooner or later force the West to make common cause with us against communism."[50] The word "us" in this sentence is ambiguously interesting. Most immediately it referred to the intelligence staff of Foreign Armies East. Beyond that, it referred to the German Army, or at least the General Staff itself. And beyond that, it referred at least to all those elements in Germany that saw the Second World War as an anti-Communist crusade. This view of things in early 1945 was held by a variety of historical actors: Himmler; Allen Dulles, perhaps; certain members of the Curia. Gehlen had not been a member of the Nazi Party, nor, as he tells the story, much of an admirer of Hitler. He was (or thought of himself as being) a typical representative of the General Staff, an organization with its roots in the Prussian garrison state, which it was said was not so much a country with an army as an army that happened to be stationed in that country. For members of the General Staff, the continuity of the army was more important than that of any particular regime to which it was formally responsible. The unforgivable sin of the Nazis, in the eyes of such men, was to have threatened that continuity. (Hence the generals' revolt in 1944.)

As Gehlen went about his planning in the closing days of the Second World War, his first priority was to preserve his unit of Foreign Armies East through the interregnum. He went to much trouble to legitimate his plans with this in mind. The problem was that "it was questionable in April 1945 whether we could succeed in establishing with one of the three Western powers a working basis that would prove acceptable to a later German government. We could not work purely as mercenaries for a former enemy if we were not to burden the future intelligence service with the psychological stigma of having been a quisling organization. I therefore later tried to establish a degree of formal legality for our plans; in the last weeks of the war I outlined the plans to General August Winter, deputy chief of the OKW [General Staff]'s operations staff, and secured his blessing for them . . . After the war I chanced to meet Grand Admiral Dönitz in the prison camp at Wiesbaden. Dönitz was formally Hitler's successor as head of state. He also approved my plans."[51]

The ironic muse falls silent before such scenes.

Late in the spring of 1945, as the German Army was collapsing, Gehlen scattered his staff and its records in remote mountain hideaways. Wishing to appear in the camp of the victors on his own terms, he surrendered to the Americans only when the initial U.S. Army sweeps ended. After being shuttled among various prisoner of war camps, Gehlen and his chief officers were secretly brought to Washington for interrogation. The interrogation turned into a negotiation, during which Gehlen persuaded U.S. Army Intelligence to take on his unit of Foreign Armies East as "the Gehlen Organization" (a Nazi locution, as it happens), with responsibility for reactivating his agent networks in Eastern Europe and the Soviet Union. Returning in triumph to Germany, Gehlen established a headquarters in the Bavarian village of Pullach, near Munich, in the summer of 1946. For the next three years he was in the pay of the U.S. Army. This was satisfactory at first, but as the United States demobilized the financial resources available to the Gehlen Organization decreased; this eventually brought about a crisis and, with it, an opportunity. Weary of supporting his organization by black market business deals, Gehlen decided that "Only one thing could rescue us from our chronic financial crisis—the rapid transfer of the Gehlen organization from U.S. Army control to . . . the Central Intelligence Agency . . . From as early as November 1948 . . . we were involved in negotiations with the CIA's representatives . . . It was not until the late spring of 1949 that our talks with the CIA finally reached a positive outcome; the terms were formally settled in English on May 13 and in German on the twenty-third, in a new gentlemen's agreement that this time was put in writing. On July 1 . . . the CIA took over responsibility for us."[52]

Under this "gentlemen's agreement," Gehlen was now working for the Office of Special Operations, which meant that he was working with, if not strictly for, James Angleton. Association with Angleton brought with it association with Jay Lovestone and Allen Dulles.[53] Work with Dulles probably seemed routine for Gehlen; Dulles was a well-known pro-German, anti-Soviet figure. But Lovestone must have given pause. It is a tribute to Gehlen's General Staff discipline that he was able to bring himself to cooperate with a Jewish ex-Communist. One is not sure what it meant about Lovestone that he was willing to work with Gehlen.

It took Gehlen some time to achieve his desired level of autonomy in his arrangement with the CIA. He explained that "Life was not a bed of roses with the CIA at first . . . [T]he essence of the [CIA's] project system was that the probable outcome of every operation and its requirements in time, manpower, and money had to be submitted for clearance in advance."[54] Apparently little accustomed to bureaucracy during the Third Reich, Gehlen desired a more freewheeling approach that would give him more control of operations, money, and manpower. Eventually he was able to persuade the CIA that their rules should not apply to his organization. He was in a strong position. The CIA did not have his experience with the Soviets, had no networks of its own in Eastern Europe, could not match (or dispute) his claim to networks in the Soviet Union itself. The intelligence he provided and the analysis that went with it were of tremendous importance to the Agency in those years. Not that the CIA was Gehlen's only customer: "From the end of 1950 onward . . . [w]e were de facto serving two masters . . . one in Washington, the other in Bonn."[55] There were others, less official. The Gehlen Organization was employed by the CIA until 1956, when it became in name as well as de facto the foreign intelligence unit of the West German Government. The success of Reinhard Gehlen's plan for the survival of Foreign Armies East was astonishing, as were the implications of that success for the course of the Cold War. It is difficult to think of a parallel achievement: to take a military secret intelligence unit intact from a defeated army, virtually lease it out to the victors, civilianize it, then detach it from its foreign caretakers and make it a unit of a completely new regime.

Beyond that, what Gehlen did, in effect, was to place the interpretive filter of the Second World War German General Staff between the actions and imagined intentions of the Soviet bloc and, first, the U.S. Army, then the Central Intelligence Agency, and finally the West German government.[56] Insofar as the Cold War was a matter of shadow play, of the interpretation of intentions, this intervention was crucial. Gehlen's appreciation of the Soviet Union had been formed in the agony of the Nazis' long retreat from Moscow. His Red Army was the ever-victorious, irresistible "horde" of "Asiatic barbarism," which, in the ultimate realization of Goebbels's propaganda, had sent Mongolian horsemen into the ruined streets of Berlin. Gehlen's view of the Soviet Union coincided with that of American observers like Frank Wisner. If the Soviet Union had been able to overwhelm the previously unchallengeable German armies, what hope was there for a West weakened by democracy and demobilization? The only viable strategy was continuous vigilance and suspicion, the construction of each month's situation report as a warning of imminent war, the seizing of any instrument at hand, no matter how discredited, to slow the inexorable advance of Red barbarism.

Gehlen had believed that he had discovered the secret of victory in the East in the employment of nationalisms such as the Ukrainian against Communist hegemony. Hitler had rejected his counsel; the CIA would embrace it.[57] Part of the value of Gehlen's organization to the Americans, in addition to intelligence procurement, was that it also offered the possibilities of covert operations, building on the foundation of the Russian Liberation Army and similar Baltic, Ukrainian, and Polish groups. "Gehlen supported regional insurrections in the Baltic countries and opened courier channels via Austria and Switzerland through Hungary to the Balkans, swapping accommodations with White Russian relics in Paris and Armenian separatists."[58] The 1945 reversal of alliances included not only the absorption of Gehlen's unit of German army intelligence, but the absorption of various Eastern European anti-Soviet organizations formerly supported by the Germans and the creation of still others from the displaced persons camps. After Potsdam, "the emerging intelligence community had begun undertaking small- and medium-scale campaigns using former Nazis and Axis collaborators as operatives in the attempted coup d'état in Romania, the subversion of elections in Greece and Italy, and attempts to manipulate favored political parties throughout the Soviet-occupied zone of Eastern Europe."[59] There was a cover story, picked up by Peter Grose in his biography of Allen Dulles, that the beginnings of the CIA's use of refugees and Eastern European national committees in the United States and Europe was a private endeavor.[60] In fact, the private efforts were a sideshow. The real action was in the CIA/SIS alliance intended to roll back the Soviet Union by quasi-military means.

Matters looked promising, particularly in Poland, when an emissary appeared in London in 1949 with the news that the Polish Home Army had survived and was ready under the name Freedom and Independence (Wolnosc i Niepodleglosc—WiN) to resume against the Red Army the role it had played during the German occupation. The following year the CIA began to ship arms, radio transmitters, and cash to this anti-Communist underground. Frank Wisner was optimistic. The reports of successful actions encouraged ever larger shipments of supplies until finally WiN asked that an American general parachute into Poland in order to complete the organization of the opposition forces.[61] At this point Angleton intervened. He went directly to General Walter Bedell Smith, then director of central intelligence, and argued that WiN was a creature of Soviet intelligence. Smith and Wisner accepted Angleton's arguments and no American general was parachuted into Poland. It was just as well. The remnants of the Polish Home Army had been destroyed in 1947, and, as Angleton suspected, the CIA's supplies and funds had gone to building up Communist forces in Poland. The WiN fiasco spelled the end of the CIA's effort to create resistance networks in the Soviet Bloc.[62]

Angleton and his colleague Ray Rocca began a study of the WiN affair and its original, the Trust organization of the 1920s (see chapter 3).[63] Later, Angleton would extend his historical studies to the Okhrana, the Tsarist predecessor organization of the KGB. These efforts were controversial in the Agency, pointed to by some as evidence of Angleton's irrationality. Later, after the Cold War ended, it was found that the KGB and its associated agencies had indeed used Okhrana and Trust materials and methods. Paranoia—not to mention a liberal education—has its uses.

In the fall of 1949, as the CIA was taking over responsibility for the Gehlen Organization and as the Polish drama was winding down, James Angleton's Ryder Street colleague, Kim Philby, was posted to Washington. Philby was very pleased with the assignment as SIS liason with the CIA and FBI because, as he wrote, "The intention was to upgrade the job for a significant reason. The collaboration between CIA and SIS at headquarters level (though not in the field) had become so close that any officer earmarked for high position in SIS would need an intimate knowledge of the American scene."[64] Even the KGB, in a quite disinterested manner, approved of the choice, Philby's controller, Modin, commenting that "the CIA . . . had serious organizational difficulties . . . A completely fresh structure was needed. Philby, who had an excellent knowledge of covert operations against both Fascism and Communism, was just the man for the job."[65] Philby's predecessor as SIS liaison in Washington, Peter Dwyer, was felt to have favored the FBI at the expense of the CIA. Therefore, in addition to helping out the CIA with its bureaucratic problems, and in that process gaining the familiarity with the CIA thought necessary for a possible future director of the SIS, Philby was charged by SIS with rebuilding good relations between MI6 and the CIA without offending J. Edgar Hoover.[66] Philby had his work cut out for him. Not offending Hoover would have been a full-time job in itself.

Britain was rapidly becoming manifestly the junior partner in the Atlantic Alliance, and the secret intelligence services were no less eager than the Foreign Office to do all that they could to maintain their position of at least surface equality with the upstart cousins. Philby's relationship with Angleton played out, in part, as a series of "friendly" struggles for dominance in one sphere or another. For example, Philby had one strong card in his hand, the SIS's worldwide communications system, which was better developed than that used by the CIA. Philby "would turn up at meetings with an operational report from a British source which he knew the Americans would not have yet received from their own man, toss it casually on the table with a tight smile and say: 'Wonder what you make of this, old boy?' And then, not too often and with the right degree of diffidence, he would suggest that SIS would be delighted to allow the CIA to use its communications any time it liked. But senior CIA officers, led by Angleton, were against the idea because they did not want SIS reading their messages."[67] Or so it was said.

The display of superior communications, and the use of privileged information, for bureaucratic maneuver were tricks of the trade that Angleton would have appreciated. He countered with one of his own, arguing to Philby that the primary location of liaison between SIS and the CIA should be in London, not Washington. As penetration is the point of liaison, even between allies, the service operating on the other's home ground will have more opportunities for acquiring information not strictly needed for matters at hand. Philby says that he yielded the point in order to increase his personal influence over Angleton.[68]

Another point of contention between the services was control over anti-Communist émigré organizations, most of which had spent the war in London as clients of the British government. According to Philby, he and Angleton "had many skirmishes . . . over the various Russian émigré organisations . . . There was the People's Labour Alliance (NTS) . . . There were the Ukrainian Fascists of Stepan Bandera, the darlings of the British. Both CIA and SIS were up to their ears in émigré politics, hoping to use the more promising groups . . . Although the British put up a stubborn rearguard action in favour of the groups with which they had been long associated, the story was one of general American encroachment in the émigré field. The dollar was just too strong. For instance, although the British had an important stake in the NTS, SIS was compelled by financial reasons to transfer responsibility to CIA."[69]

We might note, given the patronizing tone of Philby's stories, that Angleton won about communications, about the point of liaison, about control of the émigré organizations.

Angleton and Philby fell into the habit, soon after Philby's arrival in Washington in early October 1949, of having lunch with one another in downtown Washington each week, sometimes at Harvey's Seafood House ("Many of Harvey's lobsters went to provoke Angleton into defending, with chapter and verse, the past record and current activities of the von Gehlen organization"), sometimes at the Army and Navy Club.[70] The great ground-floor dining room of the Army and Navy Club in Washington is the closest thing in that city to the club-land dining rooms overlooking London's Pall Mall. Angleton's lunches there and at Harvey's with Philby mark a change in his routines from Rome as we have them, a reversion, perhaps, to London patterns. Hostile observers, noting that he drank wine with lunch, cocktails before, and brandy afterwards, and that over the years the lunches prolonged themselves into the late afternoon, took this to indicate a certain lack of seriousness about Agency business. Less hostile witnesses saw these lunches as an extension of his office hours during which he cemented relations with domestic contacts like Jay Lovestone, and with representatives of foreign intelligence services, such as, yes, Philby.

Philby's dual responsibilities gave him good cause to drink his lunch with Angleton. While going through his London briefings, Philby had discovered that he would have a much more difficult task than courting the CIA and not offending Hoover on behalf of SIS: the hunt for "Homer."

> FBI cryptographers . . . working on [wartime] radio transmissions from the Soviet consulate in New York, had come across the code name of another Russian spy, "Homer." What the FBI knew about "Homer" strongly suggested that there had been a leakage from the British embassy in Washington during the years 1944–5 and that among the material that had found its way out of the embassy had been the telegraphic traffic between Churchill and Truman . . . [T]he FBI and MI5 had been narrowing down the list of people who had been working at the embassy at the time and who might have had access to such material. Soon, and certainly during Philby's spell of duty in Washington, the case would come to a head and Philby should prepare himself to handle the British end of it. As soon as he could Philby contacted his KGB control in London and told him about the "Homer" case . . . Within a few days Philby had the answer . . . "Homer" was . . . Donald Maclean.[71]

Maclean, who at that moment was back at the Foreign Office in London and once more in line for an ambassadorship and, quite probably, a knighthood to match his father's. Philby, then, in the summer or early autumn of 1949 knew that the FBI had evidence that someone, code-named Homer, had provided information to the Soviet Union during the Second World War. And he knew that Homer was Maclean. Once in Washington, Philby kept a close watch on the progress of the investigation. Having arrived at the penultimate step in his rise within British Secret Intelligence, he knew that a decade's work was teetering on the edge of catastrophe. Philby played his weak hand coolly enough. Peter Wright, of *Spycatcher* fame, recalled that "Meredith Gardner [the FBI's cryptographic genius, who broke VENONA] . . . used to tell me how he worked on the matches in his office, and of how a young pipe-smoking Englishman named Philby used to regularly visit him and peer over his shoulder and admire the progress he was making."[72] We might here note the level of Philby's access to American secrets.

It appears from the VENONA material that it was on August 21, 1950, that the Arlington Hall cryptographers translated the fragments of a Soviet intelligence document dated August 2–3, 1944, reporting on the work of a certain committee: "The Committee is . . . on . . . political and economic questions for drawing up instructions to EISENHOWER and WILSON."[73] The FBI now could see that the Soviets had in 1944 an agent with access to the planning process for the post-war zones of occupation and who was in a position to decipher personal communications between Churchill and Roosevelt concerning postwar strategy as well as the discussion over the location of the Western Front invasions. In addition to this basic information, which could point equally to code clerks at the White House, in Downing Street, or at the embassies of each country, the message included a fragment of a commentary on the meaning of the material, which indicated a more highly placed source.

On March 9, 1951, Arlington Hall was able to read a message of September 7, 1944, giving "HOMER's report of 2nd September." This one included a summary of British negotiating positions concerning postwar economic prospects for Britain, immediate plans for intervention in Greece, occupation zones in Germany, and the debate concerning the status of Germany after the war. Homer reported that the British and Americans were discussing breaking up Germany into at least three states, whether to help Germany to recover economically or leave it in chaos, and related questions. This message made it apparent that Homer had been a high-level British official in Washington. Finally, VENONA contained references to an agent (again Homer) with access to British diplomatic traffic who frequently visited New York.[74] When Maclean worked in the British Embassy in Washington, his KGB contact had been through the New York office of Soviet intelligence. He had at first had his wife, who was pregnant, remain in the New York area, which gave him a good cover reason for frequent trips to the city.

The specifications were exact; it was only a matter of time before the investigators turned from their initial favorite suspicions of code clerks and the like to the very small number of senior British diplomats who enjoyed access to the highest levels of Allied discussions. Maclean's name was prominent on that short list.

The closing years of the Truman administration were notable for the return of triumphalist anti-Communism. That atmosphere was so pervasive, and so noxious, that it reached even into the genial correspondence between the Angletons and the Cummingses. E. E. Cummings—a more than conservative figure—wrote to Cicely Angleton that "Trumantown (never my favorite clime) must closely resemble Moscouw [*sic*] at this writing—everybody suspecting everybody without any time-off for a good honest hate."[75] Cicely Angleton responded that she and her husband had given up Wisconsin beer as a way to express their disapproval of that state's junior senator, Joseph McCarthy. The Angletons avoided McCarthyite society, exchanging visits instead with CIA couples, with sympathetic journalists, poets, and visiting foreigners with intelligence ties. The Philby household was a slightly more complex venue for such occasions than most, as it included, as well as children, Philby's assistant: none other than Guy Burgess, who—against all retrospective probability—had been posted to the British Embassy. Alcoholic, devoutly homosexual, anti-American, aristocratic British intellectuals were not as familiar in Washington as in London, nor, naturally enough, as well understood. (Except, possibly, by alcoholic, homosexual, anglophile types like Joseph Alsop.) Philby had taken him in, a natural, compassionate gesture for Philby the British official, but inexplicable for the Soviet agent whose safety depended on his protective camouflage as precisely a member of "normal" young Washington officialdom. Burgess began at once to misbehave to an extraordinary degree: continually drunk, dirty, insulting—normal behavior in London's Chelsea, but attracting unwelcome attention in Washington. One explanation was that he knew that he was endangering Philby by his mere presence, and wished, by this behavior, to demonstrate to the Foreign Office that he was urgently needed elsewhere than in Washington. Another was that he was simply unhappy to find himself so emphatically a queer fish out of water in an alien and hated country.

One well-known occasion when the Philbys took their turn as hosts for an intelligence community dinner party was January 19, 1951. The two or three dozen guests included the Angletons; William Harvey, the ex-FBI agent who was then responsible for counterintelligence at the CIA, and his wife; Robert Lamphere, FBI liaison to the CIA, and his wife; Robert Mackenzie of MI6; and Dr. and Mrs. Wilfrid Mann. Mann was a nuclear expert and the British liaison officer with the CIA on atomic energy matters. According to Lamphere, "I remember sitting next to Cicely Angleton, who had a cigarette in her hand, and having her ask me, 'What Freudian impulse causes you not to smoke?'"[76] Burgess did not appear for dinner, but made his entrance when the group was gathered in the Philbys' living room for (more) drinks. Someone mentioned that Burgess was a talented caricaturist. Mrs. Harvey, who had been keeping up with the drinking, demanded a caricature of herself. Burgess was glad to oblige, producing a drawing of the lady with her dress hiked up to her waist, her facial features "beastily distorted." Harvey was enraged; there was shouting; the Harveys left, not quietly, and the Philbys dissolved in tears, Aileen Philby in the kitchen, attended by Cicely Angleton and the other women, Kim Philby on the living room sofa attended by James Angleton and the remaining men. Philby had good reason to cry: Burgess had made him a powerful enemy. An odd, memorable detail of this somewhat over-recorded incident was that, when "Mann returned to pick up his car around ten the next morning [he had been too drunk to drive home], he discovered, to his amazement, Burgess and Philby in bed together, downing a bottle of champagne."[77] Aileen Philby assured Mann that it was all perfectly normal, just a manifestation of an old school friendship. And so it probably was.

The dinner party story is recounted in most books about the milieu. It is precisely dated, in a context where precise dates are few. The participants are known and named. The activities are reviewed in convincing detail. The verisimilitude is remarkable. But we might ask, as we must ask of all such stories in the peculiar literature of secret intelligence, what function does the story serve? To give Harvey a reason for disliking Philby? To give readers reason to share the contempt of the more sophisticated guests for the Harveys? To imply that Burgess lived with the Philbys because Guy and Kim were lovers? And, more importantly, what does the story conceal? It is interesting that it is Mann, the atomic energy expert, who tells the story of Philby, Burgess, the bed, and the bottle of champagne. Mann, who had been too drunk the night before to drive home. Had he been drunk enough to talk about his work during dinner? Had they *all* been drunk enough to talk about their work at dinner? Perhaps the next morning Philby and Burgess were celebrating the *success* of the dinner party. Gathered at the Philbys' were those responsible for U.S. foreign intelligence collection, for liaison between CIA and the FBI, for liaison between the British and the U.S. intelligence services, and for liaison between the British and the American atomic programs.[78] What was spoken about at dinner between rounds of drinks? We are not told. That question, of course, relates to a more important question: How much did Philby know? He knew what Maclean knew about British/American policy matters. He knew, according to Angleton, what Mann knew about nuclear technology. Perhaps Philby did choose, among all possible occasions and locations, to have sex with Burgess in the middle of the day in his own bed, with Aileen, cheery enough, nearby. Or perhaps this is what we are meant to believe, to turn our attention to, so that we do not notice something else, that the hard-drinking Dr. Mann was for turning.[79] Such is the art of much of the literature concerning secret intelligence agencies.

The day after the Philbys' dinner party, Alger Hiss was convicted of perjury, and three days after that Klaus Fuchs confessed to atomic espionage. Both these events were connected to the intelligence gathered from the VENONA material, although very few at the time knew it. (Crucially, one of those few was Philby.) Then, in May 1951, British and American cryptanalysts finally decided that "Homer" was Donald Maclean, noting that Maclean's qualifications filled out Homer's checklist: a Foreign Office expert on atomic energy matters, among other things, then head of the American section of the British Foreign Office, in a position to review all diplomatic exchanges between the British government and those of the western hemisphere.[80] Philby would have learned of this very soon after the decision was made.

It had taken nearly two years to go from the break into the VENONA traffic with its references to "Homer" to the identification of "Homer" with Maclean. Burgess, meanwhile, had continued to cultivate his customary social life in Washington as best he could, picking up young men here and there and, in more easily obscured quarters, perhaps cultivating in Washington, Oyster Bay, and Charleston that part of the American aristocracy introduced to him by Joseph Alsop.[81] And then, as the FBI came closer and closer to identifying "Homer" with Maclean, either because he had been ordered back to London by the KGB to warn Maclean of his danger, or because he had gone totally off the rails, Burgess got himself into serious trouble during a journey to South Carolina to lecture at the Citadel: collecting traffic tickets, falling asleep on the rostrum, insulting his hosts. The local authorities were satisfied that they, through clever interrogation of one of his pick-ups and similar strategies, had forced Burgess out of the country. Burgess's story seems to have been that he had set up a charade to get himself ordered out of the country so that he could warn Maclean. The stories are not incompatible. In any case, the result was the same: the State Department complained to the British Ambassador and Burgess was sent back to London to universal satisfaction, not least his own.

The saga of the Cambridge spies was reaching its climax. Once in London, Burgess contacted Maclean, through Blunt, to warn him of his danger. It was decided (by whom is not clear) that Maclean should disappear for a while. There was a coded telephone message from Philby. There were obvious signs that the British authorities were about to make their move. Burgess set out a series of false clues: "On the morning of Friday 25 May [1951] . . . Burgess pottered around, calling friends, including the poet Stephen Spender, whom he might have known had contacts in the Agency. Did Spender, by any chance, have W. H. Auden's address in Ischia?"[82] On the last weekend of May, Burgess and Maclean took a boat for France, and then vanished. To Moscow—as everyone involved immediately theorized—to an early death from alcoholism for Burgess, lonelier in Russia even than in America; to a long career as a Soviet intelligence and foreign policy academic for Maclean.

There was consternation in Bloomsbury. Rosamond Lehmann said that she was going to tell MI5 that Burgess was a Soviet agent. "The poet Stephen Spender had been jabbering away that Guy wasn't a spy so my brother took the chance to snub him. He wrote to Spender in Italy, saying, keep your mouth shut, but someone we know well has told me that Guy is a communist agent.' Spender then gave John Lehmann's letter to the *Daily Express*, which promptly splashed it over the front page."[83] If Burgess were associated with Auden, then he was associated with Spender, something Spender could not—literally—afford, as he was beginning to depend for his livelihood on the CIA-funded journal *Encounter*. In any case, the letter in the *Daily Express* was a good ploy to frighten Burgess into staying out of England.

There was equal consternation in the secret world on both sides of the Atlantic. Maclean was to have been called in for questioning on the "Homer" matter on the Monday, yet he was not watched over the weekend: MI5 had let him slip through their fingers. (Helped, no doubt, by the expertise Soviet intelligence had gained from Blunt about British secret intelligence's watchers and their habits.) Washington was enraged. CIA Director General Bedell Smith ordered everyone on his staff who had met Burgess to write a report about him. Angleton "reported several encounters with a drunken Burgess and said that Philby had acted as an apologist for him even when Burgess's behaviour had caused him embarrassment, explaining it away 'on the grounds that the subject had suffered severe concussion in an accident which had continued to affect him periodically.' But the tenor of the memorandum was that Philby could not be blamed for what Burgess had done and that there was no suspicion attaching to Philby."[84] William Harvey knew that it was the moment for revenge. He wrote a five-page memorandum "which traced Philby's recent career and contacts, and asserted that Philby had to be a Soviet agent . . . Smith immediately shipped off the damning Harvey material to 'C,' Stewart Menzies, in London, accompanied by a typically uncluttered cover letter: 'Fire Philby or we break off the intelligence relationship.'"[85] In August, MI6 recalled Philby "for consultations."

Philby tells an odd story concerning the day he left Washington: "Angleton rang me and arranged for us to meet in a bar before I went to the airport. He began by asking me how long I was going to be away and I said about a week. We chatted on for a bit and then he said: 'Can you do me a favour in London?' I said I would and he handed me an envelope addressed to the head of counterintelligence in London. He said he had missed the bag and wanted London to get the message as soon as possible . . . Now that's an unlikely act for a man who was already supposed to be suspicious of me . . . Unless, of course, the envelope contained a blank sheet of paper and Angleton wanted to see what I would do with it."[86]

This is rather misleading. At that point Angleton knew that Maclean had been a Soviet agent, and knew that Philby was officially considered by the CIA to be a Soviet agent. And what is the likelihood that Philby did not open the envelope? There was no doubt of Angleton's personal suspicions, only of what he was trying to accomplish by playing Philby in this way, what Philby later was trying to accomplish by telling the story in this way.

The postmortems went on for years. Angleton himself came under suspicion, if only in his own mind, for had not the very strength of his work been turned against him? Every argument for CIA rather than SIS control had been a gift of information to Philby about CIA's order of battle, personnel, methods, and liaison relations.[87] The FBI's Robert Lamphere, a guest at the famous dinner party, took these matters personally. "[I]t occurred to me that the KGB must know about my work, and, in fact, about me personally. In a sense, I had been violated because they had penetrated my office in the person of Philby . . . [T]hey probably knew my idiosyncrasies, and looked for ways to counter my every move."[88] More generally, Phillip Knightley assesses matters in this way: "Philby was at the centre of the early CIA operations and when we assess what he was able to do for the Russians during his two years in Washington, we have to think . . . of . . . political will, of the lack of it, long-term military intentions, divisions in decision-making bodies, and relations between allies—the West's grand strategy."

> His days were crowded with meetings, hearing the American view, presenting the British one, negotiating compromises, planning operations, reporting back to London. He had access to every level of the CIA, including the director, Bedell Smith, whom he saw frequently . . . To illustrate the calibre of Bedell Smith's mind, Philby wrote in his book about the time he took him a document of twenty-odd paragraphs for his scrutiny and comment. Knowing the director's "precision-tool brain," Philby had spent the whole morning learning the document by heart. Bedell Smith read it through once and engaged him in a close discussion about it, referring to the numbered paragraphs without looking at the document again. But Philby omitted in his anecdote the most important fact—the nature of the document. In Moscow he told me what it was—a detailed account of how SIS and CIA would cooperate in the event of war with the Soviet Union. Philby passed it on to his Soviet control, dictating it to him from memory, which was the real reason he had learnt it by heart in the first place.[89]

And the real reason that he told the story in his book was to communicate that fact to the CIA and SIS. Miles Copeland, one of the beneficiaries of Angleton's 1949 will a former CIA official who knew Philby, described Philby's contribution as follows: "What it comes to, is that when you look at that whole period from 1944 to 1951—leaving out anything [Philby] picked up other times—the entire Western intelligence effort, which was pretty big, was what you might call minus advantage. We'd have been better off doing nothing."[90] In Philby the Soviets had had—and the CIA now knew that they had had—the perfect agent. "What Philby provided was feedback about the CIA's reactions . . . with Philby in place, [Soviet deception planners] could . . . continually [modify] their messages to keep them credible . . . they could accurately determine whether or not reports fed to the CIA were believed or not, and what additions or revisions would make them credible. They could also find out the preconceived picture that the CIA had . . . and then fit their messages to it."[91]

Double Cross, with Philby as a human Enigma. The counterintelligence assumption that had to be made on the basis of the penetration of U.S. and

British intelligence by Philby and his Cambridge friends was that if this had happened once, it could happen again. Indeed, prudence dictated that it must be assumed that it was, at each moment, happening again.

This narrative of the early days of the Central Intelligence Agency is largely based on the agreed-upon story as found in the standard sources. Historians of secret intelligence work under unusual conditions. After all, much of what should form the material of such histories is . . . secret. The authors of the secondary material are frequently members of one or another intelligence community, or, as they say in the trade, close to it.

Some academic historians are or have been employed by secret intelligence agencies in staff positions or as talent-spotters, like Norman Holmes Pearson and his colleagues. There are occasional scandals. Some books attributed to presumably knowledgeable veterans of intelligence services have been shown to contain fabrications. Those books have been widely cited. What is to be done about them now? Aside from such luridness, how is one to weigh the evidence presented in the memoirs of intelligence operatives? Those published under Kim Philby's name were more or less overt productions of the Soviet secret intelligence services. Similar books by Western authors of similar status can only have been published with the cooperation of their services. Journalists who achieve a reputation in the field often do so by securing the cooperation of intelligence operators. In the interplay between a journalist and, say, James Angleton or William Colby, who was the more likely to be in control of the situation? Hence the set-piece stories, standing epithets, sleight of hand omissions, misleading emphases.

There are archives, it is true, some vast. These are also often unusual: edited in one way or another, made available to some researchers and not to others.[92] Much was hoped for from the archives of the former Soviet Union. And yet the way in which the material has been released has not inspired universal confidence. What, at this moment, do we know? We know what has been made public. From time to time the custodians of the history of the secret world overlook something. The correspondence between the Angleton family and the Cummings family is one such. The FBI's file on Angleton is another. In the same way, thanks to Miranda Carter, we now know much more than we had known about Anthony Blunt, his private and public lives, if not about his secret life.[93] On the other hand, practically nothing is known about Kim Philby that has not been put into the public sphere for reasons thought good by one secret intelligence service or another.

We would like to know much more about Guy Burgess, who was apparently the key figure among the Cambridge Five. Some doors have been opened by

Carter and others. Someday what is apparently a large amount of material—correspondence with lovers and friends and the like—might become available. In the meantime we have the information that has been in hand for half a century, stories told by those whose interest it was to belittle him, some other fragments. For example, there is a photograph of Guy Burgess on holiday by the Black Sea in the summer of 1962, a thin man wearing a very small swimsuit, lying on his back on an air mattress, smoking a cigarette. He is fifty-three years old. His life had not turned out the way that he might have wished. He hated Russia, longed for an England—the England of his youth in that Gothic city in the Fens, of a London that was as if invented for men of his class, education, and habits—that no longer existed. He had spent a decade in Moscow reading, drinking too much, and having sex with young men who were assigned to him or winked at by the KGB.

From one point of view, perhaps his own or that of his friends, it had not been a very successful life. From another, it had been all too successful. When barely twenty he had set out to do as much as possible to subvert the status quo in the West, the very set of arrangements that had carried him first to Cambridge and then into three of the best clubs of his time: the Foreign Office, the BBC, the secret services. It had been an arrogant, reckless gamble, a bet on Red made on a hunch by many of his generation and class. But in his case the gamble had succeeded beyond all probability. Insofar as the national security states of the postwar West were dependent on the integrity of their intelligence services, they had been badly shaken by what he and his friends had accomplished. The effects seemed out of all proportion to the cause. Who had they been? Three, four, perhaps five or more young men from the upper middle classes, barely in contact with the organizations on behalf of which they worked. And yet, empires had been shaken.

A year after posing for this vacation snapshot, Burgess was dead, but the effects of his work continued to be felt for decades more. It is said that after each debacle of that crises-ridden mid-century, Angleton would consider whether the Cambridge spies were behind it. Who knew? How could anyone know? For Guy Burgess, Kim Philby, Donald Maclean, and Anthony Blunt it had been a matter of loyalty and its vicissitudes: loyalty to an ideal, loyalty to friends, disloyalty to country or government. For Angleton and his colleagues in the CIA and the British intelligence services, the affair of the missing British diplomats and all that implied was the entrance to that Unreal City:

> Who is the third who walks always beside you?
> When I count, there are only you and I together
> But when I look ahead . . . [94]

# 7 The Business of Counterespionage

Let us visualize James Angleton's life in, say, the first week of May 1959, when he was forty years old and at the peak of his career. Arriving at his office in the old CIA buildings near the Washington Monument at ten or ten-thirty in the morning, he would have available the *New York Times* and the *Washington Post* and their various Agency supplements. Among the latter were ten daily reports, the most important of which, descending from Truman's original request for a single intelligence summary, was that prepared for the president. There was a top secret daily intelligence bulletin for the White House staff and the cabinet, with copies for officials with a "need to know" throughout the executive branch. And there was a secret Digest. These three Agency productions all covered the same territory, differing in length and the degree of secrecy. The Defense Intelligence Agency also supplied three daily reports, and the National Security Agency issued a Daily Intelligence Summary concerning their electronic intercepts. There was a report from the National Indications Center in the Pentagon, and there was the State Department's top secret Diplomatic Summary. The Foreign Broadcast Information Service published daily the full texts of significant radio broadcasts, and then there were weekly reports and occasional "think pieces" once or twice a week from each of these agencies.[1]

Angleton had access to the material generally available to intelligence officials of his rank and with his clearances (of whom there were not many), and to whatever internal Central Intelligence Agency reports and summaries were being circulated that day. He focused more closely on the reports from the Counterintelligence Staff itself, from the Israeli desk, and from his personal operations: summaries of current events and progress reports on ongoing work. Security-coded folders each morning were removed from the safes in his office and nearby and placed on his desk by his secretary, to be returned to their homes in the evening. They formed great stacks on his desk, creating the archetypical image of the intelligence bureaucrat, nearly invisible behind his papers and cigarette smoke, that is found in most memoirs that mention Angleton.

In addition to reading reports, Angleton, like most senior bureaucrats, spent much of his day in meetings. He met with his deputy and with other supervisors of the Counterintelligence Staff. He met with his assistants who handled day-to-day affairs on the Israeli desk. He also routinely met with the deputy director for plans, at that time Richard Bissell, and Bissell's deputy—and rival—Richard Helms. As the occasion warranted, Angleton would meet directly with Allen Dulles. Toward noon Angleton's secretary called a restaurant, Harvey's or La Niçoise in Georgetown, to reserve his usual table for the appropriate number of guests, and half an hour later Angleton ordered the first of his customary bourbons on the rocks and settled down to the business of the day. During a typical week, Angleton lunched with each of his FBI and foreign (Israeli, French, British) intelligence liaison officers.[2]

After lunch, no matter how late in the afternoon, Angleton went back to the office for more reading, more meetings, then home to North Arlington—where there were now three children—and dinner there, or he and Cicely would go out to one of the dinner parties at the intersection of the intelligence community and the newspaper world, perhaps at Allen Dulles's townhouse at 2723 Q Street.[3] These dinner parties were not completely sober affairs. Agency colleagues remember Angleton dancing alone to Elvis Presley records with movements borrowed from the bullring, and in a poem published long after, his widow remembered moments "Like the time / he pinched my bottom at a party when I was passing the potatoes."[4] Often, though, Angleton would work late into the night among his orchids in the hothouse he had had built in the backyard of his house, or in his basement shop, polishing and setting semiprecious stones he had picked up around the d'Autremont house in Tucson, or on his fishing tackle—or at his liaison relationships, drinking and talking among the orchids. Occasionally there would be gatherings of poets arranged by Reed Whittemore, Angleton's Yale roommate, who moved back and forth between the secret world and academe.

The close relationship between the secret intelligence services and the cultural life of the United States at mid-century has been captured (allegorically, one might say) in a photograph that journalist David Wise has published in one of his books about secret intelligence, which he describes as follows: "Angleton, standing, second from left, is shown during a lighter moment at a private party in Washington in the Spring of 1966. Others (standing) are, from left, Ambrose Gordon, poet, professor, and contemporary of Angleton's at Yale; Howard Nemerov, poet and novelist; William R. Johnson, a CIA officer and member of Angleton's Counterintelligence Staff; and (seated), left, John Pauker, poet and official of the United States Information Agency; and Reed Whittemore, poet and Angleton's former roommate at Yale."[5] All are dressed in suits, all but that worn by Nemerov are dark; Gordon, Angleton, and Johnson wear vests, Angleton's and Johnson's light in color, Gordon's dark. All but Gordon are holding drinks; at least four of the men are holding cigarettes. Pauker and Whittemore do not appear to be actually seated, but squatting, rather, at the feet of the others, Whittemore looking up and to his right to Gordon, who is returning his gaze, looking down and to his left. Angleton is slightly stooped, his head at an angle, looking down at Whittemore. Nothing much can be made out of the room, just part of a window between Gordon and Angleton and a picture, on the wall behind Angleton and Nemerov, of a girl with a braid, in profile: perhaps a copy of a Renaissance portrait. Whittemore, who was twice to hold the position now called the Poet Laureate of the United States, taught at the University of Maryland and elsewhere; Nemerov, the better known poet, taught at Washington University in St. Louis. Johnson had been at Yale, a bit behind Angleton and Whittemore, and was considering a career in the New Critical reading of English literature when Angleton recruited him for the CIA from Carleton. The photograph, taken at the height of the Cold War, is as difficult to interpret as any charred page of a Soviet code book plucked from a Finnish battlefield. All these men were poets, all but Gordon government officials of one sort or another. Most, if not all, had served in secret intelligence: Johnson and Angleton, of course, were doing so at the time the picture was taken.

Many, perhaps most, successful public careers are dependent on success in acquiring patrons who testify to the dependability of the protégé, promote that person's career, protect him or her from competitors, place their protégé in the way of preferment. James Angleton at first sought such patronage in the literary and academic worlds, developing relationships with poets Ezra Pound and T. S. Eliot, professors Maynard Mack and Norman Holmes Pearson, Empson. Pearson helped Angleton with the transition to the world of secret intelligence and nurtured Angleton's early career in that world until Pearson himself more or less left it. For a few years after the end of the Second World War, Angleton was without a major protector, as American secret intelligence was transformed from its wartime organization to its unprecedented materialization as a permanent institution of the U.S. government. He was nonetheless able to move from the Office of Strategic Services through its successor organizations into the new Central Intelligence Agency, where he worked with colleagues like William King Harvey and Kim Philby to create a peacetime counterintelligence structure for the United States in alliance with that of the United Kingdom.

During this period Richard Helms was following a parallel path in the specialty of foreign intelligence collection. Allen Dulles had left government service, after serving with OSS in Switzerland and, briefly, in Berlin, to return to the practice of law on Wall Street. By December 1950, however, Dulles was back in secret intelligence as deputy director for operations (a title that Dulles changed to deputy director for plans: "a less revealing designation"[6] for the official in charge of all covert operations of the Agency.) Less than a year later, General Walter Bedell Smith, then director of central intelligence, promoted Dulles to the second-in-command position in the Agency and Frank Wisner replaced him as deputy director for plans.[7] Angleton, who had friends in both the Office of Special Operations and the Office of Policy Coordination—and had become close to Dulles—was able to claim the credit for Wisner's promotion.[8] The merged OPC and OSO were committed to "rollback," to active measures to combat the Soviet threat, but not everyone who had been in the Foreign Intelligence division of the Agency was equally enthusiastic about this interpretation of the role of the organization. Some OSO survivors—such as Richard Helms—gravitated to the classic intelligence activities of agent running. Others, including Angleton, bridged the gap between the two traditions.

Angleton had a good relationship with Dulles, going back to their meetings in Italy at the end of the war. Rumor had it that when Dulles came into the CIA this relationship was strengthened by Angleton's expertise in the surreptitious gathering of information, a talent he exercised on home ground as he had in Rome. In Washington it was thought that Angleton, as a favor to Dulles, had bugged the offices and homes of both those considered a threat to the CIA and the CIA's employees. Angleton's legend includes a story concerning Tom Braden, who coordinated the cultural policy of the CIA from its International Organizations unit. Braden "and his wife [Joan] were in their bedroom one evening when Braden relayed some office gossip."

> "Beedle doesn't like Allen," he told her . . . "The next day," Braden said, "Dulles called me in. He asked, 'What's this about Bedell and me?'" . . . "You'd better watch out," Dulles warned him. "Jimmy's got his eye on you." Angleton was known to have bugs all over town . . . "Angleton would come into Allen's office first thing in the morning and report what his bugs had picked up the night before. He used to delight Allen with stories of what happened at people's dinner parties . . . Jim used to come into Allen's office and Allen would say, 'How's the fishing?' And Jim would say, 'Well, I got a few nibbles last night.' It was all done in the guise of fishing talk . . . Everybody assumed he bugged CIA staff officers too . . ." At a bugged dinner party, Braden said, "some senator or representative might say something that might be of use to the agency . . ." Stories such as Braden's—and they are legion—helped to make Angleton a sinister and mysterious figure inside the CIA, and in the tight social circles in Washington in which he moved.[9]

Fishing.

There are quite a few of these stories. It is difficult to know what to make of them. Angleton was not head of the CIA's Office of Security. Are we to believe that he somehow was running operations within Washington, against Agency personnel and other members of the government, simply on his own, as a favor to Dulles? Perhaps, or it might be that Angleton had picked up information from someone in the FBI (to which he was close, as we shall see later) who *was* running such operations, and, later, when he had grown entrenched in his job and the favor of Dulles, the stories seemed explanatory. Or perhaps Angleton's persona was such that it simply attracted such apocryphal stories. They meant something, but not necessarily what they seemed to mean. As David Wise has commented in this regard, "In a city in which information is power, secret information is the most valuable of all. And it was the belief within the CIA that Angleton possessed more secrets than anyone else, and grasped their meaning better than anyone else, that formed the basis of his power. Angleton understood this very well, and he cultivated an aura of omniscience . . . The secrets that Angleton did not share not only enhanced his power within a secret agency, they gave him the advantage in bureaucratic infighting. Secrecy served as an unassailable fallback position in any argument."[10]

Allen Dulles was the heir apparent to General Smith at CIA, but after Eisenhower's election in November 1952 it was not at all clear that he would succeed to the position. There were complications within the Republican Party—and complications having to do with the appearance of impropriety if John Foster Dulles were to be Secretary of State while his brother ran the Central Intelligence Agency. "So insecure was Allen [Dulles] about realizing his aspiration that he looked about for a safety net in case he was not chosen. He set up a lunch date in New York for January 21, the day after the presidential inauguration, with his Council on Foreign Relations friend David Rockefeller. He learned that if he gave the word, he could abandon the Washington power game and return to New York to become president of the Ford Foundation—already usefully engaged as one of those organizations that Allen [Dulles] had years before mobilized for political warfare against communism."[11]

"In a city in which information is power, secret information is the most valuable of all." There may be a link between this story of gentlemanly patronage and that concerning the Bradens' bedroom. Joan Braden was said by many to have been a mistress of David Rockefeller's brother, Nelson, who had a variety of official and unofficial connections with the secret intelligence establishment. Had Angleton been looking for information about Nelson Rockefeller on Dulles's behalf?[12] Had he succeeded? Had this facilitated Dulles's conversation with David Rockefeller? These matters are probably at this date unknowable. Be that as it may, Allan Dulles's apparently petitionary visit to David Rockefeller demonstrates yet again the close interrelationships among the seemingly independent great private foundations in New York, and between them and the foreign policy establishment and, as we have seen, with the CIA itself.

The operations of patronage networks, and interlocking directorates, that are assumed behind the scenes in Europe (whether based on class, as in Britain, or on a mandarin system, as in France) were (are?) as common in the United States. Seen from a sufficient distance, a government run at its highest levels by a fairly stable elite of Whig grandees and their nominees spanning the distance, say, from Harriman to Rockefeller in those years, and the organs of civil society, finance, and industry run by the same people, form virtually a single structure within which one can trace the networks as strongly among institutions—from Chase to the Council on Foreign Relations to the Ford Foundation to Yale to the State Department—as within them. Or, as William Corson put it, "Individuals and their interrelationships with one another have had a strong effect on the development of America's intelligence heritage and the intelligence community itself. As intelligence operations expanded rapidly into the mid-twentieth century, these personal relationships came to form a powerful and unofficial intelligence net of influences and alliances which operated in and outside official government channels."[13]

There is a name for this form of governance. It is not democracy, of course: it is oligarchy.

Allen Dulles, assured of the presidency of the Ford Foundation as a fallback (and, behind that, his ultimate retreat at his brother's law firm of Sullivan and Cromwell), finally became Director of Central Intelligence in February 1953.[14] The Clandestine Services at this time included a Foreign Intelligence Staff, within which Angleton was chief of the Special Projects unit, "special," having its usual Agency meaning of "secret." Whether or not Angleton and Dulles had been willing to spy on their colleagues, they were willing to go much further in pursuit of their goals in relationship to the Soviets.

> [Allen Dulles] had long since overcome scruples about the means by which a grand and noble purpose is furthered, and with his ascendancy, practices that might have raised questions before became the acceptable norm. Examination of the international mails, for instance, to get the names and addresses of those who corresponded with people in the Soviet Union might turn up useful leads for espionage. Accordingly, late in 1952 the CIA asked the chief postal inspector in New York for a discreet facility inside the post office to study the international mail traffic. Only the envelopes would be examined, the CIA men implied, but their internal planning memo was

> more candid: "Once our unit was in position, its activities and influence could be extended gradually, so as to secure from this source every drop of potential information available." Within just a few months selected letters were being opened and analyzed by CIA in violation of all postal regulations; indeed, their actions were a crime under federal statute.[15]

We will have occasion to look more closely at this postal program, but first there is yet another episode of "Kim" to consider.

After a London newspaper (*The People*) published a story claiming that they had been Soviet agents, the Foreign Office, which had been resisting such a move for four years, were forced to publish a White Paper about Burgess and Maclean. Exactly a month later, the New York *Sunday News* named Philby as the Third Man. Prime Minister Harold Macmillan felt obliged to make a statement to Commons on November 7. It was somewhat disingenuous: "No evidence has been found that Philby was responsible for warning Burgess or Maclean. While in government he carried out his duties ably and conscientiously. I have no reason to conclude that Mr. Philby has at any time betrayed the interests of this country, or to identify him with the so-called 'third man,' if, indeed, there was one."[16] This did not go down well with the Central Intelligence Agency, where Angleton, along with most others, was convinced that Philby was indeed the Third Man. Liaison activities between the U.S. and British secret intelligence services frayed. Philby was, for the moment, triumphant on two counts: the prime minister himself had vouched for him, which was a personal victory, and the Western alliance, from the secret intelligence point of view, had been weakened. The prime minister's statement convinced the British intelligence services that Philby had to be handled gently. He was found a place as a journalist and given some connection with MI6—as a concession, or as a way to keep him under observation.

It was not a good career move, and senior officers in the British Secret Intelligence Service, worried about their old friend, looked for a way that he could get back into the game without being on the regular payroll. They decided to send him to Beirut. "SIS was taking an increasing interest in the Middle East, and to have an experienced agent in what was then the centre of intrigue for the area seemed a good idea. Even Philby's enemies were not entirely against the scheme, arguing that making Philby active again might lead him to provide the evidence necessary to prove his guilt and close the case."[17] The plan was for Philby to be an *agent*, not an SIS officer. It was quite a comedown in terms of an intelligence career, but, of course, he still had official status with another secret intelligence agency. Philby's British cover in Beirut was as a stringer for the *Observer* and the *Economist*. SIS had vouched for his bona fides with those newspapers. In Beirut during the late 1950s, then, Philby filed stories on international affairs, was reunited with his father, remarried, collected information for Moscow and London. His old skill had not completely faded: "the CIA believed that Philby had a top-level source within the Agency who revealed to him in Beirut some of its covert actions."[18] A quiet, productive life for an aging spy. Virtually simultaneously with the settling of these arrangements, the search for Burgess and Maclean, which had involved thousands of working hours by British and American intelligence, came to an end when they gave a Moscow press conference in February 1956.[19] The matter of the Cambridge spies then receded from the press's attention, if not that of James Angleton, for a few years.

As covert action eclipsed psychological warfare in the thinking of the Clandestine Services, James Angleton assumed the role that made him famous—or, more precisely, secretly famous for twenty years, then more widely notorious. On August 18, 1954, Angleton gave a briefing for the group working under General James Doolittle, which President Eisenhower had commissioned to make recommendations about the Central Intelligence Agency. According to a top secret FBI report discovered by Ted Morgan, he

> was subjected to several questions which led to his open criticism of many of CIA's operations . . . He was highly critical of Gen. Walter Bedell Smith's administration at CIA. When Angleton finished his briefing he was asked numerous questions by the Doolittle group. Nearly all the questions were predicated on what was wrong with CIA and how it could be improved. Angleton "opened up" and said exactly how he felt about his agency. The present setup which allows for joint operations has led to confusion, duplication, and waste of manpower and money. Angleton placed great emphasis on the fact that his agency has suffered because of the many directors and the inevitable changes in policy and thinking. The changes in leadership had led to one revolution after another, which had affected production and morale. Angleton was openly and strongly critical of Gen. Walter Bedell Smith's administration and claimed that Smith had been hoodwinked by the psychological warfare experts like Frank Wisner. Smith forgot espionage and counterespionage operations and devoted his time and attention to psychological warfare projects, many of which failed miserably.[20]

Angleton's comments, as reported to the FBI, presumably by Angleton himself, were meant to strengthen the hand of those like Allen Dulles, Richard Helms, and Angleton who had devoted their careers to intelligence collection. Such sentiments would have been welcome at the Bureau, which saw itself as an intelligence collection agency. We need not take these comments at face value.

Perhaps they were made as reported, perhaps not. In any case, Dulles's covert projects were ultimately on a scale far beyond those Wisner had attempted under Smith.

The governmental reviews of the Central Intelligence Agency during the Truman administration, including Dulles's own reports, had emphasized the importance of upgrading the counterintelligence functions of the Agency. The report of General Doolittle, presented to Eisenhower in September 1954, repeated earlier admonitions to strengthen CIA's counterintelligence activities: "Most signally, the report urged CIA to assume the country's leading counterintelligence role . . . The United States needed to abandon the law-enforcement route for a 'more ruthless' approach, the Doolittle Report stressed, and that new ruthlessness must be applied to 'intensification of CIA's counterintelligence efforts to prevent or detect and eliminate penetrations.' The situation required a new strategy, a new concept for American life, one which would spill across normally restricted areas, legal channels, and departmental lines."[21]

In December of 1954, Dulles acted on the recommendations of the Doolittle Committee by creating a Counterintelligence Staff within the clandestine services and making James Angleton its chief. Angleton, who had helped establish the Soviet branch of the CIA, when his career had seemed to be following that of Richard Helms in Foreign Intelligence collection, found his proper niche in counterintelligence: to one side of the main currents and the conflict between intelligence procurement and covert action, in some sense isolated, in every sense independent. He was to become, in Robin Winks's phrase, counterintelligence's chief theoretician as well as its most famous practitioner.

When Angleton took the position of chief of the Counterintelligence Staff of the Central Intelligence Agency he took responsibility for ensuring that the Agency's secrets would not be known to enemies. The difficulties of the task had just been made dramatically clear by the Burgess and Maclean cases, by that of Fuchs, as they had been first—more happily—pointed up by the accomplishments of the British secret intelligence services during the Second World War. As we have seen, Angleton was a student of the history of the KGB's deception operations and its ability to penetrate opposing intelligence services. Closer at hand he had the example of the British services, their great wartime success with Double Cross, which demonstrated that under the proper conditions a counterintelligence operation could identify *all* the opposition's agents, and, playing them back, control their parent organization. And then there were the equally significant catastrophic failures of British intelligence, the Cambridge and atomic spies.[22]

It was in this context that in 1954 Angleton proposed that "whereas the Soviet Division might see a Soviet diplomat as a possible CIA mole, the Counterintelligence Staff would view him as a possible disinformation agent. What division case officers would tend to look at as valid information, furnished by Soviet sources who risked their lives to cooperate with them, counterintelligence officers tended to question as disinformation, provided by KGB-controlled sources."[23] Angleton's was a rhetorical approach to the close reading of intelligence reports: instead of being understood as narratives, they should be contested in dialogue. The bureaucratic implication of Angleton's proposal was that in this dialogue the Counterintelligence Staff would be equal in authority to its intelligence collection interlocutor. Although Dulles placed Angleton under the deputy director for plans, on a level with the division chiefs, Angleton's view of the matter was that the Counterintelligence Staff was an independent bureau. That is how he ran it, and that is how Dulles and his immediate successors allowed him to run it, for that is what they wanted.

For Dulles and Helms, for other ex-OSS officers in the CIA, "the lesson of X-2 was that it's preferable to have unfounded suspicions than to be duped by a bogus source."[24] This is a judgment call, a calculation, it might be noted, made by the British when they appeared to be losing the war, when to be "duped," even once, might have been fatal (a lesson neglected by the Special Operations Executive). The Church Committee's report two decades later, echoing, no doubt, Angleton himself, stated that counterespionage is "a discipline of great importance, for the rock-bottom obligation of an intelligence service is to defend the country; meeting this obligation is the very *raison d'être* of counterintelligence. The discipline also represents the most secret of secret intelligence activities—the heart of the onion."[25] John Masterman, theorist of the wartime Double-Cross system, earlier had pointed out the challenges of peacetime counterespionage, which "is a matter of the utmost difficulty; it is immensely hard to secure proof; it is impossible to act on suspicion however strong; the whole tenour of life in this country is antagonistic to overregimentation and to rigid classification; it is better to let many spies 'run' rather than to risk one mistake."[26] Counterintelligence or counterespionage, Masterman continued, is inherently frustrating, all its efforts essentially indeterminate. "No counterespionage service, however well organised and however efficient, can hope to prevent all espionage, but it can keep its controlling finger on all espionage and be ready to strike at it at any moment . . . it is therefore of paramount importance to keep a firm hold on the enemy's own system of agents and informers. Knowledge of his methods, knowledge of his intentions, and knowledge of the personnel of his organisation are all vitally necessary . . . [I]n peace as well as in war a carefully cultivated double agent system is the safest and surest weapon of counterespionage, and the one most easily adaptable to changing conditions, changing problems, and even changing enemies."[27]

Angleton himself suggested to his protégé Epstein, "imagine a wife, attempting to deceive her husband, who bribed his psychiatrist into telling her how her husband interpreted all the lies and misleading clues she furnished him. Those he believed, she could elaborate on; those he disbelieved, she could cease providing or modify. Eventually, through trial and error, the wife and psychiatrist would supply the husband with a story that perfectly fit in with what he believed. Through such strategies, as Angleton put it, 'the deceived becomes its own deceiver.'"[28] This is an arresting image. Applying a New Critical "close reading," as if Angleton were a character in a novel, would yield questions about the choice of the metaphor by a man whose marriage was often in difficulty, whose wife had precisely sought a psychiatrist's help about that marriage. In any case, it was probably a good enough crosslight on the matter. Raymond Rocca, Angleton's disciple, explained the relationship between counterintelligence and intelligence collection using a different marital image: "What you had in actuality was a marriage that went across the board . . . On the one hand we were supposed to be a shield for the Agency, but in a way we were the most exposed."[29]

People on the intelligence collection side of the Agency could be frustrated by Angleton's efforts to ensure the security of their operations: "We never had a successful Soviet operation that Angleton and his crowd didn't cast some doubt on," complained John Maury, chief of the Soviet Union Division at the time. "In house it was all right to raise doubts, but Jim and a few of his close colleagues allowed his suspicions to be widely known around the Hill."[30] A most serious charge.

The theory of counterintelligence begins with an audit, as it were, of where the secrets are held and who has access to them. Who were likely to be the most damaging spies? Counterintelligence officials like Philby; crucial government officials like Maclean and Burgess; possibly, intelligence service chiefs like Hollis, head of MI5, and suspected, if never proven, to be an agent. David Wise thought that "to Angleton . . . it made perfect sense to assume that the KGB had succeeded in planting a mole or moles inside the CIA . . . [T]he CI Staff argued that the intelligence services of other nations—notably the British—had been penetrated by the Soviets. Why should the CIA be exempt? . . . Angleton also had personal reasons to press the search for penetrations with such ferocity. He had been taken in by the supreme mole of the century, Kim Philby, and he was not about to make the same mistake twice."[31] Who were the positionally possible American parallels to the Cambridge spies? Angleton drew up a list. It necessarily included his key colleagues. Logically, it included Angleton himself, and such influential figures as Averell Harriman, not because Angleton actually had reason to think them (or himself) disloyal, but simply because of the amount of damage they could have done if, in fact, they were Soviet agents. It was and it was known to be his job to be universally suspicious.[32] Of course. The British—and the German—experience had pointed out the risks of not thinking about the unthinkable. It was a lesson Angleton had learned well.[33] According to Rhodri Jeffreys-Jones, "To some, Angleton's obsession with compartmentalization and his suspicion of the Soviet Union's every move smacked of paranoia, but chronic skepticism is no fault in a counterintelligence chief. Angleton helped to ensure that—as far as is known—the CIA was not penetrated."[34]

The dialogic approach to counterintelligence worked well enough (or was simply accepted) in the postwar CIA until, with time and the accumulation of power, Angleton's views came to outweigh those of his intelligence interlocutors. His vocational "mind-set," that all contacts with foreign intelligence services must be viewed with suspicion, became dominant over what he himself would have assumed to be the equally necessary mind-set that intelligence collection must proceed. The "necessary duality" broke down. Out of balance, by the late 1960s the machine had run off the rails and Angleton was blamed. His defenders would counter that he was doing the job he was paid to do. The problem, they said, was the weakness of the necessary countervailing voices. The greater, the urgent problem, he said, was the penetration of the Western intelligence services by those of the Soviet bloc. He was right, as it happened—but at least in regard to the CIA, just because he was right, he was right too soon.

One of James Angleton's primary responsibilities as chief of the Counterintelligence Staff of the Central Intelligence Agency was liaison with the Federal Bureau of Investigation. This was a more complex relationship than appeared on the surface: Angleton seems to have been, in a sense, an FBI agent within the CIA. As early as June 10, 1953, in a memorandum from the FBI's V. P. Keay to A. W. Belmont, a senior member of Hoover's staff, Keay wrote that "during the past year [Angleton] has been very cooperative and has volunteered voluminous information of interest to Bureau. At the present time he more or less falls in category of Confidential Informant. In order to handle his material in a more efficient and secure manner, it is being recommended that a control file be created." Such are the terms of praise of the bureaucrats of the secret police.[35] From the point of view of the Central Intelligence Agency, Angleton was their liaison officer with the Federal Bureau of Investigation, while from the point of view of the FBI, he was a Confidential Informant, their penetration agent, as it were: a convenient situation for the Bureau, which received information from him through official channels, and additional information more directly. Angleton was in fact designated "Confidential Informant T-2" by the FBI that year, and continued to furnish "voluminous" unofficial information to the Bureau into the late 1970s.

Former colleagues of James Angleton, when asked to describe him, almost inevitably talked about his orchids or his bass or trout fishing techniques. Mark Riebling, giving one of the many accounts of Angleton's trout fishing, notes that he was careful to study the local insect life before deciding which lure to use for the fish in a particular stream.[36] The fishing was natural enough for Angleton—he was from Idaho, after all; his father fished, and his wife's family were originally from Wisconsin, where they maintained trout fishing rights near the Brule River.

> . . . Even in August you need a fire in these
> north woods. I see the wicker rocking chair,
> a lamp that needs rewiring. Bats hang
> upside down from curtain folds, suspended
> until night. They look like withered figs.
> On the wall, rubber waders nudge each other
> when the kitchen door bangs shut. They're split
> like the bamboo rods that flicked
> and bent above the Falls at midnight. Like the post
> along the fence that made me call your name
> one evening after sunset . . .
> Cicely d'A. Angleton, "Brule in August"[37]

Cord Meyer, when asked in 1995 about his memories of Angleton, replied with similar trout fishing stories. Others varied the routine with references to bass fishing or the cultivation of unusual orchids.

The orchids, like the trout and bass fishing, were part of Angleton's "legend"—both in the common meaning of the word and as it is used in the intelligence world to mean a misleading biographical narrative. Edward Jay Epstein, the journalist closest to Angleton after his retirement from the CIA, quotes Angleton as saying, almost too perfectly in character, "With most species of orchids, it is not the fittest but the most deceptive ones that survive."[38] David Wise quotes a similar story: "Angleton . . . used orchids as a cover . . . He bred and named a couple of orchids. He named one for his wife. A cattleya called 'Cicely Angleton' . . . Jim used to sit for hours and talk about orchids . . . He was never without his trench coat."[39] The trench coat is a nice touch.

The orchids had their own cycle of stories, emphasizing their ambiguous beauty, the patience needed to breed them, the nocturnal attentions they received. These influenced Aaron Latham's novelistic treatment of Angleton: "[He] wore black shoes, black socks, a black suit, a black tie, a white shirt, and a black homburg. He was not a man who had much affinity for greys. Tall and thin with a stooped, slightly twisted body, he looked like a crooked black snake in a garden of brightly colored orchids."[40] But do not all these stories about Angleton's orchids hearken back to a classic model? In Raymond Chandler's *The Big Sleep*, Marlowe encounters a secretive, powerful man who manipulates society from a hothouse filled with orchids. It is a suitably sinister image of artificiality, the cultivation of the orchids pointing to the cultivation of other matters.

The stories about Angleton's orchids and other hobbies are bridging images, equating Angleton in the popular mind with figures like Chandler's omniscient quasi-villains, who spend sleepless nights in arcane research, infinitely patient, demonstrating through the painstaking breeding of exotic flowers, long days beside remote streams, the possibility of other efforts, equally hidden and painstaking. Insofar as our image of Angleton is romantic in this way, it is slightly removed from the day-to-day reality of his professional activities. One might argue that a function of such stories (perhaps of most of the literature of espionage) is to remove their subject from the field of political and historical analysis. If so, they serve a useful purpose for secret intelligence agencies.

The information from the FBI's files on Angleton demonstrates that he functioned virtually as a second FBI liaison officer, in this case *within* the CIA, for over twenty years. Especially when Sam Papich was Angleton's partner, communications flowed well in both directions between the domestic and foreign intelligence services. To pick another example, not quite at random, in October 1955 Hoover suggested that Donald Maclean might have compromised CIA employees. Maclean had been "a frequent visitor" at CIA, according to a Bureau source, and was alleged to have "dated" two stenographers. An FBI search of logs kept by the guards at the CIA's building on the Mall showed that Maclean was often there after business hours.[41] The FBI's suspicions that Maclean had been a kind of male Mata Hari are, to the say the least, surprising. Nonetheless, the FBI's information probably served to remind Angleton of the success of Maclean and Philby in infiltrating the CIA, heightening, perhaps, the "dissociation of sensibility" between the CIA and the British intelligence services.

Papich told writer Mark Riebling stories about some of the information provided by Angleton to the FBI, presumably through official channels, as an indication of why Angleton was highly valued by the Bureau: "In one case, Angleton got the Bureau access to a New York mob lawyer. The man was a rascal, but there was no counting the cases the FBI prosecuted on the basis of his cooperation, all involving corruption within unions and city government—and all for *free*, just given over by Angleton. Papich also worked with CIA people on projects spearheaded by Angleton in the cryptographic field, while the Agency, for its part, serviced countless FBI requests for coverage of American communist leaders traveling abroad . . . Angleton would ask the Bureau to undertake 'black bag' jobs against certain domestic targets, and the Bureau would sometimes do so."[42] However, this passage raises more questions than it answers. Why did Angleton, head of foreign counterintelligence, have "access to a New York mob lawyer"? What cryptographic projects were "spearheaded" by Angleton? Why—and on what authority—was Angleton requesting "black bag" jobs against domestic targets? We are not told. It is quite possible that we will never know. Some records are presumably maintained, inaccessible to historians, in the depths of Langley; others have been destroyed.

In order to combat the threat of foreign enemies, Angleton's Counterintelligence Staff acquired a worldwide network of agents who were charged with confusing and thwarting hostile intelligence services.[43] These hostile intelligence services represented a considerable, and very real, threat to the United States and its allied intelligence services. Writing at the very end of the Cold War, Loch Johnson accepted a figure of "over a thousand Soviet officials . . . on permanent assignment in the United States alone. Among these, more than 50 percent have been positively identified as members of the KGB or GRU, the Soviet civilian and military intelligence units. Conservative estimates for the number of unidentified intelligence officers raise the figures to over 60 percent of the Soviet representation; some defector sources have estimated that as many as 70 to 80 percent of Soviet officials in the United States have an intelligence connection."[44] If we are going to go that far, counting Cold War–era Soviet officials with "an intelligence connection," it would be difficult to find grounds to exempt any of the thousand. And then, as Anatoli Golitsyn was to point out, we must add the representatives of the governments of the remainder of the Warsaw Pact countries. All these, not only in the United States (in cooperation with the FBI) but worldwide, were Angleton's responsibility, his particular bit of the threat to counter. He could not stop even there, for once all the legal residents abroad of the Soviet Union and its allies were accounted for, there were the illegal residents, followers in the tradition of the organizers of the Red Orchestra of the 1930s.[45] Angleton is said to have tipped off the FBI about the KGB's Rudolf Abel, one of the more important illegals to operate in the United States. Abel was arrested on June 21, 1957, after a ten-year run.[46] This was a good example of coordination between the domestic and foreign secret intelligence agencies of the United States government, or, perhaps, an indicator of illegal domestic surveillance by the CIA, depending on the source of Angleton's information about Abel and one's view of these matters.

Angleton's survival and success within the Agency were a mystery to some observers. "What outsiders couldn't factor in was the compelling quality of Jim Angleton's presence," writes Burton Hersh, "the dutiful, devoted, *authentic* mannerisms he'd evolved to convey the urgency of the crisis, the sacrifices which he and his men were prepared to continue to make to seal the ramparts of the West."

> Who presumed to rebut, watching Jim wind one long pinstriped shank ever tighter around the other, tap out one more Virginia Slim, attempt one last time not merely in words but more, really, by way of that knitted, knotted, weaving, bobbing, wincing, stalking *lexicon* of body language—who undertook to challenge that? Angleton's small, sculpted head—each hair combed back, wet, to expose a central part of Edwardian integrity—craned forward: Angleton's mocha eyes shone, and as his lips parted, without warning, a grin would irradiate that famously hollow face. A boon, utterly unexpected, to complement the fillip of true warmth that flickered and burnished Angleton's genuine midwestern inflections.[47]

We are meant to believe, by such portraits, that Angleton's role and power were derived from his earnest presentation skills, as, so often, his trout and bass fishing were presented—are still presented—as somehow an explanation of his place in the world of secret intelligence. Such presentations are functional. In this way the inquirer is shunted off to picturesque sidings, amused, inquiries halted or at least delayed.

For, of course, those inquiries had to be parried, as it was precisely Angleton and those other gray men who survived the purges after the Bay of Pigs who would manage the most secret of the Agency's covert operations—and who would, at the end of the decade, turn it into an instrument of a government at least partially at war with its own people.

# 8 Foreign Liaisons

James Angleton is known—inasmuch as he is known—as the "Molehunter," a story to which we will turn later. His career from 1948 to 1954 had been that of a foreign intelligence officer with line authority in a number of areas, authority he retained after returning to his métier of counterintelligence. These areas included the Israeli "account" and what was in effect his own foreign intelligence network. A principal part of the latter was based on his relationship with Jay Lovestone. As we have seen in an earlier chapter, Lovestone was a useful agent, having built his own networks on behalf of the American Federation of Labor, with well-established contacts and funding conduits to anti-Communist trade unions and such useful allies as waterfront thugs in Europe and elsewhere. Lovestone had not restricted himself to trade union politics. In Germany, for example, in April 1947, he provided ten thousand dollars for Kurt Schumacher's Social Democratic Party for "office equipment."[1] (Schumacher's offices must have been peculiarly well equipped in an era when a carton of cigarettes could purchase the good will of any given sector of the local populace.) This support for the German Social Democratic Party was aligned with the CIA's general strategy of providing resources to both center-left and center-right parties throughout Europe, funding Socialists and Christian Democrats so that their grateful anti-Communist deputies were likely to dominate the government of the day without regard to the particularities of electoral results.

The AFL's foreign policy and that of the U.S. government converged in 1947 when Schumacher went to Washington seeking direct U.S. support. As he made his rounds he was accompanied by Lovestone, which is how Lovestone met James Forrestal. Lovestone told Forrestal that his trade union programs had penetrated every country in Europe, making the AFL "a world force in the conflict with world Communism in every field affecting international labor."[2] It was a very effective sales pitch. At the end of 1948, William Donovan recommended Lovestone to now Secretary of Defense Forrestal, "who was looking for an advisor familiar with the methods of subversion and fifth columns."[3] On December 10, 1948, an AFL official wrote to Frank Wisner, then head of the Office of Policy Coordination, introducing "Mr. Jay Lovestone . . . He is duly authorized to cooperate with you in behalf of our organization and to arrange for close contact and reciprocal assistance in all matters." According to Lovestone's biographer, "With this letter began a period of collaboration between the AFL and the CIA that lasted for more than twenty years . . . Lovestone used a simple device to cook the Free Trade Union Committee's books. Before the CIA funding he had itemized the contributions of affiliates union by union. In 1949, when Wisner started paying, contributions from 'individuals' were also listed, with numbered receipts giving the amounts and the made-up names of the supposed donors. Thus, that year contributions from affiliates amounted to $56,000, while contributions from 'individuals' were $203,000. The individual's real name was Frank Wisner."[4]

The next year Wisner decided to protect his investment by assigning the ever useful Carmel Offie as Lovestone's liaison to the CIA, thus guaranteeing a certain measure of transparency, at least from Wisner's point of view, in the relationship between the Free Trade Union Committee (FTUC) and the CIA.[5] Lovestone's biographer appears to believe that this most sophisticated of political operatives, capable of surviving a personal attack by Stalin himself, "never fully grasped that he and the CIA had different agendas. His aim was to promote free trade unions as a way of checking Soviet expansion. The CIA agenda was to infiltrate all the significant groups in a given country."[6] It is difficult to believe that Lovestone did not understand this.

Lovestone's conception of his role, and his possible belief in the differing aims of the AFL and those of the CIA, did not prevent him from accepting what was in effect a position as an agent of James Angleton, to whom Lovestone's network was given by Allen Dulles, as the Israeli desk had been given earlier. Angleton dealt with this bureaucratically by establishing a Special Projects Section for his Israel and Lovestone responsibilities.[7] Lovestone had a particular importance, as he was linked to a special interest of Allen Dulles. According to the internal CIA history of the Dulles years, "Dulles took a great personal interest [in operations concerning] international labor. These operations were of great domestic sensitivity, particularly since CIA worked with and through both the CIO and the AF of L before their merger. As a result, special arrangements for their handling were in force and policy guidance and approval was limited to contact between Dulles and specified CIA officers, primarily in the [Braden/Meyer] I[nternational] O[rganizations] Division, and the Under Secretary of State for Political Affairs, with the Assistant Secretary of Labor for International Affairs consulted on occasion."[8] Angleton, who secretly read the international correspondence of the AFL, satisfied himself concerning the uses to which the CIA's money was put and developed "a close, mutually respectful association with Jay Lovestone himself [with] many undisclosed tradeoffs."[9]

According to Ted Morgan, "In passing Lovestone to Angleton, Allen Dulles made an inspired personnel decision."

> In Angleton, [Lovestone] finally found a CIA man he truly liked. Jim Angleton was not only a colleague but a best friend and kindred sprit. Each found in the other a deeply compatible mirror image. Lovestone, who had no family and spent three days a week in Washington, found himself practically living at the Angleton house. He was made welcome by Angleton's spirited and attractive wife, Cicely, who recalled that "Jim was devoted to Jay. He thought that Jay had struggled all his life to make his ideas prevail. Many were the times when Jay came to dinner and he and Jim sat up talking into the night. Jay was the only person Jim didn't call a cab for. Even in the driving rain or snow he would drive Jay back to the Statler" . . . The bond between Jim and Jay was founded on the conviction that they had a higher understanding of the Soviet threat. They were the guardians at the gate, with access to information others did not have. As Cicely Angleton put it: "They saw what others did not see. They knew the enemy and how he operated. They could put the pieces together, draw the inferences."[10]

From 1954, Lovestone collected intelligence from agents in Europe, India, Japan, and Africa which he turned over to Angleton, who paid for Lovestone's—and the AFL's—foreign operations.[11] The relationship was not entirely one-way. The AFL would occasionally use Lovestone to obtain assistance from the CIA for its political efforts. For example, Lovestone wrote to Angleton in March of 1959, stating that union chief George Meany wished to be appointed to the U.S. delegation to the United Nations General Assembly and asking for Allan Dulles's intervention. Angleton did as asked and Meany got the job.[12] It is of some interest that at least one expert believes that as late as 1959 positions on the U.S. delegation to the United Nations General Assembly were in the gift of the Central Intelligence Agency. The AFL, the Ford Foundation, Yale and Harvard, parts of the Department of State, the Museum of Modern Art—what U.S. institution in those years was alien to the Central Intelligence Agency?

We know of two other members of Angleton's personal spy networks. One was the glamorous Louise Page ("Pagie") Morris, a Boston debutante and sometime New York model. Morris had joined the OSS in 1942 and after the war she continued to work for Donovan. (And for a time was Donovan's mistress, tolerated by his wife because the latter was concerned to prevent her daughter-in-law, Mary Pinchot Donovan, from taking that role.)[13] When, in mid-1949, Angleton, as chief of Foreign Intelligence Operations, decided to set up something of his own agent network, "his first recruit was Pagie Morris . . . Most of the time, Pagie was engaged in a bewildering array of assignments for

Angleton, from whom she never knew what to expect. He might say, 'Would you like to go to Jordan and look around?' Or, 'My people want to turn so-and-so.' Or, 'There's a woman in Italy giving me trouble.'" This pattern continued long after Angleton's responsibilities changed to those of chief of the Counterintelligence Staff. In 1954 Angleton sent Morris to Cairo, Karachi, Bombay, Rangoon, Bangkok, Djakarta, and Taipei. She went to Iraq for him in 1959 and 1963, and, no doubt, to many other places through the years.[14] Her cover was that she worked in the Gompers Research Library at 406 East 58th Street in New York City, ostensibly part of the Free Trade Union Committee. The small, usually empty reading room was paid for and stocked with books from Angleton's budget.[15]

We owe an account of another of Angleton's networks of agents to Angleton's nemesis William Colby. Colby, who, when posted to Italy to lay the groundwork for the 1958 elections, worked under the direction of Gerald Miller, CIA chief of station in Rome. The effort that Colby led in Italy was even more extensive than that which Angleton had run five years earlier: pumping money into the Christian Democratic Party, fending off the Communist-Socialist alliance, running agent networks, developing contacts throughout Italian society.[16] Colby found a system of "cutouts" left in place by Angleton to pass funds to those in need.[17] According to Colby's account of the art of secret influence, "this sort of thing was so effective that often the Italian recipients of our aid themselves were not certain where the aid was coming from. Some believed that they were in contact with private American groups who had taken an interest in their cause. And those who had an inkling that they were in touch with the United States government in some way, though not knowing exactly in which way, were discreet enough not to ask . . . Americans could present the flimsiest reasons for being in Italy at that time without raising a single incredulous eyebrow. They could be businessmen, free-lance journalists, students, artists, aspiring film actors, or just well-heeled drifters who had come to partake of the sweet life."[18]

In order to learn something about Angleton's agent in Italy, we can profitably give Colby's memoir the sort of close reading Angleton's teachers at Yale developed. It is the sort of thing that CIA archives show Angleton himself doing in similar circumstances.

The political situation in Italy, when Colby arrived, was one in which the CIA-backed Christian Democrats were faced on the right by a variety of neo-fascist and monarchist parties, and on the left by the allied Communists and Socialists. The position of Ambassador Clare Boothe Luce, and of Angleton, was that the Socialists were completely under Communist control. Colby saw promise in what became known as the "opening to the Left," the policy of certain Christian Democrats to split the left alliance and develop a relationship with the Socialists, the strategy that had brought them victory in the 1948 elections. Colby's explanation of this first conflict with Angleton was, therefore, at one level political: Colby was a "liberal," Angleton a rigid anti-Communist conservative. On the other hand, there was something more to it than that—or less. There was a bureaucratic conflict.[19]

Most CIA agents in Italy in the mid-1950s were run as members of networks ultimately controlled by Colby. But others were run by Angleton's Counterintelligence Staff. This was standard practice, a continuation of X-2's operations during the Second World War.[20] On the other hand, it was also routine that the intelligence acquisition and covert action sides of the Agency did not like it. Colby writes in his memoir that sometime before the fall of 1956 his boss, Gerald Miller, asked to see him.

> He said he wanted me to meet a very secret American contact whom I should handle for him in the future. We went out to a small bar where no one would notice us and shared a *cappuccino*. I learned that my new friend (and he is still my friend) had come to Italy with the OSS and had gotten to know a number of young political leaders when they were trying to establish their new political system. A liberal Catholic by background, and fluent in Italian, he had befriended a number of them and helped them to formulate their ideas on how Italy should develop. He had returned to the United States after the war, but had kept his friendships not only with the Italians but with some of the OSS veterans who also had operated in Italy during the war and later had helped to form CIA, in particular James Angleton. They had asked him to return to Italy from time to time to keep in touch with his old friends and report to Washington on their views and hopes. He had done so regularly, but it was clear that the struggle in Italy was moving into high gear, and Washington had sent him to Rome to live, so that his information could be continuous. Gerry had tried to meet with him and keep him compartmented from the rest of the station, and from my political operations, but had come to the conclusion that it could not be done. The problems of briefing and debriefing him, ensuring that he both understood and thus followed the ambassador's policies, yet operated without apparent connection with the embassy were too demanding in time and too difficult to conceal for one in Gerry's prominent position as one of Mrs. Luce's principal advisers as well as in official liaison with the Italian security services. So Gerry obtained Washington's approval to bring me in on the secret of his friend's activities and authorized me to help in handling him thenceforth.

Colby's memoir does not present the issues here very clearly. They boil down to the fact that this "individual," who at first is referred to as if he were simply a cooperative American citizen, was actually a CIA official ("Washington had sent him to Rome to live"), in some way or other one of Angleton's agents.

To this point in Colby's account, what is being done is a managerial change: that instead of being "handled" by the chief of station, the agent was to be handled by Colby, briefed and debriefed, informed of the embassy's policies. Colby goes on to describe his new agent: "'Charlie,' as we referred to him when necessary, was a fascinating individual. Totally devoted to Western freedom and the United States, he had a circle of Italian friends that made me green with envy, as they covered a number of political currents. Well-educated and widely read, he could discourse with ease on medieval philosophy and the Pope's social encyclicals." Colby admired Charlie, but—and here he is going beyond his brief from Miller—Colby believed that the way in which "Charlie's" reports had been handled was in error. This was, in Colby's view, because "his very closeness to his Italian friends had an impact on his judgments about them. He looked as much at their personal attributes as at their political roles, and he formed strong opinions about whether their personal standards were of the high quality needed, inevitably measured by his own, which were high indeed. As raw information feeding into an over-all assessment of Italian affairs, his contribution was of great value."

The key term here is the phrase "feeding into an over-all assessment of Italian affairs." In other words, Charlie's reports had gone through the Rome station only for communication to Washington, and Colby—perhaps because he disagreed with "Charlie's" analysis of the Italian situation—thought this an error. "But I learned that it was more than this, and in my view dangerous. I learned that the secrecy of his operation as a classic 'singleton,' an individual agent operating alone rather than as a member of a net or through a chain of intermediaries, produced the impression in Washington that it reflected the direct truth about events and personalities in Italy. And the professional intelligence operators who managed him, to ensure that this direct truth reached policy levels, had arranged that his reports be forwarded in their raw form in sealed envelopes to Washington and laid on the desk of senior policy-level officials as the real story direct from the source."

This "stovepiping" is a typical Washington tactic to get information and views at varience with the professional consensus to policy makers. It was the route used, for example, in the second Bush administration in connection with Iraqi matters.

"I learned that he had even been picked up on a Washington street corner by a black limousine so that he could orally brief the Secretary of State, John Foster Dulles, as they drove through the city . . . Obviously such a meeting and the dramatics of clandestinity that surrounded it enhanced the impact of Charlie's views, vastly beyond the effect of the judgments of the many other reports, also from direct conversations with Italian leaders, but passed through the careful screening and collaboration process of the corps of experts on Italian political affairs not only in the editing staffs of our station, but in the analytical components of the embassy, the State Department and the CIA."

Colby took action. "I adhered to Washington's strictures that his identity be kept totally hidden, but I began to insist that his product (but, of course, not his identity) be circulated to those who needed to know the results of his unique access in Italy."

> This began with the Ambassador and the political officers of the embassy, and then spread naturally to the other CIA officers in the station, the operational desk at home, and finally the analytical staffs of CIA's Directorate of Intelligence and the other intelligence "customers" in Washington. Charlie's material then reached all its proper readers, but arrived without a special aura of mystery, and was put in proper proportion in the jigsaw-puzzle collection of information needed to understand the variegated Italian political scene. *I could not be accused of suppressing it*, but only of ensuring that all points of view were reported. To the extent that Washington or the embassy adopted his views and his recommendations for policy, *even over my arguments to the contrary (and they were many as the opening to the Left loomed)*, I at least knew that the policies he espoused had official approval. Moreover, Italians were not subject to confusion at hearing one policy from the embassy and its unofficial spokesmen and another from a mysterious representative of some unstated authority in Washington, perhaps the CIA.[21] (Emphasis added.)

The final sentence adds another piece of information: Charlie was not only reporting on his conversations with Italian leaders, he was attempting to implement policy, a policy, most probably, at odds with that favored by Colby.

All is fair in bureaucratic intrigue. Angleton, it seems, had attempted to run his own agent in Italy and that agent's reports and other actions were at odds with Colby's support for the "opening to the Left" of the Italian Social Democrats. Colby, when he had the chance, shut down this effort, pleading, as was his habit, procedural reasons. There is something rather defensive about this detailed, if veiled, account of what appears to have been a very minor incident in Colby's five-year tour of duty in Rome. Unless of course, there was more to it than is revealed in that account. Colby had, in effect, gone beyond what his chief had asked him to do; he had even, perhaps, gone against his instructions to maintain the security and special status of the agent, by circulating his reports within the embassy. Hence the rationalizations for that violation of instructions. There might be something else.

Who was "Charlie"? We are told that he was an ex-OSS agent, obviously bilingual, very well connected in Italy, who had after the war joined the CIA. It sounds very much like Angleton himself—and even more like Angleton's younger brother, Hugh, who had served in the OSS, and had, after the war, returned to Italy, and had also, at some point, been employed by the CIA. We know, for example, that Hugh Angleton was in Rome in 1955. If "Charlie" was Hugh Angleton, then that would explain his special relationship with James Angleton, and his special access in Washington—as well as his opposition to Colby's political strategy. This is an unlikely but not entirely impossible hypothesis. In any event, Colby and Angleton had clashed on Angleton's home ground, and Colby had won—not for the last time.

Responsibility for the Israeli "account" within the Agency was a vital component of Angleton's position. For the most part this involved responsibility for liaison with the Israeli secret intelligence services, which, like many elements of Israeli society, predated the Israeli state itself. Angleton's connections with the men who were later to run the Israeli intelligence establishment began in Italy during the Second World War with the reports that crossed his desk about the efforts of Italian Jews who were part of the partisan resistance to the Germans and Italian Fascists, and of the Italian and non-Italian Jews who later established escape routes from the occupied areas and eventually from the camps. These groups were useful to the Allied war effort, and were, at the same time, yet another faction that bore watching. In the infinitely complex flow of events from 1944 to 1946 they were considered under various headings: Allied units, which included the Jewish Brigade of the British Army; partisans, possible Communist formations; chance colleagues on specific operations. Toward the end of this period the Jewish Agency was working, in opposition to the British, to move Jewish refugees through Italy to Palestine and to move arms with them. Angleton watched and, perhaps, assisted with these matters. In any case, he established strong personal relations with some of the leaders of the fledging Israeli secret intelligence services: Teddy Kollek, for one, and Meir Deshalit, for another.

In June 1948, a month after Israel became independent from Britain, the now-Israeli intelligence unit, the SHAI, was divided into four sections; all these were designed by and under the overall control of the special advisor to the prime minister for foreign affairs, Reuven Shiloah, a cofounder with Isser Beeri of the SHAI and one of the founders of the Jewish Brigade of the British Army.

It is useful to remember that, although for the past generation the United States and Israel have been the closest of allies, for a few years after the Second World War it had appeared that the new State of Israel would become part of the Soviet bloc. At that time, both "Soviet diplomatic support and the arms supplied to the Zionists from Czechoslovakia with Soviet blessing, during their war with the Arabs, were of crucial importance in the birth of Israel. In May 1948 the Soviet Union was the first to give the new state *de jure* recognition . . . Israel, the Kremlin believed, was destined to become the vanguard of the anti-imperialist revolution in the Middle East and to help the Soviet Union gain a foothold in the Mediterranean. Within the new state the left-wing Mapam Party described itself as 'an inseparable part of the world revolutionary camp headed by the USSR' . . . The emigration of Russian Jews to Israel offered an ideal opportunity to send Soviet agents to work both within Israel and against the 'Main Adversary' and other Western targets."[22]

This state of affairs came to an end with Stalin's 1948 anti-Semitic campaign. By 1950, when it was clear that there would not be an Israeli-Soviet alliance, the Israeli government turned to the United States for assistance. A reorganization of Israeli secret intelligence led in 1951 to the creation of the Mossad, "the Institute for Intelligence and Special Tasks," which was modeled after the CIA and was particularly concerned to maintain close liaison relations with that Agency. In 1953, Amos Manor, a Hungarian émigré who had been head of counterintelligence for another unit, Shin Bet, became director of the Mossad.

According to Seymour Hersh, Angleton's responsibility for Israeli affairs "was one of the most important assignments in the 1950s and early 1960s, the height of the Cold War, because of the continuing flow of Soviet and Eastern European refugees into Israel . . . It was the Jewish refugee operations, as many in the CIA understood, that provided the West in the early postwar years with its most important insights into the Soviet bloc."[23] Angleton decided that it was in the American interest to build up the Israel intelligence services, both as a defense against internal Israeli threats, and as an instrument of the American intelligence services: more eyes and ears in the Middle East (and, indeed, in Eastern Europe) and more operational forces available in situations not offering easy access to the CIA.[24]

In May 1951, David Ben-Gurion and his intelligence advisor, Reuven Shiloah, traveled to Washington to meet with President Truman, DCI General Walter Bedell Smith, and then Deputy DCI Allen Dulles. Shiloah proposed a special relationship between the Mossad and the CIA, which was accepted by Smith and Dulles.[25] In June, Shiloah was in Washington to work out the formal arrangements in meetings with "Smith, Dulles, and especially James Angleton."[26] As the relationship developed, Angleton expressed discomfort with the security implications of the emigration of Jews from Eastern Europe, some of whom he believed were working for the Soviets' intelligence services. The Israelis persuaded the CIA that the situation might be played back to the advantage of the West, using the émigrés as sources for information about the Soviet Bloc. Under the U.S.–Israeli intelligence agreement the two countries agreed not to spy on one another and began to exchange information between their secret intelligence agencies, using liaison officers stationed at their embassies in Washington and Tel Aviv. Two Israeli intelligence officers were sent to Washington: Teddy Kollek, who became counselor in the Israeli embassy, and the former AMAN chief Colonel Chaim Herzog as a military attaché.[27] Teddy Kollek had a public reputation as the jovial, long-time mayor of Israeli Jerusalem. The roots of his career are to be found in the secret world.

It was about the time that Angleton was moving from foreign intelligence collection duties to the post of chief of the Counterintelligence Staff of the Central Intelligence Agency that he was—most unusually—given the independent post of head of the Israeli section of the Directorate of Intelligence. It was said that the CIA official who would normally have been the case officer for Israel, the director of CIA Near Eastern operations, as an Arab-American, was not acceptable to the Israeli government. So it is said. Angleton made the first of many visits to Tel Aviv in April 1953, meeting the Shin Bet chief, Amos Manor, among others.[28]

For some observers, Angleton's work on Israeli matters was fully as important as his other responsibilities. Tom Mangold asserted in a note to his *Cold Warrior* that "Angleton's closest professional friends overseas . . . came from the Mossad."[29] Angleton was considered, to adapt the Chinese usage, "a friend of Israel." William Hood noted that after his death, not one but two monuments to Angleton were dedicated at memorial services in Israel. They are large stones mounted with bronze plaques. "One is on a hillside, a few miles from Jerusalem and the scene of a major battle in the early days. The other is in a park near the King David Hotel in Jerusalem. The ceremonies were attended by the surviving chiefs of Israeli intelligence and various public figures. A future prime minister dedicated one monument . . . I know of no country that has given such public recognition to a foreign intelligence officer."[30]

The first generation of American intelligence officers, to which Angleton belonged, was not known for its friendship with the Jews, in general, or with Israel in particular, rather the contrary. Angleton would have been a good candidate for harboring the country-club anti-Semitism of his class, especially in light of his friendship with Pound and Cummings and his admiration for Eliot. On the other hand, there may have been the influence of his wife's family, with their liberal sentiments. However, staff of the Church Committee investigating the CIA in the mid-1970s found some of Angleton's personal files showing that "Angleton had constructed what amounted to a matrix of the position and Jewishness of senior officials in the CIA and elsewhere who had access to classified information of use to Israel."[31] Anyone in a sensitive position who was active in Jewish affairs or who had Zionist relatives was investigated. A former member of the Church Committee staff was still outraged by this when interviewed twenty years later. Others had, earlier, arrived at a less emotional position: "Samuel Halpern, a Jew who served for years as executive assistant to the director of the CIA's clandestine services, was under constant investigation by Angleton . . . 'Jim looked at me real hard,' Halpern recalled with a laugh, 'but I told him, "I'm not going to muck up your desk." The Israelis never approached me. Why should they when I'm sitting on the third floor . . . and Jim's on the second?'"[32] Meaning, among other things, that Angleton himself was the chief conduit for information to the Israeli intelligence services.

There was surveillance of Jews, as individuals who might have some loyalty to Israel that would call into question their loyalty to the United States (not a completely irrational supposition, as it turned out, given the Pollard case), and surveillance of the operations in the United States of the Israeli government itself and groups professionally aligned with it. Angleton was the sponsor of a CIA operation involving the purchase of a trash collection company in Washington, D.C., that had contracts with the embassy of Israel and the office of B'nai B'rith. The trash from these stops (and how many others?) was delivered to the Agency for sorting and analysis.[33] Angleton, in his role of chief of the Counterintelligence Staff of the CIA, was professionally suspicious of American Jews employed by the CIA, of Israeli diplomats in Washington, of Jewish organizations with international interests. However, in his role as head of the Israeli "account" he acted in quite another fashion. The Israeli secret intelligence services were useful allies for the CIA in its work to counter the secret intelligence services of the Soviet Union and its allies.

Which brings us back to those monuments. What was it that Israel owed to Angleton that led to the construction of two monuments to his memory? Perhaps two monuments were necessary, on a symbolic level, at least, because his services to Israel were of two kinds: routine and extraordinary. The first of these was the enduring relationship, dating from before the founding of the State of Israel, based on the connection between Angleton and the Israeli intelligence services. Angleton told the reporter Daniel Schorr that he had been to Israel thirty times,[34] amounting, let us say, to three visits every two years over the time that he was chief of the Counterintelligence Staff of the CIA. He even used Israel as a location for what, as an old soldier, he would have thought of as "rest and recreation." But what brought Angleton again and again to Israel was the business, his business, of intelligence liaison and counterintelligence. Angleton's relations with the Israeli intelligence services will be possible to trace in full only when the files of those services and those of the CIA itself are open to public view. This may mean, in practical terms, never, but if we use Angleton's own method of triangulation, and a few scraps of evidence that have come incidentally to light, we can at least delineate areas of interest.

In addition to the regular exchanges of information between Angleton and his Israeli liaison contacts, there were three extraordinary events: the affair of the Khrushchev secret speech, Angleton's role in preserving Israeli secrecy in connection with Suez, and his role in relation to the Israeli nuclear program.

Arguably, 1956 was the most intense year of the Eisenhower administration's Cold War, with revolts against the Soviet occupation of Poland and Hungary, then the nearly simultaneous effort by Britain and France to reassert their claims to influence in the Middle East. From the point of view of certain elements in the American government these were parallel events, the efforts of empires to control restive territories (or ex-territories), each in its own way a challenge to America's own hegemonic claims. In the end it was the Anglo-French efforts that were more strongly opposed, as lèse-majesté on the part of American client states unwilling to accept the postwar settlement.

Suez and the revolt in Hungary were preceded by the story of Khrushchev's "secret speech" to the Twentieth Congress of the Communist Party, February 24–25, 1956, in which he denounced—and separated himself from—Stalin's crimes. Allen Dulles's biographer gives a colorful account of what happened when Washington heard of the speech. Dulles, it is said, "summoned his top deputies and issued a challenge. Robert Amory, deputy director for intelligence analysis, recalled the merry mood of that staff meeting. 'In the words of the ancient bawdy ballad, [Dulles] offered "half his kingdom and the royal whore, Hortense," to whoever brought home the bacon.'"[35]

There are many, contradictory, stories about how a copy of the speech was obtained. The most circumstantial account turns on Angleton's special relationship with Israeli secret intelligence. This account claims that copies of the fifty-eight-page speech were sent by courier from Moscow to the various Communist parties. The Polish First Secretary, Eduard Ochab, had it translated into Polish and sent, in numbered copies, to the leaders of the local Polish Communist Party units. (This pattern is likely to have been followed throughout the Soviet Bloc.) The Warsaw party leader, Stefan Staszewiski, had thousands of copies of the translation distributed, giving copies to three Western news correspondents, including Philip Ben, said to be "close to Israeli intelligence." Meanwhile, "Shin Beth in Warsaw was already in congenial contact with a circle of former political prisoners gathered around the figure of Wladyslaw Gomulka . . . Gomulka's wife, who was Jewish, [had] readily accepted the friendship of the Shin Beth representative in Warsaw, known as 'Victor' . . . One day in April 1956 a responsible intimate of the Gomulka circle handed their Shin Beth friend a bulky Russian typescript. After taking one look at the papers, Victor drove straight to the airport to catch the first plane out. Landing in Vienna, he called Tel Aviv to say that he would be on a connecting flight to Israel. He arrived late on Friday afternoon," April 11.[36] Amos Manor, head of Shin Bet, a Hungarian who did not read Russian, had the typescript translated into Hebrew, taking it to Prime Minister Ben-Gurion on Sunday the 13th. The next morning, Ben-Gurion, after deciding that the text was authentic, ordered Manor to have a courier fly to Washington with the original Russian version and deliver it to Angleton.[37] With "a flourish that his detractors would later disparage, Angleton declared to Allen [Dulles] that he had 'brought home the bacon.' Two days later he called Manor personally, speaking in the guarded tones required on the international circuits, with the unadorned message, 'Thank you.'"[38]

"A flourish that his detractors would later disparage." Perhaps those others had heard a belated echo of the "furious" young Angleton, who by now had long since otherwise disappeared beneath layers of responsibility, authority, and legend. It is not recorded whether Angleton received Hortense, but he did receive—or, rather, was confirmed in his unfettered possession of—those parts of Dulles's kingdom which had to do with counterintelligence and Israel. He also became, for many years, untouchable in the Agency.

Concerning the controversies about how the speech reached the West, it is apparent that there were multiple routes. There is the copy in Russian (the Gomulka text) sent to Angleton via the Israeli connection, but if the story about the Polish translation (the Ochab text) and distributions is true, these also would have come out in various ways, not least through the three Western correspondents who received copies, and there were probably parallel routes in each of the Soviet Bloc countries and each Western country whose Communist Party had a representative at the Moscow meeting where they heard Khrushchev's speech.[39]

Be that as it may, once the speech, by whichever route, was in Washington, there ensued a debate about what to do with it. "While presenting textual evidence that there was plenty to substantiate Khrushchev's authorship of the document, [Ray] Cline found himself arguing against both Wisner and Angleton's preference for leaking this material piecemeal. 'They kept saying they wanted to "exploit" the speech rather than simply let everybody read it.' . . . As Angleton remarked afterward, the best imaginable use for Nikita's mea culpa was months—years—off, when they'd had time to 'organize and update' their 'vast preparations for refurbishing operational groups' secretly training in West Germany under 'a born leader, a Yugoslav, whose schooling was in the Hapsburg military academy.' Only after these client armies of Poles and Hungarians and Rumanians were 'up to snuff,' Angleton argued, should teasers excerpted from the Khrushchev statement be doled out to the captive populations as incitement to revolution, a means of discrediting the entire Bolshevik leadership and provoking a wide-scale political chaos into which to feed the paramilitaries the Agency was shaping up."[40]

As Cline presents the discussion, it was his own scholarly arguments that carried the day. But according to Burton Hersh, "Angleton disparaged Cline's input. 'He wasn't a party to the discussions on the clandestine side . . . The decision to publish the Khrushchev speech was made by Eisenhower, Allen Dulles, and John Foster Dulles. They decided its significance should take precedence over political action.'" On the other hand, Cline claimed that "Jim Angleton much later admitted I was right, but that day he tried hard to keep his secret paper secret."[41] Angleton may have wished to use the speech in support of the great Central European revolt, or he may have just wanted to have it on hand in case something came up. But there was another complication to the handling of the speech, in Angleton's view, which was exactly that the Agency *had* been successful in obtaining a copy of the speech. He said that at least six different Communist diplomats offered Khrushchev's secret speech to the CIA and other Western intelligence services.[42] This would have inevitably raised in Angleton's mind the possibility of a disinformation effort on the part of the KGB. On the one hand, the speech seemed important; seemed to have been a closely held secret; seemed to offer a variety of possibilities for exploitation. On the other hand, perhaps the speech was a move in a KGB disinformation campaign. Why else would it have been so widely reproduced in Poland, and perhaps elsewhere? Why else had it been offered by so many sources? Yet despite his doubts about its provenance—or perhaps because of those doubts—Angleton does seem to have presented the speech in familiar theaters. According to William Colby, Angleton leaked a copy of it "sourced in Italy, with subtle variations in the original text to increase suspicions and backbiting among Communists."[43]

It is at this point that the story of the Khrushchev speech and that of the Hungarian revolt begin to entwine. According to the East German foreign intelligence chief Markus Wolf, "Filtered through Eastern Europe via the Western media and word of mouth, Khrushchev's volcanic speech helped escalate the dissatisfaction in Poland and Hungary. The Hungarian uprising of October–November was a direct result of Khrushchev's denunciation."[44] But there were other factors, presumably well known to Wolf. According to David Murphy and his colleagues, as early as 1952 the CIA operated a "defector inducement" program, called "Red Cap" after the railroad baggage porters.[45] Some of the defectors were organized into replacement formations for those of the collaborationists left over from the Second World War. William Corson attributes much of the anti-Soviet activity in Central Europe in 1956 directly to the CIA's Operation Red Sox/Red Cap, which "resulted in a frantic expansion of the CIA's training center outside of Munich. Under the direction of Mike Ray and Charlie Katek, Eastern Europeans from Hungary, Poland, Rumania, and Czechoslovakia were trained to become the CIA's entry in anti-Soviet struggles."

It is said that clandestine services chief Frank Wisner and James Angleton had dual responsibility for Red Sox/Red Cap. If true, this indicates that Angleton had European covert action operational responsibilities beyond those associated with his positions as chief of the Counterintelligence Staff and head of the Israeli desk. Angleton's argument in relationship to the uses for the Secret Speech was one in which he was representing not only his own staff, but Wisner's as well. According to Robin Winks (which probably means according to Angleton), as we have seen, since Angleton had found a man to lead an Eastern European revolt, he wanted to hold the speech until this paramilitary group was trained and ready.[46] At this time, Burton Hersh relates, "CI paperwork especially was replete with reports of resistance groups coalescing throughout the Balkans picked up by Angleton's listening posts. The top administrators heard what they wanted to hear, and in the battle over policy 'there was a hell of a lot of shystering,' [Howard] Roman could see. His bosses craved action. 'I'm only intimating here,' Howard [Roman] says, 'and there *were* sources, but even Angleton was not above having sources that were not all that . . . reliable, you know. He had so many.'"[47]

Let us look at the complicated chronology of public events in 1956. Khrushchev's speech took place in April. At that point events in Poland had been moving toward a crisis for some time. Inadequate food supplies and mishandled labor disputes were exacerbated by tension between the Polish and Soviet governments and military. The crisis came on June 28, 1956, when a revolt of workers in Poznan was crushed with nearly fifty killed and a hundred wounded. For a moment it appeared that the Red Army would move into Poland, but—not without drama—this was avoided (only to be replayed twenty years later). Demonstrations in Warsaw beginning on October 19 overthrew the pro-Soviet regime, and the reformer Wladyslaw Gomulka (one of Angleton's putative sources for the secret speech) became secretary general of the Polish Communist Party. On October 23 (three days before Suez), Imre Nagy came to power in Budapest. Both Gomulka and Nagy were Communists, but they were, first of all, nationalists. It appeared for a few weeks that Stalin's postwar arrangements in Central Europe were coming apart.

Just at this moment, prewar Anglo-French imperialism in the Middle East was reviving in the form of the Suez Crisis. The Suez Crisis and the Hungarian revolt were intimately related: "The start of fighting in the Middle East on 29–31 October, which left Moscow's political ally Egypt in a precarious state, caused even greater complications for the Soviet leaders. They worried that a failure to act decisively in Hungary would compound the damage to Soviet foreign policy . . . Khrushchev himself expressed the dominant sentiment at the [October 31] Presidium meeting: 'If we depart from Hungary, it will give a great boost to the Americans [whom he assumed were backing the British], English, and French—the imperialists. They will perceive it as weakness on our part and will go on the offensive. We would then be exposing the weakness of our positions. Our party will not accept it if we do this. To Egypt [the imperialists] will then add Hungary.'"[48]

Frank Wisner's liberationist wing of the CIA thought their day—long awaited—had arrived. Radio Free Europe and Radio Liberation, as it was then still called, went all-out to report each nuance of the struggle of the new regimes—and in a few instances went further, implying that NATO aid would be furnished to the rebels, in spite of the fact that Eisenhower had "instructed the CIA to maintain caution and avoid giving Moscow any reason to suppose that the United States had either instigated or would support the Hungarian rebels . . . Cord Meyer [instructed] . . . the newscasters of Radio Free Europe . . . in the subtle process of encouraging the Hungarian rebels without—as he later insisted—inciting them to revolution."[49] It is said that General Gehlen, less scrupulous and under lighter control, sent arms into Hungary.

We turn again to the omniscient William Corson. "In the several months between Poznan and Gomulka's election, the CIA pushed ahead with plans for uprisings in Hungary, Czechoslovakia, and Rumania, in that order. Red Sox/Red Cap groups, like latter-day Trojan Horse forces, were inserted into those nations' capitals and plans were made final for the 'freedom fighters' to throw off the evil yoke of communism . . . On October 23, just two days after Khrushchev's order to the Red Army to stand down [in Poland], the Hungarian revolt against the Soviet-dominated regime began. Unlike Gomulka's threat to pit Polish communists against Soviet communists, the Hungarian revolutionaries, aided and abetted by the Red Sox/Red Cap forces, declared their enemy to be not simply the Russians occupying their country but communism itself."[50]

Corson's report is seconded by Stephen Ambrose. "The CIA sent RED SOX/

RED CAP groups in Budapest into action to join the Freedom Fighters and to help organize them . . . Radio Free Europe, and the RED SOX/RED CAP groups, encouraged the rebels." Often since denied, this was something known at the time to those in the know. For example, on November 10, 1956, the FBI tapped a conversation between Pagie Morris and Jay Lovestone. Morris said, "I know the whole thing . . . Do you remember when I said to you that it was criminal to incite a revolution and a rebellion, and not to follow it through? . . . Well, the Wisner crowd incited it . . . And the Horthy crowd has been in it . . . That Radio Free Europe is the crowd that's behind it."[51] The Horthy crowd being the party of prewar Hungarian Fascism.

There were negotiations, a few days of hope and despair, then, on November 4, Khrushchev sent the Red Army into Budapest, crushing the revolt. There were thousands of fatalities; many more Hungarians went into exile. Wisner flew to Vienna, and in a classic scene of the Cold War stood at the border watching the refugees cross. A manic depressive, Wisner suffered a breakdown.[52] Bipolar syndrome follows its own path, but, again according to Ambrose, "Many ex-agents . . . today believe that Frank Wisner's tragic mental breakdown and subsequent suicide date from the failure of the RED SOX/RED CAP program."[53] Evan Thomas notes that when he inquired after them, oddly enough, "Full copies of Wisner's [Hungarian Revolution] cables could not be located by the CIA. Interestingly, the covering letter on the Cable Log, dated November 26, 1956, is a request from Richard Helms, who was the chief operations officer of the DD/P, to James J. Angleton, chief of the counterintelligence staff, to pull together Wisner's cable traffic. Since Angleton was not in the normal chain of command and was sometimes used for special projects requiring discretion, it is a reasonable guess that Wisner's cables were disturbing to their recipients in Washington, and that Helms quietly asked Angleton to pull them together for review."[54] And, perhaps, discreet disposal.

After the failure of the Hungarian revolt, General Lucian Truscott, the CIA's deputy director, reviewed Operation Red Sox/Red Cap, finding that in spite of the Hungarian debacle the CIA was planning to use Red Sox/Red Cap in Czechoslovakia. Truscott recommended disbanding Red Sox/Red Cap.[55] When the playbook was run through again five years later, in Cuba, one of the arguments for going ahead with the invasion was the difficulty of resettling the Cuban exile cadres, perhaps because of this precedent. Bad faith cuts both ways.

There is a certain way of doing things that appears to have been institutionalized in the CIA in its first phase: the encouragement of exiles from a target country; the organization of some of those exiles into quasi-military formations; the launching of a "liberation" campaign spearheaded by those formations: Albania, Poland, Hungary, Cuba. It was not a very successful methodology. In any case, the result insofar as Hungary was concerned seemed definitive. As latter commentators have it: "By reestablishing military control over Hungary and by exposing—more dramatically than in 1953—the emptiness of the 'roll-back' and 'liberation' rhetoric in the West, the Soviet invasion in November 1956 stemmed any further loss of Soviet power in Eastern Europe . . . Any lingering U.S. hopes of directly challenging Moscow's sphere of influence in Eastern Europe thus effectively ended."[56] One wonders what became of Angleton's Yugoslav, Hapsburg-trained "natural leader."

That was one part of the drama in the fall of 1956. The Israeli contribution to the CIA's effort to obtain a copy of Khrushchev's speech, the CIA's resulting debt of gratitude to the Israeli secret services, and the heightened prestige of those services and James Angleton that resulted were factors in another of the interwoven events of the year: Suez.

The roots of the Suez crisis can be traced back to the 1952 overthrow of the United Kingdom's client king in Egypt, Farouk I, by a group of Egyptian army officers who had—or soon obtained—CIA backing. After Colonel Gamal Abdel Nasser eventually came to power in October 1954, his security forces were organized by the CIA, then handed off to the Gehlen Organization, which had access to certain personnel—torturers and the like—unemployed since the Second World War. In the mid-1950s, U.S.–Egyptian relations cooled (while British–Egyptian relations grew steadily worse). When, in May 1956, Egypt granted diplomatic recognition to the People's Republic of China, the American government retaliated by withdrawing financial support for the Aswan Dam. Nasser found an alternative source of funding by nationalizing the Suez Canal.[57] John Foster Dulles finally decided that, given events in Central Europe, the time was not right for intervention. And the CIA men, who had helped train the Egyptian secret police, were reluctant to offer agents to the attention of that now expert cadre.

Meanwhile, the British were taking Middle Eastern matters back into their own hands. Prime Minister Anthony Eden, who had developed what many observers believed to be an excessive fixation concerning the threat to British interests represented by Nasser, decided to remove the Egyptian leader either through assassination—an alternative that was discarded not for ethical reasons but only after it failed—or intervention. The mechanism for this intervention was rather complicated. The Israelis were to launch a preemptive attack across the Sinai Peninsula "in response" to ongoing Egyptian military threats, then the British and French were to seize the Canal Zone "to separate the combatants," and, incidentally, regain the canal and so humiliate Nasser that he would be forced from office. The British would be rid of Nasser; they and the French would recover their prestige, and investments, in the Middle East; and the Israelis would both collect a debt of gratitude from the European powers—to be paid in nuclear technology—and secure their border with Egypt. The British, lost in dreams of imperial grandeur, kept the whole matter from the Americans, who were known to be opposed to military intervention by other Western powers in the Third World, especially at the moment when the Soviets were sacrificing their anti-imperialist credentials in Central Europe.

The first indications reaching the CIA of what came to be called the Suez Crisis were negative. "The British intelligence services had 'crawled into a shell,' Allen [Dulles] learned from his liaison officers; they were unwilling to share anything with their American counterparts." Angleton's liaison sources with the Israeli secret intelligence services were also silent, although there were rumors that the Israeli army chief, Moshe Dayan, had been in Paris and that the French were supplying the Israelis with Mystère fighters. Angleton nonetheless reported that the Israelis would not launch an attack on Egypt.[58]

On October 8, 1956, Allen Dulles returned to Washington from one of his periodic world tours of CIA stations. Kermit "Kim" Roosevelt, Jr., of the CIA's Middle Eastern division briefed him about conversations he had had with British officials at the United Nations, who had hinted at an imminent major military operation. Roosevelt predicted that the British would launch an attack on the Suez Canal by the end of the month.[59] The war plans in fact had been finalized a week earlier. After some tinkering, everything was settled among the Israelis, British, and French by the middle of October.[60] At which point the CIA was telling the president that the Israelis were planning to invade *Jordan*.[61] However, there was at least one report pointing to the true target: the U.S. military attaché in Tel Aviv, whose over-age, war-mutilated chauffeur had been called up, sent word that Israel was planning to attack Egypt. James Angleton intervened, saying that the information was not accurate.[62] Another warning came from London: "The Agency's deputy director for intelligence Robert Amory . . . predicted the attack to within twenty-four hours . . . Amory's liaison man in London, Chester Cooper, complained that Washington simply did not listen."[63] The word from London is said to have led to a dramatic scene in Allen Dulles's office. "Dulles summoned Angleton. 'Look what Bob [Amory] has brought in,' he told Jim [Angleton] . . . 'Doesn't mean a thing,' Angleton said. 'I've just spent all night with our friends in the Israeli embassy' . . . Amory blew up. 'This is where the buck stops,' he rounded on the Director. 'You either believe me or you believe this coopted Israeli agent!'"[64] It is difficult to imagine anything worse Amory could have said about Angleton in the presence of the director of central intelligence. Nonetheless, Dulles believed Angleton rather than Amory. When, on October 29, 1956, Israel attacked, Allen Dulles called the Sinai invasion merely a "probing action."[65]

Playing out their scenario, the British and French called for a disengagement of the Egyptian and Israeli forces, then launched their own air attacks on Cairo and Suez. The Americans, despairing of conventional intelligence sources, turned to a new technological source of information, the U-2. One of the pilots of the CIA's exotic aircraft was to become well known a few years later. Francis Gary Powers had begun in September 1956 flying the U-2 regularly over the Mediterranean, where he was to "watch for and photograph any concentration of two or more ships." The ships he was looking for were British and French: "what the CIA, and Ike, wanted to know was how quickly and in what strength London and Paris were preparing for an attack on Egypt . . . On a flight on October 30, 1956, Powers saw and photographed black puffs of smoke in the Sinai—the first shots in the Israeli invasion of Egypt."[66]

Dulles now had cause to rue his trust in Angleton's Israeli contacts. According to Rhodri Jeffreys-Jones, "There has been considerable speculation about this presumed intelligence failure. For example, some accuse James Angleton, who had close links with Israeli intelligence, of suppressing some indications of the attack because he sympathized with its objectives, while others report that he was furious at being kept in the dark by his Israeli friends. But there is some doubt as to whether the CIA was, in fact, caught unawares."[67]

The implication here is that the story of the confrontation between Amory and Angleton may have been fabricated. Be that is it may, Eisenhower was angry with the British, but not, as far as is known, with the CIA. When, on November 5, British and French troops landed in the Suez Canal Zone, the Soviets, who the day before had sent tanks into Budapest, announced their intention of sending peacekeeping forces to Egypt. In order to forestall the Soviets and punish the British, the United States had the United Nations condemn British aggression and compelled British withdrawal. Eisenhower refused Eden's request for consultations and threatened to cancel credits, which would have broken the British financial system.[68] Prime Minister Eden gave in and went on medical leave and the crisis gradually wound down, but not without continuing enmity between the U.S. and British governments and their secret intelligence services, which were increasingly in conflict throughout the Third World.[69]

One monument set up by the Israelis after Angleton's death, then, the public monument, might be taken to memorialize his long operational relationship with the Israeli intelligence services.[70] The other, the more obscurely situated monument, perhaps could be taken as memorializing, in part, a quite specific service to Israel that was performed by Angleton: his help with the Israeli atomic bomb project.

As a quid pro quo for Israeli assistance with the Suez matter, France had provided Israel with a large reactor, and then continued with supplies of nuclear material in the following years. The Israelis turned to Angleton for help with the development of weapons from the French material. Journalist Tad Szulc publicly quoted sources "close to Angleton as saying that he had indeed secretly aided Israel with technical nuclear information during the late 1950's." Seymour Hersh claims that Angleton provided the Israelis with similar information in the 1960s.[71] The Israeli decision to "go nuclear" had been made by David Ben-Gurion himself, for whom it became something of an idée fixe, the magical weapon that would ensure a balance of forces against the immensely larger populations and armies of Israel's neighbors. Relations between nations in the Middle East in those years (and the years since) moved in a familiar and rapidly escalating dialectic, each side always seeing itself as threatened by the other. For example, when, "on February 28, 1955, Ben-Gurion responded to a cross-border attack by Palestinian guerrillas, or *fedayeen*, by authorizing a large-scale retaliation against an Egyptian military camp at Gaza, Nasser responded to the increased tension by turning to the Communist world for military aid. He traveled in April 1955 to the Bandung Conference of African and Asian nations and received a promise from Chou En-lai, the Chinese premier, for as many arms as Egypt could afford. In July, Soviet delegations arrived in Cairo to offer military aid . . . [French premier Guy] Mollet agreed later in the year to begin secretly selling high-performance French bombers to Israel . . . Arms continued to flow from France to Israel for the next twelve years . . . In return, Israel agreed to begin sharing intelligence on the Middle East, the United States, and Europe with the French."[72] A guerrilla raid leading, tit for tat, to a somewhat one-sided nuclear arms race.

The Israeli nuclear program was built on twin technical foundations, that of the American "atoms for peace" program of disseminating nuclear reactor technology on a tightly controlled basis, and that of the French strategic and economic relationship which Ben-Gurion and Shimon Peres, with CIA aid, manipulated to obtain weapons technology. The first gave Israel a small experimental reactor as early as 1954.[73] It is evident that Israeli intentions in regard to nuclear research aroused suspicion somewhere in the American government, as in January 1956 Israel was put on the list for atomic intelligence collection.[74] This was perhaps prescient, or perhaps there was beginning to be some gossip in Western intelligence circles, for within a few months Shimon Peres had negotiated a comprehensive security understanding with the French government, working through the defense and interior ministers.[75] Also early in 1956, Prime Minister Ben-Gurion ordered the creation of a special intelligence relationship between French and Israeli military intelligence.

Now the development of the Israeli atom bomb began to overlap with the Suez crisis. The month after Nasser nationalized the canal, the first Israeli nuclear science liaison officer was sent to Paris. In mid-September the French and Israelis reached an agreement in principle on the sale to Israel of a research reactor. This was signed at the Sèvres Conference at the end of October, when the Anglo-French-Israeli plans for the Suez operation were completed.[76] Israeli participation in Suez was thus enabling for the Israeli nuclear program, while at the same time Suez itself provided another motivation for the program.

The Israeli nuclear bomb was to defend Israel not only, or perhaps not even primarily, against the Arab states, but also, perhaps primarily, against the Soviet Union. The need for this had become evident when the Soviet Union issued an ultimatum to Britain, France, and Israel on November 6, 1956, stating that the government of Israel was "criminally and irresponsibly playing with the fate of its own people . . . which puts in jeopardy the very existence of Israel as a State." Soviet Prime Minister Nikolai Bulganin warned Ben-Gurion in a separate communication that this was a threat of a Soviet missile strike against Israel. Ben-Gurion immediately sent Director General of the Ministry of Defense Shimon Peres and Foreign Minister Golda Meir back to Paris, where Peres requested French nuclear assistance in return for an Israeli withdrawal from the Sinai.[77] The French agreed to provide the technology and the technicians needed.[78] From that point the Israeli bomb project went down the path since followed by other second- and third-generation atomic powers: obtaining "peaceful" nuclear reactor technology from one of the four initial atomic powers, then modifying it for weapons production.

The American government made an effort to keep track of this process. For example, early in 1958 the U-2 photographed construction under way near Beer Sheba in the Negev Desert. President Eisenhower was personally briefed on this, but "did not say a word." There were no follow-up orders from the White House or the CIA for additional photographs of the site. Rumors reached the American Embassy in Israel in May 1959 that the chief of the Israeli Ministry of Defense's Development Authority, Dan Tokovsky, had resigned, supposedly as a consequence of his opposition to Shimon Peres's determination to obtain nuclear weapons, but the rumors were not confirmed and no action followed. The next month the U.S. Atomic Energy Commission (AEC) was notified that Norway had agreed to sell Israel heavy water, but no effort was made to investigate this, nor was the matter pursued when the CIA found that the amount of heavy water in question was twenty tons.[79] (It will be recalled that German interest in Norwegian heavy water had been one of the impulses behind the Second World War's Manhattan Project.)

The French, on the other hand, were no longer so sure that they wanted Israel to join the nuclear club, notifying the Israeli ambassador in May 1960 that France had decided to end its nuclear relationship with Israel. However, a distinction was made between government-to-government ties and commercial interests. French companies were allowed to continue working on the Dimona reactor and did so until it was completed in 1963 or 1964, at which point, with blueprints acquired from the Saint-Gobain enterprise, the Israelis were working on the reactor's fuel reprocessing plant.[80] The continuing French "private" support for the Israeli nuclear weapons program had not gone unobserved: "In late October and early November [1960] the United Kingdom informed the United States that it believed a reactor was under construction near Beer Sheba. On 8 November British intelligence provided CIA/PIC with ground photography of the site. The next day, based on a hurried analysis of the photography, a preliminary assessment was made in the CIA—'the site was probably a reactor complex.'"[81] On December 2, Allen Dulles informed the National Security Council that Israel was building a nuclear complex in the Negev, probably including a reactor capable of producing weapons-grade plutonium. This was made public on December 18 when the chairman of the AEC, John McCone, announced it on the television program *Meet the Press*.[82] The next day the *New York Times* carried the story on its front page.[83]

Why did it take more than three years for the American intelligence establishment to reach the conclusion that Israel was planning to build nuclear weapons at the "peaceful" nuclear research station at Dimona? According to Avner Cohen's account in *Israel and the Bomb*, "Information about Israel was jealously held within the CIA, where James Jesus Angleton was in charge of the Israeli desk. Angleton did not share sensitive information with other agencies, and also withheld much of it from other CIA sections."[84] While John Loftus and Mark Aarons in *The Secret War against the Jews* have argued that Angleton played an active role in the Israeli acquisition of the nuclear technology necessary for the production of atomic weapons, and protected that effort, Seymour Hersh has made the more conservative claim that Angleton was aware of the weapons program from its inception but did not actively sound the alarm. "Angleton's close personal ties with the Deshalit family and others in Israel made it inevitable that he would learn about the construction in the Negev. One senior official recalled that Angleton's first intelligence report on Israel's plans to build the bomb was filed routinely in the 1950s, and not by back channel, and thus could be made available to those who needed to know inside the CIA's Directorate of Operations, the unit responsible for clandestine action . . . Over the next few years Angleton continued to produce intelligence on Dimona, also based on information supplied by his personal contacts . . . 'Jim kept saying, "Yes, they've got it," and the analysts would say, "I don't believe it,"' one former intelligence official recalled."[85]

Angleton, it turns out, knew of what he spoke. In Top Secret testimony to the Church Committee Tad Szulc outlined Angleton's own account of U.S. assistance to the Israeli atom bomb program:

> I was told by one of my news sources that a situation had occurred in the 1960's in which the CIA delivered to the Israeli government classified information, technical knowledge, know-who, the services of distinguished physicists and fissionable material in the form of plutonium to assist in the development of an Israeli nuclear weapon at the Dimona Israeli Nuclear Testing grounds . . . I have raised the subject in a private conversation with Mr. James Angleton in the spring of this year [April 1975]. Mr. Angleton told me that essentially this information was correct.[86]

This apropos of an article by Szulc then forthcoming in *Penthouse* magazine.

Angleton corrected Szulc on two points, saying that the events had taken place in the late 1950s, after the Suez War, and that no fissionable material had been delivered. Szulc then asked Angleton "whether he could confirm that a British born scientist . . . Wilfrid Basil Mann . . . was indeed one of the scientist involved in this operation. Mr. Angleton confirmed that indeed this was the case."

Angleton asked Szulc not to publish Dr. Mann's name, as he (Mann) might commit suicide if this were done. Angleton went on to explain that Mann, who in the early 1950s had been a British representative to the joint U.S.–British nuclear group in Washington, had been found by the CIA's counterintelligence staff to have been involved with Burgess and Maclean and had been "turned," became a double-agent, was paroled and given U.S. citizenship.[87] According to his biography on the website of the National Institute of Standards, "Wilfrid Mann was the most influential radionuclide metrologist in the world." The official biography does not note his relationship to Burgess, Maclean, and Philby, nor his services to Israel.

By the mid-1960s the CIA station in Tel Aviv was convinced, for good reason, that the Israelis had an atomic bomb program.[88] These field reports became official in March 1963, when the head of the Office of National Estimates, Sherman Kent, released a report on "Consequences of Israeli Acquisition of Nuclear Capability." Kent wrote that "Israel's policy toward its neighbors would become more rather [than] less tough . . . [I]t would . . . seek to exploit the psychological advantages of its nuclear capability to intimidate the Arabs and to prevent them from making trouble on the frontiers . . . [Israel] would use all its means at its command to persuade the US to acquiesce in, and even to support, its possession of nuclear capability." Kent predicted that the Arab countries would be dismayed and frustrated and turn from the United States to the Soviet Union for support.[89] Three years later the CIA predicted that Israeli "assembly of a nuclear weapon could be completed in 6–8 weeks,"[90] a prediction that came true when, just before the 1967 war, Israel put together two nuclear weapons.[91]

The effect of the Israeli nuclear program was to make it possible for this relatively small state to survive even such a near-catastrophe as the Yom Kippur War and go on to become the dominant actor in the region. Much of this was attributable to Angleton. He is known to have gone some distance to help Israel in related activities, such as the Suez Crisis. Later, he worked with Israeli and British intelligence on Operation Babylon, the project to infiltrate—and finally destroy—Iraq's nuclear program.[92] The Szulc testimony seems to point to Angleton as having played at the very least a valuable role in assisting Israel to go nuclear.

Angleton believed, or said he believed, that U.S. support for the Israeli nuclear program was a requisite quid pro quo for continuing cooperation between the two countries in matters of secret intelligence. He had developed that relationship to the point where much of the U.S. intelligence effort in the region was contracted out to Mossad. According to Seymour Hersh, the CIA gave millions of dollars annually to Mossad. "In return, Mossad authorized its agents to act, in essence, as American surrogates throughout North Africa and in such countries as Kenya, Tanzania, and the Congo. Other intelligence agreements with Mossad revolved around the most sensitive of Israeli activities in the Middle East, where American dollars were being used to finance operations in Syria, and inside the Soviet Union, where the CIA's men and women found it difficult to spy. Some of the Soviet activities apparently were financed by regular Agency disbursements—and thus cleared through the appropriate CIA congressional oversight committees—but the complex amalgamation of American financing and Israeli operations remains one of the great secrets of the Cold War."[93]

And then there was Cuba (for which see Chapter 10).

As a consequence of his close relationship with Mossad, Angleton was trusted enough by the Israeli intelligence services to be recruited by them for help with an intragovernmental struggle over war aims in 1967. "James Critchfield, a longtime CIA official who was chief of the Near East Division in 1967, recalled that Dayan and Zvi Zamir, then head of Mossad, joined forces with him and James Angleton at the end of the Six-Day War in a brief and ill-fated attempt to stop the abuse in the West Bank and elsewhere."

> The goal, said Critchfield, was to reach a quick accord on trading land for peace before the Israelis began settling the occupied territories. Dayan and Zamir were convinced that such a step would be "a disastrous development," said Critchfield. "We had to reverse it immediately, or it'd be a *fait accompli.*" The goal was to start negotiations with Jordan's King Hussein, who had entered the war reluctantly and late, and was eager to negotiate an end to Israeli attacks on his country and palace. "We started talking and we were making progress," said Critchfield. "I'd kept Mac [McGeorge] Bundy [who had returned briefly to the White House as Johnson's special national security assistant for the Middle East] informed and he'd approved it. Twelve days after the end of the war, I thought we ought to remind Mac that we were doing it." A White House meeting was arranged with Bundy and Nicholas D. Katzenbach, then the Under Secretary of State. "We were told to knock it off," Critchfield said. "They thought it was not well prepared. Angleton argued that if we do not act now with Dayan's and Zamir's support, there will be settlements in the West Bank. As we walked out, Mac said to me, 'I'd forgotten how passionable Angleton could be. We were at Yale together.'"[94]

The story, if true, is quite extraordinary, and extraordinarily revealing about the personalities involved: the trust in back channels as means to major geopolitical ends; the ties among intelligence agencies; and the reduction of policy disagreements to glib and demeaning psychological generalizations, a specialty of Bundy's from his Red-baiting days at Harvard. In this way an opportunity for less bloodshed in the Middle East was lost with the dismissive, "I'd forgotten how passionable Angleton could be."

There were many forces at work in the American-Israeli alliance; the relationships, sympathies, and efforts of one person, even a person as strategically placed as Angleton, cannot be the whole story. Nonetheless, those efforts might well have been at least part of the story. They were certainly part of *his* story. Through his control of the Israeli account Angleton had virtually a second career in the Agency, supporting operational activities quite distinct from his main counterintelligence responsibilities. It is difficult to exaggerate the importance of this second power base for Angleton within the CIA. It made him virtually unassailable.

However, given Angleton's view of the world, all matters were subordinate to those directly related to the great game of U.S.–Soviet rivalry. The Israeli secret intelligence services were for him simply enabling of the American effort to peer through the Iron Curtain. Parochial Israeli matters, and even, to some extent, wider Middle Eastern matters, were clearly of minor concern by comparison. Angleton was not alone in Washington in this regard. For nearly half a century, successive administrations—and national security advisors such as Henry Kissinger—found it impossible to consider any events in the Middle East as other than so many occasions for Soviet challenges to American interests.

Information, particularly secret information, has a certain multiplier effect. Angleton's good relationship with the Israeli secret intelligence services in the matter of intelligence collection could, from time to time, serve as a resource when he donned his more customary hat as chief of the Counterintelligence Staff. On at least one occasion he used it to help the FBI in its stateside spy-catching efforts.[95] As his Israeli connections strengthened his position with the Bureau, that position became a useful addition to his resources for the continuing Washington power games. It may be significant that only after both Helms and Hoover left their respective positions—the latter through death—that Angleton was vulnerable.

In the mid-1950s Angleton's legend, and power, still were growing. Based on his experiences with X-2, Angleton believed it important that counterintelligence have its own secure means of communication, separate from that of the remainder of the Agency.[96] Within two years of becoming chief of the CIA's Counterintelligence Staff, he had achieved that goal.[97] In a field where knowledge is quite literally power, Angleton's command over his own communications channels meant that no one else in the Clandestine Service would have the knowledge of his affairs necessary to control the operations of the Counterintelligence Staff, which meant, in turn, that the organization chart was a fiction: Angleton, from 1956, was not answerable to the deputy director for plans (Wisner, at that date), but only to Dulles and his successors.

# 9 Illegalities International Mail

*Thank you so much for sending* [E. E. Cummings, a Miscellany] *to us and for inscribing it . . . Jim reads it in bed and for a while escapes bombs and pashas in the poems & the world of the twenties which he loves . . . It was wonderful to see you both again and to hear the beautiful poems. And no, no more enfant terrible? He is back in Italy again, so we read, declaring that we are all mad! Have you heard from him?*[1]

One of Angleton's first tasks when he had returned to Washington from Italy had been to lay the foundations for a CIA "registry"—the heart of an intelligence organization—along X-2 lines. These efforts culminated, shortly after he became chief of the Counterintelligence Staff, in a program that computerized documents on first-generation, punch-card-driven IBM computers.[2] Angleton envisioned something like Yale's Horace Walpole project—that effort to interpret the writings of a minor eighteenth-century figure against the totality of what was known about his times—applied to the tasks of counterintelligence.

For such an enterprise no piece of information was irrelevant. He included in his files, for example, every American interested in Soviet matters, by the simple expedient of intercepting, noting, and sometimes opening their mail. This program was one of the closest-kept secrets of the CIA. It began early in 1952 as an effort to examine mail sent between the United States and the USSR and then gradually extended to other destinations of interest to the Agency. Each evening, mail addressed to interesting locales arriving at Idlewild Airport in New York on its way overseas was brought to the nearby Federal Building No. 111, the Jamaica Airmail Facility, and then taken by courier to the CIA's office in New York City. In the early days of the project each envelope was held in the steam from a teakettle, a stick was slipped under the flap and the letter removed, photographed, replaced in the envelope, which was resealed and sent on its way the next morning. Approximately two-thirds of the letters that were examined were selected at random. Others were selected from a watch list that included Linus Pauling, Bella Abzug, Senator Hubert Humphrey, John Steinbeck, Edward Albee, Thomas Merton, Jay Rockefeller, Martin Luther King, and, of course, Richard Nixon.[3]

The mail-opening program was given the cryptonym HT/LINGUAL and eventually was a prominent item on the list of "family jewels" of illegal operations revealed by William Colby in the early 1970s. Angleton told the Church Committee, in Top Secret testimony, that he thought the mail-opening program "was probably the most important overview that Counterintelligence had."[4] According to Mark Riebling, Angleton thought that "*precisely because the enemy regarded America's mails as inviolate*, mail coverage was likely to provide clues to the identities of Soviet agents . . . Angleton understood that the mail-opening operation was illegal, and that if it were ever exposed, 'serious public reaction in the United States would probably occur' . . . Angleton believed that any restrictions on government mail-opening must similarly have read into them an exception that would allow CIA to cover mail in time of secret war."[5] (Emphasis added.)

In spite of the Post Office Department's and the American public's understanding that the contents of international mail were inviolate, the 1975 *Report to the President* by the Commission on CIA Activities within the United States (the "Rockefeller Commission") found that from February 1953 mail was being opened and the contents analyzed by the CIA.[6] By late 1955 the CIA had eight full-time and some part-time employees opening the mail. Angleton asked Helms, then chief of operations in the Plans Directorate, on November 21, 1955, for formal approval of a mail project to "gain access to all mail traffic to and from the USSR which enters, departs or transits the United States." He requested that "raw information acquired be recorded, indexed, analyzed and that various components of the Agency be furnished with items of information." The project was approved in January 1956, but organizational difficulties delayed operations until November 1956.[7]

There is, among the exhibits to the Church Committee hearings, a memorandum from Angleton to Helms laying out the bureaucratic mechanisms necessary for HT/LINGUAL.[8] It recommends expansion of an existing illegal mail-opening program so as to cover *all* mail going through New York to the Soviet bloc, not just a sample selected at random and those from and to people on the watch list. Angleton does not comment on the legal or ethical questions at issue, nor does he spend much time arguing for it. He assumes that the only questions at hand are those bureaucratic issues of budget, staffing, and space, and deals with them by emphasizing the importance of the project for the Agency's largely unstated purposes. The memorandum establishes Angleton's central role in the mail-opening program, from at the latest November 1955, and his bureaucratic authority, or at least strong influence, over the Agency's Security Department in this regard. Richard Helms accepted Angleton's reasoning, approving HT/LINGUAL on December 7, 1955, with a budget of $86,722.50 for 1956. After a laboratory was added in 1960 and the entire operation was moved to Idlewild Airport in 1962, the operation could process "two to six bags of mail a day, from five thousand to fifteen thousand items."[9]

The potentially explosive HT/LINGUAL program came to light—if that is the phrase—within the intelligence community itself in 1958. As if illustrating the maxim that any promising invention will be independently arrived at by those interested in the matter, the Counterintelligence Staff of the FBI, "having learned . . . that when illegal agents wished to meet their principals they wrote to a particular address in the Soviet Union . . . reasoned that if they could intercept communications directed to that particular address, they might net a good number of spies." Therefore, FBI Director J. Edgar Hoover in January 1958 authorized his staff to meet with Post Office officials to discuss opening mail from the United States to the KGB's Moscow address. The chief postal inspector, David Stephens, no doubt somewhat nonplussed, refused cooperation as "something had happened in Washington on a similar matter."[10] Stephens then informed Angleton that the Bureau wanted to begin a mail opening program. Angleton talked with Dulles, and they decided to let the FBI know about HT/LINGUAL. Angleton invited Papich, the FBI's liaison officer for the CIA, to his house for drinks late that night. He took Papich into his orchid greenhouse (as, no doubt, he had done many times before) and told him that CIA was opening mail. Angleton said that the project was aimed at identifying people behind the Iron Curtain who had family members in America. (That was not true. As we have seen, HT/LINGUAL had a steadily expanding range of interests.)

The discussions in Angleton's greenhouse led to an agreement for the CIA to send the FBI those letters which were of internal security concern and for the FBI to facilitate the selection by providing the CIA with its watch lists. "Eventually, the FBI would become, by far, the principal recipient of mail project materials outside of the CIA's Counterintelligence Staff."[11] Thus, from the late 1950s much of the international mail of Americans was being read by both the CIA and the FBI. Angleton later claimed to have been responsible for HT/LINGUAL only for "quarters and rations" from 1953. The phase "quarters and rations," a military usage, indicates responsibility of an administrative nature not including operational responsibility. This was disingenuous of Angleton. In 1955 he had assumed moral responsibility for HT/LINGUAL by arguing for its continuation and funding. In bureaucracies the official responsible for the budget of a program is responsible for the program itself. Angleton may not have had day-to-day administrative involvement with the program—hardly surprising, given his other responsibilities—but it was his program, he supported it, and he kept an eye on it. It is said that Angleton in later years would often answer casual inquiries as to his work by claiming to be a Post Office employee. A taste for irony was one of many things he had acquired at Yale.

HT/LINGUAL ran smoothly into the 1960s, when it was briefly interrupted in late 1964 and early 1965 while Senator Russell Long began looking into allegations that government agencies illegally spied on Americans.[12] According to the Church Committee report, the deputy chief of the Counterintelligence Staff argued that "under the most unfavorable circumstances . . . it might be necessary after the matter has cooled off during an extended period of investigation, to find a scapegoat to blame for unauthorized tampering with the mails. Such cases by their very nature do not have much appeal to the imagination of the public, and this would be an effective way to resolve the initial charge of censorship of the mails.' This strategy of complete denial and transferring blame to a scapegoat was approved by the Director of Security in February 1962."[13]

This strategy was indeed followed by DCI Colby in 1974. The scapegoat at that point was James Angleton. But that was still a decade in the future. We might note, for continuing reference, that the Agency adopted, as a legitimate response to congressional inquiry, a "strategy of complete denial and transferring blame to a scapegoat."

After the Long Committee investigation—which did not uncover HT/LINGUAL—the CIA's mail-opening program again expanded, paralleling the expansion of National Security Agency monitoring of overseas telegraph traffic, in part because of more requests for coverage from the FBI.[14] The NSA program was, if anything, an even more closely held secret than HT/LINGUAL. It was not made public until it was revealed in testimony to the Church Committee in the mid-1970s. According to then director of the National Security Agency, General Lew Allen, "The activity in question is one in which U.S. names were used systematically as a basis for selecting messages, including some between U.S. citizens when one of the communicants was at a foreign location . . . Beginning in 1967, requesting agencies provided names of persons and organizations, some of whom were U.S. citizens, to the NSA in an effort to obtain information which was available in foreign communications as a by-product of our normal foreign intelligence mission . . . The initial purpose was to help determine the existence of foreign influence on specified activities of interest to agencies of the U.S. Government, with emphasis then on Presidential protection and on civil disturbances occurring throughout the Nation . . . Later, because of other developments, such as widespread national concern over such criminal activity as drug trafficking and acts of terrorism, both domestic and international, the emphasis came to include those areas . . . [A]t the height of the watch list activity [1967 to 1973], there were about 800 U.S. names on the 'watch list' and about one third of these 800 were from the narcotics list."[15]

Committee Counsel F. A. O. Schwarz, Jr., then asked, "General Allen, were any warrants obtained for any of the interceptions involving U.S. citizens which you have recounted in your statement?" General Allen: "No."[16] Later in the hearings Senator Church himself added some details to General Allen's testimony about what the NSA called SHAMROCK: "In the early 1960's . . . RCA Global and ITT World Communications began to store their international paid message traffic on magnetic tapes, *and these were turned over to NSA* . . . [T]elegrams to or from, or even mentioning, U.S. citizens whose names appeared on the watch list in the late sixties and early seventies, would have been sent to NSA analysts, and many would subsequently be disseminated to other agencies . . . [I]t is estimated that NSA in recent years selected about 150,000 messages a month for NSA analysts to review."[17] (Emphasis added.) In other words, messages were not *intercepted* by NSA. *All* messages, every telegram sent by means of the American telegraph companies, were simply delivered to the NSA by those companies.

Early in 1969, as chance would have it, a senior CIA official was appointed to the office of Chief Postal Inspector (a title that was something of a redundancy, under the circumstances). On April 8, 1969, Angleton reported to Helms that when he had spoken to "Bill Cotter," the official in question, Cotter had expressed concern that, as he knew about HT/LINGUAL, he might have to brief the postmaster general on it. Angleton wrote to Helms, inter alia, that "COTTER regards HT/LINGUAL as CI [Counter Intelligence] Staff business rather than Office of Security business . . . While Mr. COTTER will undoubtedly inspect the HT/LINGUAL activity in his new capacity and may even find it necessary to brief the Postmaster General, he has given us assurance that he will consult with us prior to taking any action. Therefore, the CI Staff sees no requirement for concern at this time and would not want any action taken to suspend the HT/LINGUAL operation."[18] (We should note that in this internal CIA document Angleton did not contest Cotter's view that HT/LINGUAL was "CI business," that is, under Angleton's direction.)

The following year, as part of the activity around the Huston Plan, "the heads of [the CIA and FBI] signed a document for President Nixon, which correctly stated that mail opening was illegal, falsely stated that it had been discontinued, and proposed that the illegal opening of mail should be resumed because it would provide useful results."[19] As a matter of fact, there had never been any question within the Central Intelligence Agency that the mail opening program was illegal. "In surveys of the CIA's New York mail opening program, the [Central Intelligence Agency's] Inspector General reported on issues of management and security, but failed to raise any question about the program's legality with either the General Counsel or the Director, even though the Inspector General 'knew' the program was 'illegal.'" In a footnote to this observation, the Church Committee report goes on to quote the deposition of the inspector general at the time in question, Gordon Stewart: "The IG under whose auspices the survey was conducted [Stewart] believed it was 'unnecessary' to raise the matter of illegality with the Director 'since everybody knew that it was [illegal] . . . and it didn't seem . . . that I would be telling Mr. Helms anything that he didn't know.'"[20] [Elision in original.]

In 1971, at the height of the anti–Vietnam War agitation, when the operation threatened once more to come to light, Helms called a meeting of senior staff responsible for HT/LINGUAL: the deputy director for plans (DDP, in the memorandum of the meeting), the director of security (D/S) and the chief of the Counterintelligence Staff (C/CI), James Angleton: "The DCI opened the meeting with a reference to an inquiry as to possible mail tampering by Government agencies, addressed to the Chief Postal Inspector, Mr. Cotter, by Dr. Jeremy J. Stone on behalf of the Federation of American Scientists."

> On the question of continuance [of HT/LINGUAL], the DDP stated that he is gravely concerned, for any flap would cause CIA the worst possible publicity and embarrassment. He opined that the operation should be done by the FBI because they could better withstand such publicity, inasmuch as it is a type of domestic surveillance. The D/S stated that he thought the operation served mainly an FBI requirement. The *C/CI* [emphasis added] countered that the Bureau would not take over the operation now, and could not serve essential CIA requirements as we have served theirs; that, moreover, CI Staff sees the operation as *foreign* [emphasis in original] surveillance.
>
> Mr. Helms then asked what should be done: do we want to continue the operation in view of the known risks? The C/CI replied that we can and should continue to live with them . . .
>
> As the meeting closed, the DCI told the C/CI/Project to monitor the operation most discreetly, and bring any problem or difficulty directly to him.[21]

The director of security believed, inaccurately, that the mail opening program was a service that the CIA performed for the FBI. Angleton corrected him: it was *his* program, justifiable, in his view, in terms of the foreign intelligence information uncovered. It allowed the CIA to monitor mail from Soviet exchange students in the United States and from American students and scholars in the Soviet Union; it allowed the CIA to read the mail of antiwar fugitives like Kathy Boudin; it enabled Angleton to track mail to and from Philby's Moscow post office box.[22] He thought it sufficiently important to balance the risks of disclosure to the American public.

A couple of weeks later Helms reported at another meeting that he had secured support for the mail-intercept program at the highest levels:

> Mr. Helms stated that on Monday he had briefed Attorney General [John] Mitchell on the operation . . . Mr. Helms indicated that Mr. Mitchell fully concurred in the value of the operation and had no "hang-ups" concerning it . . .
>
> The DCI then indicated that yesterday, 2 June 1971, he had seen Postmaster General [Winton] Blount. Mr. Blount's reaction, too, was entirely positive regarding the operation and its continuation. He opined that "nothing needed to be done," and rejected a momentarily held thought of his to have someone review the legality of the operation . . . Mr. Helms showed the Postmaster General a few selected examples of the operation's product, including an item relating to Eldridge Cleaver, which attracted the PMG's special interest . . .
>
> It was obvious that all present were gratified by the favorable reception Mr. Helms had met in briefing the two mentioned Cabinet officers.[23]

The program's rationale was that it was a matter of "foreign surveillance," and yet when DCI Helms wished to convince the Postmaster General of its value, he displayed an item concerning the Black Panther leader Eldridge Cleaver. It may have been true that Angleton's interest in HT/LINGUAL was for its utility in protecting the Agency against Soviet spies; others, including Helms, Mitchell, and Blount, saw it as a useful instrument against black activists and the antiwar movement. It could be argued that Cleaver was traveling abroad, had been in contact with foreign governments, and so forth, but Cleaver's importance for the government and the intelligence community was not a matter of interest to the Soviet desk of the CIA. He was of interest because of his standing as a "Black Activist," in the vocabulary of the FBI.

HT/LINGUAL operated through a dual process of selection. The FBI and other agencies provided the CIA's post office group with lists of names, the so-called "watch list," accumulated from the Bureau's Security Index and other such documents going back a generation or more, and "the CIA opened vast numbers of letters on an entirely random basis; as one agent who opened mail in the CIA's New York project testified, 'You never knew what you would hit.'"[24] The scale of this can be grasped in that during its last year of operation, the mail interception program in New York processed "approximately 4,350,000 items of mail and examined the outside of 2,300,000 of those items. Photographs were taken of the exteriors of approximately 33,000 items. Some 3,700 items were opened and the contents analyzed."[25] There were then about six hundred names of individuals and organizations on the Watch List, "many of them American citizens and organizations who were engaged in purely lawful and constitutionally protected forms of protest against governmental policies."[26]

> By 1972, the FBI's list of targets for CIA mail opening included:
>
> New Left activists, extremists, and other subversives.
>
> Extremist and New Left organizations.
>
> Protest and peace organizations, such as People's Coalition for Peace and Justice, National Peace Action Committee, and Women's Strike for Peace.
>
> Subversive and extremist groups, such as the Black Panthers, White Panthers, Black Nationalists and Liberation Groups, Students for a Democratic Society, Resist, Revolutionary Union, and other New Left Groups.
>
> Traffic to and from Puerto Rico and the Virgin Islands showing anti-U.S. or subversive sympathies.[27]

The list of organizations of interest to the FBI cited by the Church Committee in the quotation above is derived from a Routing Slip from J. Edgar Hoover to James Angleton dated March 10, 1972, which is an indication that Hoover thought Angleton responsible for the HT/LINGUAL program. And Hoover should have known.

It was only after William Colby was moved in March 1973 from the executive directorship to become deputy director for operations (DDO, head of the Clandestine Services) that there was a change in the climate of opinion within the CIA as to the value and appropriateness of the mail-intercept program. Colby's account of the matter is that, since as DDO he was in charge of Counterintelligence, when he was briefed about HT/LINGUAL he "got into the mail-opening thing and wrote a memo saying it should be terminated . . . The Post Office guy running it was getting scared. I couldn't find it had produced anything. Angleton objected. [Then DCI James] Schlesinger cut the baby in half and said, 'Let's suspend it but not terminate it.'"[28] Apparently, the "Post Office guy . . . was getting scared" because he was reading the *Washington Post*'s Watergate coverage.[29] Be that as it may, Chief Postal Inspector Cotter gave the CIA "a deadline of February 15, 1973, to 'get superior approval' for its illegal mail-interception program or discontinue it"[30]—which was when, and why, Schlesinger suspended the program.

A few weeks later, when Colby himself became director of central intelligence, he asked James Angleton for an account of the project. Angleton submitted a lawyerly brief on the matter:

A program of intercepting mail between the United States and the USSR has been in existence since 1952. While the recording of addresses and return addresses is totally legal, the opening of first-class mail is in conflict with 39 U.S. Code, Section 4057. A contention can be made that the operation is nonetheless within the constitutional powers of the President to obtain foreign intelligence information or to protect against foreign intelligence activities (powers statutorily recognized in 18 U.S.C., Section 119, with respect to bugging and wiretapping) . . .

The political risk of revelation of CIA's involvement in this project is in any case substantial. In my view, this political risk is not justified by the operation's contribution to *foreign* intelligence and counterintelligence collection . . .

Pending resolution of the above [assumption by the FBI], the project is suspended.[31] [Emphasis in original.]

As it was clear that Colby wanted HT/LINGUAL stopped, Angleton decided to reverse his position and recommend transfer of the project to the FBI. He nonetheless went on to justify the illegal opening of the mail.

The mail intercept Project is a basic counterintelligence asset designed to give US intelligence agencies additional insight into Soviet intelligence activities and interests. It provides information about Soviet-American contacts and insight into Soviet realities and the scope of Soviet interests in the academic, economic, scientific and governmental fields unavailable from any other source . . .

The Project is particularly productive in supporting both the Agency and the FBI in pursuing investigative and operational leads to visiting Soviet students, exchange scientists, academicians and intellectuals, trade specialists and experts from organizations such as the USSR Institute of the USA. The basis for exploiting the Project for this purpose is the knowledge we have from every Soviet Bloc intelligence service defector that each visitor to the West is approved by the respective Security Service. The Project, limited to mail to and from the USSR and the USA, is basically concerned with individuals the KGB approves because it controls them, their passports, their foreign exchange, their education, etc. . . .

The Project provides information otherwise unavailable about the Soviet contacts and travel of Americans to the USSR which is often important when checking applicants for Agency or other Government employment and in confirming reports from Clandestine Service, Domestic Contact Service and FBI agents, contacts and informants.[32]

This reiterates Angleton's basic position about the project: as the Soviets (like the American people) believed that the U.S. mail was secure, they used it to communicate with their agents or "cooptees," that is, according to Angleton, every Soviet citizen coming to the U.S. The Central Intelligence Agency could therefore learn by reading their mail what they had done in the U.S. and whom they had met. The names of the latter could then be placed on lists of Americans suspect to the Agency and the FBI. "The FBI has benefited from leads to American students who have been in the USSR and, in particular, from the knowledge that the sons and daughters of CPUSA and Front Group officials who they expect will be the left leaders in 5 to 10 years have studied in the USSR . . . The Project maintains a compartmented machine record system which includes about two million names of persons involved in USA-USSR contact . . . The total cost of the operation is approximately $260,000 per annum."[33]

The project generated a list of "about two million names": two million people who were thereafter of interest to the CIA and the FBI, subject to special attention when applying for government employment, for example, or visas, or when writing letters to the editor of their home-town newspaper. After reading Angleton's memorandum, Colby terminated the program in its twenty-first year.

Angleton's memorandum stated that the mail-opening program was illegal and known to be illegal to Angleton, his staff, and his superiors.[34] The project was also unconstitutional, in violation of the Fourth Amendment regarding illegal search and seizures. The Church Committee found the "covert mail opening programs in violation of Sections 1701–1703 of Title 18 of the United States Code which prohibit the obstruction, interception, or opening of mail . . . All of these activities . . . also infringed the rights of countless Americans under the Fourth Amendment protection 'against unreasonable searches and seizures' . . . did serious injury to the First Amendment guarantee of freedom of speech and the right of the people to assemble peaceably and to petition the government for a redress of grievances."[35]

HT/LINGUAL was a successful effort by the Central Intelligence Agency to conduct illegal searches, to use exactly the belief in the security of the U.S. Mails as an inducement for people—some spies, some not—to entrust their communications to a channel open to the Agency. There is no record that the Justice Department was informed by Angleton, Cotter, Helms, or Colby that they had knowledge of and were involved in an illegal, unconstitutional, activity for which penalties existed in statute. The mail opening program and the related NSA program concerning international telegrams were begun, in Mark Riebling's phrase, "precisely because the enemy regarded America's mails as inviolate." The American people—and many in their government—shared that belief. Such matters were imagined to be part of the very fabric of American freedom, which agencies like the CIA, NSA, and FBI were supposed to be defending by means of the Cold War. If these institutions were not defending the Constitution, what was the meaning of their work? What was the raison d'être of the Cold War—that "Crusade for Freedom"—itself? These questions have a certain resonance in the first decade of the twenty-first century.

The HT/LINGUAL enterprise, although of crucial importance from one point of view, was only an ancillary activity for Angleton himself. It was significant to the FBI for its potential in identifying Soviet Bloc activities in the United States and, perhaps more significant for Angleton as a source for the CIA's version of the British Registry, which he had nourished from his earliest days in counterintelligence. The more names known to secret intelligence the greater the chance that any query submitted to the Registry would result in a "hit." This is part of the librarianship of counterespionage, unglamorous, but an essential component of professionalism. That is its—and Angleton's—justification. Someone had to do it.

There was, in a phrase often used by Angleton's teachers at Yale, a "moral unity" to the Cold War. The activities of the Central Intelligence Agency abroad were considered by its leaders to be the "moral equivalent" of war. It was important to the conduct of that "war" that Soviet agents operating in the United States were identified. An effective method of doing so was to screen, then open, the international mail. But the effects of this activity could not be contained. Opening the mails for one purpose led to the accumulation of information not only about foreign nationals, but also about citizens of the United States, which was illegal and known to the officials involved to be illegal.

The pursuit of illegal activities, in this regard, had wider implications. Unknown to most Americans, it changed the nature of American society. The great register of names at the Central Intelligence Agency began to fill with increasing numbers of the names of Americans, annotated with accounts of their lives. Such collections are among the foundations of a police state. A suggestive parallel is to be found in the record of the German Democratic Republic, which notoriously used large numbers of ordinary citizens as informers about the others. This had certain obvious effects at the time, when it was known to few, and other effects later, after the collapse of that state, when it became generally known. People found, retrospectively, that their lives and freedom had been limited without their knowledge. Which is more important, the felt state of affairs from day to day, or the "actual" state of affairs, revealed, perhaps, years later? German courts will work for decades to sort out these matters. The parallel in this country did not attract continuing attention. It may yet.

What, then, was the legal status of American officials like James Angleton who in the course of their work knowingly violated the law and the Constitution? International precedents, from Nuremberg to Pinochet, and especially the prosecutions of officials of the former German Democratic Republic, point to an obvious conclusion: they should have been tried for those violations and, if convicted, sent to prison. How it came about that they were not called to account in these matters is a topic to which we will return.

# 10

# Cuba, the Kennedys, and the Molehunt

The Eisenhower administration ended, as it had begun, with covert action campaigns attempting to contain the Soviet Bloc in Europe and prevent its extension into the Third World. In Africa, the overdue and precipitous Belgian action in granting the Congo independence resulted in what might well have been well-anticipated chaos and civil war. The disintegration of the new state seemed for a time to be taking place in order to allow continued exploitation of the mining areas by Belgian interests (a condition and a possibility that remain remarkably persistent). That unhappy country continues to be tormented from time to time by civil war and invasion by neighboring states. Forty years ago, it was intervention by more distant powers, the United States, Cuba and others, that exacerbated warfare between nationalist and secessionist groups. In the Congo, as elsewhere in Africa during the Cold War, Israeli units served as the Agency's surrogates, the CIA providing funding to underwrite Israel's international clandestine activities. These were signs and results of Angleton's influence in both the American and Israeli secret intelligence worlds.

The Congolese nationalist leader Patrice Lumumba was a target of CIA assassination plans, which, like those involving the Dominican Republic's Rafael Trujillo and others, ended with the death of the person in question at the hands of people known to the Agency. But as it was said, in the case of Lumumba, that different weapons were used than those the Agency provided, the American government claimed a certain juridical innocence, perhaps a more or less plausible deniability. There are stories from the time of CIA officials driving about the capital of the Congo with Lumumba's corpse in their car trunk, stories, more recently told, of direct Belgian intervention to insure that the victim was tortured before execution, that embrace of barbarism typical of our times. There is a certain overdetermination in the pattern of these assassinations. Various powerful interests wish to be rid of one foreign leader or another; plans are put *en train*; leaders of action groups attract a cloud of secondary gunmen—and when the trigger is pulled, who is responsible? Lumumba died, as would Trujillo (as would Diem and Allende), in an atmosphere of confusion about direct responsibility that usefully obscured the genealogy of assassination.

During the Eisenhower years there was a belief at home that it was unthinkable that such old-world customs as political murder could be adopted by the genial president. And yet, political assassination as an instrument of policy was not unknown to, might almost be said to have been habitual for, that former military man. During the Second World War, in Tunisia, among the complexities of the Allied invasion of North Africa and various would-be leaders of France, General Eisenhower, "angry at Darlan, Juin, and Giraud for putting their 'individual fortunes and opportunities' ahead of the Allied cause . . . [c]onfessed that 'a situation such as this creates in me so much fury that I sometimes wish I could do a little throat-cutting myself!' Ike meant it as a tiny joke, but joke or not, the subject of assassination kept coming up in conversations between the Allied leaders on Gibraltar . . . The Governor of Gibraltar told Ike that 'he had a good body disposal squad if needed,'" for the French General Darlan. Again: "When a message came into Gibraltar . . . saying that Darlan would talk to Eisenhower but to no one else, most especially not Giraud, . . . [Eisenhower] swore, 'What I need around here is a damn good assassin!'"[1] Assassins were not scarce on the ground. Darlan *was* killed, not, apparently, as a consequence of a direct order from Eisenhower, but by the soon-to-be-customary secondary actors, who were themselves customarily and rapidly removed from the scene. A decade and a half later, President Eisenhower apparently had the same impulses or policies as he had when in uniform. According to the Church Committee report, "The chain of events revealed by the documents and testimony is strong enough to permit a reasonable inference that the plot to assassinate Lumumba was authorized by President Eisenhower."[2] In the Congo, the American candidate, Mobutu, emerged victorious from horrors sufficient to madden Guevara himself, preserving freedom and democracy in central Africa for the next thirty years. Guevara later succumbed to secondary or tertiary instruments of the American president, but his compatriot, Fidel Castro, survived not only Eisenhower's wrath and possible intentions, but those of his successors. The consequences of this continuing demonstration of American official ruthlessness, and its failure in regard to the Cuban leader, would cast a long shadow over the 1960s.

It was a decade that did not begin well for James Angleton. In May 1960 he had a flare-up of tuberculosis and was confined to a Virginia sanitarium.[3] We can trace from FOIA-released files how J. Edgar Hoover followed the vicissitudes of Angleton's illness through reports from the field to his deputy, Alan H. Belmont, ending with: "You will recall that in May of this year Angleton was confined to a sanitarium because of a tubercular ailment. For your information, Angleton returned to his home on November 4, 1960, where he will continue his convalescence. The lung infection has been cleared but he will be required to rest and continue some drug treatments for several more weeks. He very likely will not return to active duty before April 1, 1961."[4]

Thus Angleton had not been present, but was no doubt informed, when on January 26 his friend and agent, Jay Lovestone, gave some significant testimony to Congress concerning the secret Moscow conference of Communist parties the previous December. "This threat is very serious," Lovestone said. "The Communists have recovered much of the ground they lost in the Polish revolt and the Hungarian revolution." The Moscow meeting, he said, came up with "an extremist, adventurous program for world conquest" and war against the United States, deemed "an enemy of the peoples of the whole world."[5] We will hear much more of that Moscow gathering, but let us simply note here that the first account of it comes from a man who was one of Angleton's closest friends. If Lovestone thought the threat "very serious," Angleton would have taken it seriously.

On February 28, 1961, the Bureau learned that Angleton had "returned to duty" a month or so early.[6] Eight or nine months of inactivity after sixteen years of work under the highest pressure would have been a difficult emotional experience. According to Thomas Powers, Angleton dealt with it in part by adding leather work to his hobbies during that term of enforced leisure.[7] And that summer, Cicely Angleton, pursuing her interest in the Cathars—attributable in part, perhaps, to Angleton's old association with Ezra Pound—sent "Mr. and Mrs. E. E. Cummings," as a trophy, a postcard with a color photo: "L'Ariège Pittoresque, 9/113, Le Chateau de Montségur (Alt. 1201 m.) dernier bastion de la religion Cathare. Les Albigeois y furent massacrés en 1244." Her ecstatic message was, "We did it! Climbed the mountain, all in black of course, with flowers in our hands. We love the Languedoc, the people, the heat & have searched for Cathars under every rock and bush, besides swimming in the Mediterranean, seeing plays in Carcassonne, meeting live Cathar bishops—love—Cicely."[8] The dry heat of the Languedoc—reminiscent of Tucson's—would have been good for Angleton's lungs. It does seem remarkable he was able to go mountain climbing, with flowers in his hands, so soon after leaving the hospital; certainly cause for celebration in the wineries of that pleasant, haunted countryside.

The Angleton marriage continued over forty years to shelter such fragments of a life of letters that the husband had abandoned for counterintelligence in wartime Rome (if not earlier still, in London), but which neither he nor his wife ever quite forgot. Social life in the Washington of the Kennedys exhibited many such layerings, symbolized, to choose one example, by the salon run by the socialite and journalist Joseph Alsop.[9] The worlds of journalism and diplomacy mingled at Alsop's home with those of scholarship and secret intelligence; Arthur Schlesinger, the champion, if not the creator, of the non-Communist Left, sitting on the right hand of those who had been present at the creation of the Cold War. Down one notch, as it were, the Angletons and their friends attended similar parties, where poets mingled with national security bureaucrats, painters like Kenneth Noland dining at Cicely Angleton's table with men like Cord Meyer and their wives. This cozy, compromised world would shatter at the end of the decade when the poets, the wives, and the children, to the surprise of all concerned, turned on their patrons and on those patronizing husbands and fathers. In 1961, however, the postwar Establishment was at its zenith: the men in their dark suits, white shirts, thin ties, sipping martinis on one side of the room; the women with their hair sprayed in varnished helmets, their twinsets and pearls like armor, their smiles like ramparts, sipping gimlets on the other.

When Angleton returned to Washington in the spring of 1961 he had found the new administration preoccupied with what would become known as the Bay of Pigs, the effort to overthrow Fidel Castro's government, an adventure which President Kennedy only halfheartedly supported. (Cicely Angleton commented, "Prince Hamlet is in the White House.") The CIA itself was split on the Cuban invasion scheme. Richard Bissell, an economist who had helped design and run the Marshall Plan and who had then gone to the CIA, where he had guided the U-2 project, had been made head of the Clandestine Services after Frank Wisner's collapse. He allied himself with Wisner's old group of covert warriors, including Tracy Barnes and Desmond FitzGerald, who remembered the CIA's Guatemala intervention, PB/SUCCESS, as, well, a success. The intelligence collection specialists, who looked to Richard Helms, now chief of operations for the Clandestine Services under Bissell, were once again more skeptical, Helms famously withdrawing from discussions about Cuba (when not already excluded from those discussions by Bissell).[10] Angleton, in the Helms camp, saw disaster in the offing: "Through Mario Brod in New York, Angleton had some Mafia sources who knew Cuba, and they all told Brod that it would never work."[11] Apparently no one thought it odd to look to the Mafia for intelligence expertise. They were, it would turn out, something of a CIA "asset." Or vice versa.

The ex-OSS group around Helms not only quietly withheld their support from Bissell; they made sure that those seconded to the Cuban effort were not the most capable members of their staffs. Why throw good men into a doomed adventure? On the other hand, Bissell's sidelining of the Counterintelligence Staff in 1960–61 had its roots much earlier. As in OSS, where X-2's veto on agent recruitments had been deeply resented by other parts of the organization, in the CIA circa 1960 "Bissell and Barnes resented the delays imposed by Angleton's investigators, and they blamed Helms for the fact that they had to put up with them."[12] They made sure that they did not have to put up with them in Cuba. A single counterintelligence officer was assigned to the Bay of Pigs project, and the job was simply beyond him.[13] The suppressed CIA inspector general's report on the Bay of Pigs noted this simultaneous passive opposition by one group and deliberate exclusion by the other as a contributing cause for the failure of the project, and specifically listed lack of active involvement of the Counterintelligence Staff as a significant factor.[14] Helms and Angleton did not entirely abdicate responsibility, but Helms's insistence on a role for counterintelligence was countered both by Bissell's resistance and his own reluctance to be involved. In the days immediately before the invasion the Cuban police arrested virtually every CIA asset on the island.[15] Blinded, the invasion went forward to its doom.

The operation that became the Bay of Pigs is identified with President Kennedy, but that is rather unfair. It began during the Eisenhower administration, soon after Castro took power.[16] Planning, down to and including such matters as air support, was already well advanced by the beginning of 1961. No experienced military commander would authorize an assault on a beach in the absence of air cover. (Eisenhower himself had been particularly insistent on the point at Normandy.) The post-mortems recorded, however, that the invasion of Cuba took place without adequate air support, without a unified command, without the integration of military assets with those of the CIA; under the direction, not of an appropriate officer, a Marine perhaps, but of an economist—Bissell—and his buccaneering lieutenants who had drawn the wrong lessons from their PB/SUCCESS operation in Guatemala. Hence the events on a Cuban beach and the swamp beyond it unfolded with the inevitability of classical tragedy.

After it was over, John Kennedy famously told Richard Bissell that in a parliamentary system Kennedy would have had to resign, but under the American presidential system it was Bissell and, of course, Dulles who would have to go. And how close was the Agency itself to termination? According to one observer, "After the Bay of Pigs, President Kennedy said that he wanted 'to splinter the CIA into a thousand pieces and scatter it to the winds.'"[17] On May 16, 1961, "the Cuba Study Group met at luncheon with the President to give orally an interim report on their conclusions to date . . . There was some discussion of the desirability of changing the name of CIA in order to reduce its visibility. Mr. Dulles undertook to study the matter and see if he could make a recommendation."[18] Close enough.

Allen Dulles was told in August that he was to be replaced; on September 27 it was announced that John McCone, a wealthy Republican defense contractor, was to become director of central intelligence. (Cicely Angleton commented in a letter to the Cummingses that "Jim likes his new spy-master."[19]) Dulles occupied himself for a month or two with overseeing the completion of the new Agency headquarters in Langley, Virginia, then took his successor on a tour of Europe. The new headquarters was dedicated on November 28. The next day Dulles retired to write books, nurse his gout, correspond with Rebecca West about "the meaning of treason," think about Kim Philby. It seemed as if a generation had passed, that the charismatic founders had left the scene and that colorless bureaucrats had inherited Dulles's grand new headquarters building. Richard Helms remained (an expert in the *collection* of intelligence, not the more glamorous covert action), and, of course, James Angleton remained. They appeared to represent the "minimum" option for an intelligence service—the collection of intelligence and the protection of the organization that did the collecting: a worthy, worthwhile, noncontroversial mission performed by gray men. Such was how the thing appeared.

The debacle in Cuba reverberated for months through the American government. In a way it has not yet ceased to do so. How could we (the most powerful nation in the world, etc.) have failed? Who was to blame? How were we to be avenged? The reasons for failure were investigated by General Maxwell Taylor on behalf of the president, and, less publicly and more accurately, by CIA Inspector General Lyman Kirkpatrick. Kirkpatrick's report was presented to the incoming director of central intelligence before it was seen by Dulles. The story told was that this breach of protocol, with its supposed roots in Kirkpatrick's bitter ambition, robbed the report of a hearing. In any case it was suppressed. When disinterred from the vast cellars of Langley, it turned out to be moderate, realistic, and accurate. The project had been doomed, according to Kirkpatrick, by poor planning, inexperienced leadership, incompetent staffing, and passive opposition within the Agency. (Angleton would have added that its Miami base had been riddled with Cuban secret intelligence agents.)[20] There was, however, another factor involved, not mentioned by Kirkpatrick or Taylor. The invasion had not been intended to topple the Castro regime. It had been intended to fill a vacuum left *after* that regime had been decapitated.

Planning for the assassination of Castro had begun under President Eisenhower as an integral part of the preparations for the Bay of Pigs operation. This planning had involved that seemingly ubiquitous ally of the American government of the day, the Mafia.[21] In August 1960, CIA Deputy Director for Plans Richard Bissell contacted the Mafia, offering $150,000 for the assassination of Castro. The Mafia, in the persons of Messrs. Rosselli and Giancana, accepted the assignment, but declined the payment. It was, then, under the Eisenhower administration that the CIA first tried to arrange a Mafia "hit," as if that were a routine, although no doubt sensitive, governmental endeavor. (The president knew what he wanted. As he had said years earlier, in wartime, "What I need around here is a damn good assassin!" Where better in time of peace to find one than in the Mafia?)[22]

According to David Wise, "the well-bred old boys at the CIA, the adenoidal gentlemen at the top, with their reversible names and consciences to match, did not stop at murder . . . Living in their own clandestine world, safe in the dark, weird cocoon of Langley, accountable only to themselves, they had been schooled at St. Grottlesex but learned their political morality from Eichmann. In their ignorance of the very system of government they professed to serve, they confused their arrogance with patriotism."[23] The inspector general of the CIA commented more calmly on such matters in an April 25, 1967, report: "CIA twice (first in early 1961 and again in early 1962) supplied lethal pills to U.S. gambling syndicate members working on behalf of CIA in a plot to assassinate Fidel Castro." As it happens there were three assassination attempts in 1962: in late February–early March, in late March–early April, and in April–June.[24] There was a fourth attempt late in 1963.

As was the custom, much was done afterwards to conceal the reasons for the Bay of Pigs failure. Kirkpatrick's report was buried and the inspector general himself libeled and belittled in the memoirs and insiders' histories of the period for having uncovered the incompetence of the planning for the operation. Revisionist historians accepted that it was President Kennedy's cancellation of the air strikes that sealed the fate of the invading brigade, shifting the blame from the CIA. Others, under the influence of the military, shifted it back, citing military amphibious warfare doctrine. And all the while there was another field of research and speculation, that concerning tit-for-tat the assassination attempts. Preoccupied by the tragedy in Dallas at the end of that path, researchers have not concentrated on its beginning in Washington. The assassination of Castro was a precondition for the Bay of Pigs operation. Failing that, neither a better invasion site nor better air cover would have helped. Failing that, Bissell saw no reason to request, and the president saw no reason to grant, air strikes around the Bay of Pigs to support the landing. Which is why Bissell did not ask. They both knew that the project was doomed before it was launched.

Among the ruins of the Bay of Pigs operation there was this capacity, as it was called, for assassination, intact and ready at hand as an instrument of revenge. The Kennedys did not let it lie idle. They made a third attempt on Castro's life a year after the Bay of Pigs. And then a fourth.

As graceful statements were made by the president in public, Robert Kennedy was treating senior officials of the Departments of State and Defense as if they were clumsy family retainers: raging at everyone within reach, demanding his revenge. At the same time the Kennedys began projecting a Cuba in which they were victorious and Castro was dead, as if they could retroactively triumph by sheer force of will. Within two weeks of the failed invasion a covert annex to a policy paper prepared for the National Security Council on May 4, 1961, by a committee chaired by Paul Nitze tasked Angleton's Counterintelligence Staff to cooperate with the exiled Cuban Revolutionary Council to "create, train and support a highly motivated and professionally competent apolitical and career security service which will be dedicated to the preservation of the democratic form of government."[25] In other words, to create a secret intelligence agency for the Cuban exile groups. Angleton was to "assign carefully selected and qualified Agency personnel to work with the service during the current and *post-Castro eras*."[26] (Emphasis added.) And again: "*If Fidel Castro were to be eliminated* from the scene the regime might collapse for lack of this central rallying point . . . *if Castro were eliminated*, the US would be in a much stronger position to insist upon adoption of a program of moderate, evolutionary change by the ruling groups in Latin America."[27] (Emphasis added.) In November, an "Inter-Agency Staff Study" noted hopefully that "*the disappearance of Castro* from the Cuban political scene under widely-known conditions of chaos and open resistance to his regime will help destroy the Castro myth and the appeal his regime has had for the peoples of many underdeveloped nations."[28] (Emphasis added.) All of which sounds as if something more than calculations based on chance and the actuary tables were involved.

The president himself was careful to go on record as opposed to the assassination of Castro. During "a conversation on November 9, 1961, between President Kennedy and Tad Szulc of *The New York Times* . . . President Kennedy asked him: 'What would you think if I ordered Castro to be assassinated?' Szulc indicated that he felt that would be a terrible idea and Kennedy responded, 'I'm glad you feel the same way.'"[29] Implying, but not saying, that he had not already issued the order, when in fact he had, or, more to the point, that he had reconfirmed the order of his predecessor.

On November 3, 1961—six days before the Szulc interview—President Kennedy had ordered the creation of a program to overthrow the Cuban government. Robert Kennedy took notes at the meeting: "McNamara, Dick Bissell, Alexis Johnson, Paul Nitze, Lansdale (the Ugly American). McN said he would make latter available for me—I assigned him to make survey of situation in Cuba—the problem and our assets. My idea is to stir things up on the island with espionage, sabotage, general disorder, run & operated by Cubans themselves with every group but Batistaites & Communists. Do not know if we will be successful in overthrowing Castro but we have nothing to lose in my estimate.[30]" The CIA assigned approximately four hundred people at CIA headquarters and in Miami for the implementation of Operation Mongoose, which, under General Edward Landsdale, was to accomplish America's—the Kennedys'—revenge on Castro's Cuba.[31] It was to be the instrument that would accomplish what the Bay of Pigs invasion had failed to achieve: not only the liberation of the Cuban people from totalitarian Communism, but the destruction of Fidel Castro himself, for lèse majesté if nothing else. Under Landsdale, the CIA officer in charge of Operation Mongoose was Angleton's old colleague William King Harvey, who had been introduced to Kennedy as "America's James Bond."

MI5's Peter Wright describes a scene in the fall of 1961, adding some color to these bureaucratic arrangements. At a lunch with William Harvey and James Angleton, Wright was asked, "What would the Brits do in Cuba? . . . Would you hit [Castro]? . . . Harvey and Angleton questioned me closely about every part of the Suez Operation [to assassinate Nasser] . . . 'We're developing a new capacity in the Company to handle these kinds of problems,' explained Harvey, 'and we're in the market for the requisite expertise' . . . 'Have you thought of approaching Stephenson?' I asked. 'A lot of the old-timers say he ran this kind of thing in New York during the war . . . ' Angleton scribbled in his notebook, and looked up impassively . . . Harvey was not the kind of man to laugh at a joke. Come to that, neither was Angleton."[32] Which implies, if Wright is to be trusted, that Angleton as well as Harvey was involved in the CIA's attempts to assassinate Fidel Castro. The president ordered that the Mafia were to be enlisted for active service to the same end.[33]

The CIA appears to have taken two attitudes in regard to assassinations. DCI McCone was opposed to the deed on "moral or ethical grounds," while the action officer, William Harvey, was opposed to *talk* about the matter. American policymakers' focus on the goal of assassinating Fidel Castro himself can be traced in this *Alice through the Looking Glass* world by their decision to conceal the fact that such discussions were taking place.[34] There *were* discussions about assassinations under way in the summer of 1962, and they included senior members of the cabinet of the government of the United States.

Operation Mongoose, designed by General Landsdale and operated by William Harvey, landed small raiding parties, printed propaganda leaflets, sabotaged factories, enlisted Mafia assassins, all to no avail. Angleton, worried, placed an agent in Havana to watch Harvey's back. The provenance of that agent is of interest. Angleton told the Church Committee, in a secret session only much later declassified, the following story:

> So when Bill took over in the Cuban business, then I decided that since we were very close friends that I would try to help him out by getting him a source totally unknown to everybody. And I went to the Israelis. And I had them assign a man to Havana, whom I happened to know very well. He was born in Bulgaria. He can speak Russian and the Balkan countries' languages. He is today their senior man on Soviet intelligence. He was a young officer in the days I am speaking of. And he was sent to Havana, which meant that there he was—and the communications were from him in a one time pattern, I mean total security, from Havana to Tel Aviv, to me, and from me to Bill. And no one knew of his existence or his identity, except Harvey and myself, and of course, Dick Helms.[35]

Angleton went to the Mossad, as if to another department in the CIA, and had them place an agent in Havana, something that no one else in the CIA had been able to do. So intimate were Angleton's relations with his old friends in Tel Aviv.

Harvey continued to run his covert operations on the island after being ordered to stop by (and having lied about it to) Robert Kennedy. Harvey was only saved from forced retirement by Helms, who packed him off to Rome, where he rapidly descended into the final stages of alcoholic paranoia: grossly overweight, alternately spinning bottles of Jack Daniel's and revolvers on his desk to amuse himself and intimidate his visitors. America's own James Bond.

Meanwhile, on November 22, 1963, AM/LASH himself, Major Rolando Cubela Secades, one of the CIA's would-be assassins of Fidel Castro, met in Paris with Desmond FitzGerald, who gave him a fountain pen modified as an injection device and poison to fill it.[36] Castro apparently knew about this plan, as he had—as he would—know of others. Here the movie screen of history must be split into three parts, as in Abel Gance's *Napoleon*: on the right, say, FitzGerald handing the assassination devices to Cubela in Paris; on the left, Castro in Havana reading reports about such preparations; in the center, the motorcade making its slow progress through Dallas. The president died, as had Lumumba, as had Diem, as would Trujillo, at the hands of one of a cloud of those secondary figures whose swarming screened their principals. In this case, perhaps, that cloud included right-wing Texans, agents of the Cuban secret police, renegade CIA officers, Mafia figures enraged by having been used and double-crossed by the Kennedys. The great library of research and speculation on the assassination of Kennedy is a swamp as dismal as that behind the beaches of the Bay of Pigs. The grassy knoll in Dallas has with passing time become ever more crowded with these phantom assassins, their identities seemingly lost to history with the convenient murder of the Fair Play for Cuba Committee's most famous member, Lee Harvey Oswald, and Jack Ruby's silence and the obscurity of files held or destroyed deep within Dulles's monument at Langley.

President Johnson said, "What raced through my mind was that if they had shot our President, driving down there, who would they shoot next? And what was going on in Washington? And when would the missiles be coming? I thought it was a conspiracy and I raised that question, and nearly everybody that was with me raised it." [37] The key to the mystery was that seeming nonentity, Oswald, the "loner" whose connections with the Soviet Union and Cuba were well known to the CIA—in part through Angleton's mail surveillance program.[38] Had Oswald been a KGB (or Cuban) agent? In other words, had Kennedy been assassinated by "the Communists?" It seemed that the CIA thought so: for it was after he was briefed by Helms, in 1964, that Johnson had become "convinced that the Kennedy assassination represented Castro's revenge for attempts on his life." [39] In the bipolar world of the Cold War, Cuba meant the Soviets. It was inconceivable in Washington that the Cubans would have acted independently. But here the chain of reasoning broke down: a motive was obvious for the Cuban pawn; Soviet motivations were less clear; the rules of the Cold War seemed to preclude assassination of major political leaders. And yet, the FBI's liaison officer to the CIA, Sam Papich, "had driven to Langley and was in Angleton's office by 10:30 A.M. on the day after the assassination, where the CI chief apprised him of certain 'sinister implications.' Angleton was bothered by [a] 1961 warning about the KGB's plotting to kill a 'Western political leader,' by the mystery of Oswald's travels in the USSR, and by other unresolved questions." [40]

Immediately after the assassination, in an attempt to resolve such questions, President Johnson had the CIA undertake an investigation of Oswald's history of contacts with Cuba and his stay in the Soviet Union. Raymond Rocca, who had worked with Angleton since OSS days, was at first put in charge of coordinating the operation. Then, in January, 1964, after the appointment of the Warren Commission, Angleton himself was made the CIA's liaison to the Warren Commission. It was then that

> Angleton contacted William Sullivan of the FBI, saying that "it would be well for both McCone and Hoover to be aware that the commission might ask the same questions wondering whether they would get different replies from the heads of the two agencies." Angleton gave examples of what questions might be asked and how they should be answered:
> (1) Q. Was Oswald ever an agent of the CIA?
> A. No.

(2) Q. Does the CIA have any evidence showing that a conspiracy existed to assassinate President Kennedy?
A. No.[41]

Coordinating answers in this way is a routine procedure for institutions or individuals anticipating an adversarial investigation. In other words, Angleton (and presumably Sullivan) anticipated that the Warren Commission would assume that the Bureau and the Agency were not only among its instruments for exploring the assassination, but at some level were themselves suspect. Otherwise, why was it necessary to practice denying that Oswald had been a CIA agent and that the assassination had been the result of a conspiracy?

If these answers satisfied the commission, they failed to convince the new president. In the following quotation from testimony before the Senate committee that investigated the CIA in the mid-1970s, Cartha D. DeLoach, an aide to FBI Director Hoover, was being questioned by Senator Richard Schweiker:

SENATOR SCHWEIKER: [In] a memorandum from [Mr. DeLoach] to Mr. Tolson, dated April 4, 1967, . . . it says: "In this connection, Marvin Watson called . . . late last night and stated the President"—President Johnson—"had told him in an off moment that he was now convinced that there was a plot in connection with the assassination"—this is the Kennedy assassination. You [Mr. DeLoach] go on to say, "Watson requested that any further information that we could furnish in this connection would be most appreciated by him," the President. Then you say, "I reminded Watson that the Director had sent over to the White House some weeks back all of the information in our possession in connection with the CIA's attempts to use former agent Robert Maheu and his private detective outfit, in contacts with Sam Giancana and other hoodlums relative to fostering a plot to assassinate Castro." . . .

MR. DELOACH: . . . the President felt that a certain Agency may have been involved in a conspiracy.[42]

President Johnson was briefed by the CIA in 1964 and concluded that President Kennedy had been killed by the Cubans. Discussing the matter with the FBI three years later, he felt that the CIA itself had been involved, conspiring, it seems, with the Mafia. Which, of course, was true, at least in part. The CIA *had* conspired at assassination with the Mafia.

The commission's files in the National Archives contain more than two hundred documents indexed under Angleton's name. He brought to his work on the assassination of President Kennedy his specialist interests in the matter. As a printer shown a book will inspect the pages for "rivers" of type ineptly set, before reading it, so Angleton, given Oswald's file, held it up to whatever dim light was available in his office and looked for the identifying marks of espionage. Thus, "mysterious aspects of Oswald's odd character, which the FBI and the Warren Commission casually dismissed, seemed perfectly explicable to Angleton as espionage 'tradecraft.' Oswald used aliases and post-office boxes, and lived apart from his family. His possessions had been found to include a book which had certain letters cut out, giving the impression that this might have formed the base or key for a cipher system . . . One possibility, taken seriously by Angleton and many others at CIA, was that Oswald had learned his tradecraft in Russia . . . CIA analysts . . . considered whether he might not have been 'programmed' or brainwashed by Soviet mind-control specialists using LSD."[43]

After having decided that Oswald's way of life was consistent with espionage tradecraft, and having raised the possibility that he had learned to do these things while living in Russia (whether or not he had been subjected to mind-control experiments using LSD—something the CIA was exploring and therefore assumed that the KGB had already done), the next point in the argument was to attempt to answer the question of "what would the Soviets possibly gain from Kennedy's death that would be worth the risk of U.S. retaliation? From a pragmatic Western perspective, there seemed little profit indeed, but Angleton thought about the problem with more subtlety . . . Out was Kennedy, a charismatic leader who could 'sell' a socially conscious anticommunism in the Third World and even to Western liberals. In was Johnson, who would only 'heighten the contradictions' between East and West and therefore hasten . . . the ultimate collapse of late capitalism . . . Much later, Angleton would obliquely compare the Soviets' probable motivation to a famous scene in Mario Puzo's novel *The Godfather*, in which a Mafia chieftain puts a horse's head into the bed of a stubborn film producer, in order to demonstrate 'pure power.'"[44]

As the new president returned to Washington from Dallas—perhaps, as the Soviets hoped, to "heighten the contradictions between East and West"—Johnson feared almost equally that the assassination had been a Soviet action (perhaps to be followed by other killings) meant to paralyze the U.S. government before a nuclear strike, or that it would be assumed to be that by the American public, which would demand an American nuclear strike against the Soviets. Therefore, once it had become clear that there was not a wider plot to kill American officials, his policy had been to "close off public speculation about Oswald's foreign connections to forestall public outrage that might lead to pressure on [President Johnson] to wage some kind of revenge assault against Cuba or the Soviet Union."[45] Reflecting the president's concerns, three days after the assassination one of his aides wrote to another that "it is important that all of the facts surrounding President Kennedy's assassination be made public in a way which will satisfy people in the United States and abroad that all the facts have been told and that a statement to this effect be made now. 1. The public must be satisfied that Oswald was the assassin, that he did not have confederates who are still at large and that the evidence was such he would have been convicted at trial. 2. Speculation about Oswald's motivation ought to be cut off, and we should have some basis for rebutting that this was a Communist conspiracy or (as the Iron Curtain press is saying) a right-wing conspiracy to blame it on the Communists."[46]

Thus the conclusions of the investigation of the assassination were set out before the investigation had properly begun. The problem was not the all too famous question *Who killed Jack Kennedy?* but *How was the American public to be convinced that Oswald, without help or influence from either the Right or the Left, was a lone assassin?* In this way began the gradual loss of faith in their institutions of government that was to become endemic among Americans.

And then, just as these damage control efforts were being put in place, as if summoned by the very force of the government's longing, a messenger arrived from the East. In January 1964, Yuri Ivanovich Nosenko, who had been a Soviet "defector in place" in Geneva, suddenly told his CIA contacts that he wanted to come in from the cold at once. He informed them—by the way, as it were—that he had been responsible for the KGB files on Lee Harvey Oswald and could vouch for the KGB having had "no involvement whatsoever with Oswald or with the assassination." He was brought to the United States the next month.[47] Much of the American government, including the president, would have been only too pleased to accept Nosenko's message, but Angleton and his colleagues found that they could not swallow its implications: "On the face of it, Nosenko's assertion that the KGB had no interest in Oswald seemed to defy logic . . . Oswald had been stationed at Atsugi, Japan, a base for the U-2 aircraft. Since 1956, the CIA spy planes had been overflying the Soviet Union to collect intelligence data; and to the CIA it seemed improbable that the KGB would not want to debrief Oswald about the U-2."[48] If the KGB said that Oswald had been of no interest to them, that was good, as that meant that the president had not been murdered on orders from Moscow. On the other hand, if the proof of Oswald's bona fides was based on the word of the KGB, that was bad, as it was an article of faith in the CIA that the KGB was never to be believed. And it was not only the CIA that was doubtful. Francis Gary Powers, for one, believed that Oswald had given the Soviets the information necessary for their successful interception of his aircraft.[49]

Nosenko, who had been working with the CIA for nearly two years when he delivered his message about Oswald, was a remarkable catch. He was the son of a Soviet minister of shipbuilding who had been a member of the Communist Party's Central Committee, a deputy to the Supreme Soviet, and close to members of the Politburo.[50] Nosenko himself had joined the GRU, Soviet military intelligence, in 1949, transferring to the KGB in 1953, where he worked in counterintelligence, first in the American Department, then, in 1955, transferring to the Tourist Department, where, after an intervening tour back in the American Department, he became deputy chief of the Tourist Department. (The duties of the Tourist Department of KGB counterintelligence included surveillance of foreigners in the USSR. Nosenko, as an American specialist, had responsibility for Americans such as Oswald.) In the spring of 1962 Nosenko received his first foreign assignment, as a security officer attached to the Soviet disarmament delegation in Geneva.[51]

Contacting the CIA, Nosenko began to provide information about KGB operations against the United States and Great Britain. Richards Heuer, writing thirty years later in a CIA house organ, stated that "Nosenko provided identification of, or leads to, some 238 Americans and about 200 foreign nationals in whom the KGB had displayed varying degrees of interest, and against whom they had enjoyed varying degrees of success. He provided information on about 2,000 [!] KGB staff officers and 300 Soviet national agents or contacts of the KGB. His information on the methods and scope of Second Chief Directorate operations against foreign diplomats and journalists in Moscow and visitors to the Soviet Union filled a large gap in our knowledge and had an enormous impact on the raising of CIA's consciousness of these operations; the result was important improvements in the physical security of U.S. installations and in the personal security of U.S. officials and visitors to the USSR."[52] During his first Geneva period Nosenko had insisted that he did not wish to defect. He went back to the Soviet Union for a time, during which he was not in contact with the CIA, stating that their operations in Moscow were not secure, was transferred back to Geneva and then made his sensational jump to Washington.

The arrival of this messenger, and the message he brought, threw the CIA into a prolonged crisis. Nosenko seemed to prove his bona fides as a defector by providing the CIA with vast quantities of valuable information. Along with this information, he claimed that he had been nearly uniquely positioned to know about Oswald's relationship with Soviet secret intelligence. The average counterintelligence officer would reason that each additional piece of important information passed by a defector increased the probability both that he was a genuine defector and that any given piece of information he provided was as likely as not to be accurate. Thus, the sheer mass of verifiable information provided by Nosenko tended to increase the probability that his unverifiable claim to knowledge about Oswald was also true. One line of reasoning, then, was that Nosenko was telling the truth: Oswald had not worked with the KGB and therefore the Soviets were not responsible for the president's death. Another line of reasoning, perhaps more sophisticated, was that Nosenko's assertion about Oswald was possibly untrue—in any case difficult to believe—and that therefore the other information he provided was meant as a decoy, as a sacrifice to gain belief in the false message about Oswald and to conceal the truth that Oswald *had* worked with the KGB, if only to provide information about the U-2, and therefore Nosenko was not telling the truth about that and he was not a defector but an agent and Oswald, too, in some sense had been a Soviet agent.[53] Or, as Richard Helms put it, if Nosenko gave the CIA false information about Oswald, "it was fair for us to surmise [additionally] that there may have been an Oswald-KGB connection in November 1963, more specifically that Oswald was acting as a Soviet agent when he shot President Kennedy"[54]

And yet, ultimately, neither Angleton nor the CIA's Soviet Russia Division believed that Oswald was under the control of the KGB when he shot Kennedy. Angleton thought it more probable that Nosenko was attempting to conceal Oswald's earlier relationship with the KGB having to do with the U-2.[55] According to one-time CIA Director Admiral Stansfield Turner, "Angleton concluded that since Oswald had worked on the U-2 spy plane when he was in the U.S. Marine Corps, it was unlikely that the KGB would have overlooked him entirely when he was in the Soviet Union. There was, then, cause to be suspicious of Nosenko's story about Oswald. It appeared to Angleton that the Soviets might have sent Nosenko to plant a story that would absolve them of any complicity with Oswald in the Kennedy assassination."[56]

Angleton had constructed a probability distribution for the Oswald/Nosenko matter. At one end was belief in Nosenko's story: the KGB had nothing to do with Oswald and therefore nothing to do with the Kennedy assassination. On the other end was the belief that Nosenko was lying and that therefore the KGB had controlled Oswald and was responsible for the assassination. In between was the most probable interpretation: Nosenko was lying, the KGB had been in contact with Oswald, but about the U-2, not the assassination, and it was concerned that if the U-2 matter were known, the United States would believe that the KGB had used Oswald to assassinate Kennedy. Complicated enough; however, given what was at stake, what seemed only more likely was not good enough.

Under the circumstances prevailing in Washington in the spring of 1964 Nosenko's bona fides were indeed of the highest importance. How were they to be verified—or discredited? The CIA could not then, as far as we know, directly access KGB files. All that could be done was to question Nosenko until his interrogators were satisfied that he was telling the truth, or until he "broke" and confessed to lying. Angleton's confidant Edward Jay Epstein tells us that "the CIA decided that there was a strong possibility that Nosenko might break and might even unravel Oswald's tangled web before the Warren commission put out its final report." With the backing of Attorney General Robert F. Kennedy, Nosenko was put under "hostile interrogation," during which Kennedy repeatedly telephoned the Agency to ask whether Nosenko had been broken. The answer was always "Not yet."[57]

There are three issues to be considered at this point. Who was responsible for the decision to subject Nosenko to "hostile interrogation"? What did the nature and fact of hostile interrogation imply about the American government? And, finally, was Nosenko telling the truth?

The issue of the responsibility for the decision to subject Nosenko to hostile interrogation is the least difficult to untangle. When Nosenko defected, Richard Helms asked both the CIA's Soviet Division and its Counterintelligence Staff how he should be treated. The Soviet Division "argued that conditions should be 'Spartan' and should coincide with 'hostile interrogation.'" Helms agreed with that recommendation, since it promised a resolution to the problem.[58] Angleton's position on this decision has been much debated. The most recent opinion is that he had been opposed to hostile interrogation.[59] Angleton told Epstein that he had been against hostile interrogation "not because he believed Nosenko was a legitimate defector, but because he considered it advantageous that the KGB believe Nosenko had been accepted. He viewed Nosenko simply as a Soviet postman, delivering a message. He assumed that he would not have been dispatched on such a mission by the KGB if it did not have an 'inside man' in the CIA to feed back to it the CIA's assessment of Nosenko. He had hoped to play the game out, seeing where it might lead."[60]

In this version of the story, Angleton is said to have believed that it was the play of the interpretation of the text that mattered. If there was a text, there had to be both a sender and receiver, there had to be, as he had learned in London, an observer to note the interpretation. There had to be a Philby, leaning over the shoulder of the analyst deciphering the message. The possibility that Nosenko's defection pointed to the existence of a mole in the CIA was much more important to Angleton, professionally, as a molehunter, than the more sensational matter of Oswald's connections with the KGB.

Angleton thought it vital—that there was nothing more vital—to discover whether there was a penetration in the Agency and whether Nosenko's appearance was linked to such a penetration. When advising as to whether Nosenko was on a mission from the KGB, or when advising as to whether anyone else who had come under suspicion was in fact an agent, it was his perception of his duty to err on the side of caution, to err, that is, against the suspect and for, as he saw it, the greater cause of national security. Therefore, "Angleton went to Dulles, laid out the evidence, and said the one thing which sealed the Suspect's fate: not that there was a 50–50 chance he was guilty, nor even that there was a 10 percent chance. All it took was *a* chance, and in Angleton's view the evidence pointed in that direction. It was possible."[61] Given that, it would not be surprising if he voted in favor of continued interrogation of Nosenko. That does not necessarily mean he was in favor of extreme measures. However, if Angleton was opposed to the hostile interrogation of Nosenko, he was not sufficiently opposed to intervene officially.

To sum up the matter of the responsibility for the hostile interrogation of Nosenko, the decision was, in the first instance, that of the chief of the Soviet Russia Division, David Murphy, and approved up the line to, as we have seen, Robert Kennedy.[62] It would not have happened without the approval of others in the chain of command, including Angleton (in at least an advisory capacity) and Helms. But ultimately the person behind the decision to subject Nosenko to hostile interrogation was the same person who drove the campaign to kill Fidel Castro: Robert Kennedy.

As we have, of late, become once more sensitive to such matters, what was the meaning of the phrase "hostile interrogation" in Angleton's time at the CIA? This question can be answered on two levels, the first of which is simply to describe what happened to Nosenko, the second of which is to think about the wider significance of these affairs. What was done to Nosenko was dreadful and illegal, if not as dreadful and illegal as what has been done to dozens, if not hundreds, of people more recently in the name of the government of the United States. Its significance extends beyond the treatment of Nosenko himself to the secret heart of mid-twentieth-century American history. Yuri Nosenko was imprisoned and interrogated by the CIA for nearly five years. He was kept in solitary confinement, eventually in a one-room prison, a purposefully ill-heated, un-air-conditioned structure where he was deprived of books and writing materials, sometimes not allowed even so much as a toothbrush, ill fed, and subjected to extraordinarily prolonged questioning.[63] He was subjected to invasive physical examinations and questions he found humiliating, bullied, lied to, cajoled, deprived of sleep. On the other hand, unlike more recent guests of the Agency, he was not beaten or otherwise subjected to physical pain.[64] He was not "water-boarded" or placed in "stress positions." He was not threatened by attack dogs. However, hostile interrogation did mean for Nosenko years of dread and debility, the destruction of his life. He went in a matter of weeks from being an upper level bureaucrat living in comfort in Switzerland to the life of a political prisoner, living in conditions that were meant to imply that at any moment those conditions might worsen, perhaps fatally. This was the meaning of the phrase "hostile interrogation" in the mid-1960s. Its significance lies not in that it happened to Nosenko, but that such actions were as integral to the nature of the Central Intelligence Agency then as they are today.

But fortunately for him, Nosenko's treatment was done literally by the book—the book in question being *KUBARK Counterintelligence Interrogation* (July 1963), a manual prepared for Angleton's interrogators—and not by whatever understandings pertained in the Agency's secret prisons forty years later.[65] The manual affects a calm, reasonable, quasi-scientific tone, with arguments and evidence (including citations both to the open literature and to the CIA's own research) for and against each coercive technique. Solitary confinement, for example, is recommended not as an end in itself, but because of its effects: "to deprive the subject of many or most of the sights, sounds, tastes, smells, and tactile sensations to which he has grown accustomed." It is, to use one of the manual's favorite terms, "debilitating": it weakens the power of a person to resist the wishes of his interrogators.

*KUBARK Counterintelligence Interrogation* had two primary purposes. It was an interrogation textbook, giving the novice interrogator the basic information he or she needed to conduct interrogations, and it was a way of forming the character of the interrogator, an instrument, not to put too fine a point on it, of moral corruption. For example, in a section called "Legal and Policy Considerations" we find a comment on the procedures for detentions such as Nosenko's: "The legislation which founded KUBARK [i.e., the CIA itself] specifically denied it any law-enforcement or police powers. Yet detention in a controlled environment and perhaps for a lengthy period is frequently essential to a successful counterintelligence interrogation of a recalcitrant source. [Approximately three lines deleted.]" And then a page later: "Interrogations conducted under compulsion or duress are especially likely to involve illegality and to entail damaging consequences for KUBARK. Therefore prior Headquarters approval at the KUDOVE [Office of the Director] level must be obtained for the interrogation of any source against his will and under any of the following circumstances: 1. If bodily harm is to be inflicted. 2. If medical, chemical, or electrical methods or materials are to be used to induce acquiescence." Then approximately three lines are again deleted, about which we can only wonder. The novice interrogator was told quite clearly that the actions that form the subject of the manual were (then) illegal, from "detention in a controlled environment" to "bodily harm."

But where one might anticipate that the invocation of the law would be followed by a prohibition against the activities in question, instead the novice interrogator was told that these illegal activities may be undertaken with approval of "Headquarters." This amounts to an assertion that the Central Intelligence Agency is outside the legal structure of the United States. Or to put it another way, the view of the CIA, which it taught its staff, is that "it is inconceivable that a secret intelligence arm of the government has to comply with all the overt orders of the government," as James Angleton famously remarked to the Church Committee's investigators. The point of this was to assure Agency interrogators that, although the actions associated with hostile interrogation are illegal, *they* are not at risk: responsibility for this violation of the law was assumed by the Agency, by the very existence of the manual and through the indicated approval process at the senior staff level. This line of reasoning, unacceptable at Nuremberg (or, more recently, at the Hague), was presumably offered to assure the interrogators (Angleton's subordinates) that the Agency was sufficiently powerful to protect its employees from the consequences of their illegal actions. This view was not something that the CIA wanted known outside the Agency. Public documents, including such unofficial but CIA-approved accounts as ex-CIA counterintelligence officer William Johnson's *Thwarting Enemies at Home and Abroad: How to Be a Counterintelligence Officer*, make explicit statements claiming that the CIA interrogator is "not in the torture business."[66] The publication of *KUBARK Counterintelligence Interrogation* and more recent events in Iraq and elsewhere have made it clear that this was—is—not the case. The CIA interrogator is *expected* to be in the torture business, as is, perforce, the Agency itself.

A person who has accepted and internalized *KUBARK Counterintelligence Interrogation* has become quite a different type of person than one who has not. He is no longer a member of civil society, of the constitutional order. He belongs to a society of men, not a society of laws, as Angleton pointed out. The publication date of *KUBARK Counterintelligence Interrogation* is convenient—July 1963—it was then, at the latest, that "we" became indistinguishable from "them." If, even in a single manual, the Counterintelligence Staff of the Central Intelligence Agency taught and sanctioned torture, then the Agency itself did so. And if it did so, this was, perforce, the position of the government of the United States. It was, in those years, as we have seen, a government that used assassination as an instrument of policy. It was a government that trained its officials in the techniques of torture. This was the moral center of the Cold War. It continues to contaminate and corrupt American life, a steadily spreading moral and ethical decay of the foundations of the Republic.

Because a "penetration agent" or trained intelligence officer like Nosenko was taken by the authors of *KUBARK Counterintelligence Interrogation* to be immune to torture, the fact—or report—that Nosenko himself was not tortured, but simply subjected to imprisonment, humiliation, and conditions leading to "debility" is a red herring. If Nosenko in fact was not tortured this strongly indicates that he was dealt with in accordance with the documented procedures of Angleton's Counterintelligence Staff. At that point Angleton's attitude toward the matter becomes academic—or Jesuitical—no matter what, many years later, he wanted believed about the matter. The hostile interrogation of Nosenko was the way in which the Agency sought to unravel what was seen as the most important counterintelligence issue it had yet faced. In this the Agency failed. It was unable to prove that Nosenko was lying when he said that Oswald was not under KGB control, and it was unable to satisfy itself that he was telling the truth.[67] Late in June of 1964, Helms reported as much to Chief Justice Warren.[68] The matter was bracketed: as it could not be resolved, it was left out of the Warren Report. Here the silence of the official historical record cannot be taken to mean that the government believed Nosenko's account. Much of the government, including President Johnson and, crucially, that Agency charged with investigating the matter, did not believe it.[69] But the chief justice had to file his report, and it was decided that, absent Nosenko's cooperation, it would not refer to him and his information at all. The Warren Commission told the American public that Oswald was a "loner," that "conspiracy theories" were inappropriate, that there had been no Soviet, no Cuban, no right-wing plot. The public, then, learning the phrase and learning to laugh at "conspiracy theories," did not call for war with the Soviet Union or Cuba. Johnson's nightmare of forty million Americans dead in twenty-four hours was averted.

In his concern to discover whether the assassination of his predecessor had been directed by the Soviets—or by the Cubans—President Johnson had asked the CIA to conduct a domestic investigation in violation of its charter. The significant point was not so much the actual result of the investigation, but the nature of the investigation itself. From that moment the Agency had a domestic investigation capacity and a precedent, authorized, as they said, by the "highest authority." The action officer was James Angleton.

After the CIA decided that nothing decisive could be learned from Nosenko concerning the assassination, the attention of the Counterintelligence Staff turned to Angleton's theory that the reception of Nosenko's "message" as a matter of tradecraft, would be monitored by a "penetration agent," a mole, at a high level within the CIA itself, as the Venona decryption had been monitored by Philby. At this point the Nosenko narrative, a man sitting in a badly heated concrete cell, his teeth rotting, intersects with the molehunt.[70]

If the name James Jesus Angleton is known to the common reader—say that five percent of the population who, according to Lewis Lapham, sometime editor of *Harper's*, read his magazine, the *Atlantic*, the *New Yorker*, and the *New York Review of Books*, watch public television, and listen to public radio—he is known for the Great Molehunt. Angleton's campaign in the 1960s to discover if there was one or more Soviet agents in place in the Central Intelligence Agency has been described in melodramatic terms by David Wise in his eponymous *Molehunt*, by David Martin in *Wilderness of Mirrors*, and in Tom Mangold's *Cold Warrior* as something like the first stages of the Stalinist Great Terror, with the secret intelligence services of the state consuming themselves in a search for traitors. Angleton has been depicted as an Ahab, obsessed and unhinged by fantasies of treachery. But as the old joke goes, even paranoids have enemies—and think they have friends. Angleton had once had a very good friend named Kim Philby.

It was just about this time, as it happened, that Philby himself reemerged. Philby's career in MI6 had been ruined by the KGB's effort to save Donald Maclean. And yet, although Maclean was known to be a Soviet agent, Philby was simply suspected of being one. There was no proof, not even an ambiguous World War II decrypt. Although, as we have seen, Philby had been put out to grass by MI6 (at U.S. insistence), he had powerful protectors, including Prime Minister Macmillan. He was allowed to return to his alternative—or cover—career as a journalist, this time in Lebanon, where he filed stories and reports for the *Observer* and the *Economist*, MI6 and the KGB. Conditions changed in 1960 when Dick White, a man of impeccably bad judgment, became head of MI6. Philby was encouraged by the British secret intelligence service's man on the spot, Nicholas Elliott, an old friend (yes), to become more active: "The idea was to force Philby out into the field, to give him the profile of an active and industrious intelligence officer and thus force the Russians to use him again. Philby would be taken into Elliott's confidence; he would be made a part of SIS operations; he would learn information so important that he would have to pass it to his Soviet control. But although some of that information would be genuine, some of it would be a plant and Western counter-intelligence would be waiting to see where it surfaced. If it could be traced back to Philby, and only to Philby, then the British authorities would at last have proof of his treachery."[71]

Philby's father, who had become his companion in Lebanon, died, and after George Blake was arrested and sentenced to a surprisingly long prison term in 1961, Philby became depressed and worried, began drinking—even more—heavily and his health deteriorated. In the autumn of 1962 another member of the Burgess–Blunt set from the Comintern period, Tomas Harris, was killed, it is said, in an automobile accident in Spain. MI6 decided that time was running out.[72] In January 1963, Roger Hollis, head of MI5, sent Nicholas Elliott to Beirut to confront Philby. Robin Winks, who may be taken as relaying Angleton's account of the matter, writes that Angleton had two agents in place in Lebanon, planning to have Philby detained by the CIA's station chief in Beirut and interrogated "by someone Philby did not know," presumably an American, but was frustrated in this by Hollis's appointment of Elliott.[73] When Philby told Elliott that he was indeed a Soviet agent and that it was he who had alerted Burgess and Maclean to their danger, the news was immediately sent to Angleton, raging in Langley.[74] Elliott returned to London with a typed two-page confession for Hollis,[75] while Philby thought about Elliott's offer of immunity, took his decision—and his opportunity—evaded various watchers, boarded a Russian freighter, and sailed from Beirut through the Straits to Russia.

The way the Beirut interview of Philby was handled, and Philby's escape, convinced Angleton, Peter Wright, and Arthur Martin that there was a mole inside MI5.[76] In March 1962, the CIA had sent MI5 a list of ten "serials," identifications of KGB agents. One concerned the "ring of five," including Burgess, Maclean, and a third, code-named "Stanley," who had something to do with the Middle East.[77] This seemed to point to Philby. But who were the others? Martin decided the Fourth Man was Sir Anthony Blunt, by then holding the title of Surveyor of the Queen's Pictures. Charred ancient MI5 Registry files, which had been recovered from the ruins of Wormwood Scrubs Prison during the Second World War, were pulled from the bags in which they had been stored for nearly twenty years and examined, their pages painstakingly separated with tweezers and wooden spatulas.[78] These archeological studies were supplemented by the confession of Michael Straight, a wealthy American who had been a member of the Cambridge set led by Guy Burgess before the war, who confirmed Blunt's identification as the Fourth Man.[79]

Burgess and Maclean, Philby and Blunt made four. The mystery of the Fifth Man was to occupy British intelligence for a generation. For some it was solved when John Cairncross was identified as a long-serving Soviet agent. For others it was never solved. In a sense it was a misleading question. Anthony Blunt "was asked if it was correct that there had been twenty-five people in positions similar to his. He replied: 'My guess would be that there must have been a great many more people involved in this . . . I think it is common knowledge that the network was considerable.'"[80] According to Peter Wright there were between one hundred fifty and three hundred spies active in Britain in 1945.[81] Giving, say, two hundred spies during the war. New revelations continue to appear, but as yet none have touched on the matter that obsessed the British molehunters: Had one of those hundreds of spies reached the top of the British intelligence services undetected, succeeding where Philby had—just—failed?

As for Philby himself, now in Moscow, "In those early years he was fully occupied with his debriefings . . . Philby was emptying his mind of *everything* he knew about the workings of British and American intelligence . . . [W]hen an intelligence officer as senior as Philby defects there is not a lot that *can* be done. Intelligence agencies are big, bureaucratic organizations employing thousands of highly trained people, many with specialist skills. The way these organizations work cannot be changed overnight; the people they employ cannot be quickly replaced; operations under way for years cannot be immediately aborted."[82] In 1965, at long last, Kim Philby received recognition from the Soviet intelligence services for his great services to their cause: the Order of Lenin and the Order of the Red Banner.

As Philby sat at his desk in Moscow, emptying his memory into the archives of the KGB, James Angleton settled down to work in his new office at Langley—curtains drawn, files piled on his desk, cigarette smoke further obscuring the shadows—thinking about Kim Philby in Moscow, about what he was then doing, about what he had done. As Nina Burleigh put it in her book about Mary Meyer, "The revelation that his British friend Kim Philby actually worked for Moscow would propel Angleton in the sixties from garden-variety suspicion of the Soviets to a state that some in the CIA have compared to clinical paranoia. 'That [defection] was a shattering experience to Angleton,' [CIA psychiatrist John] Gittinger recalled. 'From that period on he was the most suspicious man in the agency. My own feeling is the emotional wreckage of that close friendship made him mistrust everybody and colored his life from that point on.'"[83]

Of course, Angleton was paid to be "the most suspicious man in the Agency": the role of counterintelligence is to see anyone coming to its attention as a potential threat. Angleton had long been known for his zeal in this regard.[84] But as America in the 1960s descended into a maelstrom of assassinations, failed war, cultural revolution, and counterrevolution, the usual efforts—"meticulous, tireless and endless" though they were—began to appear to Angleton to be insufficient. The Soviet and their allied secret intelligence services had become increasingly aggressive. General Gehlen's intelligence apparatus, begun as part of German army intelligence on the Eastern Front during the Second World War and smoothly completing a transition to postwar life under the patronage of the CIA, was penetrated at the highest levels. And if the CIA itself seemed secure, its even more secret counterpart, the National Security Agency, was not. In June 1960 two cryptanalysts employed by NSA defected to the Soviet Union, via Havana, just after Gary Powers's U-2 was shot down. Their work for the Soviets overlapped and was replaced by that of an army driver, Staff Sergeant Jack E. Dunlop, who stayed in place for five years, chauffeuring generals and secret documents to and fro, until his suicide in 1963.[85] The threat was real.

In the early 1960s, just as Philby's story was coming to its conclusion, a wave of defectors began to arrive in the West, each with his or her story of penetrations of Western secret security services.[86] At a meeting in a Washington, D.C., Chinese restaurant, Angleton and Peter Wright "talked until 4 A.M. . . . Who was true, and who was false? Who defected, and who was sent? . . . 'This is Kim's work,' [Angleton] muttered."[87]

The most significant defector, for Angleton and for the CIA, was Anatoliy Golitsyn, who had arrived a bit earlier, defecting from the KGB on December 15, 1961. This was a year after "the secret gathering in Moscow of eighty-one Communist parties" that Jay Lovestone testified had determined on what amounted to a secret declaration of war against the West. Golitsyn had been serving in Helsinki, as a certain "Klimov," ostensibly as vice consul in the Soviet Embassy, with the actual rank and duties of a major in the KGB.[88] Ten years younger than Angleton, he had been formally educated as an intelligence officer, attending a Soviet intelligence school from 1948 to 1952 while Angleton was establishing himself in the CIA, then spending two years in Vienna in the mid-1950s before returning to Moscow for more studies in the KGB's higher education system, earning a law degree, spending a year or two on a desk as an analyst in the Anglo-American and NATO sections of the KGB, then moving on to Finland for his second overseas tour. He was a highly educated intelligence analyst, not an operations officer. In the CIA order of things he would have been in the Directorate of Intelligence, not in the Clandestine Services. Or, to look at it in another way, he was what in the United States would be called a defense intellectual.

Golitsyn paid for passage to Washington for himself, his wife, and daughter by bartering the KGB's Helsinki order of battle (organization chart). Beyond such specific information, his value to the CIA was that he was that rare thing in the West, a serving KGB officer, a breed that showed up only every couple of years. It was his routine knowledge of the KGB gathered over fifteen years of experience that at first interested his interlocutors in Washington.[89] That, and his claim to have prepared a second dowry for himself in the form of memorized KGB documents on KGB sources in NATO.[90] As there is much debate—among people who debate such things—about Golitsyn's importance, it is notable that the KGB itself took Golitsyn's defection very seriously.[91]

Most of the accounts of Golitsyn emphasize his peculiar psychology, his sense of his own supreme importance (at first he insisted that he would speak only to the president), his paranoia. Unusual psychological manifestations are not uncommon with defectors and many defectors were, like Golitsyn, heavy drinkers. Of course, it sometimes seems as if in those years all intelligence professionals, from Dulles on down, were heavy drinkers. And what does it mean to say that a counterintelligence professional is paranoid? Seeing enemies everywhere is a professional duty. It could be a rational approach to an uncommon form of everyday life, or it could be a certain form of natural selection. If you are trying to find people to work in a profession where identifying hidden enemies is the point, those psychologically prone to suspicion are a likely class from which to draw. Hence, Angleton, it is said, hence Golitsyn. In any case, Golitsyn was difficult. And important.

Golitsyn worked with Western counterintelligence for more than a decade, causing havoc according to one interpretation, saving the West from the massive Soviet campaign planned at Lovestone's "secret gathering in Moscow of eighty-one Communist parties," according to another: according to Angleton—and himself. He claimed to be unique among defectors in that he contributed not only the usual lists of agents and order of battle information about the KGB, but a new system, a "methodology" for interpreting Communist intelligence. The occasional references to Golitsyn's methodology in the books that mention him are mostly derisive. This is a mistake. Golitsyn, whatever his degree of sanity, was an educated and serious intelligence professional.

He had spent his career in the KGB reviewing files and had a good memory, but it was not photographic. As time passed after his defection, Golitsyn relied on reviewing CIA (and MI5) files to trigger memories of what he had read in Moscow. This sort of thing is probably a reasonable, if poor, substitute for total recall. It is, for example, standard in police interrogations: witnesses being shown, say, sheaves of photographs to jog their memories. However, as the KGB files faded from Golitsyn's memory, his reactions became less reliable, "theory" would substitute for memory, and confusion—or delusion—became the mother of denunciation. His accusations against the Rothschilds were a case in point: certain spies were Jews, the Rothschilds were Jews. . . .

Golitsyn's other, more interesting, "methodology" was a mode of interpretation with fairly clear rules, which Golitsyn detailed in the book published under his name in the 1980s, *New Lies for Old*. A careful reading of the book is surprisingly rewarding. It is, for one thing, rather well written, in an expository prose of the sort taught in Jesuit or English public schools: lists of propositions, arguments logically and fully laid out following from those propositions, an air of reason or at least of rationality. It is not the prose of a fanatic. Of course, there is no particular reason to believe that it is the prose of Golitsyn himself. It might just as well be the house style of MI5. Or, as some say, the style might point to Angleton.[92] Be that as it may, it does cast some light on the perspective Golitsyn brought to the CIA.

Much of *New Lies for Old* is taken up with an exposition of an argument that the evidence for post-Stalinist disturbances within the Communist world—Khruschev's secret speech and all that followed from it—had been wrongly interpreted by Western analysts. Instead, according to Golitsyn, those disturbances should all be seen as part of a "weakness and evolution" pattern of deception such as that decided upon at the secret gathering in Moscow of Communist parties in December 1960. Some of Golitsyn's detailed claims are persuasive, some are not; some are presented in such a way as to appear at first to be stronger than a closer reading indicates. The most notorious, the claim that the Sino-Soviet split was "disinformation," turns out to be merely a claim that the split occurred later than usually assumed.[93] In general, Golitsyn argued that the Western view of Soviet Bloc events at the height of the Cold War was based on a projection (misinformation) emanating from Moscow itself, an effort to present—through press reports, diplomatic cocktail conversations, controlled defectors—a view of the Soviet Bloc as divided, weak, reasonable, peace-loving, etc.

Efforts of this sort do from time to time occur. An early Soviet parallel was the "Trust," the supposed counterrevolutionary organization invented by the KGB's predecessor, which had been carefully studied by James Angleton. The supreme achievement in this regard—that of projected interpretation, as it were—was not, as it happens, a Soviet campaign, but the invention by the Western Powers of FUSAG, the notional World War II Allied invasion force created by Allied intelligence out of thin air, coded messages from double agents, the pearl-handled revolvers of General Patton continually visible in Whitehall. Twenty divisions were summoned from the empyrean in this way to protect Eisenhower's left flank, pinning down an equal number of very real German divisions awaiting the arrival of those sprits of the air at the Pas de Calais: a triumph that in Eisenhower's view determined the course of the war in the West.

Golitsyn's theories, and his reflections on various stories he had heard while working in Soviet intelligence, underlay his sensational claim that the Western services and governments had been penetrated by the KGB. He had heard in various Moscow corridors that there were long-term Soviet agents in the various Western intelligence services; he thought, or at least claimed, that the lack of success of Western efforts in the Cold War, from, say, 1960, was attributable to the penetration of Western secret intelligence services and he believed that the deception operation he posited required for their success such penetrations, as FUSAG had depended on British intelligence's control of German agents.[94] Hence, Golitsyn believed that there were agents in place, moles, as they are called, in the highest regions of Western intelligence. When Golitsyn first arrived in the West he said that there was a KGB agent at one of the Agency's European stations; that the French secret intelligence system (as well as De Gaulle's cabinet) had been penetrated; that a Canadian ambassador had been blackmailed into cooperation with the KGB; that there was a "ring of five" agents in England; and so forth.[95] All of these allegations were later confirmed by the Western intelligence services concerned.

This confirmation is more impressive, and more believable, today than it was ten years ago. We now know much more about the scale of Soviet-era intelligence operations than we did when writers like David Wise and Tom Mangold were examining Angleton's mole hunt. For example, we now have a KGB report to Khrushchev recording that in 1960 alone, "375 foreign agents were recruited, and 32 officers of the State Security were transferred abroad and legalized."[96] And, as the proof of the pudding, as it were, there is the plan presented to the Central Committee by KGB chairman Alexander Shelepin in March 1961, in which the KGB proposed "to carry out disinformation measures on the information that American intelligence obtains about the Soviet Union; to pass along the channels of American intelligence disinformation on economic, defense, and scientific-technical issues; to disinform the USA intelligence regarding real intentions of Soviet intelligence services, achieving thereby the dispersion of forces and means of the enemy's intelligence services."[97] This is pretty much the plan reported by Golitsyn to his CIA interrogators and described in *New Lies for Old*.

But the mere report of a coordinated Soviet misinformation effort was not a sufficient basis for Golitsyn's extraordinary effect on the Western intelligence services. It was not what was going on in Moscow that was their primary concern: what worried them was what might be going on in their own agencies. According to David Wise, "The real danger would be a mole high enough up in the Clandestine Services to have access to a wide array of CIA operations and plans,"[98] as had Philby, as had been Angleton's nightmare for a decade by the time Golitsyn appeared in Washington, as would in fact be the case some years later when the counterintelligence officer on the Soviet desk was Aldrich Ames.

Golitsyn was at first interrogated by the Soviet division of the CIA, as was standard practice, but Golitsyn was difficult, suspicious of his interrogators—thinking them to be Soviet spies if they could speak Russian, naive if they could not—and in October 1962 responsibility for Golitsyn was taken over by the CIA's Counterintelligence Staff. Angleton had long since become preoccupied with Golitsyn, telling the Church Committee staff that "for a year or so" he had worked on the case "full time," seven days a week.[99] The elegance of Golitsyn's intellectual constructs appealed to Angleton; their text-centered method of interpretation was familiar. He had, after all, once been to school with teachers who had worked on a similar basis. During his interrogations, Golitsyn "said he had seen some material at KGB headquarters that could only have come from a very sensitive area of the agency. From someplace high inside the CIA. The implication was plain, and frightening. If Golitsin was right, the KGB had an agent inside the CIA. Pressed for a name, a description, a clue—anything—Golitsin could only provide tantalizing fragments . . . The mole, he told his CIA interrogators, was someone of Slavic background whose name might have ended in '-sky.' He had been stationed in Germany. His KGB code name was Sasha . . . And there was something else, Golitsin said. The mole's true last name began with the letter K."[100]

The immediate suspect was the CIA representative to the State Department's new crisis operations center, a technical expert named Peter Karlow. The identification with Golitsyn's Sasha seemed obvious: "Karlow had run [a CIA] laboratory in Hochst. Sasha had a Slavic background, and a name that might have ended in '-sky.' When the CIA's investigators pulled out Karlow's file, they discovered that his name at birth was Klibansky, and that his father at times had claimed to have been born in Russia . . . By January 15, 1962, wiretaps had been secretly installed at Karlow's home . . . He was, the CIA files made clear, the 'principal suspect.'"[101] The FBI was called in, Karlow's telephones were tapped, he was followed, questioned, harassed, but never told what it was of which he was suspected. The irony of the initial "K" was sufficiently labored.

The investigation of Karlow led to a characteristic conflict between the Bureau and the Agency. The FBI wanted evidence that would lead to a conviction in court. The CIA wanted information. "One year of obvious surveillance, capped by a 'hell week' of interrogation, was not CIA's way of doing things. Angletonian CI would have preferred to see Karlow transferred to an out-of-the-way station where CIA could quietly wait for him to make contact with the Soviets. Perhaps, after a time, CIA would obtain data exonerating him; or, if damning evidence was obtained, Karlow might be asked to become a double agent. But because the FBI had made Karlow aware of the suspicions against him and forced him out, none of that was possible."[102]

Karlow, somewhat pathetically, eventually turned to James Angleton himself for help. Around February 1963 he went to see the counterintelligence chief. "Angleton, chain-smoking as usual, sitting stooped over his desk, had a warning for Karlow. He spoke deliberately. 'This is a very uncertain and highly dangerous situation,' he said. 'There is more that goes on here than I can possibly explain to you. It has to do with a Russian defector.' Angleton leaned forward and added: 'Please don't discuss this with anyone,'"[103] enlisting the fly to assist in the spider's work. On April 3, Karlow decided to appeal to Richard Helms. Helms reported to the CIA's deputy director, General Marshall S. Carter, that Karlow "felt a web had been woven around him based on circumstantial evidence and that he was finding it extremely difficult to untangle the web and come to grips with the exact nature of his alleged derelictions."[104] Matters were not clearer to the CIA than they were to Karlow, but since Karlow had been investigated and not *proven* to be innocent, General Carter decided that "he should be authorized to resign," which he did on July 5, 1963. More than a decade later, after Angleton himself had been forced out of the CIA, Karlow had a series of meetings with Angleton, seeking an explanation for the destruction of his career. Angleton finally said, "There was literally a panic when Golitsin said there was a mole. We were under so much pressure after Burgess and Maclean."[105] ("This is Kim's work.") Finally, in 1989, nearly a quarter of a century after his career in the CIA had been destroyed (he went on, it should be said, to a very successful second career in the private sector), Karlow was vindicated under the "Mole Relief Act" and given half a million dollars—and a medal—in compensation.[106]

Meanwhile, "As the investigation grew . . . to include literally dozens of suspects, the demands on Angleton's staff, and that of the Office of Security, were overwhelming. By 1964 Angleton realized he needed more manpower just to handle the 'Golitsin serials' . . . Angleton brought in Newton S. Miler, who was then the CIA station chief in Ethiopia, to help run the mole hunt . . . Angleton . . . assigned him the title of deputy chief of 'special investigations,' the euphemism that Angleton gave to the mole hunt. The work was carried out by a unit of the Counterintelligence Staff known as the Special Intelligence Group, or SIG."[107]

Karlow had actually been cleared by the FBI of the mole charge in 1963. (No one bothered to tell him. It was a secret.) This left Angleton in a quandary. If Golitsyn was to believed, and if Karlow was not "Sasha," then who was? The CIA once more turned to the FBI for help. "Angleton asked for telephone taps on suspected Soviet agents, but Hoover would not allow it, as he thought the CIA did not have enough evidence to justify a warrant."[108] Hoover was occasionally punctilious about such matters, especially when they involved the rival Agency. Angleton, with Miler's—and Golitsyn's—help, continued the hunt. In Miler's "view, every possible suspect had to be scrutinized, for a mole could be anyone, anywhere."[109] Eventually Miler and his staff investigated more than one hundred twenty CIA officers.

From time to time Golitsyn's "methodology" would yield new suspects. For example, a year after Peter Karlow's resignation, Golitsyn identified a new "mole," Richard Kovich, third national officer in the Soviet Bloc division, a recruiter of third-nation citizens for work in Moscow on behalf—knowingly or not—of the Agency. As he had recruited Ingeborg Lygren, a secretary in Norwegian military intelligence, this made Lygren, in her turn, a suspect. On Golitsyn's "evidence" the Norwegian police arrested Lygren in September 1965.

There were the usual interrogations and humiliations, but after a few months the case was dropped. In July 1968 the Norwegian parliament, not as generous as the American Congress, gave Lygren $4,200 in compensation.[110]

On the other hand, it turned out that Golitsyn had been right about there being a spy named Sasha. Just after the Second World War the CIA's Berlin office had looked for people who would work for it in East Germany. One member of this Berlin CIA group was Igor Grigorievich Orlov. "The name Orlov had used since Vlassov Army days was Aleksandr Kopatsky (in German transliteration, Kopazky), and he was known to friends and his CIA case officers as Sasha, the diminutive for Aleksandr."[111] According to David Murphy, co-author of one of the recent Cold War histories based on Soviet archives, "Orlov was the man described by Golitsyn."[112] Murphy had a personal interest, in that, in the late 1960s when he was head of the Soviet division, he was accused of being a possible Soviet agent by Peter Kapusta (that "K" again), one of his own officers. In 1968, Murphy was replaced as head of the Soviet division and sent to Paris as chief of station.[113] Assignment to Paris is not exactly a punishment in the Soviet tradition for suspected spies, but, in spite of the obvious compensations, it was a demotion for Murphy, who remained bitter about the incident.[114]

David Wise, who first wrote about the Great Molehunt, called the effort "the secret search for traitors that shattered the CIA," blaming Angleton for the damage to the Agency. But even Wise admits that "Angleton may have been the point man, but it was Helms who had presided over the period of the mole hunt, first as the deputy director for plans from 1962 and then as the Director of Central Intelligence from 1966 to 1973. Little of importance could have occurred during that period without his personal approval."[115] Angleton's deputy, Miler, who was actually in charge of the molehunts, drew their bureaucratic map: "The Counterintelligence Staff . . . did not do the investigations. We did the research. OS [the Office of Security] did the investigation if it became a good case. OS, the DCI, chief of CI, and the DDP [deputy director for plans] would know about it. In almost every instance of a referral to the FBI the DCI gave the approval."[116] A few years later the crisis within the CIA reached its climax when, out of despair of ever positively identifying "the" mole, the entire Soviet division of the CIA "was cleaned out. Literally hundreds of people, all of the Russian-speaking officers, were transferred." Some fifty of these were career officers, of the approximately three hundred in the division.[117] It was this experience, it is said, that led so many in the Agency to ignore the evidence of spying by Aldrich Ames. They could not bear the thought of another purge.

Nonetheless, some of Golitsyn's leads had spectacular results abroad. During this period, the FBI and the CIA collaborated on a "black-bag job"—a burglary—of the French Embassy in Washington, D.C. "This operation had the cooperation of Philippe de Vosjoli, the French Western Hemisphere intelligence chief, who remained inside the embassy after midnight and let the team in. The objective was apparently to see what material French intelligence agents in the U.S. might be passing to their superiors in Paris, some of whom Golitsyn and Vosjoli suspected were working for Moscow."[118] Philippe de Vosjoli said that Angleton had been showing French intelligence officials reports that came from their own secret files. "They had been supplied, Angleton explained, by a recent defector from the KGB [Golitsyn]. This leak meant, as de Vosjoli instantly realized, that the KGB had one or more sources in French intelligence. The defector then provided data suggesting that the penetration not only was widespread but involved de Vosjoli's superiors in SDECE. Then, in November 1963, de Vosjoli was tipped off by a colleague in Paris that he himself would be assassinated on his return to France. De Vosjoli resigned from SDECE, went into hiding, and, with Angleton's help, relocated himself in the United States."[119]

Angleton's suspicions concerning the security of the French intelligence apparatus, and the clumsy way that he dealt with them, did nothing to benefit relations between France and the United States at the time. "'The whole French thing was a mess,' [a] former CIA man said. 'Some of the leads pointed to personalities in S-deck [SDECE] who'd been involved in operations with us and about whom there had been some suspicion, but no proof. Jim [Angleton] weighed in against these people, and it caused a lot of friction.'"[120]

From Angleton's vantage point, the French services did not seem to be moving aggressively to weed out Golitsyn's supposed nest of spies. Others in the American government shared his concern. "On one occasion in 1963 Kennedy shared what had been for him a delicious moment—an opportunity to goad his European nemesis, Charles de Gaulle, in the name of protocol."

> "Joe [Alsop], I have the best joke to tell you," said the president. It seemed that a Soviet defector [Golitsyn], then in the hands of the CIA at a New York safe house, had revealed that French military intelligence services were riddled with Soviet spies . . . "Our people believe him," said the president with a laugh, "and so I had the pleasure of sending our friend de Gaulle a handwritten letter by courier telling him that he had a problem." . . . Kennedy had added that de Gaulle's office had called immediately to request an opportunity to debrief the defector . . . "They're sending a top general over next week," he said . . . "Who is it?" asked Joe . . . "You've probably never heard of him—fellow named Jean Louis de Rougemont." . . . "Oh," exclaimed Susan Mary [Alsop], "he and his wife Louise are two of my closest friends." . . . They all laughed at the small

world they inhabited. But for Kennedy the biggest laugh came from the jab he had administered to de Gaulle while fulfilling diplomatic courtesies.[121]

A small world indeed, given that Susan Mary Alsop had been the mistress of Duff Cooper when he was British ambassador to France—and similar complications. Despite the attentions of General de Rougemont, "the CIA suspected the French were more interested in covering up the potential political scandal than in finding and punishing the moles."[122] Perhaps they were right. In any case, no one in the French intelligence services was convicted of spying.

Meanwhile, matters in the wider molehunt accelerated. "By 1968, American intelligence was, as Helms described the situation, 'a house divided against itself.' The Soviet Division was paralyzed by charges and accusations over the Nosenko case. The FBI had broken off its liaison with the CIA. The British security service was in disarray, with its own Director [Roger Hollis] under suspicion as a mole. German, French, and Dutch intelligence services were rated 'insecure' by the CIA. Pressure was building in the CIA to dissolve Angleton's staff. J. Edgar Hoover characterized Golitsyn as 'paranoid' and a possible 'provocateur.'"[123] Hoover, who was otherwise close to Angleton (who was, after all, one of his secret informants), had a methodological dispute with him in regard to Nosenko and Golitsyn. "There seem to have been two pillars to Hoover's position. First was the fact that Golitsyn kept asking to see FBI files. If Golitsyn redefected, or was in contact with Soviet agents, or even if he was genuine but was kidnapped by the Russians, FBI secrets could be lost; therefore, the intensity of his interest in Bureau files evoked great distrust. Second, Golitsyn's disinformation thesis had led to a situation where, as Angleton's deputy, Miler, put it, 'You had a bunch of CIA guys throwing darts at the FBI's sources' . . . The . . . interagency dispute over Nosenko's bona fides crystallized twenty years of difference over CIA philosophy. Angleton's pattern-recognition method, which found in the study of poetry a relevance to the detecting of strategic deceptions, was set squarely against Hoover's criminal-evidentiary approach."[124] It was not to be the end of such disputes.[125] A recent commentator, reviewing the entire matter, concludes, "I remain firmly opposed to the view that the master plot was an irresponsible, paranoid fantasy. Given the information available at the time . . . it would have been irresponsible not to have seriously considered this possibility. The mistake was not in pursuing the master plot theory, but in getting so locked into a position that one was unable to question basic assumptions or to note the gradual accumulation of contrary evidence."[126]

Evidence of Soviet Bloc penetration of Western intelligence services continued to mount. In December 1967, the Czech deputy minister of defense Bittman defected to the United States. After the Soviet invasion of Czechoslovakia in August 1968, two other high-ranking Czech military men followed. "As a direct result Rear-Admiral Herman Luedke, SHAPE's logistics chief, shot himself. On the following day, 9 October, Host Wendland, the Deputy Chief of the West German intelligence service, shot himself in his office at his headquarters at Pullach in West Germany. On 14 October Hans Schenke of the Ministry of Economics hanged himself. He was followed, four days later, by Colonel Johann Grimm of the West German Ministry of Defence. Three days later Gerhard Boehm, also of the Ministry of Defence, was found drowned in the Rhine near Cologne . . . All these individuals had been identified as moles by Bittman."[127]

And Nosenko, like some Cold War Rip Van Winkle, who had all this time sat in his very own, and very illegal, CIA prison, was released, "rehabilitated," and in the spring of 1969 became a paid CIA consultant by way of amends.[128] After so long, after so much suffering for Nosenko himself and so much disruption in the Agency, one would have thought that would be the end of the matter. It was not. Even Angleton's retirement did not stop the debate about Nosenko's bona fides, a debate which continued into the 1980s.[129]

According to the teachings of Angleton, "discovering the disinformation which the enemy was attempting to plant was in many ways as important as any real information which might be divulged."[130] The Nosenko case was important within the Agency and within the FBI not only for the light it might have shed on the Kennedy assassination, but also because it became a central factor in interpreting all counterespionage cases under way.[131] For example, as the CIA's Soviet Russia Division believed that Nosenko had deliberately lied about his rank and lied about his reasons for defecting, and as his word on those matters had been supported by "Fedora," the FBI's double agent in New York, Fedora came under suspicion.[132] Fedora, who had contacted the FBI in March 1962, providing information about Soviet espionage operations, was of the highest importance in the continuing quarrel between CIA and FBI counterintelligence.[133] He and his colleague "Top Hat" (cute names are an occupational hazard of the spy business), were the FBI's prize informants. According to Edward Epstein's account of this affair, "If Nosenko was now ruled a fraud, then Fedora would seem to be part of the same Soviet deception. And if Fedora were really under Soviet control, it would bring down the entire FBI counterespionage structure."[134]

Angleton thought that Fedora, Top Hat, and Nosenko were all part of a KGB plot.[135] The end of the Fedora story seemed to support Angleton's view. Fedora returned to the Soviet Union in 1977 and died, it was said, of natural causes about 1983. It was fairly unusual for a genuine Soviet defector to return to the Soviet Union and die of natural causes, particularly a defector as famous in the small world of counterintelligence as was Fedora. If "Nigel West" is to be trusted on this point, Fedora was Viktor M. Lessiovski, the personal assistant to the secretary-general of the United Nations, U Thant. In 1980 the FBI decided that he indeed had been a KGB *agent provocateur*.[136] If Fedora was not genuine, as now appears to be the case, the syllogism would lead us to side with Angleton, that as Fedora had supported Nosenko's bona fides, Nosenko was not genuine . . . and Golitsyn was.

One of the more exotic but not necessarily unreal offshoots of the molehunt involved the connected mysteries of the death of Hugh Gaitskell and, a decade later, the sudden resignation of Prime Minister Wilson. Gaitskell, the leader of the right wing of the British Labor Party, was one of the British leaders closest to the CIA.[137] He died suddenly at the beginning of 1963, apparently from lupus. But "the post-mortem on Gaitskell carried out on January 18, 1963 had shown that he was not in fact suffering from Lupus. No Lupus cells had been found in his body: 'It was a condition like Lupus. What he actually had was what we call an immune complex deficiency. His immune system broke down as the cells degenerated.'"[138] Gaitskell's doctor was puzzled by this and for reasons best known to himself he contacted MI5. According to Peter Wright,

> Arthur Martin, as head of Russian Counterespionage, went to see him. The doctor explained that he was disturbed by the manner of Gaitskell's death. He said that Gaitskell had died of a disease called lupus disseminata, which attacks the body's organs. He said that it was rare in temperate climates and that there was no evidence that Gaitskell had been anywhere recently where he could have contracted the disease . . . We did not know where to go next because . . . it wasn't known how the disease was contracted. I consulted Jim Angleton about the problem. He said he would get a search made of Russian scientific papers to see whether there was any hint of what the Russians knew about this disease. A month or two later he sent us a paper about lupus which he had had translated from a Russian scientific journal. The paper was several years old and Angleton reported that there were no other papers in the Russian literature that they could find.[139]

Perhaps remembering how American physicists ceased to publish their research findings concerning atomic energy as they embarked on the Manhattan Project, Angleton and his colleagues took the *absence* of Soviet publications on lupus as pointing to an interest in the disease on their part. Of course, an extensive Soviet lupus literature would have led to the same conclusion.

Harold Wilson became leader of the Labor Party in February 1963. Wilson had been involved in Russian–U.K. trade matters in the immediate postwar period, traveling to Moscow on occasion, thus placing himself on the secret intelligence world's "watchlists." When he became prime minister in 1964, "Angleton made a special flight to London to see his friends in MI5. He told them that he had some very secret information from a source he could not name. This source alleged, according to Angleton, that Wilson was a Soviet agent."[140] It is said that these seeds bore fruit ten years later, when "Wilson was . . . reelected to a second term as Prime Minister early in 1974. It was then, according to Wright, that unnamed colleagues in MI5 tried to enlist him in a plot to leak information from the files of the security service to the press in order to oust Wilson from office . . . After only eighteen months in office during his second term, Wilson suddenly resigned in March 1976."[141] David Leigh has argued that this resignation was the consequence of what he has called the "Wilson Plot" to overthrow the British government. Perhaps. Or perhaps Wilson was tired.

NATO was another field for molehunting in the early 1960s. Golitsyn said that the KGB had a spy high in NATO. Georges Paques, deputy head of NATO's press office, was arrested in August 1963 and convicted of treason. And then there was Canada. First, Hugh Hambleton, a Canadian economist, who worked for NATO from 1956 to 1961, was found to have worked also with the KGB. He was arrested in London in 1982 and sentenced to ten years in prison. Then there were other, more serious, Canadian alarms. According to David Wise, the bidding went something like this: During the 1960s some efforts by the Royal Canadian Mounted Police against the Soviet Union failed. In one of these, Angleton's opposite number at the RCMP, Leslie James Bennett, the head of counterintelligence, thought that a Soviet intelligence agent normally stationed in Canada, while traveling in South America, had met with a West German secret intelligence official stationed in Washington. Bennett reported these suspicions to the CIA. The CIA concluded that Bennett was working with the KGB to frame the West German. Angleton, therefore, asked the RCMP to investigate Bennett. "The RCMP finally confronted Bennett in 1972, subjecting him to a harsh interrogation that proved nothing. Although Bennett passed a polygraph test and maintained under oath that he was never a Soviet agent, he was forced out after eighteen years and moved to Australia."[142]

And so forth, and so on, for years: the business of counterespionage.

In the midst of these matters of grand strategy and incipient international catastrophe occurred what seemed to be, in contrast, a simple domestic tragedy. In October 1964, Mary Meyer, estranged wife of Cord Meyer, sister-in-law of Ben Bradlee of the *Washington Post*, was murdered while walking near her Georgetown home. Mary Meyer (née Pinchot, a prominent family active in the Republican Party) was an artist and, with Cord Meyer, part of that social set of postwar Washington where the artists, poets, and journalists drank with the congressional staffers and their younger bosses and the more cultivated officials of the Central Intelligence Agency. Bradlee, for example, said that he first met the Angletons at one of Mary Meyer's dinner parties.[143] According to her biographer,

> Rather than make small talk with diplomats at Polly Wisner's, the younger families—the Meyers, Janneys, Truitts, Pittmans, Lanahans, and Angletons—spent a great deal of leisure time together. There were evening get-togethers, and sometimes the families took weekend camping trips to nearby beaches or mountains when the husbands could get away. They went to the Delaware shore and the Blue Ridge Mountains with their children. On Saturday mornings in the fall, the adults got together and played touch football in a park north of Georgetown while their children biked around the sidelines, then all retired to someone's house for lunch and drinks . . . Jim Angleton and Cord and the boys fished together at Milford and in the Washington area . . . Cord often accompanied Angleton to his retreat in northern Wisconsin. Angleton made his own dry flies and raised trout fishing to a pursuit as complex as the hunt for Communists.[144]

Fishing.

In the late 1950s "Jim Angleton came to play a greater role in the Meyer family affairs. He took it upon himself to be a second father to the boys, taking them fishing and checking in on them periodically. Eventually he was overseeing their trusts and intervening for them at their colleges."[145] His evident affection was returned. "Mary's sons and nephews idolized Angleton. 'He had more depth than any man I'd ever met,' said one of Tony Bradlee's children. 'He had extraordinary sensitivity and an interest in people.' He was so nurturing of his friends that one of his nicknames was 'Mother.' Angleton was a hugely entertaining friend who saw life through the lens of classical literature. Mundane events—a family poker game or the way a dinner was cooked—often drew a cryptic scholarly allusion. Those who didn't know their Homer had to guess at his meaning. The spymaster played the piano at family gatherings at his suburban house and sometimes cooked barley stew with marrow bones for the Meyers."[146]

Painter Kenneth Noland, one of Mary Meyer's lovers, "vaguely remember[ed] seeing one of Mary's paintings at Cicely Angleton's."[147] Which of course means that Noland, too, was a friend of the Angletons: poets and painters, scholars and spies. It was not a simple world; it was a world in which high politics and espionage were inseparable from the life of barley stews, fishing, college tuition, who gets published, whose paintings are shown. In this world, "Angleton made it his business to stay on top of the private affairs of the denizens of Georgetown, men and women with complicated lives so intimately connected to the heart of the national government that they seemed obvious targets for any enterprising Communist looking to do blackmail or, worse, recruit a traitor . . . Angleton would boast that he had . . . bugged Mary Meyer's telephone and bedroom."[148] As he had Joan Braden's.

Mary Meyer's telephone conversations, and the bedrooms she used, were of particular interest—indeed, of national security interest—during the Kennedy administration. "Cord was aware as early as October 1961 of [President] Kennedy's interest in his ex-wife. Jim Angleton was paying keen attention to the young president's personal life and he had obliquely warned his old friend, although it doesn't appear he told Cord all he knew at the time . . . Cord wrote [in his diary] that Angleton had told him Mary 'baffles' Kennedy and that even with money and power, Kennedy 'still yearns for a respect that eludes him from such as myself.'"[149] Kennedy had many lovers, of course, although it seems that Mary Meyer was exceptional in having maintained that status for most of his presidency. Meyer, with her cashmere twinsets and pearls, came from the Protestant ascendancy that had despised the Kennedys, with their rum-running money and Mafia connections. This was reason enough to make the divorcee (and her friends whose names have not yet become part of the public record) attractive to him. The president betrayed his wife with Mary, and Mary with others of her set, and them with others not of their set . . . with, it seems, nearly any woman. "James Angleton, when asked by journalists in the 1980s how Kennedy could have felt strongly about Mary and still carried on affairs with other women, replied, 'There's a difference between sex and love.'"[150] And there is a difference between both and social climbing, or resentment, or revenge.

On October 12, 1964, James and Cicely Angleton went to hear Angleton's Yale roommate Reed Whittemore speak at the Library of Congress on "Ways of Misunderstanding Poetry and Being Dismal." "One of the misunderstandings about poetry was the notion that poetry must be 'pure,' he told his listeners. He compared the sterile concept of pure poetry with the lifeless center of Washington, 'all those monuments, all that turf, all those inscriptions, all those marble pillars and steps and busts—and not a delicatessen or sidewalk café for miles.'"[151] It must have been a pleasant return to old times for the Angletons, to hear Whittemore, to think about the negative aspects of purity.

The next day, not quite a year after Kennedy's assassination, as the molehunt was reaching its peak, Mary Meyer, while walking on the towpath that runs past Georgetown, was murdered. According to Ben Bradlee, "Two telephone calls that night from overseas added new dimensions to Mary's death. The first came from President Kennedy's press secretary, Pierre Salinger, in Paris. He expressed his particular sorrow and condolences, and it was only after that conversation was over that we realized that we hadn't known that Pierre had been a friend of Mary's. The second, from Anne Truitt, an artist/sculptor living in Tokyo, was completely understandable. She had been perhaps Mary's closest friend, and . . . she told us that Mary had asked her to take possession of a private diary 'if anything ever happened to me.'"[152]

There are two accounts concerning what happened next. According to Bradlee, when they heard about her sister's murder, he and his wife Tony went to Mary Meyer's to look for the diary. They arrived to find James Angleton in the house, looking about, and embarrassed to be found there. (Particularly embarrassed to be found inside the locked house.) He explained that "he, too, was looking for Mary's diary." The three of them found nothing and returned home. Later, it occurred to the Bradlees that the diary might be in "Mary's studio, which was directly across a dead-end driveway from the garden behind our house . . . [W]e walked toward the studio, only to run into Jim Angleton again, this time actually in the process of picking the padlock . . . [H]e left almost without a word." This time the Bradlees found the diary. "It was small (about 6″ × 8″)—with fifty to sixty pages, most of them filled with paint swatches, and descriptions of how the colors were created and what they were created for. On a few pages, maybe ten in all, in the same handwriting but different pen, phrases described a love affair, and after reading only a few phrases it was clear that the lover had been the President of the United States, though his name was never mentioned . . . The next day, Tony gave the diary to Angleton, because he promised to destroy it in whatever facilities the Central Intelligence Agency had for the destruction of documents." When, "some years later," Tony Bradlee asked Angleton if had indeed destroyed the diary, he said he had not. She asked him to give it back to her; he did, and she burned it.[153]

Which seemed to be the end of the story—but Bradlee tells us that "Anne Truitt and Cicely Angleton have disputed this version of the discovery and disposition of Mary Meyer's 'diary.' They say they 'told' Jim Angleton 'to take charge of this diary.' They acknowledge Tony Bradlee gave the diary 'and several papers bundled together' to Angleton 'and asked him to burn' them. They say Angleton 'followed this instruction in part by burning the loose papers,' but 'safeguarded' the diary itself. Some years later, they say, Angleton 'honored a request from Tony Bradlee that he deliver the diary to her.'"[154] Bradlee, experienced in the ways of the CIA, later said that he thought it unlikely that all copies of the diary had been destroyed.[155]

We can rewind the tape and hear a fuller version of this scenario from Mary

Meyer's biographer, Nina Burleigh, as she refers to a letter to the editor of the *New York Times Book Review* from Anne Truitt and Cicely Angleton.

> Anne Truitt and Cicely Angleton contend that when word of Mary Meyer's death reached the Truitts in Tokyo, Anne Truitt called and reached *Jim Angleton at the Bradlees' house* on N Street. Anne Truitt claimed Mary had explicitly requested that if anything happened to her while Anne was in Japan, she should instruct James Angleton to take charge of her private diary . . . It is . . . conceivable that Anne Truitt deemed Mary's relationship with Kennedy a matter of national interest and took it upon herself to involve the CIA man . . .
>
> In Cicely Angleton and Ann Truitt's account of the diary search, *a group of Mary's friends, including Tony, the Angletons, "and one other friend of Mary Meyer's,"* together searched for Mary's diary. At some point, according to the two women, Tony Bradlee discovered the diary and "several papers bundled together" in Mary's studio. After she and Ben looked at the diary, Tony gave the bundle and the diary to Angleton and asked him to burn it all . . .
>
> Angleton later [said] that he went through the papers, catalogued them, and offered some letter writers the option of repossessing their letters. Angleton said he had read the diary, that two other people, whom he cryptically identified . . . as "M" [Cord Meyer?] and "F," had read the diary, and that Mary's eldest son, Quentin, was also allowed to read it.[156] (Emphasis added.)

Which account is true? If Bradlee is to be believed, how did Angleton know about the diary? How did he know about the relationship? That Bradlee includes part of Anne Truitt and Cicely Angleton's version in his own account, without giving further evidence against it, interestingly tells against his own story. The preponderance of evidence favors the two women's version: the Angletons were visiting the Bradlees when they heard about the diary and the two couples went together to Mary Meyer's house. That leaves the question of why Bradlee told the story in the way that he did, which makes Angleton seem a rather amateurish villain. Why should Bradlee wish to defame his old friend?

The police found a suitable young Black man with a record of petty crime to accuse of the murder of Mary Meyer, but, to their surprise, he was acquitted by a District of Columbia jury, the Black members of which, according to Burleigh, were tiring of such judicial conveniences.

We are left with the question, Who killed Mary Meyer, and why? Was it a random act of violence? Or were there those who, sophisticated in the technique of murder, wished her secrets hidden beyond the reach of investigations? Those secrets were of at least three kinds: the fact of her affair with the president; information about the CIA she might have picked up from her former husband, Cord Meyer, and friends such as the Angletons; and whatever the late president might have told her. The death of Mary Meyer would not have concealed the first of these—the affair was too widely known. Concerning the second, there were other CIA wives, many as disaffected as Mary Meyer, who were not mysteriously murdered. That leaves two possibilities: her murderer in fact did not know her, but simply came across a solitary middle-class white woman, panicked during an attempted rape or robbery, and killed her, or she was killed because of something only she knew. Hence the importance of the diary, which, of course, has been destroyed. Or so we are told.

In any case, the death of Mary Meyer can be our marker for the end of the early 1960s. When she attended the trial of Mary Meyer's accused murderer in July 1965, Cicely Angleton "was unnerved by the racial tension in the room."[157] The Sixties proper were well under way. During the "long, hot summer" the previous year, President Johnson had been determined to prevent the South's "massive resistance" to desegregation—and, on the other hand, the efforts of the Freedom Riders and their Southern Black allies—from derailing his domestic policy. According to the transcripts of Johnson's White House conversations, the president turned to the very willing director of the FBI for help.

> LBJ: I asked Hoover two weeks ago, after talking to the Attorney General, to fill up Mississippi with FBI men and infiltrate everything [a footnote here reads: "Meaning the Ku Klux Klan and other violent segregationist organizations"] he could, that they haul 'em in by the dozens. . . . I've asked him to put more men after these three kids [Michael Schwerner, Andrew Goodman, and James Chaney].[158] [June 23, 1964; ellipsis in original.]
>
> LBJ (TO HOOVER): How many people can you bring in there? . . . I think you ought to put fifty, a hundred people after this Klan. . . . Their very presence may save us a division of soldiers. . . . You ought to have the best intelligence system—better than you've got on the Communists. I read a dozen of your reports here last night, here till one o'clock, on Communists, and they can't open their mouth without your knowing what they're saying.
>
> HOOVER: Very true.[159] [July 2, 1964; ellipses in original.]

In a July 21, 1964, conversation with Hoover, the president said, "And maybe you can put a quietus on that Muslim X [*sic transit gloria mundi*] and all that stuff. I think the Communists are in charge of it."[160] The following month, the presidential orders to the FBI had extended from the Klan and the Muslims to more powerful opponents. As of August 15, 1964, "Through Walter Jenkins, Johnson has persuaded Hoover to mount an elaborate intelligence operation at Atlantic City that will keep track of the Mississippi Freedom Democratic Party rebels and other political leaders, to ensure that 'there aren't any disruptions at the convention.' William Sullivan of the FBI's Domestic Intelligence Division found the operation particularly concerned with 'reporting on the activities of Bobby Kennedy.'"[161] Johnson was the only American president between Roosevelt and Carter *not* to authorize assassination as an instrument of foreign policy. But his orders to the FBI in the summer of 1964 renewed its authority to suppress political dissent, first on the Right, then, with much more effect, on the Left.

The open literature on Angleton, his public image, is narrowly focused on the Great Molehunt, which is an indication, among other things, of the interests of his former colleagues, the ultimate source of much of that literature. It is, in its way, insiders' history, concerned with the internal history of the Central Intelligence Agency, concerned with continuing bureaucratic battles among the file cabinets and between the covers of books, some scholarly, some not. It is, ultimately, not the history of the winners, but simply that of the survivors. Many of those who were not allies of Angleton in those battles within the Agency were willing to speak to reporters like Tom Mangold, David Wise, and David Martin. Angleton, while he lived, replied through his surrogates, in particular through Edward Epstein and Robin Winks. After Angleton's death his cause in these matters continued to be supported by those who had worked with him on the Counterintelligence Staff and those with whom he worked in the Clandestine Services, William Hood, for one, and, preeminently, Richard Helms, whose relationship with Angleton was as close as bureaucratic relationships can be: Angleton was Helms's colleague for nearly thirty years and, insofar as Helms was usually Angleton's direct supervisor, Angleton's actions were those of Helms as well. If there had been a problem with those actions, after Angleton's death the problem was Helms's.

The Great Molehunt mattered for Helms, as head of the Clandestine Services, in two ways. If Angleton and Golitsyn were right, if there were in fact moles in the Agency, then it was Helms who would be held responsible, as was evident from the British experience. More importantly, penetration at the level that Angleton suspected would have meant that the entire effort of the CIA's clandestine intelligence program over years or even decades had been wasted. There is a central paradox in the dynamic of secret intelligence and counterintelligence in that where the former impinges on a wider world, it is justified entirely in terms of that world. Success for the secret intelligence division of an intelligence service is to know that which others would not have known. Success for the Counterintelligence Staff, on the other hand, is in what others do not know. To be "unwitting" oneself is the greatest failure for a counterintelligence officer; to ensure that others are unwitting the greatest victory. It ensues that, as secret intelligence operations and counterintelligence activities grow closer, in the classic model of the British XX Committee, the importance of any particular secret becomes merely notional. Each secret, on this level, is equivalent to all others, as it is the fact of concealment, the fact that one thing or another *is* secret, that is crucial. The most successful intelligence operation, in these terms, is one that remains unknown.

Thus, Helms could not afford to allow any possibility of guilt to linger about the personnel files of any member of his department.[162] That the process of removing those doubts also removed many valuable career officers, that it destroyed the Soviet Bloc group in the Agency, that it interfered with operations and intelligence collection was a very high price to pay, but, in counterintelligence terms, it was arguably not an excessive price. So much more important, Angleton and Helms believed, that the Soviets knew nothing about the secrets of Langley than that the CIA knew anything about the secrets of the Kremlin. An indication that this judgment was widely held within the Agency, even by those most opposed to Angleton, is that neither Angleton nor Helms was ever seriously considered as a candidate for the role of an American Philby, as had their opposite numbers in Britain been suspected Fifth (or Sixth or Seventh) men. They might have been thought wrong, but they were not thought duplicitous.

It is, say, early in the evening toward the end of 1964 or early in 1965. Lyndon Johnson has won reelection on his own, running on a peace platform. Only a small part of official Washington is thinking about the war in Vietnam. James Angleton sits at his desk in his dimly lit office, the curtains closed. His secretary has taken the stacks of files to their safes and left for the day. He lights another Virginia Slim cigarette. Was Nosenko a double agent? Was David Murphy? Was Hollis? His damaged lungs fill with smoke, then expel it. Who killed Mary Meyer, and why? Who ordered the assassination of President Kennedy? He watches the smoke swirl above the table lamps. What is Kim doing at this moment?

He lights another cigarette, looks up from his desk to the mirror that might have hung on the wall opposite, reflecting other mirrors behind him, stands, and—he was a brave man—walks across the room and through the mirror, into that other world, searching among the reflections in ever more mirrors for his old friend, his old enemy.

Or not. Or he simply leaves the office, drives home in his black Mercedes, and has dinner with his wife, talking, as others at dinner with their families were talking, of the party they were planning for Saturday and, perhaps less like others, of Cathars and painters and poets. And of the war.

# 11

## Illegalities CHAOS

There is a certain wholly admirable America: a world of beautiful landscapes cherished by a serious and decent people. It can be found in poems nearly forgotten now, Yvor Winters's "California Oaks," or some of the lines about her Pennsylvania childhood by H.D. Everyone who knows this country will have their own cherished landscape, their own memories of those gestures of loving kindness that occur everywhere in our exhaustingly complicated society, their own literary touchstones of nostalgia. We can recall Cicely Angleton's mother, for example, doing her best to be helpful to those she was in a position to help in mountain-shadowed 1940s Tucson. It is easy to be supercilious about such efforts—the charities of bankers' wives—but it would be wrong to do so. For we must consider what happens in the absence of such gestures, when we cease to be conscious of individuals and think only of groups; when we cease to be aware of individual objects in the landscape—the marine fog slowly enveloping those ancient oaks—and think only in abstractions, of, for example, the state; when we push the poem aside for the memorandum. It is then that the harmony of reciprocal relations among individuals—cornfields tended as if they were gardens, white sand lanes between hedgerows—becomes the chaos of state power in a landscape of fear.

The "long" 1950s, which might be said to have spanned the twenty years following the Second World War, were just coming to an end in 1965. Although the repression of women that Cicely Angleton felt in the 1940s was still pervasive, the economy and the military still oriented toward the possibility of a Third World War, country club culture still producing and seeing itself in glossy magazines, on television, at Yale and at Ohio State University, there were signs of change. African Americans were pressing against legal and customary discrimination, the immense population bulge of the Baby Boom generation was passing through adolescence, and the Johnson administration seemed more ambitious to improve the lives of poor and working-class Americans than any since that of Franklin Roosevelt. The men in their Brooks Brothers white shirts and dark suits who ran the country from New York and Washington, Detroit, San Francisco, and Los Angeles still believed that America—and much of the rest of the world—was theirs to run. But the gods, who delight in frustrating the ambitions of proud rulers, willed that the troubled affairs of small countries in Southeast Asia would arouse the hubris not only of the outsized Texan but of an entire generation of Imperial Guardians, blinding them to the implications of their actions, leading them and their world to destruction as they struggled to save their Imperium.

Director of Central Intelligence John McCone, who had succeeded Allen Dulles after the Bay of Pigs fiasco, lost the confidence of President Johnson in 1965 because of his opposition to the president's policy of slow escalation in Vietnam. McCone had argued, in an early version of what later would be known as the Powell Doctrine, that if the United States was to intervene, it should do so on a large scale, with a full commitment of ground troops and few or no limits on the bombing of the North. The president's policy, on the other hand, was that the war should be conducted in such a way as to minimize attention from the American public, a policy that precluded any action that would have led to significant American casualties.

McCone was soon replaced by Admiral William F. Raborn, a Navy technocrat. On April 28, 1965, "Johnson took it into his head to invite all the top officers of the CIA to the ceremony" for Raborn's swearing-in, "the Deputy Directors, the head of the Board of National Estimates, a whole raft of people who had only the shadowiest existence in official Washington."

> One of the men in the crowd was James Angleton . . . "Oh, my God!" said Angleton as photographers trooped into the room, "Those people are going to take our picture!" He squeezed himself back into a corner, trying to hide his tall, lanky frame behind a much shorter fellow CIA officer. Then President Johnson entered the room, glanced around, and strode directly to Angleton's corner . . . Angleton's is a face of exquisite refinement, finely chiseled, striking and expressive. His long mouth is so sensitive to inner mood that he can express two emotions at the same time, registering a dourness close to despair at one end, while turning up in sardonic comment at the other. But when President Johnson planted himself directly in front of Angleton, and the cameras all focused in, Angleton's face expressed nothing whatever but pure horror.[1]

According to a passing comment in the Church Committee report, Angleton spent "considerable time in the Far East at the height of the Agency's effort there."[2] It was in Vietnam, as the Sixties reached their midpoint, that Angleton came into conflict once more with William Colby. Colby was then head of the Phoenix Program, which sought to destroy the Communist infrastructure in

South Vietnam. Angleton thought that the South Vietnamese government and intelligence services were heavily penetrated by agents of the North, and Colby denied it.[3] Eventually the conflict became so intense that Colby was not allowed into certain of the CIA's offices in Saigon.[4]

Throughout this period Angleton also continued to be officer-in-charge of the Israeli "account," supporting the Israeli atomic bomb project and watching over other matters that would not be revealed until much later: what amounted to a personal intelligence-gathering service directed by Jay Lovestone, ostensibly of the American Federation of Labor; the HT/LINGUAL project of tampering with the U.S. mails; and, of course, the Great Molehunt. Later in the decade Angleton was to become the CIA representative on both the National Advisory Commission on Civil Disorders and the National Commission on the Causes and Prevention of Violence. (One of his staff, Richard Ober, whom we will be considering at some length, was his alternate on the latter body.)[5] But before civil disorders and such reached a level requiring national commissions—which would be soon after the Raborn photo session, in fact—Angleton was to have another responsibility added to this formidable list: the creation of a capacity within the Central Intelligence Agency first to monitor, then to counter, the gathering antiwar movement that came into being, as McCone had predicted it would, in opposition to the President's Vietnam policy.

By early 1966, when American forces had reached two hundred thousand, support for the U.S. presence in Vietnam had begun to fade among policy and opinion leaders. Walter Lippmann came out against the administration's Vietnam policies in February. In the same month, Senator J. William Fulbright began hearings on the war before his Foreign Relations Committee, and on April 21 gave a speech on the "Arrogance of Power."[6] While opposition to the president's Vietnam policy was building at this rarefied level, it was also gathering momentum among unprecedented numbers of students on college campuses, in the so-called underground press on those campuses and elsewhere, and in certain comparatively mainstream publications. The intervention of the Central Intelligence Agency against the debate about the Vietnam War began with the last of these, not in the street, but on the newsstand. In a way, this was natural enough: the Agency had long been accustomed to thinking of cultural matters as an integral part of its mission, an aspect of what was called psychological warfare. It was under this rubric that James Angleton and his colleagues, notably Cord Meyer, had participated in the formation and implementation of CIA's cultural policy.[7] But that had been abroad and therefore legal.

The California-based liberal Catholic magazine *Ramparts* had become a center of opposition to the Vietnam War. Early in 1966, "information reached the CIA" that Stanley K. Sheinbaum was about to publish an article in *Ramparts* revealing the CIA's activities on college campuses. (Which meant, of course, that the CIA was already monitoring the American press with some degree of intensity.) According to Angus Mackenzie, "Word of Sheinbaum's forthcoming article caused consternation on the seventh floor of CIA headquarters. On April 18, 1966, Director of Central Intelligence William F. Raborn Jr. notified his director of security that he wanted a 'run down' on *Ramparts* magazine on a 'high priority basis.'" [8] Raborn's order was a clear violation of the 1947 National Security Act, under which the Director of Central Intelligence, if he believed an investigation of an American magazine warranted, should have asked the FBI to investigate the matter. But Admiral Raborn, perhaps unfamiliar with the Agency's charter, decided to handle the matter within his own organization. Howard J. Osborn, the CIA Director of Security, was told that "the Director . . . is particularly interested in the authors of the article, namely, Stanley Sheinbaum and Robert Scheer." [9] More generally, Director Raborn was interested in anyone connected with the magazine. Two days later Osborn had put together dossiers on twenty-two or so of the fifty-five writers and editors of *Ramparts*.

It is remarkable in itself that the CIA had files on hand concerning nearly two dozen *Ramparts* writers and editors. Apparently the Agency believed even before Raborn's order that it was authorized to assemble dossiers on Americans not all of whom, presumably, were at that point individually known or suspected of involvement with foreign intelligence services. The investigation was an effort to develop information about *Ramparts* as if it were the target of an Agency foreign covert operation in Rome or Tegucigalpa. The director wanted to know about the lives and connections of its staff and supporters, and whether the magazine was a vehicle for foreign, that is, Soviet, funding and influence.

One of the CIA's first reports about *Ramparts*, which concerned Sheinbaum's co-author, the magazine's managing editor, Robert Scheer, was sent to Walt W. Rostow, special assistant to President Johnson.[10] (Johnson became even more intensely interested in the investigation when the CIA reported that Scheer and another editor of *Ramparts* were planning to run for Congress on antiwar platforms.) Rostow would be the key recipient of CIA reports on *Ramparts* and other domestic security matters until he was replaced by Henry Kissinger as national security advisor. It was unusual that the White House's foreign affairs specialists would be kept informed of an operation of this type, as Berkeley, where *Ramparts* was published, was not literally a foreign capital. With its reports on *Ramparts* and that magazine's staff, the CIA had moved fully into the business of collecting information within the United States on matters that had nothing to do with foreign governments; that is, on what in those comparatively innocent times many Americans would have thought was quintessential constitutionally protected activity.

The Agency's investigation of *Ramparts* was combined, nearly from its inception, with what the KGB called "active measures" intended to damage the magazine. Intervention in press matters was a well-established Agency procedure, much practiced during the preceding twenty years in Europe and the Third World. The lessons learned abroad were now applied in the United States. Edgar Applewhite, who was assigned by Deputy Director for Plans Desmond FitzGerald to discredit the editors of *Ramparts*, later told Evan Thomas that he "'had all sorts of dirty tricks to hurt their circulation and financing. The people running *Ramparts* were vulnerable to blackmail . . . We were not the least inhibited by the fact that the CIA had no internal security role in the United States.' When Applewhite . . . brief[ed] FitzGerald on his dirty tricks . . . the clandestine chief was bemused. 'Eddie,' he said, 'you have a spot of blood on your pinafore.'"[11]

The clandestine chief, according to Thomas, was "bemused" by the illegal activities of his subordinate. Thomas's book is entitled *The Very Best Men*, in the tradition of phrases like "the best and the brightest" and Thomas's own *The Wise Men*. He refers to FitzGerald as "the Cavalier" and comments that "he would perhaps have been happier as a nineteenth-century British gentleman."[12] Perhaps. After all, a nineteenth-century British gentleman would not have had the obligations to the American Constitution and legal system that FitzGerald so "cavalierly" ignored, about which he was "bemused," as it is impossible to be a traitor to a foreign country. On the other hand, FitzGerald and Applewhite were not British gentlemen; they were American officials sworn to uphold the Constitution.

Applewhite found that the financial underpinnings of *Ramparts* were fragile. The CIA's investigation in the late spring of 1966 therefore expanded from developing information about the magazine's staff to "identifying the source of *Ramparts's* money." Although eager, the Agency was not yet mobilized for this type of task. Therefore, "On June 16, 1966, [DCI Raborn] ordered Osborn to 'urge' the FBI to 'investigate these people as a subversive unit.' Osborn forwarded this request to the FBI, expressing the CIA's interest in anything the FBI might develop 'of a derogatory nature.' One CIA officer, who later inspected the CIA file of the *Ramparts* investigation, said that the Agency was trying to find a way of shutting down the magazine that would stand up in court, notwithstanding the constraints of the First Amendment."[13] What they found was that the magazine was financed by contributions from sympathetic individuals, U.S.

citizens, with no involvement of foreign governments. At that point, by statute, the Agency should have closed down its investigation of the finances and staff of the magazine (not to mention the "dirty tricks" campaign). It did not.

It continued on the basis of a February 7, 1966, "agreement concerning 'coordination' between the CIA and the FBI [that] permitted CIA involvement in internal security functions."[14] There were safeguards in the 1966 agreement, mainly to ensure that the FBI did not feel that its prerogatives were being infringed: "Under the agreement, the CIA would 'seek concurrence and coordination of the FBI' before engaging in clandestine activity in the United States and the FBI would 'concur and coordinate if the proposed action does not conflict with any operation, current or planned, including active investigation of the FBI.'"[15] The Agency had over the years violated its charter's prohibition against domestic covert activities in many ways, with its mail-opening program, with the exchange of information and good offices between FBI and CIA counterintelligence staffs (of which the computerized compilation of lists of names was one example), campus and cultural activities. These, like the 1966 agreement, were viewed as matters of mere routine and as routine actions of governmental officials, not singular actions of private individuals, little noted and never referred to the Justice Department for prosecution under a criminal complaint. Continued for a decade or more, such illegal activities were compartmentalized in the bureaucracy of the Agency and the minds of its responsible officials: known and acknowledged to be illegal, but somehow, as long-standing practice, thought permissible.

Sheinbaum's story, published in the June 1966 issue of *Ramparts*, "disclosed that Michigan State University had been secretly used by the CIA to train Saigon police . . . When scholars are forced into a conflict of interest, he wrote, 'where is the source of serious criticism that would help us avoid future Vietnams?'"[16] The Agency knew as well as Sheinbaum that scholars and other intellectuals involved with the execution of governmental policy are not in a very good position to criticize that policy or to wish to do so. Their involvement with the government's business need not be as overt as training foreign secret police and keeping an inventory of their weapons. It could be something as seemingly innocuous as accepting a fellowship apparently funded by a private foundation to study a language or country of "strategic importance," rather than one not pointed to in the same manner. It could be something as innocuous as *not* writing an article unlikely to be published in *Encounter* rather than writing one that *would* be published there, so as to finance a vacation in Europe, or, better yet, enter the lists of those routinely invited to the Congress for Cultural Freedom's posh conferences and be *paid* to vacation in Europe. As Sheinbaum well knew, not to put too fine a point on it, in 1966 the U.S. government was not in the business of seeking to encourage serious criticism. It was in the business of actively suppressing criticism.

On June 20, 1966, Richard Helms, Angleton's contemporary and patron, was sworn in as director of central intelligence in succession to Admiral Raborn, who had not managed to win the trust of the Agency and had soon lost that of the president. The old boys were back in charge. This time there was no embarrassing photo session. Helms, who knew whom he could count on to get things done, immediately took the *Ramparts* operation away from Osborn and gave it to James Angleton. Robert Kiley, "who was the last CIA official in charge of the NSA, said that James Angleton was more aggressive than [Deputy Director for Plans] FitzGerald in looking for a way to stop *Ramparts* from publishing. Angleton believed the [Sheinbaum] article was a 'Soviet plot.'"[17] Angleton's undergraduate career as a literary journalist would make him a natural choice for countering what was seen by the administration as a threat from a magazine. He knew the territory. On the other hand, it had been a long time since he had been an undergraduate. "When [Edgar] Applewhite returned from his mission to dig up dirt on the *Ramparts* editors, 'I [Applewhite] told him [Angleton] that the *Ramparts* hippies had reached a journalistic threshold in describing the incidence and practice of fellatio on the West Coast. He asked, what is fellatio? When I told him he cracked up. The practice was not new to him but that word was. In his weekly staff meeting a few weeks later he regaled his nonplussed division chiefs with an explanation of fellatio.'"[18]

Sheinbaum's article turned out to be merely the opening of a campaign by *Ramparts* against the CIA's involvement in American universities. Returning to their offices after the New Year's holiday at the beginning of 1967, CIA officials "heard rumors from 'N.Y. publishing circles' . . . that *Ramparts* was doing [another CIA] story."[19] (We note that the CIA had contacts in "New York publishing circles" sufficiently kindly disposed to the Agency to keep it informed about the publishing schedule of *Ramparts*.) *Ramparts* was not alone in its interest in the Central Intelligence Agency. The muckraking newspaper columnist Drew Pearson published a column on February 20, 1967, "which said that the CIA paid out $100 million a year to the labor movement. 'No CIA money for labor is spent without Lovestone's approval,' Pearson wrote, 'and few labor attachés are appointed to American embassies abroad without his OK.'"[20] As Lovestone was Angleton's agent, the Pearson column was a direct attack on the Counterintelligence chief, who was, and knew he was, on shaky ground. Seymour Hersh put it clearly: "The CIA was not mandated to collect domestic intelligence; by having agents inside the AFL-CIO it was breaking the law."[21] Pearson was a recurrent irritant, recurrently the object of CIA and FBI attention. But he did not know of the connection between Lovestone and Angleton, and for the moment, nothing more came of Pearson's revelations. The CIA was free to continue its investigation of *Ramparts*.

In an internal memorandum filed March 22, 1967, the CIA reported that

> It has been learned that *Ramparts*, a California based monthly magazine, is planning to publish in its March issue an expose of CIA involvement with the *National Student Association* and with a number of foundations which are either Agency owned organizations or cooperate extensively with the Agency. The *Ramparts* article will also probably mention CIA involvement with a number of other domestic private voluntary organizations, as well as with two or more international organizations in the youth & student field. Although the article will probably contain some false information, it will almost certainly accurately identify a number of ostensibly private foundations as funding channels used by the Agency in covert operations, and name a number of Agency employees who have been involved with clandestine youth and student operations.

The next paragraph of the memorandum was deleted when it was released by the CIA in 1997 (perhaps because it concerned "sources and methods" in relation to such matters as suppressing critical segments of the press). The third and fourth paragraphs substantiated the forthcoming article's information and sought to justify the activity described in it: "CIA has cooperated with and subsidized a number of domestic and international voluntary organizations in the youth and student field since the early 1950's . . . CIA assistance to these pro-Western organizations was given at the request of the responsible officers of the groups involved . . . The subsidies they received from CIA were used only in international activities, and only in cases where assistance was necessary if the organizations were to be able to counter effectively the efforts of the international communist front groups." Paragraph 5 is a damage appraisal: "It is considered likely that the *Ramparts* article will be picked up by respected domestic newspapers, such as the New York *Times* and the Washington *Post*, and that there will be an extended public controversy over CIA involvement with private voluntary organizations and foundations. The CIA will probably be accused of improperly interfering in domestic affairs, and of manipulating and endangering innocent young people. The Administration will probably come under attack for permitting this kind of activity."[22]

The CIA's subsequent damage control efforts involved commissioning stories unfavorable to *Ramparts* and implying foreign influence over the magazine. There was a pro-CIA article in the *Washington Star* by Carl Rowan and a press conference was scheduled with the intention of preempting the *Ramparts* story by having the leaders of the National Student Association "admit to their

CIA relationship and . . . say it had been ended at their insistence."[23] Warren Hinckle, the magazine's editor, learned about the planned press conference in advance. Determined not to be scooped on his own story, he took out full-page advertisements in the *New York Times* and the *Washington Post* with a summary of the article. One of the NSA student leaders told a reporter that the *Ramparts* story was accurate, which caused Hinckle to comment, "It is a rare thing in this business when you say bang and somebody says I'm dead."[24] Members of Congress protested the CIA's involvement with the National Student Association, and by summer the Agency had to sever its connections with the student group. As would happen with the Congress for Cultural Freedom under similar circumstances, the organization changed its name and funding arrangements, but never recovered its former influence.[25] The fact that both the National Student Association and the Congress for Cultural Freedom withered away after their CIA funding ended demonstrated, if demonstration were needed, that they had flourished primarily as instruments of the secret foreign intelligence service of the United States: they were fronts.

The CIA redoubled its secret investigation of *Ramparts* after the NSA article. Angleton's action officer for the investigation was the aforementioned Richard Ober (Harvard, not Yale, 1943).[26] On April 5, 1967, Ober, who by that point had twelve CIA officers working on *Ramparts* at CIA headquarters, reported that his unit had "identified and investigated 127 *Ramparts* writers and researchers, as well as nearly 200 other American civilians with some link to the magazine."[27] The investigation of *Ramparts* was, if anything, a greater violation of the CIA charter than the matters reported by *Ramparts*. If someone at the time had suggested that the CIA was investigating over three hundred Americans merely because of their connections with a magazine, the report would no doubt have been discounted as typical "conspiracy theory" paranoia. On April 7, Ober submitted a forty-nine page report to Angleton (who initialed it on the 14th), including a history of the magazine, its publishers, finances, content, and contributors. Files deposited at the National Security Archive by Angus Mackenzie include an extraordinary number of reports about the *Ramparts* investigation. One series, from August 2, 1967, to May 1969, approximately two hundred seventy pages in all, gives a running account of each issue of *Ramparts*, including changes in the magazine's masthead, a cumulative file of names, and annotated tables of contents. Typical is a memorandum of March 7, 1969: "In the first year under HINCKLE's management [June 1967—], a total of twenty-seven new staff members joined *Ramparts* as replacements and additions. Twelve of this total were associated with Students for a Democratic Society (SDS), and ten of the twenty-seven were associated with groups or individuals characterized as subversive . . . On the current staff of *Ramparts* fourteen members are known to be associated with subversive organizations . . . The foreign travel and contacts of selected *Ramparts* staff members are as follows: [Three listings blanked out]."[28]

In order to complete the *Ramparts* file, Angleton himself wrote a thematic analysis of *Ramparts* articles. "In an attachment to a memo he sent to the FBI, Angleton wrote that the magazine had hardened 'from a New Left organ to an outlet for standard Soviet propaganda.' He based this on the percentage of times certain themes appeared in the magazine's articles—how many times they said the United States was 'sick,' for example; how many times they said the present U.S. government was fascistic; how many times the magazine said the Catholic Church was reactionary and hierarchical; and how many times the publication said the FBI and CIA were 'evil.'"[29]

Angleton, having been trained at Yale in the analytical techniques of the New Criticism, applied those techniques to the analysis of this somewhat unusual text, comparing it with others in the standard manner of literary-influence studies. It is a well-done piece of work, well done, especially, given the years that had elapsed since last Angleton had written a thematic analysis of a piece of prose. It is, perhaps, a matter of opinion whether reiterated statements that the United States was at the time "sick" or "fascistic" and the FBI and CIA "evil" were more characteristic of New Left journalism or Soviet propaganda. In this case, Angleton took the step from establishing parallel vocabularies to the conclusion that, for *Ramparts*, they implied not only influence but control. A move of this sort, submitted in a paper to the Yale English Department, would not have received top marks: the evidence did not warrant the conclusion. On the other hand, it was a clever argument, convincing, in all probability, for those already or already wishing to be convinced. The Central Intelligence Agency's investigation of *Ramparts* widened in the summer of 1967 to include other aspects of the antiwar movement, converging with the far broader, and far older, efforts by the Federal Bureau of Investigation to track and if possible counteract what it took to be domestic threats to national security.

During the Second World War, the Roosevelt administration had illegally dispossessed one hundred ten thousand American citizens of Japanese origin and imprisoned them—adults and children—in detention camps for the duration of that conflict. In 1946, even as the unfortunate and unconstitutionally detained citizens and legal U.S. residents of Japanese origin were released from their wilderness camps, the Federal Bureau of Investigation informed then Attorney General Thomas Clark that it had in secret assembled what it called a "Security Index," a list of "potentially dangerous persons." As a matter of fact, President Truman's Department of Justice had not merely listed these presumably infamous citizens, it had created plans for the detention of such people without regard to the right in common law—and, at that time, statute—of *habeas corpus*, in camps similar to those just vacated by their Japanese-American fellow citizens. The secret lists and the plans for the detention of those listed became public, to general approval, when in 1948 Congressmen Karl Mundt of South Dakota and Richard Nixon, then also a congressman and just beginning his unparalleled governmental career, introduced in the House Un-American Activities Committee a bill calling for the registration of "radicals," such as members of the Communist Party. In effect, they would be asked to register themselves for imprisonment. Senators Kefauver and Humphrey, liberals both and the latter a renowned champion of civil rights, "supported an alternative version . . . which included provisions for '. . . concentration camps to intern potential troublemakers on the occasion of . . . "Internal Security Emergency."' . . . [T]he Internal Security Act of 1950 (also known as the McCarran Act, after its sponsor) . . . passed relatively intact, and was sustained over Truman's veto."[30] (Truman explained that he wished to veto the McCarran Act because it *allowed* habeas corpus.[31]) The question of camps—concentration or internment—is important, as they were integral to the set of procedures that begin with the compilation of lists of suspect persons. The lists are not an end in themselves. The ultimate end, the goal, of the lists is to reserve places in the camps for those listed. In this way the liberties defended from Fascist onslaught in the Second World War were to be guaranteed against a more subtle enemy at home; guaranteed, in Senators Kefauver and Humphrey's opinion, by concentration camps.[32]

When in 1950 the Congress of the United States duly passed, and the president in this case signed, an Emergency Detention Act, that law included, despite the president's objections, procedures allowing that detained persons might appeal first to a review board and then to the courts—before, if necessary, taking up involuntary residence as guests of their careful government. Congress appropriated $775,000 in 1952 to establish six detention camps.[33] Here was an illustration, no doubt, of the superiority of a democracy, at that time, to the totalitarian system against which it was engaged in desperate struggle: the congressional appropriations for the establishment of camps for dissidents and the procedures for the appeal of detention were a matter of public record. In spite of this congressional action, and contrary to law and contrary to the traditions of the Republic, Attorney General J. Howard McGrath authorized the Federal Bureau of Investigation to "proceed with the program as previously outlined," that is, without the impediment of habeas corpus or other cumbersome procedures. McGrath's illegal and unconstitutional instructions were endorsed by two subsequent attorneys general, giving those instructions, in the eyes of some, a certain prestige and legitimacy—apparently on the well-established theory that a single crime committed by a private citizen should as a matter of course be punished, but that a long-continued series of crimes by governmental officials constitutes policy. This particular policy provided the framework for the anti-dissident activities of the police power at all levels of government for the next quarter-century (and then again in the early twenty-first century).

The FBI shared the KGB's inelegant practice of abbreviation through the use of the initial few letters of words composing bureaucratic titles. Thus the Bureau's *co*unter*intel*ligence *pro*gram was designated COINTELPRO; that part of it devoted to the Communist Party, USA, was therefore COINTELPRO-CP, USA. The COINTELPRO-CP, USA program was a great success.[34] By the mid-1950s the Federal Bureau of Investigation had so thoroughly infiltrated the American Communist Party that it was said that the FBI had a majority on the Party's governing committee and could have, if it had so desired, moved the dissolution of the organization.[35] The effective destruction of the American Communist Party during the McCarthy-era persecutions meant that there was room on lists and camp reservation forms for non-Communists.

During the administration of President Eisenhower the number of persons on the Bureau's Security Index to be proscribed in the case of national emergency reached 26,174. This great number was reduced between 1955 and 1958 to a mere 12,870. The Bureau then established a second list (which in 1960 was named the Reserve Index), conveniently including the names of those previously removed from the Security Index and then expanded to include additional "influential" persons deemed *likely*, because of their "subversive associations and ideology," to "aid subversive elements" in the event of a hypothetical emergency. The individuals included on the Reserve Index, equally liable to proscription as those on the Security Index, included "Professors, teachers, and educators; labor union organizers and leaders; writers, lecturers, newsmen and others in the mass media field; lawyers, doctors, and scientists; other potentially influential persons on a local or national level; individuals who could potentially furnish financial or material aid" to dissent. Such definitions offered great scope to an energetic Bureau. Persons so defined and listed would receive "priority consideration" for "action" after the detention of those more dangerous citizens whose names appeared on the Security Index proper. The breadth of the reserve list is illustrated by the inclusion of the names both of author and activist Norman Mailer and a certain professor, unnamed even in this literature of naming, who had praised not COINTELPRO, but the Soviet Union, to his class.[36] Members of Congress, authors, teachers, feminists, woolly-minded liberals, all were to be swept up together and deposited in secure facilities in the western deserts and

Gulf Coast swamps. Nothing like it would have been seen since the departure of the Decembrists from St. Petersburg.

During the administration of President Johnson, Attorney General Ramsey Clark (the well-known liberal, not to be confused with Thomas Clark, President Truman's attorney general), again in violation of the overt traditions of the republic, common law, and the Constitution, revised the 1950 Emergency Detention Act so that any person might be deprived of their freedom who had been a member of a "basic revolutionary organization" during the previous five years, or, failing that, who had been a leader or participant in "a front organization" during the previous three years, or, failing that, who "could be expected," in a national emergency, to engage in "interference with or threat to the survival and effective operation" of the government; all this without regard as to whether they had either through act or speech indicated that these activities were in fact their intentions.[37] (The figure used in this order was apparently borrowed from Queen Victoria, famous for her innovation of rhetorical triplets that did not build, say, from misdemeanor to treason, but diminished from treason to misdemeanor—or innocence. It is an effective figure for the purposes of the FBI: the opening category of the statement coloring the following with a pink tint.) The police power of the state was by this decree extended from the realm of civic action to that of personal intention, a doctrine familiar to the Church but hitherto novel in the history of any republic since the Venetian. The apparatus of lists and detention camps was in place, as was the tradition and practice of using such means, along with wiretaps, illegal entries, informants, and surreptitious opening of the mails, should a new generation of dissidents appear. This was the internal security policy of the Republic of the United States of America during the Cold War, a policy intended to contain the grave threat of a practically nonexistent American Communist Party and of such other activities by American citizens deemed undesirable by the president, his advisors, and some dozens of bureaucrats able to act in the name of the president. On the shelf, as it were, in case of need.

The Communist Party fading in importance toward the end of the 1950s, the civil rights movement attracted the attention of the FBI as a possible substitute threat to internal security and practical justification for the Bureau's staffing, reputation, and funding formulae. In October, 1962, as a kind of milestone marking this realization, the name of Martin Luther King was inscribed in Section A of the FBI Reserve Index, securing his place in the array of those to be moved from that list to the more select Security Index, and then, in the event of a national emergency, onto the roll of those to be housed in the detention camps themselves.[38] The other growth area for the Bureau in those years was its New Left program, in connection with which, in addition to compiling lists for internment, the Bureau attempted to prevent the indiscreet exercise of constitutional rights. According to the U.S. Senate's Church Committee Report, "In the [FBI's] New Left program . . . approximately thirty-nine percent of all actions attempted to keep targets from speaking, teaching, writing, or publishing."[39] So vigilant was the FBI in its efforts to ensure domestic tranquility.

The ever-expanding lists of citizens teaching, writing, and publishing during the 1960s were typed on the Bureau's specially ordered paper—thicker than that used by other governmental agencies—requiring vast supplies of (ordinary) manila file folders, which in their turn filled the gray drawers of filing cabinets, which, in ever proliferating numbers, created a crisis of storage. Eventually the "Justice Department established a unit for storing and evaluating intelligence about civil disorders which was designed to use non-intelligence agencies as regular sources of information, which, in fact, drew on military intelligence as well as the FBI, and which transmitted its computer list of citizens to the CIA and the IRS."[40] (The partially successful attempts to turn the Internal Revenue Service into an adjunct of the government's internal security system is a largely untold story of the time.) "Field offices were instructed that 'proper areas of inquiry' regarding the subjects of 'New Left' investigations were 'public statements, the writings and the leadership activities' which might establish their 'rejection of law and order' and thus their 'potential' threat to security. Such persons would also be placed on the Security Index (for detention in a time of emergency) because of these 'anarchistic tendencies,' even if the Bureau could not prove 'membership in a subversive organization' . . . Quarterly reports were to be prepared, and 'subfiles' opened" under eighteen different headings, including that of "Education ('courses given together with any educational outlines and assigned or suggested reading')."[41]

It is little known that the archives of American higher education in those years were committed to the safekeeping of the Bureau, where, no doubt, they reside to this day, overflowing with such glacier-frozen mammoths of academic pride as "educational outlines and assigned or suggested readings"—and perhaps the readings themselves, which in turn (that being the polysemous nature of the beast) would have suggested yet other readings to be copied onto the FBI's special paper and filed.

Hoover's bureau made a fetish of counting, which allows us to learn that from late 1956 through mid-1971 the FBI "engaged in a total of 2,218 separate COINTELPRO actions, many of them coupled directly with other sorts of systematic illegality such as the deployment of warrantless phone taps (a total of 2,305 admitted) and bugs (697 admitted) against domestic political targets, and receipt of correspondence secretly intercepted by the CIA (57,846 separate instances admitted)."[42] In addition, "During the 1960's . . . the FBI and CIA conducted hundreds of break-ins, many against American citizens and domestic organizations."[43] This large-scale effort replicated the Bureau's success with the Communist and Socialist Workers parties. The Bureau infiltrated Black activist organizations, such as the Black Panther Party, and the groups collectively known as the New Left. Some sympathetic with the New Left think that "it is quite likely that the widely-publicized 'resort to violence' by the New Left of the late 1960s and early '70s was largely a creation of the national police establishment rather than of the radicals themselves. Certainly, of the 862 bombings and attempted bombings which supposedly occurred between January 1969 and April 15, 1970, a decided majority entailed the direct involvement of FBI and local police *provocateurs*. A good case can be made that the same rule pertains to many of the other more spectacular acts of physical confrontation attributed to the New Left in the 'friendly news media.'"[44] In this way, the threat of internal dissent was made real, retroactively justifying the activities of the Federal Bureau of Investigation in investigating that threat.

It was against this background that in the summer of 1967 the CIA, building on its experience with the *Ramparts* investigation, began Operation CHAOS, one of a number of Agency internal security initiatives developed in response to the antiwar movement.[45] Richard Helms had appointed Thomas Karamessines to replace Desmond FitzGerald in Helms's old job as head of the Clandestine Services. Acting on instructions passed down from "the highest authorities," Karamessines then asked James Angleton to set up a Special Operations Group (SOG) within the Counterintelligence Staff to investigate the suspected foreign connections of the antiwar movement. Operation CHAOS had the same official in charge, Richard Ober, and the same reporting lines—through Angleton to the deputy director for plans, now Karamessines, to the DCI, now Helms—as had the investigation of *Ramparts*.[46] Operation CHAOS was a major responsibility and as such an indication of how much Helms trusted Angleton, how close they were, how the actions of one were often the actions of both. These matters of bureaucratic and legal responsibility are important in considering the moral unity of the Cold War, abroad and at home. The Counterintelligence Staff was vast; Angleton oversaw many operations, few of which he himself ran, apart from the Israeli account and the Lovestone network. Nonetheless, he was the responsible officer—responsible to Helms—for all of its work, for Operation CHAOS as he was for HT/LINGUAL, the Agency's mail-opening program, and, of course, the Great Molehunt.

An enormous amount was riding on the CHAOS investigation from the point of view of the Central Intelligence Agency: it was a response to a—possibly illegal—presidential directive. If the Agency could satisfy the White House in this matter, it might regain the entrée and prestige lost at the Bay of Pigs.

The earliest piece of official correspondence that has been released concerning what would become Operation CHAOS is a memorandum dated August 15, 1967, from Karamessines to Angleton. The memorandum, a typical bureaucratic paper following an oral decision session, stated that, based on a discussion with Helms that day, Angleton was to take the following steps:

> a. Designation of the officers in the CI Staff who will be the responsible focal points and coordinators of operational activity in this matter. (Harry Rositzke and Dick Ober appear to be excellent candidates, as you suggested.)
>
> b. The exclusive briefing of specific division chiefs and certain selected officers in each division on the aims and objectives of this intelligence collection program *with definite domestic counterintelligence aspects.*
>
> c. The establishment of some sort of system by Dick Ober (or whatever officer you select) for the orderly coordination of the operations to be conducted, with the responsibility for the actual conduct of the operations vested in the specific [foreign] area divisions . . . [47] [Emphasis added.]

Angleton was to set up the new project in the usual way: appointing a project leader (Ober was apparently already agreed to), alerting the other branches of the Agency, instructing the project leader to set up "some sort of system." (It is interesting that at this stage Karamessines envisioned the Special Operations Group as playing a coordinating, not operational, role—rather as had been the case with the original tasking of the CIA itself. This aspect of his plan was quickly superseded.) Most accounts of Ober's assignment describe it in terms of tracking foreign influence on the antiwar movement. Angus Mackenzie, who studied the matter in considerable depth, describes instead a two-stage process: the extension of the monitoring and harassing of *Ramparts* to the remainder of the antiwar press, then a broadening of that mission to the entire antiwar movement. According to Mackenzie, Ober was "stunned" when he was told that he was to "expand his *Ramparts* investigation to encompass the entire antiwar underground press, numbering some five hundred newspapers." Nearly ten years later he told the Rockefeller Commission, perhaps with the benefit of hindsight, "I can still vividly remember saying to myself at that moment, as I walked back to my office, that I had a bear by the tail. I was convinced then that the project would ultimately leak with explosive results."[48] Others might have been more worried by the constitutional issues involved in the assignment than by its "flap potential," but, of course, such others would not have received the assignment.

Operation CHAOS, then, was first laid out in a discussion among Helms, Karamessines, and Angleton. Angleton selected its chief, Richard Ober, a long-time member of his Counterintelligence Staff. The three principals were aware from the beginning that Operation CHAOS would involve "definite domestic counterintelligence aspects" in violation of the CIA's charter. These bureaucratic details matter, as, on the one hand, Angleton later told the Church Committee investigators that he was not in fact in charge of Operation CHAOS, and, on the other, Ober told the Rockefeller Commission that the operation was not illegal. Ober said, "I wish to hide nothing . . . To my knowledge, neither my office nor I did anything illegal, anything in violation of the CIA Charter, or anything improper. I can remember no instance when my superiors, Mr. Helms, Mr. Karamessines, or Mr. Angleton or any of their successors asked me to do anything which they indicated or I understood to be either illegal or in violation of the Agency's Charter."[49]

Given that statement, it is worth reviewing the relevant section of the Agency's "charter," the National Security Act of 1947, which states that "a central intelligence agency . . . shall insure the production of the foreign intelligence necessary to enable the appropriate officials of the Government to be informed fully in their dealings with other nations, and to enable these officials to formulate national policies and plans which this Government is to pursue in order to avert future armed conflicts and assure the common defense and security of the United States . . . The Agency shall have no police, subpoena, or law enforcement powers or functions, nor shall it have any functions concerning the internal security of the United States."[50]

The historical record makes it clear that the final sentence quoted above had considerable force behind it. The last thing the founders of the Central Intelligence Agency—and in particular President Truman—wanted was for that organization to be concerned with "the internal security of the United States." And yet this is precisely what Helms, Karamessines, and Angleton asked Richard Ober to do. Operation CHAOS was not about "the common defense and security of the United States," nor "the production of foreign intelligence necessary . . . [for] dealings with other nations." It was about the actions of American citizens who were protesting the policies of their government. This was as obvious to Helms, Karamessines, Angleton, and Ober at the time that Operation CHAOS began as it is today. If the leadership of the Central Intelligence Agency knew that the project was outside its charter, and suspected that it could not be kept secret, why did they go forward with it?

Karamessines, Angleton, and Ober did it because Helms wanted them to do it. And Helms? During the Church Committee investigations of the intelligence establishment in the mid-1970s, "Helms testified that he established the program in response to President Johnson's persistent interest in the extent of foreign influence on domestic dissidents. According to Helms, the President would repeatedly ask, 'How are you getting along with your examination?' and 'Have you picked up any more information on this subject?'"[51] The president wanted it done; the CIA tried its best to do it. In a memorandum of September 26, 1967, to his deputy directors for plans, intelligence, and security (the first of whom oversaw both the Counterintelligence Staff and Ober's Special Operations Group) concerned with surveillance of that fall's antiwar demonstrations in Washington, Helms wrote, "In any event, I want to be sure that any information you gentlemen acquire through whatever channels, is promptly passed to appropriate Federal authorities, including the White House, the Secret Service, the FBI, and anyone else who counts."[52] Helms, the ultimate CIA professional, reacted to an illegal presidential directive as the much-ridiculed Admiral Raborn had: "Aye, aye, sir."

When Ober set up shop in a remote section of the catacombs of CIA headquarters, his initial actions continued to follow bureaucratic routine. Operation CHAOS was assigned a "priority" for its anti-antiwar operations equal to that of anti-Soviet and anti-Chinese operations: Moscow, Beijing, Ann Arbor, Berkeley. With this priority went extensive internal secrecy and compartmentalization arrangements. Ober took extraordinary pains to protect—and conceal—the Special Operations Group. Part of this effort was physical: the SOG offices were isolated behind vault doors—part procedural; reports were hand-carried; documents were not logged in and logged out through the normal CIA offices; plain brown covers were used whenever possible. "Ober said his security system was based on a British model. He kept a list of everyone who had been given access to MHCHAOS, and everyone had to sign [a] secrecy contract."[53] Although appointed by Angleton, Ober attempted to give the impression that he did not work for Angleton. In top secret testimony to the Rockefeller Commission, Ober said, "Actually . . . after my project was fully under way, I obtained administrative support from the Counterintelligence staff but was treated by both the chief of the Counterintelligence staff and the Deputy Director for Plans as a special project reporting directly to Mr. Helms. Mr. Angleton . . . I feel can obviously not be held responsible for my activities."[54] Later in his testimony, he qualified this declaration: "I think I oversimplified that as I look back, particularly during the first year or year and a half, things were on a much more restructured normal chain of command form than they developed later . . . In fact, I think I could say that I had four chains of command. Mr. Helms, one went from him to me, one went from him to Mr.

Karamessines, and one from Mr. Angleton to me, and it went, sometimes from Helms to Mr. Karamessines to me, and the other time from Mr. Helms to Mr. Angleton to me."[55] In other words, the Special Operations Group was physically isolated from the remainder of the Counterintelligence Staff and procedurally hidden, but—three out of four times—Ober reported to or through Angleton.[56] Nonetheless, even after both of them had left the Agency, Ober continued to attempt to shield Angleton from responsibility for Operation CHAOS, while at the same time arguing that the project was legitimate. After all, according to Ober, Angleton was misunderstood, even within the Central Intelligence Agency: "I think other people had a personal dislike, a lack of understanding of some of the people on the staff, including Mr. Angleton. He was very remote and basically a myth to most people in the Agency."[57] Apparently, Ober wished to protect Angleton from the further opprobrium that might occur if he were known to have been in control of the SOG operations against American citizens, their press, and their civil organizations.

Once the bureaucratic plumbing for Operation CHAOS was in place, its requirements were promulgated on a "need to know" basis throughout the CIA: "The first instructions to the field were in a 2 November 1967 Book Cable from the Acting DDP Cord Meyer, released by the DCI Mr. Helms and authenticated by Mr. Angleton . . . The Book Cable . . . advises that Headquarters is participating in a high-level interdepartmental survey of international connections of the anti-Vietnam War movement in the U.S. and that the purpose of the study is to establish the nature and extent of illegal and subversive connections that may exist between U.S. organizations or activities involved and Communist, Communist-front, or other anti-American foreign elements involved."[58]

The CIA's stations were required to keep "tabs on radical students and U.S. Negro expatriates as well as travelers passing through certain select areas abroad . . . to find out [the] extent to which Soviets, Chicoms (Chinese Communists) and Cubans are exploiting our domestic problems in terms of espionage and subversion."[59] The field stations sent in their reports about the activities of "radical students and U.S. Negro expatriates as well as travelers passing through certain select areas abroad," undercover agents reported what they saw, both abroad and at home, and other CIA programs and departments and outside agencies supplied reports. CHAOS received information from the Agency's own HT/LINGUAL mail surveillance program and from the National Security Agency's extraordinary SHAMROCK monitoring of international communications.[60]

The various sources providing information to the CIA about Americans became mutually reinforcing. For example, the October 1967 Pentagon demonstrations (reporting on which had concerned Richard Helms) had brought the

CIA into the domestic covert operations business on a large scale. When students at Columbia University occupied several university buildings on April 23, 1968, and subsequent days as a protest against the university's relationships with Harlem, the government, and themselves, the FBI and CIA closely coordinated operations.[61] "[O]ver two dozen CIA agents were assigned to surveillance missions in New York City . . . the CIA conducted telephone wiretaps and break-ins, and developed 'psychological assessment' profiles of student leaders."[62] In July 1968 the FBI agreed to share its files with Ober's group. "[T]he Agency was to get all FBI reports on dissidents and their known contacts, and Ober would cross-index them in a special CIA computer system, Hydra."[63] The CIA officer in charge of protecting U.S. installations of the Agency, Director of the Office of Security Howard Osborn, was requested by Ober to provide "all information about dissident groups obtained through Projects MERRIMAC and RESISTANCE, and not merely specific items suggesting foreign connections."[64] One of the groups that particularly interested both the CIA and the FBI was the Institute for Policy Studies, a left-wing think tank funded by Samuel Rubin, the founder of Faberge, Inc., and a one-time member of the Communist Party. Rubin must have been a figure from a nightmare for J. Edgar Hoover and James Angleton: a Russian émigré, independently wealthy, whose institute had been the site of meetings attempting to unify the Black Power movement with SDS, and whose daughter, Cora Weiss, was a leader of Women's Strike for Peace and one of the organizers of the 1967 Pentagon demonstrations.[65] "After October 1968, when IPS wired bail to Weathermen arrested for overturning cars and smashing windows, Angleton staffers saw the group [the Weathermen] as yet another tentacle of the Samuel Rubin octopus."[66] It was a sort of unified field theory of subversion: mirror imaging.

In September 1969, "Helms approved the development of 'new sources' to feed Hydra and Chaos. One was MK/SOURDOUGH, a project to cover mail coming into the San Francisco Bay area from communist China and Vietnam. Technical Services experts flew out from Langley for three-week shifts . . . Sourdough was soon augmented by a dramatic expansion of Chaos collection: the net was cast so wide that virtually all opponents of U.S. policy could be monitored. In October 1969, Ober for the first time 'fully tasked' CIA's Domestic Contact Service . . . to collect intelligence on 'black militants; radical youth groups; radical underground press; antiwar groups; and deserter/draft resister movements.'" This new thrust produced such silliness as a CIA memo to the FBI listing all contributors to the *New York Review of Books*, and such seriousness as the placing of CIA moles in radical groups *inside* the United States.[67]

The various programs of the American intelligence services aimed at preventing domestic dissent developed ever tighter links as the antiwar and civil rights protests intensified. "After 1969, the FBI began submitting names of citizens engaged in domestic protest and violence to the CIA not only for investigation abroad, but also for placement on the 'watch list' of the CIA's mail opening project."[68] HT/LINGUAL, which had begun as an effort to find traces of Soviet espionage within the United States through the examination of mail between the two countries, now became an instrument for the surveillance of domestic protesters. Names and information flowed in both directions between the counterintelligence branches of the FBI and the CIA: "the CIA regarded the mention of a name in any of the thousands of reports sent to it by the FBI as a standing requirement from the FBI for information about those persons. FBI reports flowed to the CIA at a rate of over 1,000 a month. From 1967 to 1974, the CIA responded with over 5,000 reports to the FBI."[69]

The flow of paper and computerized equivalents steadily increased during the late 1960s and early 1970s. A report to Attorney General Ramsey Clark recommended that FBI information "relating 'to the civil disturbance problem' under the headings 'black power, new left, pacifist, pro-Red Chinese, anti-Vietnam war, pro-Castro, etc.' be used to develop 'a master index on individuals, or organizations, and by cities.' Attorney General Clark approved these recommendations and established the Interdivision Information Unit (IDIU) . . . By 1970, the IDIU computer was receiving over 42,000 'intelligence reports' a year relating to 'civil disorders and campus disturbances' . . . IDIU computer tapes, which included 10–12,000 entries on 'numerous anti-war activists and other dissidents,' were provided to the Central Intelligence Agency in 1970 by Assistant Attorney General Jerris Leonard."[70] This put the Central Intelligence Agency in the position of maintaining files on the entire range of Americans of interest to the government, not merely those who might be suspected of relationships with foreign intelligence agencies, which was, of course, yet another violation of the spirit of the Agency's charter, another step toward the creation in fact, in not in name, of a unified American secret intelligence service—a goal later to be associated with Nixon aide Tom Huston.

Angleton's assistant Richard Ober was a talented intelligence bureaucrat, energetic and skilled at accumulating resources. His group eventually included fifty-two desk officers,[71] equivalent, say, to the strength of a middling CIA station abroad—if not Berlin, with its hundreds, surely beyond Oslo or Dublin. It was, in other words, of a size sufficient for a second-class operation: perhaps not enough for a coup d'état, but good enough for a simple pronunciamento such as the unconstitutional suppression of a protest movement. Business as usual in Africa or Central America; less usual, as far as we know, in those days in the United States itself. These dozens of desk officers were necessary in order to manage the extraordinary information flow that came into the basement of

Langley.[72] This effort required "at least several hundred FBI reports and CIA field messages every month."[73]

Such documentation and archival procedures, as we have seen, date back to those of the police in British India, who created files concerning the subversive activities of Brahmans, Untouchables, and Sikhs, Thugs, devotees of nonviolence, Communists, and members of the Congress Party, that were the basis for the yet more extensive files of MI5 and MI6 compiled during the Second World War—and which then, in their gigantic accumulation, were passed to OSS as dowry for the alliance between the British and American intelligence services. Those files, in turn, had been the core of the registry of the Central Intelligence Agency and a particular concern of James Angleton both when he first joined the Agency and all through his career. (It is in this connection that Angleton was something of a pioneer in the use of computers for large-scale data processing.)

President Johnson was convinced, as President Nixon would be after him, that the antiwar demonstrations were directed by agents of the Soviet Union, disguised as non-Communist leftists (or Faberge salesmen). Referring to Joseph Califano, the Church Committee noted that a "principal assistant to President Johnson testified that high governmental officials could not believe that 'a cause that is so clearly right for the country, as they perceive it, would be so widely attacked if there were not some [foreign] force behind it.'"[74] Johnson took the traditional precautions. He "ordered a comprehensive review of the government's emergency plans . . . One result of this review . . . was a decision to bring the Detention Program into line with the Emergency Detention Act of 1950 . . . Top priority was now given not only to leaders of 'basic subversive organizations,' [the decrepit Communist Party and the somewhat more lively Socialist Workers Party] but also to 'leaders of anarchistic groups.' It was said to be the 'anarchistic tendencies' of New Left and Black militants that made them a 'threat to the internal security'"—and candidates for detention.[75] It will be remembered that one of the most prominent victims of J. Edgar Hoover's Palmer Raids, sixty years earlier, was the anarchist Emma Goldman. No sooner had the danger of Communism been expelled from the United States than that ancient enemy reappeared, waving, at least in the imagination of the secret police, its black flag of subversion, as it would be said to, once again, after the collapse of the Soviet Union.

When Richard Nixon became President even this vast data-gathering effort was not satisfactory to the Agency's most important customers. In April 1969, Nixon ordered John Ehrlichman "to prepare a report on foreign Communist support of campus disorders. The evidence provided to Ehrlichman by the intelligence community revealed that foreign connections were virtually nonexistent. The president and his aide were dissatisfied with this finding."To remedy this unsatisfactory situation, "White House pressure . . . was brought to bear" by a young assistant to President Nixon named Tom Huston, who wrote a memorandum in June "questioning the adequacy of the CIA's efforts."[76] In response, the CHAOS program's sources of information and analytic capacity were expanded. Later in the year, "CHAOS began to develop two additional programs to increase its sources of information." In one, "CHAOS developed its own agents, who were trained in the United States and then sent on reporting missions abroad . . . Over 200 reports and other items were supplied by DCS to CHAOS between 1969 and 1973." In the other, "*CHAOS made specific requests for domestic materials* . . . For example, CHAOS asked the Chicago Field Office for information on the '28 co-conspirators' of 12 SDS members who had been locally indicted for the Weathermen riots in Chicago the previous fall. This was supplied, as well as subsequent coverage of the legal proceedings. Another CHAOS request resulted in a DCS field office obtaining from confidential sources a large report prepared by a state investigating commission on radical demonstrations in that state."[77] (Emphasis added.)

By October 1969, then, the Agency had switched from the mere processing of reports to a more active approach: recruiting and placing "penetration" agents in antiwar organizations and tasking other agencies with requests for information on domestic matters. According to the Rockefeller Commission report, "This reversal of approach appears to be attributable primarily to three factors":

> First, and most important, an increasing amount of White House pressure . . . was brought to bear on the CIA to provide more extensive and detailed reporting on the role of foreign connections with American dissident activities;
>
> Second, Operation CHAOS had been relatively unsuccessful in obtaining meaningful information through agents associated with other agencies;
>
> Third, the tempo of dissident activities had increased substantially in the United States.[78]

Ober commented during his testimony to the Rockefeller Committee that "the best way to obtain solid evidence of foreign exploitation of domestic groups was direct penetration of the leadership of these groups . . . by the FBI, or by penetration of foreign [two-thirds of a line blanked out] groups by the CIA abroad." Ober's standard account of this procedure is as follows:

> [O]ne approach I used was to develop agents who would appear attractive for use by any hostile foreign element interested in exploiting U.S. extrem-

> ists, and to put these agents abroad in circles or circumstances which would make it likely that the hostile groups would become aware of them and of their views . . . [T]he agent was either turned over permanently to the CIA for control from the FBI . . . or he was recruited initially by the Agency . . . [T]he bulk of the information gathered in this process on groups and other individuals in the United States who were his associates . . . was and is an essential part of the assessment and checking phase of a sound agent operation . . . After the acceptance of recruitment of this agent, he usually stayed in place in the United States for a few months while he was being trained . . . If during this time some of the information obtained from him appeared to be of a legitimate concern to the FBI, it was passed to the FBI.[79]

When President Johnson tasked the CIA with the investigation (and, it seems, harassment) of American antiwar activists, their magazines and newspapers, those longtime partners, Sam Papich of the FBI and Angleton of the CIA (and also of the FBI), set up what was essentially a joint operation. The dominant partner for activities within the United States was the FBI, abroad it was the CIA, but each did some work in the other's bailiwick. And yet, despite the close personal relationship between Papich and Angleton, the relationship between the two organizations was troublesome. Even in the more traditional field of counterintelligence coverage of the CIA itself, "Mr. Angleton felt that the FBI perhaps was not doing as much as it should to fill gaps, and that there was a certain attempt on his part to bring a certain degree of pressure on the FBI to produce more."[80] This was near the end of the Great Molehunt for KGB penetration agents in the CIA.

According to Mark Riebling, "In early 1971, [FBI official William] Sullivan later said, Angleton turned to the Bureau for a domestic investigation because he 'believed four or five guys were agents, including two guys still in the agency and three or four who had been high-level. They were suspected of having dealings with foreign intelligence agents.' Sullivan consulted Hoover, who 'refused on the grounds that it was the responsibility of the CIA. However, in this case he realized that he might be put in a compromising position by suggesting that the CIA conduct domestic investigations, so reluctantly he told me to go ahead, but he instructed me to conduct just the semblance of an investigation.' In other words, 'It was a brush-off. CIA was never satisfied with the FBI, and I can't blame them. We did hit or miss jobs. We were constantly cutting the throats of CIA.'"[81]

As this indicates, while the CIA became increasingly involved with domestic covert activities in the 1960s and 1970s, extraordinary internecine struggles were taking place within the FBI and between the Bureau and other American intelligence agencies. J. Edgar Hoover, reaching the age of seventy and facing forced retirement if a president were to find him an embarrassment, gradually withdrew the Bureau from counterintelligence activity, at one point going so far as to break off official liaison with the Central Intelligence Agency and all other U.S. intelligence organizations. Hoover's policy of disengagement may have increased the pressure on the CIA to replace the Bureau's covert programs with its own. "By fall 1969, in fact, President Nixon, like Johnson before him, was already beginning to 'go around' Hoover to CIA. This time it happened through the graces of Attorney General Mitchell . . . [who urged Helms] to expand CIA's domestic coverage . . . What Mitchell was asking, *as asked*, was very likely against the law, and Helms told him so . . . [T]he White House did not stop pressing."[82] Those in the White House are from time to time relatively untroubled by legal and constitutional quibbles.

These matters had their ebb and flow, and even the FBI is not monolithic. For example, those within the Bureau who were concerned about their ability to penetrate both the New Left and campus-based Black Power groups had long been arguing for authorization to recruit younger informants. "In September 1970 W. Mark Felt, a high-ranking FBI official, recommended that the age for FBI campus informants be lowered from twenty-one to eighteen." Felt wrote, in justification, "Never in our history have we been confronted with as critical a need for informant coverage. Terrorist violence is all around us and more has been threatened. Even our own doors are being threatened by Weatherman fanatics. Bombings, assassination of police officers, kidnapping and torture, murder are all part of the picture. These violence-oriented black and white savages are at war with the Government and the American people."[83]

"Bombing, assassination of police officers, kidnapping and torture, murder . . . [by] black and white savages." It is useful, perhaps, to know what images passed through the minds of senior FBI officials in the early 1970s.

The use of eighteen-year-olds as government agents was particularly repugnant on two counts: it corrupted the young and it corrupted education. It was, nonetheless, a strategy pioneered by such amphibious inhabitants of academe and the secret intelligence worlds as Angleton's mentor Norman Holmes Pearson, a strategy tenaciously pursued at Yale and elsewhere by the Central Intelligence Agency as it followed Pearson's original suggestion to develop a cadre, one eventually including thousands of academics, who could "tap" young people for the secret intelligence services, as if for acceptance by Skull and Bones. It was impossible to maintain barriers between these activities and the other enterprises undertaken by those who tapped and those who were tapped. Entire academic disciplines—such as area studies—were either largely initiated by representatives of the secret intelligence agencies or shaped to their goals and needs. The social sciences were particularly vulnerable, as was demonstrated in the case of those departments at Stanford University,[84] but the effects were pervasive, including in such seemingly unlikely fields as art history, English, and the physical sciences. The effects of penetration of the universities by the secret intelligence services could not be isolated in the freshman dormitories or the advisor's office.

Nonetheless, Mark Felt won his point. The consequences were far-reaching. As Senator Frank Church pointed out, "The 21-year limitation, which was meant to avoid student spying on students on the campuses, was eliminated, and informants were obtained on the campuses among the student body. Also, all SDS members were placed under surveillance, and 6,500 new cases were opened. Also, all black groups were placed under surveillance, even though there was no previous evidence of violence or a tendency toward violence; and that involved the opening of 4,000 new cases."[85]

The scope of the effort was staggering. *All* members of the Students for a Democratic Society "were placed under surveillance" without regard to their individual activities, *all* "black groups" were spied on. The FBI "ordered its field offices in 1970 to 'make every effort' to obtain 'informant coverage' of every 'New Left commune.' Later that year, after Director Hoover lifted restrictions against recruiting 18[-] to 21-year-old informants, field offices were urged to take advantage of this 'tremendous opportunity' to expand coverage of New Left 'collectives, communes, and staffs of their underground newspapers.'"[86]

According to the Church Committee report, "As domestic intelligence activity increasingly broadened to cover domestic dissenters under many different programs, the government intensified the use of covert techniques which intruded upon individual privacy. Informants were used to gather more information about more Americans, often targeting an individual because of his political views and 'regardless of past or present involvement in disorders.' The CIA's mail-opening program increasingly focused upon domestic groups, including 'protest and peace organizations' which were covered at the FBI's request."[87] This particular request was conveyed in a memorandum from J. Edgar Hoover himself to James Angleton in his roles as the official responsible for the illegal mail-opening program and the ultimate supervisor of Operation CHAOS.

We might pause for a moment to consider the enormity of these measures. If we assume that a plurality of African American young adults—even if that was only twenty or thirty percent—belonged to "black groups," and if we recall that SDS was a rather large organization, particularly when assimilated to New Left "collectives, communes, and staffs of their underground newspapers," it is difficult to imagine that fewer than a tenth of the young adults in the United States in those years came under surveillance by their own government. This was the capacity and ambition of the American secret intelligence services thirty years ago.

A request from the other side of the Potomac is described in an April 1970 memorandum from William Sullivan to another of Hoover's aides. Angleton had asked for a meeting with Sullivan, as if Sullivan were an official of another nation's counterintelligence service, to discuss coordination of their operations against American antiwar activists. First, Angleton wanted the assistance of the FBI in wiretaps and listening devices for the surveillance of dissidents. Second, he wanted to set up a series of interagency meetings ("seminars") to pool the information obtained from these and other sources. Sullivan replied by referring to a long-standing FBI complaint against the Justice Department and the courts. The FBI, according to Sullivan, once had an extensive wiretapping and eavesdropping program, but the evidence gathered in this way had too often (from the FBI's point of view) been inadmissible in court, the publicity had been bad, and the Bureau had not been backed up by the Attorney General. Angleton was sympathetic. He "noted that in response to CIA's request for electronic coverage of two [omitted] in the Fall of 1969, the Bureau had requested that they take this matter up with the Attorney General. He said that CIA has been giving the question of approaching the Attorney General considerable thought but this would involve a whole new set of procedures and policy considerations which would have to be carefully considered." Angleton's staff was working on a proposal to Helms to help the Bureau out in this regard. "Concerning the proposed seminar, in line with the Director's letter to Helms 3/31/70, I pointed out that we would certainly have no objection to such conferences where the occasion justified them. From Angleton's remarks, it appears that CIA is primarily interested here in the [omitted (*Ramparts* matter?)] and would like to furnish the Bureau with details of an extensive research project CIA has undertaken in recent years to correlate all available source information regarding [omitted]. This apparently would not involve any commitment by the Bureau and would represent essentially an opportunity for us to see what CIA has done in this field and how it might tie in with any current Bureau interest."[88]

Sullivan ends with a "we'll keep you posted" sentence and reiterated assurances that Director Hoover's wishes would be followed in every detail. We can conclude from this and similar documents that as Operation CHAOS matured, Angleton and his sympathizers in the FBI were doing everything they could to coordinate it with the FBI's COINTELPRO operation. The problem was Hoover, who was becoming increasingly reluctant to undertake any activities that might result in negative public reactions, which in turn might furnish the president with a reason to force him into retirement. Fortunately, from Sullivan's and Angleton's points of view, relations at the working level between the two secret intelligence organizations remained close.[89]

William Sullivan himself told his biographer that, in spite of Hoover's reluctance, "During the late 1960s and the early 1970s the bureau must have spent a million dollars maintaining informants in the Anti-War Movement."[90] We know from Ober that the Bureau did in fact receive "CIA assistance in the collection of domestic intelligence." Ober took agents where he found them, recruiting them himself or borrowing them from the vast FBI stable. Even when they were proper CIA assets, information provided by the penetration agents in question was passed back and forth between the two agencies as they worked together, and sometimes separately, to infiltrate the antiwar movement. Some contacts preferred working with one agency, some with another. "There is some evidence to suggest that . . . Timothy Leary, who was 'liberated' in September 1970 from a minimum-security prison in Lompoc, California, by members of the Weather Underground" and who later "turned state's evidence against the Weathermen who rescued him" had been working with the CIA for a number of years "in part because he did not wish to deal with the FBI."[91] Everyone has a right to personal preferences in the matter of their associations.

Abandoning the line that the CIA did not have agents in the United States and that they did not collect information on domestic matters, in his testimony to the Church Committee Ober fell back on the rationalization that "it was a question of the purpose": "Anything that was obtained by these agents was obtained not because they were directed or tasked to collect on domestic groups, but rather as a by-product of their assessment, development and training process . . . I felt that if information came to me which indicated the probability of the commission of a criminal act, it was my civil responsibility as a citizen, let alone my assignment in the CIA, to get that information to those responsible, namely the FBI, or in some cases the Secret Service."[92] Which is bland enough, if nonsensical. If it is illegal to steal, it is still illegal to steal if it is done only as "a by-product" of kidnapping. But that is neither here nor there, as what in fact actually happened was that Ober—that is, Angleton; that is, the CIA—organized an extensive intelligence network within the United States.

Cord Meyer, who was in a position to know, summed up the matter in this way: "the Special Operations Group from October 1969 to July 1972 recruited twenty-five American citizens who were active in the Anti-War Movement as agents . . . *three of these recruited agents were instructed by their Agency case officer to travel within the United States and to participate in and report on antiwar demonstrations and planning meetings. This purely domestic espionage activity resulted in the dissemination of intelligence reports to the FBI.*"[93] (Emphasis added.) The Rockefeller Commission's report went into more detail about the CIA's use of agents within the United States. In February 1968, that is, under President Johnson, the CIA's offices of Security and Counterintelligence created

> a "Project 1," which was initially entitled "An Effort . . . in Acquiring Assets in the 'Peace' and 'Black Power' Movements in the United States." The project was to involve recruitment of agents who would penetrate some of the prominent dissident groups in the United States and report information on the communications, contacts, travel and plans of individuals or groups having a connection with a certain foreign area. The proposal was rejected by Director Helms in March 1968 on the ground that it "would appear to be" beyond the Agency's jurisdiction and would cause widespread criticism when it became public knowledge, as he believed it eventually would.
>
> Shortly thereafter, the proposed Project was modified to include a prohibition against domestic penetration of dissident groups by agents recruited by CIA. Any contact with domestic groups would be incidental to the overall objective of gaining access overseas to information on foreign contacts and control . . .
>
> The modified plan was approved by the Deputy Director of Plans . . . but no evidence could be found that the project ever became operational.[94]

On the other hand, "Project 2" was begun in late 1969 (under President Nixon) by Ober's SOG in Angleton's Counterintelligence Staff.

> Under Project 2, individuals without existing dissident affiliation would be recruited and, after recruitment, would acquire the theory and jargon and make acquaintances in the "New Left" while attending school in the United States. Following this "reddening" or "sheepdipping" process (as one CIA officer [Ober] described it), the agent would be sent to a foreign country on a specific intelligence mission.
>
> Project 2 was approved on April 14, 1970, by the Assistant Deputy Director for Plans, who stated that no Project 2 agent was to be directed to acquire information concerning domestic dissident activities. Only if such information was acquired incidentally by the agents during the domestic "coloration" process would it be passed to Operation CHAOS for forwarding to the FBI.
>
> Renewals of Project 2 were approved annually during 1971–1973 . . . The Project was also reviewed and approved in the fall of 1973 by William E. Colby, by then Director of Central Intelligence.[95]

The chronology of CIA use of agents for domestic surveillance of the antiwar movement remains slightly unclear. Cord Meyer dates it from October 1969. There were, however, those CIA agents at Columbia University in April of the previous year; and then, we are told that Project 2 approval did not come until April 1970. It was probably a gradual process, the Columbia University affair being handled as an emergency (perhaps not by the Agency's Clandestine Services but by the Office of Security), while "Project 2" was not so much an initiation as a ratification of a direction of activity already under way. In any case, the approval order of April 14, 1970, established a distinction, between *directing* agents to acquire information concerning domestic dissident activities and *accepting* it, that was sufficiently flimsy. After all, everything flowed into the maw (or maws) of Hydra.

Between 1970 and 1974 two dozen agents were recruited, of whom eleven completed their training in the United States. Operation CHAOS received copies of their contact reports and those that were "deemed significant" were filed and indexed in the operation's computer system. Despite the reluctance of the Agency to have its agents involved in domestic intelligence activities, some took advantage of its good nature to secure permission to allow them to do so: one of the agents became an officer in a domestic dissident group, another became an advisor in a United States congressional campaign and submitted reports about the campaign.[96] Three agents "had an entree into anti-war, radical left, or black militant groups before they were recruited by the Operation . . . One of the three agents traveled a substantial distance in late 1969 to participate in and report on major demonstrations then occurring in one area of the country . . . The contact reports . . . provided the basis for 47 separate disseminations to the FBI, the bulk of which related solely to domestic matters and were disseminated under titles such as: 'Plans for Future Anti-War Activities on the West Coast.' The second of these agents regularly provided detailed information on the activities and views of high-level leadership in another of the dissident groups within the United States."[97]

An "officer" in a domestic dissident group would have been involved in the decisions on such matters as "plans for future anti-war activities on the West Coast." Insofar as this was the case, the CIA found itself in the interesting position of helping to plan the activities that it was seeking to follow or prevent. It is at this point that the intelligence collection agent crosses the line to become an agent provocateur. Observers at the time noted that national officers of the more radical antiwar groups, such as the Weather Underground and Prairie Fire, often advocated activities that would result in large numbers of arrests.[98] One word for this is "radicalization." Another word for it is "entrapment." But what word is there for the actions of the Central Intelligence Agency when it has a penetration agent within a congressional campaign staff?

One of the acknowledged Operation CHAOS agents, Angleton's agents, then, helped run a domestic dissident group. Another was a member of a Congressional campaign. And a third, who was to be at the center of the massive 1971 Washington antiwar demonstration, was recruited in April 1971. "Two days after the official recruitment, the agent was asked to travel to Washington, D.C., to . . . 'get as close as possible' and perhaps become an assistant to certain prominent radical leaders who were coordinators of the imminent 'May Day' demonstrations." Information from this agent went directly to Ober and from him to the FBI.[99] The theme of this third man is recurrent in accounts of Operation CHAOS. When Richard Ober was deposed by the Rockefeller Commission on the use of Americans to infiltrate the antiwar movement, he insisted that there were not many Operation CHAOS penetration agents and those that there were worked exclusively abroad. They were trained in the United States, of course, and for good operational and technical reasons "sheep-dipped" by spending some time establishing their bona fides in centers of dissident activity in the United States. He acknowledged that through force of exceptional circumstances one of these agents did in fact report extensively on dissident activities in this country, testifying that "during the May Day 1971 demonstrations in Washington, I approved the move to Washington from another city in the United States of an agent recruited by my office, then preparing for an assignment abroad . . . During this period he did uncover and report some information which was given to the FBI, including some concerning some activities abroad."[100] This is rather different from the account in the report of the Rockefeller Commission, which states quite clearly that the CIA had an agent in one American city who was moved to Washington *in order to* gather information about one of the great antiwar demonstrations and to report on that demonstration to the CIA. We have Ober's word for it that this only happened once, as we have Richard Helms's word that he was not aware of the domestic use of Operation CHAOS agents. Each is equally trustworthy. The plausible detail made available concerning Ober's agent at the 1971 May Day demonstrations is reminiscent of many such accounts of CIA activities, pointing insistently at "a single anomaly" with one hand, while using the other to push out of sight the possibly numerous other similar instances. Be that as it may, the question here, as with virginity, is not how many times the CIA committed the act, but whether it did at all.

It did.

Richard Ober's Special Operations Group was set up under James Angleton's authority to investigate *Ramparts*. It passed rapidly from that mission, from gathering information to covert action: to attempting—successfully—to suppress the magazine. The SOG's next assignment, the surveillance of the antiwar press, resulted in a similar progression. Angus Mackenzie claimed that the CIA and the FBI together largely destroyed the antiwar (or "underground") press—hundreds of newspapers. Did they? It seems implausible on its face. It is more likely, more reasonable, to assume that times changed and readership evaporated. But in quite a few cases, and those crucial, Mackenzie actually traced the chain of events that led from FBI or CIA action to the demise of the papers in question. Of course, in a sense, as with the Agency's domestic spying, it does not matter how many papers the secret intelligence agencies closed; if they did it in a single case that was enough to constitute a violation of the Constitution. Mackenzie's minimum argument seems irrefutable and we can take his thesis as demonstrated: the FBI and the CIA attempted to suppress the opposition press.

Paralleling these efforts by the Central Intelligence Agency to monitor and combat domestic opposition to the war in Vietnam, the Agency, and in particular its director, Richard Helms, attempted to satisfy the White House that all that was possible was being done to find the Red Hand behind the antiwar movement. When in the fall of 1967 President Johnson asked the CIA to prepare a study of "International Connections of the U.S. Peace Movement," the Agency reviewed its mail-opening files, polled overseas officers, consolidated these reports with the views of Richard Ober's staff. They found nothing.[101] Nonetheless, Angleton thought he could detect "some patterns suggesting foreign involvement." Some members of the New Left went to Cuba from time to time, others traveled in Eastern Europe, still others—or some of the same revolutionary tourists—went to Vietnam. Who paid for all this? And if the New Left travelers had the *opportunity* of contact with Soviet intelligence, how could Angleton rule out the *possibility* of such contact, and if contact, then influence, and if influence, then direction? On the other hand there was no hard evidence, no documentation, no photographs, no defectors' reports. Years later Angleton told Mark Riebling that "within the Agency itself, there were those who took a very staunch stand that there was no foreign involvement . . . And these were fairly senior individuals, mainly on the overt side of the business. This attitude was very definitely that there was nothing to it; namely, foreign contact."[102]

Helms balanced these views, sending the resulting paper to the White House on November 15, 1967. According to Rhodri Jeffreys-Jones, "The group found nothing to suggest that the mounting unrest was other than spontaneous and indigenous. Helms told President Johnson [that] there was 'no evidence of any contact between the most prominent peace movement leaders and foreign embassies, either in the U.S. or abroad.' He enclosed a report based on intelligence from several agencies and coordinated by the CIA. This report described Tom Hayden and other sworn enemies of Johnson's war policy as 'tireless, peripatetic, full time crusaders.' Commenting on the state of affairs, Helms said the CIA was 'woefully short of information about the protesters.'"[103]

A revision to the report was submitted on December 22, and just after the first of the year another paper—"Student Dissent and Its Techniques in the United States"—followed. Yet another report, about the worldwide student protests in 1968, was delivered to Henry Kissinger "on February 18, 1969, less than a month after Nixon took office. The paper, entitled 'Restless Youth,' was accompanied by a letter in which Helms said, 'In an effort to round-out our discussion of this subject, we have included a section on American students. This is an area not within the charter of this Agency, so I need not emphasize how extremely sensitive this makes the paper. Should anyone learn of its existence it would prove most embarrassing for all concerned.'"[104] Indeed. More has been made of "Restless Youth" than seems appropriate after a reading of the document. It is a solid piece of research, detailed and sophisticated: a country-by-country review of the youth movement of the late 1960s. Relatively little of the paper was devoted to activities in the United States and that appears to have been drawn from more or less public sources. Helms's concern, if exaggerated, is telling, showing his sensitivity to the atmosphere of the times and an apparent division in his mind between long-standing domestic operations of the Agency, such as the mail-opening program, and this special, presidentially commissioned study focusing on what was at the moment a literally explosive topic. It was, after all, a stack of paper that could be copied and published. It was, moreover, a study of a unique threat to internal security, or, at least, to internal security as the U.S. government perceived it.

Throughout the life of Operation CHAOS Helms continued to order reviews and to report negative results to Presidents Johnson and Nixon. For example, in 1967, 1968, and 1971 the CIA reported that the American student protest movement was not the result of an international conspiracy and that "the U.S. New Left is basically self-sufficient and moves under its own impetus."[105] Oddly enough, "the result of these repeated findings was not the termination of CHAOS's surveillance of Americans, but its redoubling . . . As Director Helms testified: 'When a President keeps asking if there is any information, "how are you getting along with your examination," "have you picked up any more information on this subject," it isn't a direct order to do something, but it seems to me it behooves the Director of Central Intelligence to find some way to improve his performance, or to improve his Agency's performance.' . . . Helms further testified: 'President Johnson was after this all the time . . . this was something that came up almost daily and weekly.'"[106]

The Rockefeller Commission concluded that "the intelligence disseminations and those portions of a major study ["Restless Youth"] prepared by the Agency which dealt with purely domestic matters were improper."[107] More broadly, having deployed immense resources, having violated its charter and the Constitution, having destroyed careers and parts of the press, having cooperated with the FBI in actions that went yet further in damaging American democracy, in the end the CIA concluded that the antiwar movement was not under the control of the Soviet Union. Those challenging the government were not foreign-born anarchists, easily deportable, as had been the case in the days of the Palmer Raids. As a matter of fact, some of them were the children—or the wives—of high government officials.

Remarkably early in the Vietnam War, this domestic revolt had begun among those close enough to the government and its intelligence agencies to become aware of the consequences of Johnson's policies before they had become the common currency of public opinion. For example,

> At a dinner party in Georgetown that fall of 1965, Joe Alsop began to hold forth on the nobility of America's commitment to Vietnam. The evening was a mix of generations—Des FitzGerald was there, along with his daughter Frances, and some of her friends, including Henry Breck, the young Grotonian who had signed up for the CIA partly out of admiration for men like Wisner and FitzGerald . . .
>
> "Suddenly, the younger people blew up," recalled Breck . . . "We yelled, 'Are you out of your mind? The war's a disaster!'" . . .
>
> FitzGerald was bothered to see his daughter and Breck side with the rabble. It was one thing to have scraggly antiwar protesters waving placards on college campuses; it was quite another to be rudely accosted by his own kind in Joe Alsop's dining room.[108]

Journalist Ben Bradlee remembered that in the following year his wife "was marching in the streets with one of the many anti-Vietnam protest groups while I was trying to figure out who was organizing the protests, and how well—or poorly—they were reflecting American opinion."[109] The children of Secretary of Defense Robert McNamara, those of Assistant Secretary Paul Nitze, and those of DCI Helms were all participants in the October 1967 antiwar demonstration at the Pentagon.[110] There is reason to believe that the conversations between McNamara and his children contributed to his decision to oppose continuation of the war and then to resign as Secretary of Defense.[111] James Angleton's own children, and his wife Cicely, also participated in antiwar demonstrations.[112]

Memoirs, histories, and biographies of the time have recurrent scenes where the men in their dark suits, skinny ties, and white shirts look up from their desks and see through their office windows their own families marching in protest of the policies they were attempting to implement. One of these men, William Watts, was "assigned in the last days of October [1969] to prepare further drafts for Nixon's November speech on Vietnam. Watts took a break late one evening and walked outside the White House. There was yet another demonstration against the Vietnam War going on—hundreds of protesters marching in front of the White House carrying candles. Watts strolled to the gate to get a closer look and saw his wife and children go by, each holding a flickering candle. 'I felt like throwing up,' Watts says. 'There they are demonstrating against me, and here I am inside writing a speech.'"[113] Antonia Lake, whose husband, Anthony, was working in the White House with Watts, was also a participant in that demonstration.[114]

As Christopher Lasch commented, apocalyptically, about such times: "A government faced with insuperable difficulties of every kind, a government that has already ceased in any meaningful sense to govern, will find itself increasingly dependent on its imperial police, and a panicky population will put no obstacles in the way of this dependence. For the citizens fear not only the dark, unpredictable violence of the poor but the inscrutable sullenness of their own children, the other group of rioters who have risen up to haunt respectable people."[115] More simply put, how long can men continue to toil in government offices for a policy loathed by their wives and children? It is difficult to bring to mind a parallel intersection between high policy and family life, such a collapse of the political sphere into the intimate—or vice versa.

Robert McNamara was not the only high government official made overwrought by the times. When James Angleton visited Israel in 1967, "the Chief of Station, John Denley Walker, thought Angleton was exhausted, on the verge of a nervous breakdown. He tried to send Angleton back to Washington, but Angleton instead took some time off to rest at Elat."[116] By 1968, according to Peter Wright, James Angleton "was making enemies throughout the CIA—in the CI Division, among other directors jealous of his power, and among those officers whose promotion prospects he had adversely affected." Angleton "was safe while Helms was Director, but the war in Vietnam was rapidly altering the face of the Agency, and the gathering political fashion for détente was beginning to undermine the foundations of Cold War suspicion upon which his empire was built." Angleton "was drinking far more than was good for him, and had begun to look not merely pallid but genuinely ravaged. His mood changed too. He became increasingly introspective, and the dry humor became less and less visible. He seemed pent-up and aggressive, trusting fewer and fewer people, who were turning more and more against him . . . Barry Russell Jones told me in amazement of accompanying him on a fishing trip to a stretch of river he owned in Idaho, and finding that Angleton had buried bottles of Jack Daniel's under the water at hundred-yard intervals, so that he could never be caught short."[117]

On the evening of September 11, 1968, Angleton was visiting a friend when he began hemorrhaging. He was taken to the George Washington University Medical Center, where he was diagnosed with a bleeding ulcer. The FBI, as usual, took a careful interest in Angleton's welfare. The next day D. J. Brennan sent William Sullivan a memorandum on the subject: "The purpose of this memorandum is to recommend a get-well letter be written to Angleton, a valuable liaison contact, who has been hospitalized with a bleeding ulcer . . . He is in Room 6224 South [of the medical center]. He can receive no visitors and no telephone calls. Angleton has been an extremely valuable liaison contact at CIA for many years and is well known to a number of Bureau officials."[118] A get-well note was duly sent in Hoover's name on September 13. The cause of the ulcer, or an aggravating condition, was Angleton's long-standing alcoholism. After this episode he decided to stop drinking. "The CIA veteran David Blee said: "I wouldn't have written an insurance policy on Jim, but then he quit drinking cold turkey and went on Anabuse. He went to the other extreme and would ask, 'Any sherry in that soup?'"[119]

A few months after Angleton's hemorrhage, his mentor Allen Dulles died. The Dulles Papers at Princeton University contain the documentation for Dulles's February 1, 1969, funeral services, specifying that Angleton was to carry the urn containing Dulles's ashes (a scene recorded in an often-reproduced photograph). There is also this "Procedural Document" from the Central Intelligence Agency: "Brief eulogy being prepared by Charles Murphy with Agency contribution (Mr. [James?] Hunt and Mr. Angleton responsible)."[120] The resulting eloquent "Tribute" was read by Richard Helms. It said, in part,

> We are here today to do honor to our friend, Allen Walsh Dulles. Only yesterday he walked our ways, all energy, enterprise and sage counsel, savored wit and sparkling speech welling from the springs of his own spirit . . . [I]t is as a splendid watchman that many of us saw him, a familiar and trusted figure in clear outline on the American ramparts, seeing that the nation could not be surprised in its sleep or overcome in the night . . . With Allen Dulles, what counted always were the central elements of the liberal

> tradition—liberty under law, conscience, the sovereignty of principle, the ideal of self-government, the creation of protection of democratic institutions—in short the preservation of human values . . . Perhaps we can now find it in ourselves to say that we shall always be with him: to say that for us, as for him, patriotism sets no bounds on the wider pursuit of truth and the defense of freedom and liberty.[121]

"Liberty under law, conscience . . . protection of democratic institutions." Another view, specifically about Dulles's influence on protégés like Helms and Angleton, was expressed by Benjamin Bradlee, who knew them well. He said, "Those guys were totally corrupted by Dulles."[122]

A few months later, Angleton's chief deputy, James Hunt, retired. The FBI liaison officer to the CIA, Papich, wrote to Bureau headquarters as follows: "On May 16, 1969, James Angleton, CIA, advised the Liaison Agent that Ray Rocca has been officially designated to succeed Hunt . . . The appointment of a successor to Hunt resulted in considerable controversy within CIA. Some people hoped that a top-flight intelligence officer from the field would succeed Hunt. Although Rocca is not popular within the Agency, he is a seasoned officer and merited consideration because of seniority. He has also worked very closely with Angleton for a number of years."[123] [Closing three or four lines blacked out.]

Rocca's association with Angleton actually went back to O.S.S. days. Peter Wright, as might be expected, was more melodramatic than Papich in his comments. "Hunt was a hard man, who treated Angleton's obsessions with balanced skepticism. He had his feet on the ground, and he made things happen. Angleton . . . was a hopeless administrator, and Hunt ensured that papers were circulated, requests replied to, and the day-to-day routine, upon which an efficient intelligence service relies, was maintained. Without him, Angleton became a ship without an anchor, drifting slowly toward the abyss."[124]

After Richard Nixon took office as president of the United States in January of 1969, "the abyss" became a recurrent image. In the field of foreign affairs, the president told his advisors that he wished to be seen as a leader who was out of control, a madman.[125] Some have recently concluded that those years were one of the periods in which the United States was indeed a rogue state. There were domestic parallels. Just as in international affairs the administration would accept no constraints on its actions, at home it found the rule of law increasingly troublesome, even when it was an old ally who clung to it.

J. Edgar Hoover had opposed the creation of the CIA, as inimical to his world-wide ambitions for his own organization, and continued throughout his career to minimize contacts and cooperation. This did not interfere with day-to-day activities at the working level until the combination of Hoover's nervousness about his own status, when he passed retirement age and was serving at the pleasure of the president, and about the domestic political situation at the height of the antiwar movement, caused him to become increasingly reluctant to violate the law in matters such as wire-taps and searches. As the Nixon Administration took hold of the government, officials like Angleton and William Sullivan were searching for ways to maintain cooperation between their organizations on "routine" matters—illegal wiretaps and searches—and on the extraordinary matters arising from White House pressure concerning the anitiwar movement. And the new occupants of the White House had their own activist agenda: "The Nixon White House wanted the FBI to be more aggressive, not less. Hoover's refusal to bug, tap, and open mail was the straw that broke the camel's back . . ." President Nixon appointed Tom Charles Huston to review the entire intelligence apparatus of the United States.[126]

President Johnson had expressed his concerns about the antiwar movement in a manner that would have been familiar to President Eisenhower: he spoke to his directors of central intelligence, first Raborn, then Helms. The Nixon administration worked differently, President Nixon insulating himself from cabinet officers and officials like Helms by sending messages through his assistants H. R. Haldeman and John Ehrlichman. They, in turn, used their assistants as intermediaries. Huston, a Young Republican political activist from Indiana, was one. Huston thought of himself as the Kissinger, as it were, for domestic security matters. In the summer of 1969 he called on William Sullivan at FBI headquarters, telling him that the president was dissatisfied with the work of the FBI, particularly in regard to the antiwar demonstrations. He wanted the FBI to warn him about the demonstrations before they happened. Sullivan, an old counterintelligence hand at the Bureau, looked at the young Midwestern lawyer and decided that he could be "turned," wittingly or not, to working to accomplish the FBI's goals. "[T]he entire intelligence community was undergoing budget cuts in 1969–70, and a new mandate from the White House for expanded collection operations would have given the agencies leverage with congressional appropriations committees to reverse the downtrend in intelligence spending."[127]

That was one level of Sullivan's motivation for cultivating the young man who had wandered so brashly into his parlor. Another, according to Sullivan's later account of the matter, was patriotic: "The barriers that Hoover had erected between the FBI and the other intelligence agencies had led to a condition of total isolation for each organization . . . Perhaps with my help, Huston and the White House could reorganize the entire intelligence community."[128] And there was possibly a third: someone, sometime, would succeed J. Edgar Hoover.

Why not William Sullivan? Facilitating the president's agenda could not hurt his own. For all these reasons, "Sullivan had numerous meetings and telephone conversations with Huston, tutoring him in the art of counterintelligence."[129] They became, in Huston's view, allies in an effort to bring the FBI and CIA closer together.

Huston sat at Sullivan's feet for nearly a year, preparing his "brief" on domestic intelligence matters, their intensification and coordination. In the midst of this period occurred one of the odder events in the chronicles of secret intelligence. In February 1970, "as a result of a 'flap' over the CIA's refusal to disclose information to the FBI . . . Hoover issued an order that 'direct liaison' at FBI headquarters with CIA 'be terminated' and that 'any contact with CIA in the future' was to take place 'by letter only.'"[130] The incident that caused the "flap" was (and is) rather obscure, having to do with an émigré source in Colorado used by both the FBI and the CIA. The details did not matter: sooner or later Hoover would have found an incident appropriate for his purpose. Hoover was increasingly hostile to the CIA, per se, and irritated both with its intrusions into domestic counterintelligence and its requests for intensified FBI activity of that type. He was also more and more cautious about violating the constitutional rights of his fellow citizens, something that in turn irritated both those on his own staff like William Sullivan and Samuel Papich, and their allies in the CIA, chiefly James Angleton, who saw this caution as endangering national security. They immediately set to work to nullify the effects of Hoover's order: "secure telephones were installed and working-level contacts continued."

> CIA Director Helms subsequently attempted to reopen the question of FBI cooperation with CIA requests for installing electronic surveillances and covering mail. Hoover replied that he agreed with Helms that there should be expanded "exchange of information between our agencies concerning New Left and racial extremist matters." However, he refused the request for aid with electronic surveillance and mail coverage. Hoover cited the "widespread concern by the American public regarding the possible misuse of this type of coverage." Their use in "domestic investigations" posed legal problems not encountered "in similar operations abroad." Hoover added, "The FBI's effectiveness has always depended in large measure on our capacity to retain the full confidence of the American people."[131]

It is difficult today to believe that there was a time when the director of the FBI was, for whatever reason, a defender of civil liberties against governmental intrusion.

This was the immediate background, and the atmosphere, when Huston gave the president "talking points" for a June 5, 1970, meeting in the Oval

Office between President Nixon and the directors of the FBI, CIA, National Security Agency, and Defense Intelligence Agency. The president said, reading from Huston's (Sullivan's) script, "'We are now confronted with a new and grave crisis in our country . . . Certainly hundreds, perhaps thousands of Americans—mostly under 30—are determined to destroy our society.' The president believed the domestic instability could be quieted with more complete intelligence: the government must know more about the activities of such people."[132] The president "directed that each of the agencies should join . . . a committee to be chaired by Mr. Hoover, which would prepare a report for [the president] which would cover three areas. First, it should have a threat assessment; second, it should specify the various restraints under which the agencies thought they were operating that hindered them; and, third, it should contain a series of options of how to deal with these various restraints which would enable him to make a decision."[133] Hoover followed standard governmental procedures by appointing a working committee, the Interagency Committee on Intelligence (Ad Hoc), chaired by Sullivan, with Angleton representing the CIA, to work out the details.[134] The Interagency Committee convened for its first meeting the next day, at CIA headquarters.[135]

Nixon had made Hoover head of a committee charged with drawing up a plan to institute procedures that either were already in effect or had been blocked by Hoover himself. A participant commented, "Hoover put us out of business in 1966 and 1967 when he placed sharp restrictions on intelligence collection. I was a Soviet specialist and I wanted better coverage of the Soviets. I felt—and still feel—that we need technical coverage on every Soviet in the country. I didn't give a damn about the Black Panthers myself, but I did about the Russians. I saw these meetings as a perfect opportunity to get back the methods we needed—and so did Sullie [Sullivan]."[136] Hoover was furious, but temporarily outflanked. His one-time protégés, Sullivan and Angleton, appeared to succeed in this effort to increase cooperation between the FBI and the CIA in the domestic internal security area. Their report, which became known as the Huston Plan, recommended:

> (1) "coverage by NSA of the communications of U.S. citizens using international facilities";
>
> (2) "intensification" of "electronic surveillances and penetrations" directed at individuals and groups "who pose a major threat to the internal security" and at "foreign nationals" in the United States "of interest to the intelligence community";
>
> (3) removal of restrictions on "legal" mail coverage and relaxation of "restrictions on covert coverage" . . .

(4) modification of "present restrictions" on "surreptitious entry" . . . "to permit selective use" against "high priority internal security targets";

(5) relaxation of "present restrictions" on the "development of campus sources" to permit "expanded coverage of violence-prone and student-related groups";

(6) "increased" coverage by CIA "of American students (and others) traveling or living abroad";

(7) appointment of a "permanent committee consisting of the FBI, CIA, NSA, DIA, and the military counterintelligence agencies" to evaluate "domestic intelligence" and to "carry out the other objectives specified in the report."[137]

Concerning the antiwar movement, the report of "Huston's" committee to the president stated that

> Coverage of student groups is handled primarily through live informants and it is generally effective at the national level or at major meetings of these groups where overall policy, aims, and objectives of the groups are determined . . .
>
> This is supported by information furnished by all members of the intelligence community and other Federal, state, and local agencies. Key leaders and activists are afforded concentrated and intensified investigative coverage on a continuing basis and, in situations where there are positive indications of violence, electronic surveillances have been implemented on a selective basis, informant and electronic coverage does not meet present requirements.
>
> Although several SDS chapters on college campuses which adhere to Weatherman ideology have been penetrated by live informants, there is no live informant coverage at present of underground Weatherman fugitives. There is electronic coverage on the residence of a Weatherman contact in New York City and on the residence of an alleged Weatherman member in San Francisco; however, no information has been developed concerning the whereabouts of the 21 Weatherman fugitives.

The Huston report expressed concern about "Gaps in Current Coverage."

> Established, long-term coverage is not available within student protest groups due to the fact that the student body itself changes yearly, necessitating a constant turnover in the informants targeted against these groups. His [*sic*] idealism and immaturity, as well as the sensitive issues of academic freedom and the right to dissent, all serve to increase the risk that the student informant will be exposed as such.

> Generally, day-to-day coverage of the planned activities of student protest groups, which are somewhat autonomous and disjointed, could be strengthened. Advance notice of foreign travel by student militants is particularly needed. Campus violence is generally attributable to small, close-knit extremist groups among radical students. Coverage of these latter groups is minimal.[138]

Further justification for surveillance of students was contributed by the Central Intelligence Agency, meaning, in this case, James Angleton and his deputy Richard Ober. This took two forms: an analysis of current Soviet practice, as understood by Angleton (and Golitsyn), and a history lesson.

> The Central Intelligence Agency (CIA), in its analysis of bloc intelligence, is of the view that the Soviet and bloc intelligence services are committed at the political level to exploit all domestic dissidents wherever possible. This attack is being conducted through recruited agents, agents of influence, and the use of front groups. It is established bloc policy to deploy its forces against the United States as "the main enemy" and to direct all bloc intelligence forces toward ultimately political objectives which disrupt U.S. domestic and foreign policies . . .
>
> While fostering disorder and rebellion through communist parties and fronts is a potent weapon in the communist arsenal, their past success has been evident in clandestine recruitment efforts on campuses during times of unrest. H. A. R. (Kim) Philby, Guy Burgess, and Donald Maclean were all students at Cambridge during the depression period of the 1930's and were in the vanguard of what was then the New Left. Their recruitment and cooperation with Soviet intelligence wreaked havoc on British intelligence and also compromised U.S. security in those sectors where they had authorized access.[139]

Philby! Writing in 1970, Angleton surveys an America convulsed—to use the popular term of the time—with conflict between African Americans seeking full civil rights and those opposing them, between hundreds of thousands of citizens—including his own wife and children—seeking to end a foreign war and an increasingly isolated government determined to pursue it, and thinks of the situation forty years earlier, when the radicalization of students at Cambridge provided the Soviets with recruitment opportunities.

It was not inappropriate for Angleton to produce this analysis, if asked, in his official capacity. But the offices of the Central Intelligence Agency's Counterintelligence Staff are not where national policy is best formed. The views there are only, at best, one moment in a dialectic that should weigh such possibilities against others, and in balance with the nature of democracy itself. As Tom Huston himself said a few years later, "The risk was that you would get people who would be susceptible to political considerations as opposed to national security considerations, or would construe political considerations to be national security considerations, to move from the kid with a bomb to the kid with a picket sign, and from the kid with the picket sign to the kid with the bumper sticker of the opposing candidate. And you just keep going down the line."[140] Such were the president's intentions.

But the specter of Philby might remind us that domestic security matters were not the only things on James Angleton's mind in the late 1960s. His day job was to counter KGB attempts to penetrate the CIA. As is now a matter of public record, those attempts were in fact intense. According to the KGB's 1967 annual report,

> During 1967 . . . the KGB arranged the planting of 31 agents in the enemy's intelligence; of them 12 were located by the enemy's special services and subjected to their intense scrutiny . . . During 1967, 42 agents were recruited, among them 8 diplomats . . . As part of delegations, tourist groups and exhibition participants in 1967 the KGB sent 378 operatives to the capitalist countries, and also over 2,200 agents and 4,400 persons-in-confidence . . . over 114 thousand letters and banderoles containing anti-Soviet and politically harmful printed materials were confiscated in the international mail . . . During 1967 the branches of the KGB recruited 24,952 agents, i.e. a figure constituting 15% of the total network personnel, the overall size of which did not change substantially during the year owing to the dropping of others.[141]

This appears to indicate that the KGB maintained a worldwide network of more than a hundred fifty thousand agents. The KGB's efforts were particularly successful in West Germany, where, as part of GDR intelligence chief Markus Wolf's "secretaries" program, Leonore Sütterlein, for example, who worked in the West German Foreign Ministry, gave over three thousand classified documents to her husband, an agent assigned to the task by the KGB. She was caught in 1967. At about the same time, a group of senior scientists who had emigrated to the West from East Germany returned to the East, with their accumulated knowledge and skills, and at the Karlsruhe Atomic Center, another scientist, Dr. Harold Gottfried, was arrested while in possession of more than eight hundred pages of classified documents.[142]

James Angleton's position as chief of the Counterintelligence Staff of the Central Intelligence Agency made him de facto the leader of his counterintelligence colleagues in allied countries who were attempting to resist this KGB offensive. In the late 1960s he institutionalized this relationship through a series of conferences with the representatives of the Canadian, Australian, New Zealand, and British (CAZAB) counterintelligence services. The first CAZAB conference took place in summer 1967 in Melbourne. It was attended by representatives from the CIA, the FBI, MI5, MI6, New Zealand's Secret Service, and the Australian Security Intelligence Organisation and Australian Secret Intelligence Service. Golitsin made a presentation that sufficiently impressed MI5 for them to invite him back to the United Kingdom, at the persuasive fee of £10,000 a month, tax-free.[143] That raconteur of the intelligence business, Peter Wright, called the CAZAB conferences Angleton's "outstanding achievement." "The best, the brightest, and the most senior officers in Western intelligence came together once every eighteen months to discuss his agenda—the Soviet threat, the role of counterintelligence—and to conduct doom-laden future scenarios."[144]

Wright has a less cheerful account of Angleton circa 1970, when "Angleton paid a secret visit to London" to check in on the molehunt:

> He looked worse than ever, consumed by the dark, foreboding role he was committed to playing. He viewed himself as a kind of Cassandra preaching doom and decline for the West . . . Patience with Angleton was rapidly wearing thin in London in 1970. Maurice Oldfield had an ill-concealed hostility to all his ideas and theories, and even inside MI5 he had begun to make enemies . . . We learned later just how far he was prepared to go to discredit [a defector] . . . As [the defector] was debriefed, we routinely sent over our intelligence digest containing his material to the FBI for circulation through to the CIA, and on to the National Security Council and up to the President . . . Some months later, J. Edgar Hoover took a vacation in Florida, and took the opportunity to call on President Nixon at his holiday home on Key Biscayne . . . "How do you like the British reports from their [defector], Mr. President?" . . . "What reports?" replied Nixon. He had never received them . . . When Hoover checked back with Kissinger, he had not received them either. Kissinger got on to the CIA and instituted a full search. They were finally found in Angleton's safe. He had concluded [that the defector] was a provocation, and simply refused to circulate the documents. Tom Karamessines, the CIA Director of Plans, issued a stern rebuke, and it was the beginning of Angleton's slide from power.[145]

It could not have helped Angleton's mood when, "following his election as Prime Minister in 1970, Edward Heath appointed Victor Rothschild as head of the Central Policy Review Staff . . . the [secret intelligence] Think Tank."[146] Rothschild, who had been Guy Burgess's landlord.

• • •

The report produced by Sullivan and Angleton became known as the Huston Plan, but, as Sullivan wrote, "In fact, the plan wasn't Huston's at all—it summed up the thinking of the subcommittee as a whole. Once the material was gathered from the different agencies and once the recommendations were agreed on, I turned the whole thing over to one of my men in the Domestic Intelligence Division to be written up, and I submitted his draft to the committee at large."[147] The committee met to consider this "Huston" Plan on June 25, 1970. At which point events became more than ordinarily Byzantine. First, Hoover put his colleagues through the ordeal of "going through the document page by page, and for every page, asking each person around the table for comments. Each time Hoover came to Tom Huston, he would use a different name: 'Any questions Mr. Hoffman? Any questions, Mr. Hutchinson?' and so on, getting the name wrong six or seven different ways. This was the director's way of showing his dislike for the rookie White House intellectual. Sullivan recalls that it was difficult to keep from laughing. He bit his lip and tried staring at the floor. Helms leaned back on his chair and winked at Huston behind Hoover's back." Finally, "the FBI director completed the reading and each of the four intelligence chiefs signed the document. Sullivan and Huston had achieved their goal—or so it seemed."[148] Nixon approved the report on July 14. On July 23, Huston "wrote a two-page memorandum that amounted to nothing less than a blueprint for a police state in America."[149]

When the dimensions of the Huston Plan emerged in the hearings of the Church Committee, Senator Walter Mondale questioned Huston about its legality. He received a sweeping response: "Well, as I said, Senator, it was my opinion at the time that simply the fourth amendment did not apply to the President in the exercise of matters relating to the internal security or national security."[150] The Fourth Amendment reads, "The right of the people to be secure in their persons, houses, papers, and effects, against unreasonable searches and seizures, shall not be violated, and no Warrants shall issue, but upon probable cause, supported by Oath or affirmation, and particularly describing the place to be searched, and the persons or things to be seized." Huston, a lawyer who was a staff assistant to the president of the United States, was of the opinion (like some of his successors) that unreasonable searches and seizures were legal if authorized by the president. In effect, he believed that the constitutional ban on unreasonable searches and seizures had been suspended. When had this happened?

Richard Nixon, writing in explanation of his approval of the plan, asserted that t had happened long before his administration, in that of Truman or Roosevelt.[151] In other words, the Huston Plan was simply a ratification of the status quo. Nixon, claiming, as usual, to be a victim of a misunderstanding, explained in a letter to the Church Committee:

> What many persons refused to recognize when the existence of the "Huston" evaluation became known, but what your Committee's investigation has now established beyond doubt, is that none of the recommendations contained in the Huston evaluation departed from actions taken under at least four or five earlier Administrations . . . The difference, of course, was that in utilizing the various intelligence methods suggested, such as C.I.A. informants within the United States to trace communist alliances with terrorist organizations who had threatened domestic violence to protest the Viet Nam War, my Administration was viewed as bent upon stifling dissenting political views. The intermixture of protected political activity, civil disobedience, and acts of terrorism—all under the antiwar rubric—was so great that to move against terrorism was to be guilty of political suppression. Unfortunately, the tools available to get at the one while avoiding the other were not as delicate as the surgeon's scalpel.[152]

The cost of a "move against terrorism" was "unfortunately . . . political suppression." It was a cost that Nixon believed that his predecessors—back to President Roosevelt, if not Wilson—had been willing to pay. He, too, was willing to pay it.

Senator Mondale's comment on this type of reasoning is apposite: "if criminals could be excused on the grounds that someone had done it before, there would not be much of a population in any of the prisons today, would there?"[153]

In spite of what the president viewed as its reasonableness, the Huston Plan ran into an obstacle: Nemesis, as so often at moments of triumph, stood by ready to act. In this case, Nemesis took the unusual form of the director of the Federal Bureau of Investigation. David Wise gives a colorful account of these events: "Huston, in his youthful zeal, had sadly underestimated Hoover's power. Like an old crocodile dozing in the sun, too sleepy to be bothered, Hoover finally disposed of Tom Charles Huston with one dreadful flick of his tail."[154] Attorney General Mitchell had not been kept informed of the progress of the committee by Huston. It was therefore comparatively easy for Hoover to sink the plan by going to the attorney general and expressing alarm. Mitchell was not pleased to have been bypassed by the young White House aide—and his mentors in the various intelligence agencies. Perhaps knowing that derailing the plan would change nothing, he added his influence to that of Hoover.

As President Nixon told the story, "Mr. Mitchell . . . informed me that it was his opinion that the risk of disclosure of the possible illegal actions [proposed in the Huston Plan] . . . was greater than the possible benefit to be derived. Based upon this conversation with Attorney General Mitchell, I decided to revoke the approval originally extended to the Committee's recommendations."[155] The risk of disclosure bothered the president, but not the illegal activities themselves. "The President's withdrawal of approval for the 'Huston Plan' did not, in fact, result in the termination of either the NSA program for covering the communications of Americans or the CIA mail-opening program. These programs continued without the formal authorization which had been hoped for."[156] Soon, Mr. Huston returned to the practice of law in Indiana, having learned, among other things, an important lesson about intelligence officials: "the trouble with dealing with these people is that what they say is not often so [much] untrue as it is misleading."[157] It is, perhaps, not as important a distinction as it might at first sight appear.

Senator Church summarized the strange history of the Huston Plan as follows:

> Our investigations have revealed that the Huston plan itself was only an episode in the lawlessness which preceded and followed its brief existence.
>
> First, we have discovered that unlawful mail openings were being conducted long before the President was asked to authorize them in June 1970 . . .
>
> Second, even though the President revoked his approval of the Huston plan, the intelligence agencies paid no heed to the revocation. Instead, they continued the very practices for which they had sought presidential authority, expanding some of them and reinstating others which had been abolished years before . . .
>
> Finally, the Huston plan, as we now know, must be viewed as but one episode in a continuous effort by the intelligence agencies to secure the sanction of higher authority for expanded surveillance at home and abroad.[158]

Or, as James Angleton put it, "'The Huston Plan . . . was dead in five days and therefore all of the other matters of enlarging procurement within the intelligence community were the same concerns that existed prior to the Huston Plan, and subsequent to the Huston Plan. The Huston Plan had no impact whatsoever on the priorities within the intelligence community.' . . . Angleton continued, 'People are reading a lot into the Huston Plan, and, at the same time, are unaware that on several levels in the community identical bilateral discussions were going on.'"[159] The Church Committee agreed with Angleton in this assessment: "When President Nixon eventually revoked his approval of the Huston Plan, the intelligence community nevertheless proceeded to initiate some programs suggested in the Plan. Intelligence agencies also continued to employ techniques recommended in the Plan, such as mail opening which had been used previously without presidential approval."[160] As then Senator Mondale observed, "I think a very instructive memo on this Presidential point is dated September 18, 1970, by John Dean. It went to the Attorney General. What it says, in effect, is that now that we have rejected the Huston plan, we should put it, in effect, back into place, and remove the restraints as necessary to obtain such intelligence. In other words, they rejected the formal plan, and then they proceeded surreptitiously, according to this memo, to go ahead and do it anyway."[161]

The story of the Huston Plan is an instance of the usual complexities of bureaucratic warfare. Sullivan, wishing to better secure some small part of the counterintelligence practices of the Federal Bureau of Investigation against Hoover's objections, convinced Huston that he, Huston, was creating the authority for those and a much wider range of practices that were in fact already extant. Hoover and Mitchell, thought, or at least Hoover thought, that by destroying the Huston Plan he had stopped the institution of practices advocated by Sullivan. (For example, "The final interagency report on the Huston Plan signed by Richard Helms and J. Edgar Hoover, was sent to the President with the statement, contrary to fact, that all mail opening programs by federal agencies had been discontinued.")[162] But, as a matter of fact, those practices were actually under way, and would continue.

For whom was this smoke screen created by Sullivan, Angleton, and their colleagues? Was it for Huston, the naive Nixon enthusiast? Was it for Hoover? Was it for Nixon himself? Or was it for that somewhat nebulous entity, the American people? Somewhere in these maneuvers, Nixon himself lost track of the bidding. According to the White House tapes, on June 17, 1971, during a meeting in the Oval Office between the president, Haldeman, Ehrlichman, and Kissinger, Nixon said, "Bob? Bob? Now do you remember Huston's plan? Implement it."[163]

The true importance of the Huston Plan was not its novelty—although it was intended by Huston himself to be an innovation in the practice of domestic intelligence and covert action—but in its synoptic function, summarizing in a single document the otherwise undocumented reality of domestic intelligence and covert action in the Johnson and Nixon administrations.

After the revocation of the Huston Plan, Attorney General Mitchell himself created a new group within the Justice Department, the Intelligence Evaluation Committee (IEC). The IEC was a central archive for domestic surveillance information. Although the committee met only a few times, and ceased to meet after July 1971, the committee's staff were extremely active, meeting over a hundred times between the beginning of 1971 and mid-1973. Their production included approximately thirty studies and evaluations and fifty-five summaries of significant events ("intelligence calendars"). The summaries were produced under the direction of John Dean or the committee chairman, Robert Mardian.[164] As William Sullivan observed, "Huston's failure to bring Hoover into line forced the White House to forget about the FBI and look elsewhere for men to do the kind of investigative work Nixon, Mitchell, Haldeman, Ehrlichman, Dean, and the others felt was necessary. As it turned out, they ended up forming their own group, which later became known as the Plumbers."[165] The sixty agents working for Angleton's assistant Richard Ober supplied the Nixon administration with a continuing stream of intelligence about the antiwar leadership, and Ober's commission gradually came to include assisting the White House in its efforts to gather information on the executive branch itself.[166] Ober was on Mitchell's IEC when the "top item on the committee's agenda was domestic political intelligence, and the top task—communicated directly from Nixon via Dean—was to devise better methods of preventing leaks."[167]

Looking back on his efforts and their unintended consequences, Huston concluded:

> What I did not realize then was that these kinds of programs, although theoretically and conceptually could be narrowly used in the best interests of the country by responsible people, can lead to the type of thing that happened with the Plumbers and with the Watergate . . .
>
> But it is obvious to me that this kind of thing lends itself too easily to the type of corruption that we have seen, and, therefore, I have come to the conclusion that whereas I would traditionally have taken the position that I am willing to run some small risk of infringing upon some small portion of the public's otherwise legitimate rights for the greater good security of all of the people, I now come to the conclusion that we have no practical alternative but to take a far greater risk that there are going to be these kinds of things that we cannot deal effectively against until such time as perhaps our recourse is simply to the ongoing criminal process.[168]

Nonetheless, paralleling the game of three-card monte that the Nixon administration was playing with the Huston Plan, in the fall of 1971 the Emergency Detention Act of 1950 was repealed, then the FBI's "new 'administrative index' (ADEX) was expanded to include an elastic category: 'the new breed of subversive.'" The old Reserve Index was folded into the ADEX. "It included 'teachers, writers, lawyers, etc.' who did not actively participate in subversive activity 'but who were nevertheless influential in espousing their respective philosophies.'" That brought over 23,000 people onto the ADEX lists.[169]

• • •

The Central Intelligence Agency is not simply a bureaucracy, or, at least, it has not always been that. Originally it was, and saw itself as being, a specialized function of the natural ruling class of the country ("the very best men"), drawing its top personnel from the same groups and schools that staffed the State Department, Wall Street, and the national press. These people shared a common background, a common education, common (or uncommon) tastes; they attended one another's dinner parties, married and/or had affairs with one another's sisters and wives. The great expansion of the Agency and a generational change in the 1960s and 1970s fractured this consensus. The Agency's need for specialists and, simply, for new personnel, drawn perforce from a society that itself had changed, created a new culture in the Agency, such that, for a time, orders began to be questioned, and tasks assigned began to be measured against ethical standards that did not end with anti-Communism.

It was within this changing context that Operation CHAOS, despite measures by Ober and Angleton to prevent it, became widely known within the CIA—and began to meet with opposition within the Agency itself. Ober's security precautions had attracted the attention that they were intended to avoid: "It is quite likely that certain CIA employees outside of my office falsely construed this extreme compartmentation [*sic*] and secrecy as designed to conceal illegal domestic spying," Ober said. Of course, they "could not have been more mistaken."[170] Mistaken or not, they continued to be suspicious. Word of this reached Richard Helms, disturbing him sufficiently so that on September 6, 1969, he sent a memorandum to all deputy directors of the Central Intelligence Agency, asserting that Operation CHAOS was legal and directing them to support it.[171] William Colby later wrote that this "aroused the concern of many CIA employees . . . and their constant questions about it soon made it an interdirectorate matter appropriate for me, as the [then] Executive Director, to handle. Young analysts, computer operators and operations officers were all aware that a most secret project was lodged in that most secret of Agency crannies, the Counterintelligence Staff, and that it had a great deal to do with the Anti-War Movement. And the main concern on the part of these young Agency employees was whether CIA was engaged in an activity that was clearly outside its proper charter—domestic intelligence."[172]

Ultimately, Operation CHAOS was the occasion for the closest thing on (public) record to a revolt within the Agency: "Enough information concerning CHAOS was known within the CIA so that a middle level management group of 14 officers (organized to discuss and develop possible solutions to various CIA problems) was in a position to write two memoranda in 1971 raising questions as to the propriety of the project." Nothing came of this. Helms composed a memorandum for the record on December 5, 1972: "CHAOS is a legitimate counterintelligence function of the Agency and cannot be stopped simply because some members of the organization do not like this activity."[173]

On one level, this demonstrates, as he insisted, that Ober had friends in high places. On another level it is another indication that Angleton's actions were also those of Helms. Which way the chain of causality ran might be an interesting question, but in the end Angleton was responsible for CHAOS, as well as for HT/LINGUAL and much else, and Helms was responsible for Angleton's actions in those matters. The buck stopped with Helms, and Helms was not about to allow "middle level officers" to derail an operation he had authorized, and which was, from a certain point of view, successful

For, by "the end of 1972, the mass movement which had comprised the new left had generally disintegrated, for a number of reasons, but notably because of COINTELPRO and its related forms of police pressure."[174] The underground press—and such "above ground" publications as *Ramparts*—had been destroyed, by the government's intelligence agencies and the loss of their raison d'être as the United States withdrew from the war. One after another saw its circulation drop to minuscule levels or ceased publication altogether. As its prey vanished, so did the predator: "With the decline of student demonstrations and antiwar activity in the latter part of 1972, the intensity of the CHAOS effort declined . . . In 1973, the CHAOS program was transferred from the Counterintelligence Staff to the newly formed Operations Staff within the Plans Directorate."[175] Operation CHAOS was terminated on March 15, 1974.[176]

How can we summarize this narrative of CHAOS? Between 1967 and 1974 there occurred an extraordinary series of events which might be called an "autocoup," as such events are called in Latin America—although the emergence of the military establishment as the dominant force in the Japanese government in the 1930s, not to mention more recent events in this country, might be closer parallels. The American intelligence establishment—the FBI, the CIA, military intelligence—acting with the knowledge and, to some extent, at the initiative of Presidents Johnson and Nixon, conducted a campaign to abrogate the Constitution's protection of the rights guaranteed in matters of freedom of the press and freedom of assembly. The thinking behind the system of detention camps authorized by the McCarran act was revived.[177] Not for the last time, lists of prospective detainees were compiled; newspapers and magazines opposed to governmental policy were destroyed; organizations opposed to governmental policy were infiltrated and disrupted; hundreds, if not thousands, of citizens identified with the more radical sectors of the civil rights and antiwar movements were imprisoned, and many were killed.

The consequences—and precedent—of this domestic covert action campaign are with us still. The New Left has joined the Communist Party in oblivion. Americans have grown used to a government that will not tolerate political activity outside the well-guarded channels of a political process that seems, to many, to have lost its legitimacy—to be, in the view of many, little more than a spoils system grown murderous.

# 12

# Endgame

*It is the responsibility of intellectuals to speak the truth and to expose lies.*
—*Noam Chomsky*

I have narrated Angleton's activities as chief of the Counterintelligence Staff of the Central Intelligence Agency separately: the molehunt, the private intelligence networks—Lovestone and others—the Warren Commission and the invention of that useful term of opprobrium, "conspiracy theory," the interception of mail and telegrams, Operation CHAOS, Israel. But of course they all took place simultaneously, and we have now reached a point where one after another these activities came to an end, at least insofar as they concerned James Angleton.

The Apostolic Succession in the Central Intelligence Agency led from William Donovan, the Forerunner, through the generals and admirals who assembled the Agency from the fragments of the Office of Strategic Services, to Donovan's lieutenant and true heir, Allen Dulles, through another admiral and a businessman, to Richard Helms, Dulles's protégé. Helms, who had come up through the ranks—from assisting Dulles in Berlin after the war to head of the Clandestine Services itself—represented the orthodox tradition of the secret intelligence services, those believing that the collection of secret information was the true center of the Agency. (His rival, Richard Bissell, had inherited Wiesner's covert action legacy, and, living by that sword, had died by it after the debacle at the Bay of Pigs.) When Helms was forced into what he anticipated as remunerative Iranian exile by President Nixon, he was succeeded by James Schlesinger, a usurper in the eyes of the loyalists at Langley, an outsider who decimated the Clandestine Services, retiring hundreds of officers from what he called Helms's "Praetorian Guard." Rising behind and then replacing Schlesinger was William Colby, who was, in a certain sense, as much an old boy as Helms (or Angleton, for that matter), but whose career had taken place, in the main, far from the center. It was Colby's mission to move the Agency from the charismatic to the bureaucratic stage of its development. Or perhaps, as some thought, Colby was the American Philby, hiding in the fortified hamlets of the Mekong Delta from the molehunt, emerging in the bleak end-time of the mid-1970s to betray the Agency to its enemies in Moscow and Congress.

Colby's memoir, *Honorable Men*, is a self-portrait of a liberal Catholic lawyer with a moral vision somewhat at odds with his activities, and often, he says, quite opposed to the policies of the Agency and the presidents he served. And yet his rise within the Agency was steady, unimpeded by that moral vision or even by the circumstance that he was in repeated conflict with the supposedly all-powerful Angleton. "The mutual dislike between Colby and James Angleton was no secret in the CIA," writes Thomas Powers. "Angleton had criticized Colby's support for the Christian Democratic party's 'opening to the left' in Italy in the late 1950s . . . Let in the Socialists, he argued, and the Communists won't be far behind. He darkly suspected that the Socialists and the Communists might have reached a secret agreement and thought Colby's trust of the Socialists naive."[1] Colby's work in Rome was appreciated by the Agency's personnel department, if not by Angleton; on the strength of it he became the CIA's chief of station in Saigon from 1959 to 1962, then chief of the Far East Division of the CIA from January 1963. In late 1967 Colby was appointed head of the most important component of the Clandestine Services, the Soviet and Eastern European Division, the epicenter of the molehunt.

This brought him into immediate conflict with Angleton, who had just completed the process of removing much of the division's Russian-speaking staff in that final, desperate, scorched-earth effort to eliminate the Soviet threat of subversion and penetration from the corridors of Langley itself. Colby later wrote that "As difficult as were the problems the [Soviet and Eastern European] Division faced in Eastern Europe [in early 1968], I soon discovered that it faced an almost greater problem in Washington . . ."

> The Division produced operations and intelligence, but the C[ounter] I[ntelligence] staff believed that those operations and intelligence were controlled by the KGB, that the Russians deliberately fed us and manipulated information to mislead the United States in a massive deception program . . . Our concern over possible KGB penetration, it seemed to me, had so preoccupied us that we were devoting most of our time to protecting ourselves from the KGB and not enough to developing the new sources and operations that we needed to learn secret information about the Soviets and their allies. Indeed, we seemed to be putting more emphasis on the KGB as CIA's adversary than on the Soviet Union as the United States' adversary.[2]

Which, of course, was a distinction without a difference from Angleton's point of view. Colby portrays his disagreement with Angleton as one of judgment, but it was also a matter of the desk at which each sat. Colby's job was "to learn secret information about the Soviets"; Angleton's job was to be concerned "over possible KGB penetration": Colby was the flirt, Angleton the chaperone. Furthermore, Angleton always feared that the CIA officer running the Soviet and Eastern Europe Division was the most obvious target for KGB blandishments, which did nothing to ease his relationship with Colby. However, before either of them could act against the other, Colby was sent back out to Saigon, where their relationship was to become yet more bitter.

The Vietnam War was at its height when Colby became deputy chief of Civil Operations and Revolutionary Development Support (CORDS) in March 1968, then its chief later in 1968.[3] CORDS is best known for the Phoenix operation, an effort to deprive the Viet Cong of its support in the South Vietnamese countryside. Those Americans opposed to the war said that Phoenix was an assassination program, citing 20,000 as the number of Viet Cong officials and sympathizers killed—a characterization, but not a number, that Colby denied. In Saigon as in Washington, Colby's struggle was as much with Counterintelligence as it was with the Communists. Angleton argued that the infiltration of the South Vietnamese government by the Viet Cong was a threat both to the war effort and to American security and wished to form a separate counterintelligence unit in Saigon. According to Thomas Powers, "The first step was [for the CIA] to penetrate the Saigon government itself, something Colby would not do . . . Angleton blamed the failure on Colby, but did not stop there: he said the blood of American boys was on Colby's hands."[4] There were more specific accusations, as Edward Jay Epstein tells us: "At one point, counterintelligence had even raised some questions about Colby's own contacts with a French citizen in Saigon who was suspected of being a Soviet agent. All CIA personnel were supposed to report contacts they had with foreign nationals in Vietnam and Colby failed to report meeting this person."[5]

On the one hand, Angleton was right: it appears that North Vietnam had tens of thousands of agents in the South, thoroughly infiltrating the South Vietnamese government and much of the American establishment there as well. On the other hand, given bureaucratic traditions, Angleton's desire to have a unit in Saigon reporting directly to him rather than to the Saigon chief of station was bound to be opposed by Colby.[6] The animosity became so severe that Colby was not allowed in the area of the embassy that housed the counterintelligence office, and rumors were spread by the Counterintelligence Staff that Colby had a mistress who was a suspect foreign national.[7] Eventually, Colby won, which meant, according to a sympathizer of Angleton's, that he had "terminate[d] all counterintelligence activities in that country. This meant, in effect, that the CIA could not question or evaluate the sources of its information in Vietnam."[8] From Angleton's point of view, Colby was deliberately blinding the United States effort in Vietnam. Presented with reports from sources any one of which might have been under the control of Hanoi, the CIA had no way of determining which were to be believed, which were disinformation. It is not difficult to imagine the notations Angleton made in Colby's file.

Colby returned early to Washington in mid-1971 because of the health problems of his daughter, Catherine (who was to die in April 1973, a victim, some said, of the war, which had distressed her to the point of fatally aggravating her anorexia).[9] The job Helms found for him was as executive director of the CIA. The executive director was in theory the third within the hierarchy of the Agency, but it was a staff, not a line, position. Given the tradition that the deputy director was a military man—in those years, the talented linguist and liaison officer, Vernon Walters (who, as it happened, was close to Angleton)—in effect the main operational divisions of the Agency reported directly to Helms. Colby's job was to make sure that the paper flowed well. Partially sidelined, he still saw no reason to become an admirer of Angleton: "At this stage, as Executive Director, I had no 'need to know' all the complex details of our operations against the hard targets [the Soviet Bloc] or of the supersecret counterintelligence operations," Colby wrote. "So I could not form a solid opinion on the merits in the debate whether our operations were totally suspect, as Angleton held, or whether they were being hamstrung by overcautious suspicion. But I did see clearly that a large portion of our effort was wide of the mark that we should have been concentrating on—the recruitment of Communist officials and nationals."[10]

What was more, Colby thought that "from the mid-1960's on . . . [the CIA's] Soviet operations came to a dead halt. Helms and Karamessines had launched a program we called hard targets. 'Let's recruit hard targets. Soviet. Chinese. That's what we're in business for.' It wasn't happening . . . As I understood it, it was because of the high degree of suspicion that was exhibited about any operational opportunities. The insistence of CI that defectors be looked at as probable fakes. There was an awful impasse between the CI staff and the Soviet division."[11] The argument between Colby and Angleton remained largely the same, from the mid-1950s in Rome to the 1960s in Saigon and the early 1970s in Washington. Each was presumably doing what he thought he should—Colby running spies, Angleton looking for double agents among or behind them. Their conflict could be, and usually was, presented as a policy dispute concerning matters about which reasonable men might differ. It was in fact a manifestation on the personal level of the perfectly orthodox conflict between the career intelligence officer and the career counterintelligence officer. Insofar as that was the case, in theory, it should have benefited the Agency. Each of these intelligent, dedicated men worked to balance the efforts of the other. However, prolonged differences of opinion, passionately held, have their effects on relationships and attitudes beyond the matters at hand.

Colby had returned to a Washington that was gradually becoming obsessed with the Watergate scandal, a matter in which he was to play a crucial role. In November 1972 he "failed to conceal" from investigators the fact that the White House had tried to get the CIA to block the FBI's initial investigation of the break-in (while succeeding in concealing that the CIA had in fact done the White House's bidding). But although the Agency was no longer attempting to protect the White House, it remained concerned to protect itself. A few weeks after Nixon fired him, Richard Helms, still in place as director of central intelligence, took measures to minimize the possible damage to the Agency if Operation CHAOS were to become publicly known.

> Helms called in Colby, Ober, and Karamessines for a meeting on December 5, 1972. Helms emphasized the importance of running a cleaner, less dubious-looking operation. There was a need to proceed cautiously, he said, to avoid a showdown with "some CIA personnel [in the Inspector General's office]." Nonetheless, Helms was adamant that MHCHAOS not be abandoned. It will not be "stopped simply because some members of the organization did not like this activity," he insisted . . . Helms had come up with a solution to the problem of CIA officers who doubted the legality of MHCHAOS. *Henceforth, it would be described within the Agency as an operation against international terrorism* . . . But there was in fact to be little change in targets. MHCHAOS continued to hold radicals in its sights, specifically radical youths, Blacks, women, and antiwar militants. The label "international terrorist" was designed to replace "political dissident" as the ongoing justification for illegal domestic operations . . . with Ober still in charge.[12] (Emphasis added.)

An operation against Americans was to be described as an operation against international terrorism.

Shuffling his cabinet after his landslide victory in 1972, President Nixon made James Schlesinger, formerly of the budget office, director of central intelligence in succession to Richard Helms. Schlesinger broke the tradition of having a military deputy director by appointing Colby. Colby immediately moved against his old enemy, recommending that Schlesinger fire Angleton and laying out his case against the counterintelligence chief. The director of central intelligence studied his deputy's brief and "then called Angleton into his office and went through the criticism of him point by point. Schlesinger told Angleton that Colby had accused him of being overly secretive and having a conspiratorial approach. He blamed Angleton, moreover, for confusing and demoralizing the Soviet Division. On balance, Colby [had] concluded that Angleton's relentless suspicions of Soviet infiltration had proven 'more of a liability than an asset.'" Schlesinger then asked Angleton "what he viewed as the difficulty at the CIA . . . Angleton began talking about the nature of secret intelligence: its epistemology, its vulnerability, and its ultimate value. Three hours went by . . . When Angleton emerged from the Director's office, he had not been fired as counterintelligence chief. He had now become an adviser to Schlesinger."[13] Schlesinger, like many before him, was as much fascinated by the Angleton persona as he was convinced by his arguments. Angleton had become the Scheherazade of the Cold War.

All that spring, as Schlesinger, the first civilian outsider to direct the Central Intelligence Agency since McCone, was trying to take control of the organization, the Watergate scandal had been accelerating. Finally, on April 30, 1973, Haldeman and Ehrlichman resigned and John Dean was fired. Schlesinger, learning about the Agency's connections with Howard Hunt and the Plumbers not from his staff but from the *Washington Post*, wondered what else he had not been told.[14] "He threatened to tear the place apart and 'fire everyone if necessary' to find out if other grim surprises awaited him."[15] According to Cord Meyer, "Schlesinger issued a directive to all CIA employees on May 9, 1973 . . . that read as follows: 'I have ordered all senior operating officials of this Agency to report to me immediately on any activities now going on, or that have gone on in the past, which might be construed to be outside the legislative charter of this Agency' . . . Colby was designated by Schlesinger to oversee the preparation of a report based on all available records and the testimony of those who came forward to confess . . . Colby pursued the project with penitential zeal and by May 21, 1973, had collected 693 pages describing all past instances in which the Agency's legislative charter might conceivably have been violated."[16]

It is of interest that Colby himself was among those, perhaps the principal among those, who had not been forthcoming with Schlesinger. It was Colby, after all, who had been in charge of the paperwork concerning the Plumbers. Hence, perhaps, his zeal. Schlesinger's threat to "fire everyone if necessary" was not idle. He indeed "fired or pushed into early retirement fifteen hundred employees. Of these, one thousand were from the operations side of the Agency."[17] Schlesinger thought the Agency was overstaffed, but more importantly he thought the organizational culture was wrongheaded. He sought to change it through what many viewed as decapitation, removing many of those senior members of the staff who had guided the Agency under Dulles and Helms.

Colby approved of these actions, in spite of his own status and history in the

Agency. To his surprise, there was a "senior officer who escaped the purge, and that was Jim Angleton."

> I make no secret of the fact that I recommended to Schlesinger that Angleton ought to be moved, reiterating my long-held feeling that his supersecretive style of operation had, at least in recent years, become incompatible with the one I believed essential. But Schlesinger wasn't sure. He was clearly fascinated by Angleton's undoubted brilliance and couldn't help wondering if there might not be something to his complicated theories that deserved further exploration. It may also have been that Angleton's unbending Cold War view toward the Soviets appealed to Schlesinger's own fierce anti-Communism. So he refused to let me move him. But he did agree to allow me to make some major changes in Angleton's operations.[18]

Colby "moved expeditiously to reduce the reach and size of Angleton's [180-man] counterintelligence staff. He first took away its job of determining bona fides, complaining that in the past the CIA had spent an inordinate amount of time worrying about false defectors and false agents."[19] This repeated at the center what Colby had done in the field, in Vietnam. Henceforth, the Agency was to cease to worry about vetting its sources. It is as if the CIA had found a copy of the MI6 playbook, circa 1938. When the CIA formed the Counterintelligence Staff it had done so on the theory that checks and balances were essential in the intelligence world. Intelligence officers have an interest in the reliability of their agents, an interest that can lead to conflicts in the interpretation of evidence concerning where the loyalties of those agents lie. As in the American court system, or in the traditions of the Roman Catholic Church, those who designed the structure of the CIA thought it helpful to charter a countervailing group to question the bona fides of agents proposed by intelligence officers. The tension between the two was meant to balance the faith of the one against the skepticism of the other. Colby had other ideas. He envisioned a world where every case officer was his (or, rarely, her) own counterintelligence staff.

> "I just thought CI should be an inherent part of the intelligence process," Colby later explained. "Do your counterintelligence as an aspect of your positive intelligence. Make it part of a case officer's professional background."
>
> In practice, that would mean that every case officer would have the task of establishing the bona fides of his own recruitments. Angleton's CI Staff would no longer have an automatic role in agent assessment, and would be largely cut out of the process . . . Miler [Angleton's deputy] was

incredulous. "To me, Colby's idea that every case officer could be his own CI officer was a bunch of crap. How could one man possibly know enough about foreign intelligence services to do a good job? If an agent came to you with the blueprints for, say, an Iraqi supergun, how were you going to know enough even to ask an intelligent question?"[20]

But Schlesinger had been moved up to the position of secretary of defense and Colby had finally become director of central intelligence. The argument was no longer philosophical. "Effective July 1, 1973, the CI Staff was 'decentralized,' and would serve only in an auxiliary or advisory capacity"[21] According to David Wise: "The Counterintelligence Staff was reduced to running name checks on people proposed to be used in operations . . . Colby next took away Angleton's power to review operations already in progress . . . In addition, Colby removed the small international Communism unit from Angleton's fiefdom. As each of these offices were plucked out, the size of Angleton's staff dwindled from hundreds to some forty people."[22]

The international Communism unit provided liaison to Jay Lovestone and others of that tradition. According to Lovestone's biographer, Ted Morgan, "Colby assigned one of his trusted officers, Horace Feldman, to look into Angleton's activities, and Feldman discovered the Lovestone connection and the JX reports, which had escaped the inspector general's review."

> "It was excluded for some reason," Feldman told Colby. "Excluded," Colby asked in astonishment, "how?" "It's supposed to be independent," Feldman said. "What's going on?" Colby asked. "Here we have a senior officer in the labor movement, a domestic organization outside our mandate, and he is in our pay. And he publishes a newspaper, the *Free Trade Union News*. This is a clear violation of our charter. Lovestone is collecting information on U.S. citizens" . . . "Jim fought, fought, fought. He had Horace in tears," Colby recalled . . . "But Horace doggedly investigated and gave me his report, and I said, 'This operation has out-lived its usefulness and must be terminated immediately.' It looked as though the CIA was trying to influence American foreign policy via the labor movement. And another thing, how could we run a proper agency with all the contacts Jim made on his own, such as Mrs. Morris?"[23] [For Louise "Pagie" Morris, see chap. 8 and below.]

Indeed.

Operation CHAOS survived a few more weeks, until the end of August 1973, when Colby "restricted [it] to a passive collection of information upon FBI request."[24] Three years later, the U.S. Senate's Church Committee summarized the record of Operation CHAOS and related activities as follows: "Some 300,000 individuals were indexed in a CIA computer system and separate files were created on approximately 7,200 Americans and over 100 domestic groups during the course of CIA's Operation CHAOS (1967–1973)." They judged that "throughout the administrations of Presidents Johnson and Nixon, the investigative process was misused as a means of acquiring political intelligence for the White House."[25]

Finally, Colby "managed to remove from Angleton's Counterintelligence Staff such functions as CIA's liaison with the FBI . . . and a host of procedural activities, and so [further] reduce his large staff."[26] All of which was standard bureaucratic procedure preparatory to the elimination of a rival. "As Colby would later allow, 'Taking away FBI liaison was designed to lead [Angleton] to read the handwriting on the wall.'"[27]

And yet, Colby, like Schlesinger before him, did not immediately make a decisive move against Angleton. "I thought the clandestine service had had just about all the personnel turbulence it could take for the moment and that a move against Angleton would be seen as symbolic of lots more to come."

> I decided not to move him. I spent several long sessions doing my best to follow his tortuous theories about the long arm of a powerful and wily KGB at work, over decades, placing its agents in the heart of allied and neutral nations and sending its false defectors to influence and undermine American policy. I confess that I couldn't absorb it, possibly because I did not have the requisite grasp of this labyrinthine subject, possibly because Angleton's explanations were impossible to follow, or possibly because the evidence just didn't add up to his conclusions. At the same time I looked in vain for some tangible results in the counterintelligence field, and found little or none. I did not suspect Angleton and his staff of engaging in improper activities. I just could not figure out what they were doing at all.[28]

The CIA was much occupied with changing the governments of Western democracies in the early 1970s, perhaps at home, certainly abroad. It was odd that Colby said he did not suspect Angleton and his staff of improper activities, given what Colby knew at this point about activities like Operation CHAOS and HT/LINGUAL, or, among other foreign matters, the unusual interventions of the Agency in Australian politics that were taking place just at this time.[29]

Rather than firing Angleton, Colby continued his bureaucratic salami tactics. Having reorganized Counterintelligence itself, and separated Angleton from his private intelligence collection network, Colby "resolved to move the Israeli 'account' from the Counterintelligence Staff." Once again, "In the process I hoped Angleton might take the hint and retire in time to secure certain retirement benefits which closed in June 1974. But he dug in his heels, and marshaled every argument he could think of to urge that such an important contact could not be handled in the normal bureaucratic machinery. I yielded, in truth because I feared that Angleton's professional integrity and personal intensity might have led him to take dire measures if I forced the issue of either his Israeli relationship or his continued employment."[30]

In other words, Colby, whose daughter may or may not have killed herself a few months earlier, was concerned, or wished to give the impression in his memoirs that he was concerned, that if pushed into a corner Angleton might commit suicide. This is a singular thought. There are no indications that Angleton had tendencies in that regard, unless alcoholism is taken to be a form of slow suicide. Perhaps Colby had other reasons for not moving as strongly against Angleton as he would have wished. Angleton had many friends in the Agency, and in powerful offices outside the Agency, and Colby might have felt that he was not yet in a position to exercise his will in the matter—and, in retrospect, wished to cloak his frustration (or fear) in compassion.

Later in the year, however, Colby did begin "cutting down [Angleton's] liaison duties with other intelligence services—particularly Israel." Angleton's resistance was weakened during this period. His father had died and his ulcer worsened, causing repeated stays in hospital.[31] Finally, in December 1974, Colby undertook what he said was an unpleasant personnel task. "Because another retirement deadline had been set by the Civil Service Commission for the end of December, I was determined to face up to my responsibility to remove Jim Angleton before it, so he would not miss out on its benefits."

> So, I called Angleton to my office to talk the matter out with him, saying that I had come to the conclusion that a change was necessary in both jobs, the Israeli liaison and counterintelligence, but that I wanted to retain his talents for the Agency, and especially his experience. I offered him the prospect of separate status, where he could summarize for us the many ideas he had and conclusions he had reached about counterintelligence, and where he would be consulted on, but no longer be in charge of, our Israeli liaison. Not unexpectedly he resisted both ideas with the strongest arguments he could offer. And thinking that a day or so of reflection might make it easier for him to accept the inevitable—and in my mind this time it was inevitable—I asked him to think over the matter for a couple of days to decide whether he would like to stay on in the way I described or whether he would choose to retire completely before the deadline for benefits.[32]

(The question of benefits, repeatedly raised by Colby in this account, is something of a red herring. Such matters might have been important to Colby himself, but the Angletons almost certainly were not dependent on his Central Intelligence Agency salary. The expression of concern—whether sincere or not—was typical of Colby's presentation of self, and his self-image.)

"But on the next day—it was December 18, 1974—I received a telephone call that knocked all my plans into a cocked hat, ruining not only the Christmas season for me but nearly all the next year as well." [33] The telephone call was from Seymour Hersh, an investigative reporter with sources throughout the government. One of those sources was particularly valuable: Thomas McCoy, an assistant to Colby. "McCoy told Hersh something about Angleton's reputation for intrigue and paranoia inside the CIA, and added that he'd told Colby back in May 1973, at the time of his appointment [as DCI], the first thing he ought to do was fire Angleton." [34] McCoy talked with Hersh about Angleton, and, perhaps at McCoy's suggestion, Hersh called Colby. Colby gave Hersh an interview on December 20. Hersh had "somehow" learned about Operation CHAOS, connecting it to Angleton's name, and asked Colby about it. Colby confirmed Hersh's information about Operation CHAOS and confirmed Hersh's information about Angleton's role in it, thereby making Angleton's position in the Agency untenable. McCoy to Hersh to Colby to Hersh: checkmate.

According to Colby, "On Friday, December 20, after hearing Hersh's story from him and trying to show him its true proportion, I had called Angleton back and had told him that I must make clear that my decision to remove him was firm, whatever the Hersh article might say." Colby then told Angleton "that no one in the world would believe his leaving his job was not the result of the article. But both Jim and I would know it was not, which was the important part to me." [35] This last is a typical example of Colby's self-righteousness. Another view of the events on December 20 is given by Mark Riebling. "After briefing Hersh, Colby summoned Angleton and informed him that the *New York Times* would be exposing the operations, and linking them to Angleton, who now had no choice but to resign. His old FBI friend Donald Moore was in the corridor as the CI chief shuffled out of Colby's office. Angleton's posture was more bent than ever, his face dark and defeated. Behind his horn-rimmed glasses, the usually sharp eyes were blurred with pain . . . Moore took him by the arm. 'Jesus, Jim, it can't be that bad,' Moore said. 'What's the matter?' . . . 'It's horrible,' Angleton rasped. 'It's awful. You'll soon read all about it.'" [36]

Moore read all about it when Hersh's story appeared in the *New York Times* on December 22 (datelined December 21) under the headline "Huge C.I.A. Operation Reported in U.S. Against Antiwar Forces, Other Dissidents in Nixon Years." The story's first sentence read, "The Central Intelligence Agency, directly violating its charter, conducted a massive, illegal domestic intelligence operation during the Nixon Administration against the antiwar movement and other dissident groups in the United States, according to well-placed Government sources." That is, according to, inter alia, William Colby himself.

After a reference to the "Family Jewels" list of foreign illegalities Colby had compiled for Schlesinger, Hersh returned to the domestic intelligence operations, first carefully stating that "under the 1947 act setting up the C.I.A., the agency was forbidden to have 'police, subpoena, law enforcement powers or internal security functions' inside the United States. Those responsibilities fall to the F.B.I., which maintains a special internal security unit to deal with foreign intelligence threats." Hersh then made a connection between his new information and Watergate: "The disclosure of alleged illegal C.I.A. activities is the first possible connection to rumors that have been circulating in Washington for some time. A number of mysterious burglaries and incidents have come to light since the break-in at Democratic party headquarters in the Watergate complex on June 17, 1972." He then launched into a description of Operation CHAOS, without using that name. "As part of its alleged effort against dissident Americans in the late 1960's and early 1970's, the *Times*'s sources said, the C.I.A. authorized agents to follow and photograph participants in antiwar and other demonstrations. The C.I.A. also set up a network of informants who were ordered to penetrate antiwar groups, the sources said . . . At least one avowedly antiwar member of Congress was among those placed under surveillance by the C.I.A., the sources said. Other members of Congress were said to be included in the C.I.A.'s dossier on dissident Americans." These activities Hersh firmly associated with Richard Helms: "It also could not be determined whether Mr. Helms had had specific authority from the President or any of his top officials to initiate the alleged domestic surveillance, or whether Mr. Helms had informed the President of the fruits, if any, of the alleged operations." On the other hand, James Schlesinger and William Colby were portrayed as having been "distressed" about the Agency's domestic intelligence activities, so much so that "Mr. Colby has reportedly told associates that he is considering the possibility of asking the Attorney General to institute legal action against some of those who had been involved in the alleged domestic activities." Colby, using Hersh as his messenger and the *New York Times* as his medium, was threatening Angleton, and possibly Helms as well.

According to veteran *New York Times* journalist Harrison Salisbury,

> [Hersh's story] proved to be the single most influential story published about the CIA, led to three far-reaching official investigations of the Agency, and a national self-examination into the political and ethical values which the CIA epitomized . . . It raised the question of not just

how can we bring the CIA under control . . . but can we permit the CIA to exist? . . . Hersh revealed that the CIA had conducted a "massive" and totally illegal domestic intelligence program . . . It was difficult for one like myself, who was familiar with and had lived under the omnipresent surveillance of the KGB, to detect much difference between Operation Chaos and business-as-usual within Soviet society. The ultimate triumph of the dialectic seemed to be approaching: antithesis was approaching synthesis; the harder the CIA fought KGB the more alike they became.[37]

Hersh did not rely only on Colby for his information. Parts of the article cited unnamed CIA officials who seem to have been members of the Counterintelligence Staff: "Those officials, who insisted on not being quoted by name, contended that all of the C.I.A.'s domestic activities against American citizens were initiated in the belief that foreign governments and foreign espionage may have been involved. 'Anything that we did was in the context of foreign counterintelligence and it was focused at foreign intelligence and foreign intelligence problems,' one official said." Hersh's story also included some *Casablanca* expressions of shock at his revelations. "'Counterintelligence!' one high-level Justice Department official exclaimed upon being given some details of the C.I.A.'s alleged domestic operations. 'They're not supposed to have any counterintelligence in this country . . . Oh, my God,' he said, 'oh, my God.'" One can almost hear the order to round up the usual suspects. And a "former high-level F.B.I. official who operated in domestic counterintelligence areas since World War I, expressed astonishment and then anger upon being told of the C.I.A.'s alleged domestic activities. 'We had an agreement with them that they weren't to do anything unless they checked with us,' he said. 'They double-crossed me all along.'" This distressed official was probably William Sullivan. If so, his indignation must be taken with a few shovelfuls of salt.

One of the anonymous officials furnishing Hersh with his information was quoted as naming James Angleton as the person responsible for the CIA's domestic intelligence operations: "The C.I.A. domestic activities during the Nixon Administration were directed, the source said, by James Angleton, who is still in charge of the Counterintelligence Department, the agency's most powerful and mysterious unit."

> The *Times*'s sources, who included men with access to firsthand knowledge of the C.I.A.'s alleged domestic activities, took sharp exception to the official suggestion that such activities were the result of legitimate counterintelligence needs. "Look, that's how it started," one man said. "They were looking for evidence of foreign involvement in the Anti-War Movement.

But that's not how it ended up. This just grew and mushroomed internally . . . This wasn't a series of isolated events. It was highly coordinated. People were targeted, information was collected on them, and it was all put on [computer] tape, just like the agency does with information about K.G.B. agents. Every one of these acts was blatantly illegal" . . . The source added that Mr. Angleton's counterintelligence department "simply began using the same techniques for foreigners against new targets here." Along with assembling the domestic intelligence dossiers, the source said, Mr. Angleton's department began recruiting informants to infiltrate some of the more militant dissident groups.[38]

Who was this source "with access to firsthand knowledge of the C.I.A.'s alleged domestic activities"? It was not, from internal evidence, someone on the Counterintelligence Staff. It would then have had to have been someone of higher rank than Angleton himself, that is, the head of the Clandestine Services, or perhaps Colby.

Having named Angleton, Hersh went on to name Richard Ober (ruling out Ober as a source for the story): "Most of the domestic surveillance and the collection of domestic intelligence was conducted, the sources said, by one of the most clandestine units in the United States intelligence community, the special operations branch of counterintelligence . . . 'That's really the deep snow section,' one high-level intelligence expert said of the unit, whose liaison with Mr. Helms was conducted by Richard Ober, a long-time counterintelligence official who has served in New Delhi for the C.I.A." Again Helms was implicated: "One former high-level aide who worked closely with Mr. Helms in the executive offices of the agency recalled that Mr. Ober held frequent private meetings with Mr. Helms in the late 60's and early 70's. 'Ober had unique and very confidential access to Helms,' the former C.I.A. man said. 'I always assumed he was mucking about with Americans who were abroad and then would come back, people like the Black Panthers.'" Finally, Hersh quoted Angleton himself:

Mr. Angleton, also reached by telephone this week at his suburban Washington home, denied that his Counterintelligence Department operated domestically . . . Mr. Angleton told of a report from a United States agent in Moscow who was relaying information to the C.I.A. on the underground and radical bombings in the United States during the height of the antiwar activity. "The intelligence was not acquired in the United States," Mr. Angleton declared, "it came from Moscow. Our source there is still active and still productive; the opposition still doesn't know." Mr. Angleton then described how the C.I.A. had obtained information from Communist sources about

> the alleged demolition training of black militants by the North Koreans. He also told of recent intelligence efforts involving the K.G.B. and Yasir Arafat, chairman of the Palestine Liberation Organization.[39]

According to Richard Helms's biographer, Thomas Powers, Angleton believed "that the KGB was in complete and utter control of the Palestine Liberation Organization. Angleton did not mean that the PLO was 'influenced' by the KGB, or was simply 'penetrated' by the KGB; he meant that it was a KGB creature pure and simple, and his arguments were sufficiently strong to win substantial acceptance inside the CIA."[40] That is, acceptance by Helms himself.

Hersh's interview with Angleton is an interesting text for counterintelligence training classes. Angleton brushes aside the original inquiry, and then, seizing the opportunity, uses Hersh to send a message to Moscow that the United States had an active agent in place in the Soviet capital, which may or may not have been true, but which would have usefully stirred up Moscow Center, then implies that the antiwar movement was directed from the Soviet Union, and, not to let the occasion slip, floats his belief that Yasir Arafat was a KGB asset. It was a very economical and very effective use of a difficult situation. It also demonstrates that Angleton had not yet taken it on-board that he was no longer functioning as chief of the Counterintelligence Staff of the Central Intelligence Agency.

Hersh's story made a public figure of Angleton, who emerged, literally blinking, into the light of day and the glare of television cameras when Daniel Schorr went to Angleton's home for an interview two days later, "on the morning of December 24, [1974, when] the word spread from the CIA that James Angleton, chief of counterintelligence, had resigned."

> The improper surveillance program had been under his jurisdiction—the implication seemed obvious . . . Routed out of bed by a call from my office, I looked in the telephone book for Angleton, whom I had never heard of before, and drove to his home in North Arlington, Virginia. Cameras were already staked out on his lawn, but no one had tried to ascertain if he was home. My ring was answered by a groggy-looking, stoop-shouldered man in pajamas, who pointed at the *Washington Post* on his doorstep, on which I was standing, and said, "I certainly didn't expect you, Mr. Schorr, to trample on the press!" Encouraged by the recognition and the good humor, I asked if I could come in. "Well, I've been up all night," he said, "and my family is away, but I can offer you apple juice or Sanka."[41]

Schorr's account of his extraordinary interview with Angleton gives us our first glimpse by an outsider of everyday life, chez Angleton. "Whatever the home of a chief counterspy is supposed to look like, this one resembled the home of a somewhat disorderly professor."

> Strewn about were books in many languages, mementos of Italy and Israel, worn rugs, pictures of his wife and two children. He agreed to talk to me, but not before the camera because he would be in mortal danger if recognized. For the next four hours—interrupted by telephone conversations in English, French, Italian and a "Shalom" for someone at the Israeli Embassy . . . [The question of Angleton's linguistic abilities arises from time to time in the literature about him. It is therefore interesting to note that, according to Schorr, his French and Italian were at least sufficient for telephone conversations.] "The Nixon-Kissinger détente bothers me deeply," he said. Each time I asked him about improper CIA activities in the United States, he went off on further elaboration of his cold war theories.[42]

In other words, Angleton was telling Schorr that the issue over which he had been fired was not domestic spying, but foreign policy. It would have been standard practice for Angleton to try to mislead Schorr, particularly on a matter as important as his own departure from the Agency. On the other hand, disagreements about foreign policy were probably, in Angleton's mind, much more important than the domestic application of foreign intelligence methods.

Schorr could not keep Angleton on the subject of Operation CHAOS. "When I tried to bring him back to a question put fifteen minutes earlier, he said, 'I am not known as a linear thinker, Mr. Schorr. You will have to let me approach your question my way' . . . Angleton painted the Palestinian Arab nationalists as pawns of a Communist conspiracy. He made a great point of having recognized, in a photograph, the escort of Yasser Arafat on a visit to Lenin's tomb in Moscow as an important KGB officer. Strewn through his recital were hints that Angleton's trouble with his agency had stemmed not from any CIA activity in this country, but from an internal conflict over the Middle East."

For the second time in a week Angleton used the media to send his message about Arafat, demonstrating, if there had been any doubt, that he was a true "friend of Israel." Angleton then gives Schorr the same story identified by Colby as the final breaking point in their relationship: "For twenty-two years, as a sideline to his counterintelligence work, Angleton had taken personal charge of the 'Israeli account.' He had plucked that 'account' from the pro-Arab Middle East Division, but lately had observed a growing pro-Arab drift in his agency, for which he blamed Kissinger. On Kissinger's request, Colby had canceled a trip to disputed East Jerusalem, during a visit to Israel, in order to avoid offending the Arabs. Angleton had rebuked Colby for yielding to Kissinger and thus offending the Israelis. It was then that Colby had called in Angleton, taken away the 'Israeli account,' and told him that it was time to prepare for 'new leadership' in the counterintelligence office."

Turning, finally, to the matter at hand, Angleton fed Schorr a cover story. According to Angleton, "Colby had casually mentioned that Angleton would be implicated in an impending Hersh exposé of the domestic surveillance activities."

> In fact, though the program had nominally come under Angleton's authority, it had been handled by his deputy, Richard Ober, reporting directly to Helms. Angleton, who had witnessed enough agency intrigues to understand when he had become the object of one, was ready to retire quietly—staying on the payroll for a time as a "consultant" in line with the usual CIA practice of easing the pain of ejection and minimizing hazardous resentments. The leak of his resignation two days after the *Times* story had made him appear the culprit of the spying on Americans. The episode sounded like material for a John Le Carré novel about the faithful spy thrown to the wolves to spare the headquarters embarrassment . . . Angleton voiced no open complaint about his treatment, but he defended Helms who, he said, had only started keeping files on Americans because of presidential instructions. "Helms was deeply victimized," said Angleton. "He was set up as a scapegoat for Nixon."

This was an extraordinary statement, under the circumstances. Nixon was in no position in December 1974 to victimize Helms, who had, in any case, been in Iran for nearly a year. Or was the nonlinear thinker changing the subject from his own firing to that of Helms a year earlier, and to Watergate? If he was, Schorr did not grasp what he was being told. The interview was winding down.

> It was now noon, and Angleton, still in pajamas, excused himself to dress, saying he had to go to the office. He repeated that he could never allow himself to be photographed, and I cautioned that he could hardly avoid being glimpsed by the cameras still waiting on his lawn. He shrugged, donned his diplomat-style black coat and fedora, walked out the front door and slowly across the lawn, then stopped directly in front of the three network cameras as though hypnotized. In some haste I pick up our microphone lying on the ground. Four hours of Angleton views were in my mind, but not on film.
>
> "Why did you resign?" I asked.

"I think the time comes to all men when they no longer serve their countries."

"As determined by whom?"

"By themselves and their superiors."

Another reporter asked, "Did you jump or were you pushed?"

"I wasn't pushed out the window," said Angleton cryptically, recalling heaven-knew-what covert operation somewhere back in his thirty years as a secret agent. And then the nonlinear thinker, his cover and career blown, stumbled into his blue Mercedes, looking back with a dazed smile as his car left the driveway.[43]

On December 22, when Hersh's article was published, Hersh recalls that "Angleton telephoned me very early at home and complained that Cicely, his wife of thirty-one years, had learned only by reading my story that her husband was not a postal employee, as Angleton claimed he had told her. He added: 'And now she's left me.' The call shook me up; the upset in his voice seemed real. I mumbled something about a newsman's responsibility to the truth, hung up, and telephoned an old friend who had served in the CIA with Angleton. He laughingly told me that Cicely of course had known from the beginning what her husband did for a living, and had left him three years earlier to move to Arizona, only to return."[44]

From Angleton's point of view, whether he had been fired to take the blame for Operation Chaos, as a sacrifice to Kissinger, or as part of a plot by the ultimate KGB mole, the counterintelligence apparatus he had created was doomed. It was not a good way to finish a career.

> When Angleton left the CIA on Christmas Eve [1974] . . . he fashioned three white feathers as symbols of cowardice. He planned to give them to the three top CIA executives under Colby, who had actually authorized and run the mail-opening program that he had been only nominally responsible for. They had allowed Angleton to take the blame. He looked at the feathers and decided instead to use them as fishing lures . . . Angleton wanted to hear no more about Washington—or the CIA. He left for the Arizona Desert, abandoning his prize-winning orchids and letting his greenhouse in Virginia fall into disrepair. That next year he went on a long solitary trip to a fishing camp high on the Matapedia River in New Brunswick, Canada.[45]

The story is from Edward Jay Epstein, that is, from Angleton. As such, it must be taken with some caution ("the mail-opening program that he had been only nominally responsible for"), but the tone is right. On the other hand, according to Cleveland Cram, who was not an admirer of Angleton, "When . . . Colby dismissed him in 1974, Angleton for the next six months spent part of his time at Langley, introducing members of the new CI Staff to such people as his defector friend, Anatole Golitsyn. Gradually, however, the former counterintelligence chief realized that his career with the CIA in fact was finished. The dismissal was a terrible blow; he became embittered and withdrew for a time into alcohol."[46] One narrative does not preclude the other.

Why was Angleton fired? Because of Hersh's "discovery" of Operation CHAOS, as Colby claimed? Because of policy conflicts between Angleton and Helms, on the one side, and Colby and Kissinger on the other? As part of the final moves in the Watergate affair? That last argument would run as follows: Kissinger had supported the appointment of Colby as DCI in part because Kissinger was afraid that, with Nixon bogged down in the Watergate affair, the CIA might decide to oppose his foreign policy, especially in regard to China and Israel.[47] Colby was apparently presumed by Kissinger to be loyal to Kissinger, or at least to be trusted not to take independent action. He did not, after all, have the personal following within the Agency had by Helms.

On the other hand, for those preoccupied with Israeli matters, like John Loftus and Aaron Marks, it was clear that, after the 1973 Yom Kippur War, the "first priority for the White House was to find a scapegoat for the failure to give Israel timely intelligence. By throwing James Angleton to the wolves, the White House could kill two investigations with one stone. Angleton became the scapegoat for the illegal NSA interception programs as well as for the blunders of the 1973 war . . . In addition to taking the rap for illegal surveillance programs such as Operation Chaos, Angleton became the major fall guy for all the failures of U.S. intelligence during the 1973 war. CIA director Colby announced that 'Angleton's obsessively secret and uniquely cumbersome restrictions unnecessarily slowed down vital communications, especially during the Yom Kippur War of 1973.'"[48]

Others, such as intelligence scholar Rhodri Jeffreys-Jones, trace the matter back to those Italian and internal CIA organizational matters dealt with above.

> Angleton departed because of policy differences with his boss. Though Angleton had himself cultivated center as well as conservative elements in Italy, he was known to be critical of Colby's "opening to the left" policy in that country and elsewhere. Neither did Colby and Angleton see eye to eye on the question of CIA organization. Compartmentalization in the interest of security was fundamental to Angleton's theory of counterintelligence . . . Uncompromising counterintelligence officer that he was, Angleton believed in acting on the assumption that such suspicions might be justified, just in case they were. Colby found this irritating, especially

as Angleton's stress on compartmental divisions seemed to threaten the geographic demarcations favored by himself.[49]

This view of the Italian origins of the conflict between Angleton and Colby has some support from Colby himself. "I'd had one contact with Angleton in Rome in the mid-fifties. The CI Staff was running an agent, and eventually I took over the agent. I had my doubts that was the way to run a railroad."[50] Colby's last word on the subject came during an oral history interview for the Johnson Library: "David Martin did an interesting [book] on the counter intelligence problem, *Wilderness of Mirrors* . . . That's about the [James] Angleton problem, me and Angleton . . . An interesting guy . . . He's a very, very good guy. We obviously had a difference of opinion, but it was a professional one. It doesn't bother me."[51] It had, however, bothered Angleton. Angleton's own explanation was not to look at motive but effect. After Hersh's story appeared, "Angleton called Pagie Morris to tell her that their collaboration was over and that in his opinion Colby was a mole. 'I can't understand how a Catholic who confesses to a priest can be a "sleeper,"' Jim said."[52]

How are we to disentangle these conflicting interpretations? For an intelligence officer, the first step in such an analysis is to establish a chronology. Interestingly enough, this was the procedure followed by Angleton's friend Cord Meyer in his memoirs. (Given Meyer's status in the Central Intelligence Agency, we must bear in mind that establishing a chronology implies suspicion of "penetration.")

> December 17, 1974: Colby informs Angleton that he is relieving him of his two principal duties, his function as Chief of the Counterintelligence Staff and his responsibility for liaison with Israeli intelligence. He gives Angleton the option of remaining in the Agency in a consultant capacity or of retiring before the end of the year . . . and Colby gives him two days to reconsider.
>
> December 18: Seymour Hersh . . . calls Colby to state that he has an explosive story on illegal domestic CIA activity and asks for an interview. Colby invites him to a meeting in his office in Washington two days later and alerts the White House to potential trouble.
>
> December 20: Colby meets with Hersh and . . . he admits to past improper domestic surveillance activity but claims that it was not extensive and that it has been terminated . . . After the Hersh interview . . . Colby informs Angleton of his conversation . . . [and] insists that he must retire or take the consultant job. Angleton agrees to retire.
>
> December 22: The *New York Times* publishes the Hersh story.

December 23: Angleton's retirement is announced within the Agency and the news quickly leaks to the press.[53]

Having established his chronology, Meyer then offers his interpretation: "Colby's admissions played a key role in the *New York Times*' editorial decision to give the story maximum prominence . . . By agreeing to meet with Hersh on December 20 and by confirming essential aspects of his story, Colby made a personal decision to go public with the most sensitive kind of information and again substituted his own judgment for that of the President on a matter deeply affecting the national security."[54]

Meyer, while implying by the form of his argument that he suspects that Angleton's firing had counterintelligence implications, at once avoided and pointed to the controversy about Colby's actions and motives that no doubt raged within the CIA and particularly occupied the Old Boys of Meyer's and Angleton's generation. For them, the important point would be bureaucratic rather than geopolitical. What mattered, as they saw it, was that on December 20, 1974, William Colby, using Hersh as his instrument, destroyed the counterintelligence organization of the CIA and exposed the secret intelligence apparatus of the government as a whole to a public investigation on a scale previously—and subsequently—only paralleled in circumstances of national collapse. It would have been one thing to fire Angleton; that was Colby's prerogative, and it would have followed that Angleton's chief deputies would have gone with him. But in the normal bureaucratic course of events, there might have been a reorganization, there might have been reductions in the size of the staff through transfers and firings (easily justified, given the precedents established by Schlesinger), but the complete dissolution of a counterintelligence unit was without parallel in any modern intelligence service. "'The Director of Central Intelligence *did away with* counterintelligence,' [reported] a staffer on the Senate Intelligence Committee in 1980 in reference to Colby."[55] According to Mark Riebling, "Angleton's successors had actually *burned* 99 percent of his CI files."[56] (Emphasis in originals.)

According to Thomas Powers, Angleton said that "'Colby could not have done more damage if he had been working for the other side.' Coming from such a man, this was no mere observation . . . Not only had [Colby] surrendered a huge mass of material to Frank Church, but he had literally wrecked counterintelligence."[57] We will consider the consequences that followed from this below, but for the moment they can be summed up by a remark made by Markus Wolf, head of East German foreign intelligence and perhaps the last in the tradition of the Comintern ideological intelligence officers, who thought that, after Angleton's departure, "the behavior of CIA counterintelligence . . . suggests to me that they were more concerned with quieting worries that a mole was active in the CIA than in actually finding him."[58]

By December 24, 1974 (enabled, no doubt, to collect certain retirement benefits), James Angleton was for the first time in thirty years not an employee of a secret intelligence agency of the U.S. government. Meanwhile, the chain of events begun by Hersh's article continued to detonate. Immediately after Washington awoke from the Christmas and New Year holidays, President Ford asked Vice President Rockefeller to head a commission to investigate Hersh's charges. On January 15, 1975, Colby went before the Senate Appropriations Committee and confirmed everything in Hersh's article—which probably shocked his colleagues, not to mention his president, more than anything else.[59] His predecessor, Helms, after all, was the "man who kept the secrets"; Colby, seemingly, delighted in giving them away.

> On January 27, 1975, Senate Resolution 21 established a select committee "to conduct an investigation and study of governmental operations with respect to intelligence activities and of the extent, if any, to which illegal, improper, or unethical activities were engaged in by any agency of the Federal Government." Senate Resolution 21 lists specific areas of inquiry and study:
>
> (1) Whether the Central Intelligence Agency has conducted an illegal domestic intelligence operation in the United States . . .
>
> (3) The origin and disposition of the so-called Huston Plan to apply United States intelligence agency capabilities against individuals or organizations within the United States . . .
>
> (5) The extent to which the operation of domestic intelligence or counterintelligence activities and the operation of any other activities within the United States by the Central Intelligence Agency conforms to the legislative charter of that Agency and the intent of the Congress.[60]

In other words, it was an inquiry into much of the career of James Angleton.

The committee was chaired by Senator Frank Church of Idaho (hence, the "Church Committee") and included, among others, Senators Howard Baker, Jr., Barry Goldwater, Gary Hart, Philip Hart, Walter Mondale, and John Tower, who served as vice chairman. Senator Church himself was a more or less open candidate for the Democratic nomination for president in 1976. It was a unique political moment. The Vietnam War and the Watergate affair had temporarily diminished the authority—if not the power—of the executive branch. For the first time since the presidential campaign of Henry Wallace, major American political figures believed that their ambitions could be gratified by a sharp turn to the Left. According to the committee's own final report, "Concern over the secret war in Laos, revulsion at the Phoenix program which took at least 20,000 lives in South Vietnam, army spying on U.S. civilians, U.S. 'destabilization' efforts in Chile, and finally the revelations concerning Operation CHAOS and the CIA's domestic intelligence role created a climate for a thorough Congressional investigation."[61] Which amounts to a claim that Seymour Hersh, acting on information given to him or confirmed by William Colby, had instigated the investigation. That is quite an achievement for a maverick journalist; less difficult, if more surprising, for someone in Colby's position.

Frederick A. O. Schwarz, Jr., chief counsel to the committee, directed the staff's research and worked with Frank Church on the dramaturgy of the hearings. Faced with the vast history of the Cold War itself, Schwarz recommended to the committee that they focus on ten to fifteen subjects. Rather late in the process, he recommended that the hearings include the illegal HT/LINGUAL mail openings. When interviewed twenty years later he did not then recall how he heard of the project. He did remember why it was included: "We wanted to use the mail opening as illustrative of two things: contempt of the law, and secondly, vast over-breadth—activities overly broad and wasteful." Concerning Angleton's role, Schwarz had "no doubt that Angleton was in charge of the mail opening program."[62] Working with that peculiar mixture of elation and exhaustion characteristic of the point where the legal and political systems intersect, the Church Committee (and the parallel House of Representatives Pike Committee), raced to uncover thirty years of secret history.

During February 1976, academic and temporary Church Committee staffer Loch Johnson had lunch with James Angleton at the Army and Navy Club in Washington. (Everyone involved with the investigation seems to have had lunch with Angleton.) According to Johnson, "The former CIA chief of counterintelligence became highly agitated as he discussed the congressional inquiries, comparing them to the pillaging of intelligence services in countries that had been overrun and occupied by a foreign power. 'Only we have been occupied by the Congress,' he said, 'with our files rifled, our officials humiliated, and our agents exposed.' This happened because of an 'impotent executive' that failed to 'carry out its constitutional responsibility to protect the nation's secrets' . . . I walked with Angleton from the Army-Navy Club to his car. 'Let me tell you something,' he said. 'Washington is a jungle.' His Mercedes eased into the slipstream of a Metrobus."[63]

Johnson and his colleagues did not find Angleton as amusing during the staff inquiries preparatory to the public hearings.

> Questioning him . . . was like trying to find a new planet through an earthbound telescope: it took constant probing, a sensitivity for nuance, and a willingness to endure vast oceans of silence. Angleton might begin an important story, then let it trail out like a vanishing comet and disappear into a black hole of ambiguity . . . In August 1975, Angleton said to me, in typically poetic and elusive language, that the task of the counterintelligence officer was to construct a "wilderness of mirrors" in which the opponent would be forever lost and confused. In 1975, the chief enemy of the CIA was—in the eyes of many CIA officers, including Angleton—the United States Congress. I wondered if Angleton's ploy was to lead the Church committee into his "wilderness," where everything revealed reflected something concealed, and the maddening multiplicity of images spun dizzily in the mind.[64]

Although it was initially cooperative, as the investigations progressed the Ford administration's resistance stiffened. On September 19, 1975, President Ford formed a high-level group to fend off the investigators. "From that day forward, all executive responses to the congressional committees were handled by the Intelligence Coordinating Group (ICG). This body met every day and included National Security Adviser and Secretary of State Henry Kissinger, Defense Secretary James Schlesinger, Attorney General Edward Levi, Budget Director James Lynn, Director of Central Intelligence William Colby, Chief of Staff Donald Rumsfeld, and presidential counsels Philip Buchen and Jack Marsh."[65]

At the working level, there were Thursday afternoon meetings between Attorney General Levi, his assistant, Harold Tyler, and FBI and CIA representatives, "the big chiefs," about what would be turned over to the Church Committee. According to Tyler, Angleton was there, but never spoke. On one occasion Senator Mondale asked Levi "what business it was of theirs [Justice]." Tyler said he—Mondale—was right, Justice was only conveying FBI and CIA decisions; it had no competence of its own.[66] In other words, while Schwarz and his staff planned the investigations and hearings for the committee, the Department of Justice worked with the intelligence community to transmit, and if possible enforce, the CIA's views of what the committee would be allowed to see.

On Wednesday, September 24, 1975, the U.S. Senate Select Committee to Study Governmental Operations with Respect to Intelligence Activities met, pursuant to notice, at 10:05 A.M., in room 318, Russell Senate Office Building, Senator Frank Church presiding, to hear testimony concerning the Huston Plan. After introductory remarks by Senator Church reviewing the previous day's testimony by Thomas Huston, James Angleton was introduced and sworn in. Angleton, who had never before appeared in a public setting, stepped onto the stage of history: "Mr. Chairman and members of the committee, my name is James Angleton." According to Schwarz, Angleton "looked like a scared rabbit, not an angry man, when he took the oath. He very much didn't want to be there."[67] Angleton said:

> I am appearing before the committee today, freely and without subpena [*sic*]. I am mindful of the serious issues facing the committee, and I know of your concern that they be resolved prudently and expeditiously. I have served in the intelligence community of the United States for 31 years, beginning with the OSS during World War II. In 1954, I became Chief of the Counterintelligence Staff of the CIA, a position which I held until 1974. I am now retired.
>
> My years of service have convinced me that the strength of the United States lies in its capacity to sustain perpetual yet peaceful revolution. It is the ultimate function of the intelligence community, as part of our Government, to maintain and enhance the opportunity for peaceful change.
>
> I believe most strongly that the efforts and motivations of the intelligence community have contributed to the sustaining of a Nation of diversity and strength.[68]

Thus, Angleton's first appearance on the public stage began with a soliloquy not, as might have been expected, on the nature of the threat of Soviet Communism, but on the necessity for perpetual and peaceful revolution and the role of the intelligence community to support that process and the nation's diversity and strength. Angleton would have recalled, if it had been brought to his attention, that perpetual revolution was not only a Jeffersonian concept, but also a central tenet of Lev Trotsky's doctrine. Angleton differed from them both in his emphasis on the peaceful nature of this process—Jefferson famously having called for the periodic irrigation of the tree of liberty with the blood of tyrants, and Trotsky going rather further in that regard. The linking of diversity to strength was a sign of the times, but also rather surprising for someone with Angleton's professional history. Times change, and even counterintelligence chiefs are influenced by those changes, particularly as retirement, time for reflection, and family influences bring to the fore memories of a Mexican mother and romanticized Apache ancestry.

None of this was remarked as Schwarz began an aggressive examination of the witness. Schwarz first established Angleton's knowledge of the mail-opening program and that the program had also been known to Richard Helms and J. Edgar Hoover. He had Angleton read some sentences from the "Special Report of the Interagency Committee on Intelligence" from June 1970, which stated that the covert opening of mail had been discontinued, and then said, not putting too fine a point on it, "Now, the sentence which says 'covert coverage has been discontinued,' is a lie. That is false as far as your knowledge, Mr. Hoover's knowledge, Mr. Helms' knowledge, and Mr. Sullivan's knowledge; isn't that correct?"[69] Angleton did not reply directly, but tried to establish that the covert coverage in question was that of the FBI, which had been discontinued, not that of the CIA, which had not. Schwarz, somewhat impatiently, said that no ordinary reader would have been able to interpret the sentence in that fashion, and then moved on to the two CIA memoranda concerning the CIA's mail-opening program, HT/LINGUAL, the first of May 19, 1971, the second of June 3, 1971, recording meetings in the office of then Director of Central Intelligence Helms, when he, Angleton, and others discussed the possibility that the mail-opening program would be discovered by the Post Office Department. This established that HT/LINGUAL had not been terminated in 1970 and had been known to Helms and had been under Angleton's direction.

When Schwarz turned over questioning to Curtis R. Smothers, counsel to the committee's minority members, Smothers asked Angleton about Huston's role and status. Angleton replied that "there was no question in my mind, nor in the minds of others, that he represented the Commander in Chief in terms of bringing together this plan . . . He made it very clear, and he submitted in writing that he was to have this role for domestic intelligence comparable to Dr. Kissinger's role in foreign affairs."[70] Senator Church then took over the questioning. According to Schwarz, the committee at this point was looking for a pattern of deception of the White House by the Agency, theorizing that the CIA had committed its illegalities without presidential knowledge. Angleton said that concealment from the President, if any, was unintentional.

THE CHAIRMAN: So the state of the record is that to the best of our knowledge the President had not been told that the mail was being opened. He gets a recommendation in which it is represented that covert coverage, which is mail openings, has been discontinued, and he is asked to authorize the reopening of this program. Now, you have referred to the President as the Commander in Chief. What possible justification was there to misrepresent a matter of such importance to the Commander in Chief?

MR. ANGLETON: . . . I have no satisfactory answer to your question . . .

MR. ANGLETON: Mr. Chairman, I don't think anyone would have hesitated to inform the President if he had at any moment asked for a review of intelligence operations. [Senator Church appeared to be very concerned about President Nixon's prerogatives.]

SENATOR CHURCH: That is what he did do. That is the very thing he asked Huston to do. That is the very reason that these agencies got together to make recommendations to him, and when they made their recommendations, they misrepresented the facts.

MR. ANGLETON: I was referring, sir, to a much more restricted forum.

THE CHAIRMAN: I am referring to the mail, and what I have said is solidly based upon the evidence. The President wanted to be informed. He wanted recommendations. He wanted to decide what should be done, and he was misinformed.

Not only was he misinformed, but when he reconsidered authorizing the opening of the mail 5 days later and revoked it, the CIA did not pay the slightest bit of attention to him, the Commander in Chief, as you say. Is that so?

MR. ANGLETON: I have no satisfactory answer for that.

THE CHAIRMAN: You have no satisfactory answer?

MR. ANGLETON: No; I do not.

THE CHAIRMAN: I do not think there is a satisfactory answer, because having revoked the authority, the CIA went ahead with the program. So that the Commander in Chief is not the Commander in Chief at all. He is just a problem. You do not want to inform him in the first place, because he might say no. That is the truth of it. And when he did say no you disregard it and then you call him the Commander in Chief.[71]

But in fact, Senator Church was wrong to criticize Angleton and the CIA in this way; on this issue, at least, the Agency had not been a "rogue elephant." It had been doing the president's bidding. Secretary of State Henry Kissinger told the House of Representatives' Pike Committee "that every covert action undertaken in recent years had been approved by the President himself." The Pike Committee's final report concluded that "All evidence in hand suggests that the CIA, far from being out of control, has been utterly responsive to the instructions of the President and the Assistant to the President for National Security Affairs." As Kathryn Olmsted notes, "This indictment of the presidency was potentially more alarming than any of the abuses uncovered by the Church committee . . . The Pike committee concluded that many abuses were not merely the fault of Richard Nixon or certain individuals at the CIA; instead, all presidents could abuse their power by using the secret tools at their disposal. Otis Pike realized that this conclusion threatened some of the deepest beliefs of the American public. In Watergate, he said, the American people were asked to believe that 'their President had been a bad person. In this situation they are asked much more; they are asked to believe that their country had been evil. And nobody wants to believe that.'"[72]

The Pike Committee's conclusion was supported by testimony before the Rockefeller Commission by the president's man, John Ehrlichman:

> QUESTION. Were you, Mr. Ehrlichman, aware at any time while you were on the White House staff of a program of intercepting mail in New York or any other port, mail headed into the United States from, or headed out to, any of the Communist countries?
>
> ANSWER. I knew that was going on because I had seen reports that cited those kinds of sources in connection with this, the bombings, the dissident activities.[73]

Presidential knowledge of HT/LINGUAL was confirmed by ex-President Nixon himself the following year in answer to written questions from the Church Committee

> While President, I remember being generally aware of the fact that the Central Intelligence Agency, acting without a warrant, both during and prior to my Administration, conducted mail covers of mail sent from within the United States to:
>
> A. The Soviet Union; or
>
> B. The People's Republic of China.
>
> However, I do not remember being informed that such mail covers included unauthorized mail openings.
>
> I remember learning on various occasions that, during Administrations prior to mine, agencies or employees of the United States Government, acting presumably without a warrant, conducted wiretaps, surreptitious or unauthorized entries, and intercepts of voice and non-voice communications.
>
> My understanding was that these activities, or certain of them, had taken place at various times during each of the five Administrations preceding mine.[74]

During Angleton's testimony to the Church Committee, Senator Mondale also asked about the mail-opening program, Angleton's authority for it, and his understanding of its legal status.

> SENATOR MONDALE: What was your understanding of the legality of the covert mail operation?
>
> MR. ANGLETON: That it was illegal.

SENATOR MONDALE: How do you rationalize conducting a program which you believe to be illegal?

MR. ANGLETON: To begin with, I was taking it over as an ongoing operation and there was probability that the program, through lack of personnel and funding, would have been scrubbed at some stage. From the counterintelligence point of view, we believe that it was extremely important to know everything possible regarding contacts of American citizens with Communist countries.

And second, that we believed that the security of the operation was such that the Soviets were unaware of such a program and therefore that many of the interests that the Soviets would have in the United States, subversive and otherwise, would be through the open mails, when their own adjudication was that the mails could not be violated.

SENATOR MONDALE: So that a judgment was made, with which you concurred, that although covert mail opening was illegal, the good that flowed from it, in terms of the anticipating threats to this country through the use of this counterintelligence technique, made it worthwhile nevertheless.

MR. ANGLETON: That is correct.[75]

Minutes later, Senator Mondale commented, "I see no authority for anyone in the executive or in the Congress or anywhere else for determining, on his own, that the law is not good enough and therefore taking it into his own hands. I see no way of conducting a civilized, democratic society with those kinds of rules." This was not long after Angleton had made the first of what would be a series of self-damning statements: "I believe . . . that certain individual rights have to be sacrificed for the national security."[76]

A week later, speaking in the context of other testimony, Senator Mondale would draw his own conclusions. "Without any probable cause to believe a crime was being committed and taxes being unpaid, we would throw out a huge net; we would open mail, even though we did not know what was in it, and intercept communications with no grounds, thinking we might find something. We would send out Internal Revenue agents to look at people's taxes, not because we thought they weren't paying taxes, but because we might find out something. It is that concept of counterintelligence turned in on the American people . . . [There was] a fundamental philosophy that the only way to protect this country was to start spying on a broad cross-section of Americans thought to be dangerous by someone somewhere in the bureaucracy without legal authority, without definition, without any restraints and laws."[77]

But to return to Angleton's testimony.

SENATOR MORGAN: How do you reconcile [opening the mail] with the rights of the individuals in this country under our Constitution? How did you reconcile your action?

MR. ANGLETON: Well, Senator, I reconciled it in terms of the knowledge I had, and my colleagues had, regarding the nature of the threat . . .

It was not something of an individual initiative, it was *a group of like-minded men* who arrived at similar and the same conclusions that this was an indispensable means of collecting foreign intelligence on the Soviets, who regard this country to be the main enemy, and, together with the Soviet bloc, coordinates their activities on their ideological basis. This is very persuasive to someone who has given up 31 years of their life with certain very high ideals for this country. When I left the Army, as many of us did, I believed that we were in the dawn of a millennium. When I look at the map today and the weakness of power of this country, that is what shocks me.

SENATOR MORGAN: Mr. Angleton, the thing that shocks me is that these actions could be carried on contrary to the constitutional rights of the citizens of this country.[78] [Emphasis added]

As a response to Senator Charles Mathias Jr.'s stated concerns about the "cost of intelligence," including "damage to our own constitutional process," Angleton appealed to the "nature of the threat":

I think that as far as the [Soviet] bloc is concerned, you have a unified approach to the United States as the main enemy. They are bound together by ideological ties. There has been a process of de-Stalinization which was concluded in 1959, which reconciled vast differences, and which in essence was a return to Leninism. There was enunciated the policy of the main enemy, and the main enemy was the United States . . .

The nature of the threat rests within some thousands of pages of interrogation of very-high-level Soviet and bloc intelligence officers who were, in turn, very close in their activities to the political guidance of the Central Committees. And this cohesiveness dates from the period of 1959, when the intelligence services were changed from being the protectors or the preservers of the cult of personality of Stalin, and reverted back again to the days of Duchinsky and the revolution and Lenin, where every intelligence operation has a political objective.

And it ties together with the entire philosophy—and I do not base this on reading information available at the corner drugstore; this comes from the interrogation of individuals who were in the system and had positions of high responsibility in intelligence—and the underpinning of those regimes are their intelligence and security services.[79]

Earlier in the day, Senator Richard Schweiker had spent his time with the witness attempting to establish Angleton's responsibility for Operation CHAOS.

SENATOR SCHWEIKER: Now, Mr. Angleton, you were head of the Counterintelligence Unit of the CIA and under you was a group called the Special Operations Group, headed by Mr. Richard Ober . . . [I]t is correct to say that Operation CHAOS was under your supervision, although not immediately?

MR. ANGLETON: It was technically under my supervision for "rations and quarters."

SENATOR SCHWEIKER: And you supported and went along with Operation CHAOS as an executive of CIA, is that not correct?

MR. ANGLETON: I was not familiar with all of the operations of CHAOS.

SENATOR SCHWEIKER: Did you object to it? Did you oppose it? Did you fight it in any way?

MR. ANGLETON: Those operations I knew about I approved, I mean, I was approving of.[80]

The distinction here is important to Angleton: if he "approved" operations, he was responsible for them; if he was merely "approving of them," the phrase did not imply responsibility. Schweiker, only partially successful in establishing Angleton's direct responsibility for Operation CHAOS, then tried to discover whether Angleton knew that "some of the Operation CHAOS agents were operating in the United States," which Angleton at first denied; then he qualified that denial. When asked about the "Restless Youth" report, Angleton said that he did not recall it. Schweiker began to lose patience.

SENATOR SCHWEIKER: My question is were you aware of any counterintelligence activities directed against the students of the United States of America here at home? You were in charge of supervising this whole counterintelligence unit.

MR. ANGLETON: I tried to explain, sir, that I was not in charge.

SENATOR SCHWEIKER: What does being Chief of Counterintelligence mean? You were Chief of the Counterintelligence Staff, were you not?

MR. ANGLETON: Yes.

SENATOR SCHWEIKER: And that did not come under your purview?

MR. ANGLETON: I said that Mr. Ober's unit was in the Counterintelligence staff for rations and quarters. I did not have access to many of his disseminations. We were not even on the carbon copies for dissemination. I did not know the identity of his agents. I did not have any knowledge or appurtenances of a case officer over these activities.[81]

This series of denials, which seem sufficiently definitive, were in fact references to routine bureaucratic practices that did not have the force in practice that they appeared to have as presented. Angleton was not a "case officer" for *any* of the activities of his staff, except in the most extraordinary circumstances. Case officers worked many layers below him in the hierarchy. His denial that he was a case officer in this instance was nearly tautological: the chief of the Counterintelligence Staff is by definition not a case officer, as an admiral is not a second lieutenant. And it was a firmly established principle of secret intelligence that no one *other* than a case officer knew the identity of agents. Thus, Angleton's statement was practically meaningless. Yet, while the chief of a case officer's staff would not know the identity of a particular agent, he could, if he wished, know everything about the activities of that agent.

Perhaps realizing that he was being dealt with artfully, Senator Schweiker suddenly changed the subject.

SENATOR SCHWEIKER: Let me ask you something that you did testify to that we will not have a problem of communication on. On page 109 of your September 12 testimony . . . you are quoted in your deposition [before the committee], "It is inconceivable that a secret intelligence arm of the government has to comply with all the overt orders of the government." Is that an accurate quote or not?

MR. ANGLETON: Well, if it is accurate it should not have been said.

THE CHAIRMAN (SENATOR CHURCH): That is right, Mr. Angleton.

SENATOR SCHWEIKER: It looks like we are on plausible denial again is all I can say here, Mr. Chairman . . . Mr. Angleton, do you believe that statement that you made or do you not believe it? What is your belief of whether a secret intelligence agency has the right to contradict a direct order of a President or whether it does not apply?

MR. ANGLETON: Well, I would say I had been rather imprudent in making those remarks.

THE CHAIRMAN: Do you withdraw that statement?

MR. ANGLETON: I do.[82]

Not that a statement that dramatic—and deeply felt—could ever in fact be withdrawn.

The committee later wrote the former president asking in effect whether he agreed with James Angleton, that the executive branch had a right to act without regard to the law: "*Interrogatory 34.*—Please state whether you believe that actions, otherwise 'illegal,' may be legally undertaken pursuant to Presidential, or other high-level authorization, following a determination by the President, or some other senior government official, that the actions are necessary to protect the 'national security' of the United States." Richard Nixon, referring to himself as "the sovereign," lined up with Angleton.

> I assume that the reference to "actions, otherwise 'illegal,'" in this interrogatory means actions which if undertaken by private persons would violate criminal laws. It is quite obvious that there are certain inherently governmental actions which if undertaken by the sovereign in protection of the interest of the nation's security are lawful but which if undertaken by private persons are not. In the most extreme case, for example, forcible removal of persons from their homes for the purpose of sequestering them in confined areas, if done by a person—or even by government employees under normal circumstances—would be considered kidnapping and unlawful imprisonment. Yet under the exigencies of war, President Roosevelt . . . ordered such action be taken against Americans of Japanese ancestry . . . President Lincoln confiscated vessels violating a naval blockade . . . In 1969, during my Administration, warrantless wiretapping, even by the government, was unlawful, but if undertaken because of a presidential determination that it was in the interest of national security was lawful. Support for the legality of such action is found, for example, in the concurring opinion of Justice White in *Katz v. United States*.
>
> This is not to say, of course, that any action a president might authorize in the interest of national security would be lawful . . . But it is naive to attempt to categorize activities a president might authorize as "legal" or "illegal" without reference to the circumstances under which he concludes that the activity is necessary . . . [T]he opening of mail sent to selected priority targets of foreign intelligence, although impinging upon individual freedom, may nevertheless serve a salutory [*sic*] purpose when—as it has in the past—it results in preventing the disclosure of sensitive military and state secrets to the enemies of this country.[83]

Senator Church summed up what he had learned from the hearings as follows: "Twenty-five years ago, this country had a matchless moral position from which it exercised immense leadership and influence in the world. Anything the United States stood for was automatically endorsed by three quarters of the governments of the world. Now we have had 25 years of manipulation by methods that were plainly copied from the KGB: coercion, false propaganda, bribery, abduction, attempted assassination, and where are we at the end of that 25 years?"[84]

Where we were was indicated when, during the Church Committee hearings, on November 18, 1975, Senator Philip Hart "told a story of how his family of political activists had complained to him during the Vietnam War protests in Michigan that the FBI appeared to be trying to discredit dissent."

> He had discounted their arguments, attributing them to the frustration and paranoia of a protest movement. Now, he said, in a broken and emotional voice, he saw that his family had been right all along, and he had been wrong in defending the FBI . . . "I've been told for years by, among others, members of my own family that this is what the bureau has been doing all this time . . . As a result of my superior wisdom in high office, I assured them that they were on pot—it just wasn't true. They [the FBI] just wouldn't do it." Hart paused and cleared his throat. Not a person stirred in the caucus room. "What you have described is a series of illegal actions intended to deny certain citizens their First Amendment rights—just like my children said."[85]

Senator Huddleston added, "My one point on the investigations of the 7,000 individuals on the Security Index is that it puts a person in the position of being locked up."[86]

The Church, Pike, and Rockefeller investigations had pried the lid off the secret intelligence services of the United States and revealed more about their operations than had previously been made public—about those services or any others, aside from those of defeated Nazi Germany. The Church Committee hearings seemed to have achieved enormous momentum toward a reform of the CIA and related agencies. But, after the initial shock, first the CIA, then the Ford administration itself, began to recover and seek a way to counter the congressional offensive.

First, in March 1975, David Atlee Phillips "quit" the CIA in order to organize retired CIA officers into a lobbying group.

> In ten months, he had mobilized 600 like-minded former spies in the Association of Retired Intelligence Officers (ARIO) . . . Phillips's campaign was thorough and sophisticated. Not only did he speak, write, and lobby on behalf of the CIA, but also he encouraged the hundreds of ARIO members to do the same. He helped to organize national and regional committees in charge of training speakers, conducting research, and writing op-ed articles . . . By early 1976, his organization was so powerful that its officials were pressuring news organizations into making retractions and appearing before Congress to give their views on intelligence oversight . . . In the

months to come, Phillips and the ARIO would help to promote the view that CIA officers were physically endangered by the investigations.[87]

Then, in November, President Ford fired Colby. "The consensus in Washington was that Ford replaced Colby because the White House believed he had been too cooperative with the House and Senate committees investigating the CIA."[88] When Daniel Schorr asked Senator Church what he thought of the firing of Colby, "Church . . . trembled with anger. 'There is no question in my mind but that concealment is the new order of the day,' he said, his voice quavering. 'Hiding evil is the trademark of a totalitarian government.'"[89]

The CIA gained the upper hand in the aftermath of the assassination of Richard S. Welch, CIA station chief in Athens, murdered outside his house on December 23, 1975. Welch's public funeral broke the momentum of the Church Committee's investigation. According to Loch Johnson, "Whether or not it was orchestrated in order to turn public opinion against the investigation, the ceremony surrounding the Welch burial had that effect."[90] Senator Church agreed, saying that "he believed the administration tried to use the [Richard] Welch death to 'close down the investigation as soon as possible and to try to keep control of whatever remedies were sought.' The executive branch's exploitation of the murder was so successful that one outraged writer called it a 'cold war coup d'état' . . . Thanks to the executive's shrewd decision to publicly mourn a secret agent's murder, the investigators were already on the defensive as they began drafting their final reports and recommendations."[91]

As a result, "Ultimately, the foremost problem faced by both committees was the change in the political climate . . . One institution that was consistently reluctant to challenge the nation's foreign intelligence agencies was the American press . . . Those who criticized Cold War institutions risked losing their status among their elite friends and sources."[92]

In January 1976, "prosecutors in the criminal division of the Justice Department formally requested access to the secret testimony of witnesses who had appeared before the Church committee, hoping to find fresh leads that would advance several prosecutions they had launched as a result of allegations made by the Rockefeller Commission and the Congress."

> The principal target of the Justice Department's intelligence investigation was Richard Helms. The Rockefeller Commission had revealed CIA responsibility for a break-in into a photographic studio in Fairfax, Virginia, in 1971 . . . The committee's vote on the Fairfax break-in was seven to four in favor of providing the relevant CIA documents . . . to the Department of Justice . . . This same alignment held on the second vote, on CIA Chilean documents (which Justice Department attorneys wished to review in

relation to possible charges of perjury stemming from testimony before the committee). The senators, however, proved unwilling to relinquish papers on illegal mail-opening operations; by the close vote of six to five, a motion was approved to table this request until the committee had completed its own inquiry.[93]

The next month the Department of Justice decided not to prosecute Helms on the Fairfax matter. On February 5, 1976, Senator Church "called for a special prosecutor to investigate evidence of CIA and FBI criminal activity. The Department of Justice seemed unsuited to lead a criminal inquiry into some of the abuses; the possibilities for conflict of interest were too great." But it was too late.[94] In the end, the only case that got to court was a perjury charge against Richard Helms. According to Tyler, Helms practically admitted perjury to Judge Barrington Parker.[95] In a famous scene, Judge Parker stated that Helms wsa guilty of lying to Congress and disgraced (but not guilty of the felony of perjury) and imposed a two-year suspended sentence and levied a fine, which was immediately paid by a collection taken up among Helms's colleagues. Helms was not disgraced; he was a hero, "the man who kept the secrets."[96] The reports and recommendations of the Rockefeller Commission, the Pike Committee, and, most importantly, the Church Committee, were voluminous, authoritative, and by and large ineffective. In spite of the numerous violations of law they cited, there were no significant prosecutions.[97] The Church Committee had been defeated by the alliance between the Ford administration's Justice Department and the CIA.

Years later, in a series of interviews by the author, various players offered their post mortems on the outcome. Church Committee Counsel Frederick A. O. Schwarz Jr. explained that there were no indictments because of, inter alia, the supposition of tacit knowledge of Congress concerning illegal CIA activities.[98] Judge Harold Tyler, who had been a high-ranking official in the Ford administration's Justice Department, remained convinced that "there have to be exceptions to the Constitution and legal rules" for the CIA.[99] He pointed out that, as a result of the Church Committee hearings, the Justice Department laid down new rules concerning mail openings and surveillance rather than prosecuting FBI and CIA officials. In regard to prosecutions Tyler said that, in the judgment of the Ford administration, a jury would not have convicted someone as distinguished as Helms or Angleton, "who had done what others have done. We would have spent an enormous amount of time and energy indicting people without much luck in getting convictions." This decision was made "without a big meeting . . . we kind of walked through this and came to a decision to give these guys a pass." According to Senator Gary Hart, the Church

Committee did not press for prosecutions because it "was beyond the mandate of the Senate resolution, a document that resulted from considerable negotiations with conservatives in the Senate. Senators Goldwater and Tower were on the committee to protect the Agency . . . Ultimately, it was the responsibility of Attorney General Levi. This was the period of the Cold War. People were still scared to death of Communists, the missile race was under way. The conservatives said that these people were just doing their job. There just was not a majority in the Senate in favor of prosecutions."[100]

So ended the only significant effort by the Congress of the United States to bring the CIA under the rule of law.[101]

There are those who believe in "a child's version of history." They believe, among other things, that the successful efforts of the presidents and their servants in such matters as the mail opening program, and more generally and most intensely in the period of the Vietnam War, to act without regard to the Constitution were—unprecedented—violations of the traditions of the Republic. They believed after the reforms of the 1970s that it would never happen again.

Angleton, now a private citizen, divided his time between the property of his wife's family in Tucson and the Army and Navy Club in Washington. The d'Autremont homes in Tucson dated from the 1920s, before the city grid was extended. Surrounded by untouched chaparral the size of small trees, they recall the life of small-town WASP gentry living in houses the distinguishing feature of which was more seniority than size. According to his admirer Edward Epstein, "Angleton lived in what amounted to a private park in downtown Tucson. From the porch of his ranch house, one couldn't see another house or sign of the city. He proudly showed me the furniture which he had himself designed and built; he had even commissioned the recording of the music on the stereo he had made. He evidently enjoyed designing his own world."[102]

At home in Tucson, Angleton collected and polished semiprecious stones from the Sonoran Desert. In Washington, he helped publish a newsletter for retired intelligence officers, *Nightwatch*, and became increasingly active in a series of right-wing policy groups.[103] In 1977 Angleton helped organize the Security and Intelligence Fund (SIF), originally to defend U.S. security and intelligence organizations from threats like that of the Church Committee. "Angleton then converted it into a forum for spreading information about Soviet deception. The Fund remained in effect into the 1980s until, after Angleton's death and the coming of *glasnost*, it withered away."[104] Once more an editor, Angleton returned to practices he had learned at Yale forty years earlier:

Dear Jay [Lovestone]:

Enclosed is the general set-up of your article. The advance print will look like the enclosed journal "Reality and SALT."

We need a more comprehensive biographie [*sic*]. I will try to work out a preface, and then we will be ready to go. The article will appear again in the Summer 1977 issue.

I have sent 2 copies to Virginia . . .

Best, Jim[105]

Some observers thought that in the late 1970s Angleton continued to have access to CIA headquarters. According to John Loftus and Mark Aarons, "In 1976 one of the Vatican's historians, Father Robert Graham, filed a request for the Scattolini-Vessel files under the U.S. Freedom of Information Act."

> Someone in the CIA alerted Angleton that a request for one of his old files had been received . . . [O]nce back inside the CIA vaults, Angleton took a black Magic Marker and blotted out several lines on many of the originals . . . These numbered references fraudulently indicated to U.S. intelligence that the alleged source of the JVX documents was the Vatican's secret code room. Angleton had to obliterate each of the "cipher telegram" references before the Vatican realized that no such coded telegrams had ever been sent and tipped off the U.S. government. An investigation quickly would have determined that Angleton had continued to feed the president more Vessel forgeries even after Scattolini had been discredited . . . The man who gave Angleton permission to go back into the vaults in 1976 was the director of Central Intelligence himself, George Bush . . . Angleton, though publicly disgraced and officially retired on pension, was asked to do the job . . . He was, apparently, paid a fee for reviewing the files, based on his recognized "expertise"[106]

In February 1977, James Schlesinger said to CIA Director Admiral Stansfield Turner, "I suspect that Angleton secretly still has an office out there at Langley."[107] Even after Angleton ceased to visit Langley, his aura was felt there. According to former Church Committee staffer Burton Wides, "The CIA was still opening Angleton's file cabinets—with trembling fingers—in 1978."[108]

More publicly, Angleton joined the American Security Council, a descendent of the Committee on the Present Danger, which gradually evolved into a National Security Council-in-exile for what became the Reagan administration. Angleton was co-editor of the American Security Council's journal and a member of its board, which included Richard Bissell, Ray Cline, and other retired CIA colleagues.

He also exercised the privileges of the retired public figure by attempting to influence the writing of the history of his time. He became a favorite source for journalists working on espionage matters.

> In 1978, Andrew Boyle, an English writer, came to Washington to do research at the National Archives on a book he was preparing on the career of an Englishman rumored to have been a Soviet agent during World War II. The subject was Sir Anthony Blunt . . . During his research in Washington, Boyle met Angleton, and as a result his book, *The Climate of Treason*, includes frequent respectful references to him . . . [M]any indicators in the book, especially in the chapters on Philby and "The Fifth Man," strongly suggest his influence. Angleton probably also provided some conclusive evidence about Blunt . . .
>
> To some extent the book [*Their Trade is Treachery*, by Chapman Pincher,] was the result of a conversation between Jonathan Aitken, a Tory member of Parliament, and James Angleton in Washington in December of 1979, just a few days after Mrs. Thatcher had made her admission regarding Blunt [Thatcher had been forced by the publication of *The Climate of Treason* to disclose both Blunt's 1964 confession and his grant of immunity] . . . Angleton apparently hinted to Aitken that the Blunt revelations were just the tip of a mammoth problem, which might well lead to an investigation of penetrations of MI-5 and MI-6.[109]

Angleton was also a source for journalists and scholars interested in his own career, including Epstein, David Martin, and, of course, Robin Winks.

During this period there was a curious incident, seemingly straight from a Le Carré novel. A CIA officer, John Paisley, who had been working with a group reviewing CIA intelligence estimates, "was found shot to death in 1978, chained and weighted, in Chesapeake Bay. Angleton was intrigued by the circumstances surrounding this mysterious death. He suggested that if it had not been for some of the weights slipping off the body and consequently its surfacing, Paisley's disappearance would have been written off as a presumed suicide. Because Paisley had obtained a crucial overview of the credence given by the CIA to the different methods of assessing Soviet developments, Angleton speculated that Paisley's knowledge would have been of 'great value' to the KGB, and that if they had obtained it they might also have had an incentive to hide this success by disposing of Paisley."[110] Paisley's death was remembered some years later when William Colby himself drowned in Chesapeake Bay under equally unusual circumstances.

During Angleton's retirement, his wife, Cicely d'Autremont Angleton, returned to college after an interruption of forty years and completed a doctorate in history with a learned dissertation titled "Two Cistercian Preaching Missions to the Languedoc in the Twelfth Century," combining interests in the old Provence she and her husband had learned about from Ezra Pound and other shared interests: "This paper will treat the background of twelfth-century heresy in the south, the nature of the missions, and the appropriate sources, in order to establish the effect of the missions on the counterinsurgency of the Church, resulting in the Albigensian crusade and the Inquisition in the south of France."[111] The dissertation acknowledges, "Above all, my husband and children[, who] have given me warm support and loyal encouragement which never wavered (in spite of their bad jokes and raffish teasing, patiently endured for the sake of Eternal Fame)."[112] Two of the Angleton's daughters, Lucy and Helen, had different interests in religion: in the late 1980s they were members of the Krishna group.

By the time Cicely Angleton completed her dissertation, her husband was dying. On February 20, 1986, she wrote to Jay Lovestone that Angleton had lung cancer and was under heavy medication. Not wishing to worry their old friend, she assured him that "Jim is fine."

> In fact, remarkable. This is not to say that all is hunky dory. The fact is, however, that he has no pain, he is going out to lunch occasionally, and his spirits are very good. The old steroids made him hungry all the time and he consumed meals that Paul Bunyan would have envied. ("If you give me the leg of a chair, I'd put sauce on it and swallow it" says he.) However, they're cutting down on the steroids now, as they produce anti-immunization, which leads to pneumonia. The radiation is over, and that's a mercy. Fry your brains, that's what they do. His balance is not as good as one could wish, but he gets around. Goes out to lunch sometimes and enjoys it, with his old cronies. Right now he has a breathing machine which he plugs into the wall and then gurgles around and makes misty clouds. It's called Medi-Mist. Looks like he's smoking a water pipe or hookay, old Chinee wise man . . .
>
> He is so fond of you. Last week Gen. Vernon Walters came out to see him and had tea and Jim spoke of you to him very warmly and admiringly. The General responded in kind.
>
> Shalom and Love, Cicely[113]

James Angleton died on May 11, 1987. Cicely Angleton gave Tom Mangold an account of her husband's last days:

> By the time of his final admission to the hospital a few days before his death, the sixty-nine-year-old Angleton was in pain . . . He had already

told Cicely that he wanted "to go into the woods on my own like an Indian and deal with the end of my life, like an Apache." In some fashion, he was granted this wish. Very near the end, Angleton suddenly sat up in bed, bolt upright, with his eyes closed, and began intoning an American Indian death chant, uttering incomprehensible words with an Apache inflection. When he had finished, he lay back on his bed without a word of explanation . . .

"He was an Apache to the end," Cicely Angleton observes. "He never complained. He took his punishments without a murmur."

And then "Angleton suddenly said to Cicely in a soft voice, 'I've made so many mistakes.'"[114]

If we view Angleton simply as the ideal type of the intelligence profession, his career fits within a certain typology. "As William C. Sullivan also pointed out, many intelligence officers had been imbued with a 'war psychology.' 'Legality was not questioned,' he said, 'it was not an issue' . . . Sullivan attributes much of this attitude to the molding influence of World War II upon young intelligence agents who later rose to positions of influence in the intelligence community."[115] Moving without pause from anti-Nazi efforts in London's forcing-bed of counterintelligence, the XX Committee, to chaotic Italy and then on to Cold War Washington, the Apache warrior fought as hard and as long as he could. He was finally defeated not by the KGB, but by forces within his own Agency that had gradually grown in strength in opposition to his own unyielding temperament.

As soon as Angleton had been forced into retirement, William Colby and his allies had dismantled the counterintelligence apparatus that he had created. "The intentional diminution of counterintelligence in the post-Angleton era created a culture in which most counterintelligence positions were accorded lower esteem than positions directly involved in recruitment operations."[116] This seemed, for a time, to be justified. In 1987, the year of Angleton's death, writing in the CIA's own house journal, Richards J. Heuer commented that "Concern about high-level penetration of CIA Soviet operations has been alleviated with time."[117] But Angleton's approach to counterintelligence was seemingly vindicated by events in the late 1980s and 1990s, when his worst fears were realized. There was indeed a mole in the Agency. Proof of trouble sufficient even for the post-Angletonian CIA arrived when, "after the breaching of the Berlin Wall in November 1989, West German officials captured many secret documents from the East German intelligence service, known as the Stasi . . . The East Germans had recruited Bonn's top CI officer as a mole . . . Over the last decade . . . communist counterspies had identified, exposed, or otherwise compromised every CIA agent in East Germany."[118]

As Markus Wolf remarked, with some satisfaction, "By the late 1980s, we were in the enviable position of knowing that not a single CIA agent had worked in East Germany without having been turned into a double agent or working for us from the start."[119] Not that this was all attributable to the genius of Markus Wolf. As it turned out, "a small group of officers in CIA's Soviet Division and CI Staff had been involved in most or all of the compromised operations. As in 1967 and 1986, all the suspects were quietly transferred. Among them was Rick Ames,"[120] whose father, as it happened, had worked for James Angleton. For an Agency in its dotage, such antecedents had been sufficient to place the younger Ames above suspicion. As they had once put it in MI6, "we knew his people." The problem was, "we" did not know the officer himself.

In his account of the Ames affair, David Wise wrote, "The very CIA official in charge of detecting Soviet intelligence operations against the agency worldwide, the man who knew the identities of every mole working for the CIA inside Soviet intelligence—this officer was volunteering his services to the KGB! If the senior officials of the KGB in Yasnevo could have penetrated the organizational structure of the CIA, peered inside, and reached down deep into the woodwork to select any officer they wanted, they would have chosen Aldrich Ames. It was beyond good fortune. Ames was the kind of walk-in of which spies can only dream. He was Supermole."[121]

Ames "betrayed at least thirteen major Western agents. Eight were shot; one was gaoled; two, who were stationed abroad, defected when they were ordered back to Moscow; one, the British agent Oleg Gordievsky, made a spectacular escape from Moscow . . . under the noses of the KGB."[122] At the end of the Cold War, the ultimate endgame, the Agency, betrayed from within, was left with no assets in Moscow. Such, some would say, were the fruits of Colby's labors. Or, perhaps, the consequences of Angleton's fears. Both, of course. Markus Wolf, playing the philosopher-spy, wrote that "betrayal is poison for every intelligence service . . . a poison of distrust enters the system. Agents in the field, even if their work is unconnected to the area where the betrayal has occurred, suffer a cold chill of vulnerability when they next approach a dead-letter drop . . . or tune in to coded instruction from headquarters . . . A traitor within an intelligence service betrays much more than the men or women whose names he gives away. He betrays the whole integrity of his service."[123]

Angleton had learned this lesson early on. For him, it had a poetic name, "the wilderness of mirrors," and a human face, that of Kim Philby.

For those who do not live within the airless confines of "intelligence," "the wilderness of mirrors" is simply a phrase from a poem by T. S. Eliot, which is a reminder of the mid-twentieth-century ideological struggles that took place on the odd terrain of literary studies and cultural journalism. "It's interesting," comments Noam Chomsky, "to see the extent to which U.S. intelligence itself is controlled by the ideological framework that also governs the media and academic scholarship to a large degree."[124] Interesting and, as we have seen in regard to the intellectual formation of James Angleton, not at all surprising. William Johnson, a long-time CIA counterintelligence official, who had been at Yale with Angleton and was recruited by him from a college English department, has written that "at first glance catching spies and studying English poetry do not seem to be closely related, but they have one thing in common—both, when competently done, are based on recognizing patterns."

> It is no accident that some of the most effective British and American counterintelligence officers in World War II were drafted into that war from positions as critics of English literature. They had been trained to look for multiple meanings, to examine the assumptions hidden in words and phrases, and to grasp the whole structure of a poem or play, not just the superficial plot or statement. So the multiple meanings, the hidden assumptions and the larger pattern of a CI case were grist for their mill. I do not require my young CI officers to be able to discuss the complexities of a Shakespeare play, but if I catch them studying Brooks and Warren's *Understanding Poetry*, I do not instantly send them off to the firing range. I tell them to go read Cleanth Brooks on "the Language of Paradox," because counterintelligence is the act of paradox.[125]

The New Critics, who had trained young people like James Angleton, Johnson, and their Yale classmates, didn't just teach them pattern recognition. They attempted to inoculate their students against the historicist viewpoint, against seeing culture, in the broadest sense, as unified, where poetry, for example, is not a timeless production of "verbal icons," but exactly the product of its times and predecessors. This ideology, like others, had within itself a conflict, a contradiction, that revealed the purposes for which it was instrumental. The New Criticism and its analogues in history and the social sciences spoke simultaneously of the "integrity" of the poem and of the continuity between culture and politics, seeing the former as an instrument in the service of the latter. In the immediate postwar period, according to Howard Zinn, "The Cold War against the Soviet Union was seen as a continuity of the war against fascism, of democracy against totalitarianism . . . As I took courses in 'Western Civilization,' it did not occur to me that this very choice as a basic university curriculum came out of a nationalist bias that fitted the requirements of the Cold War. In 1945, Harvard's General Education Committee issued a report (*The Reforming of General Education*), which was described by Daniel Bell as reinforcing 'the principles of a free society . . . the definition of democracy in a world of totalitarianism . . . the need to provide a "common learning" for all Americans as a foundation of national unity.'"[126] National unity to what end?

Senator Church described the illegal and unconstitutional activities of the Internal Revenue Service, the FBI, the CIA, and other agencies during the Cold War as having brought counterintelligence methods, developed to combat the Soviet Union, home to the United States. The lists of Americans to be interned upon the declaration of a national emergency, the destruction of the alternative press, epitomized by *Ramparts* magazine, the assassination of Black Panther Party leaders, the opening of letters in the international mail, audits of listed individuals, and, perhaps, the final, ironic act of a coup d'état that replaced the Nixon government were activities similar to those that ended the constitutional government of Chile or those that destroyed the Weimar Republic. The climate of opinion that had its intellectual manifestation in a certain literary reaction to the New Deal—the "Fugitive" movement and the New Criticism—both represented and contributed to the intellectual formation of a generation which saw as its task the assertion of an idea of order as against democracy itself. Habits, methods, social networks and attitudes developed in the cauldron of the Second World War in Europe came home in the postwar period with disastrous consequences for American democracy. The transplantation of the Cold War to the domestic scene had come perilously close to success. The right to free assembly, to petition the government, to a free press and free speech had been significantly abridged. What was in effect a revolution against these restrictions, in the guise of the antiwar movement of the late 1960s and early 1970s, in the end narrowly succeeded in regaining many of those constitutional freedoms. It was a close thing and less successful than it appeared to be at the time.

The Cold War is over: "they" lost; "we" won. James Angleton and his colleagues were right: the Soviet system was inimical to democracy and intellectual life. The secret intelligence services of that system had been as powerful and every bit as effective as Angleton had thought. His lectures on "the nature of the threat" had been accurate depictions of the situation then existing. It could be argued, it is being argued by many today, that the methods used to defeat Soviet Communism were justified by the evil that threatened and by their success, and that they should be used today against a similarly determined enemy.

And yet, in the words of Justice Louis Brandeis, "Decency, security, and liberty alike demand that government officials shall be subjected to the same rules of conduct that are commands to the citizen . . . If the government becomes a lawbreaker, it breeds contempt for law; it invites every man to become a law unto himself; it invites anarchy." In the same opinion, Brandeis also noted that "experience should teach us to be most on our guard to protect liberty when the government's purposes are beneficent . . . The greatest dangers to liberty lurk in insidious encroachment by men of zeal, well-meaning but without understanding.[127]

Angleton and his colleagues, the "like-minded men" of zeal who created the Central Intelligence Agency, forgot this, and for a time liberty itself was the victim. It is a danger that recurs.

This book began with a consideration of the New Criticism, taking seriously the comments of many who knew him that Angleton's education as a student of literature was formative of Angleton as the CIA's chief of counterintelligence. Societies, even societies as large and heterogeneous as ours, have a certain coherence. Patterns of domination, for example, are replicated: from the bedroom or dining room, through the workplace (even such a rarified workplace as a university English department), to the operations of the police and judiciary. What is taught to children and young adults—and particularly the manner of teaching—matters. Angleton was educated by men paid to educate men of his class to believe—and to behave as if by second nature—that protecting the interests of that class was identical with patriotism, that those ends justified any means, until the unlimited nature of those means became the end for which they worked. Those beliefs and that behavior came close to destroying the Republic. They may yet.

# Notes

### 1. THE PLAYERS ARE INTRODUCED

1. U.S. Senate, *Oversight of U.S. Government Intelligence Functions: Hearings before the Committee on Government Operations, United States Senate, Ninety-fourth Congress, second session, January 21–February 6, 1976*, 61. Excerpts here are from J. J. Angleton's testimony on September 24, 1975.
2. Ibid., 33.
3. U.S. Senate, *Hearings before the Select Committee to Study Governmental Operations with Respect to Intelligence Activities of the United States Senate, Ninety-Fourth Congress, First Session*, vol. 2, *Huston Plan, September 23, 24, and 25, 1975*, 74.
4. Ibid., 64.
5. Ibid., 75.
6. Ibid., 65.
7. Ibid., 80–81.

### 2. YALE ENGLISH

1. Mangold, *Cold Warrior*, 32.
2. Ibid.
3. Ibid., 31.
4. Winks, *Cloak and Gown*, 329. Anyone doing research concerning James Angleton must start with Winks's elegant and sympathetic chapter, "The Theorist." Much of the material in this chapter is based on re-readings of the sources pointed to by Winks.
5. Winks, 328–30; Mangold, 31–33; Hood, "Angleton's World, 2.
6. Viswanathan, *Masks of Conquest*, 56.
7. Winks, 330–31. The younger Hugh Angleton went from Chartridge to Harrow, a notch up from Malvern. Carmen went to a school in Rome, then to the Warren School in Kent. Dolores's school was in Montreaux.
8. Mangold, 34.
9. Ibid., 36.
10. Another example of Angleton's role as photographer can be found in a letter from Mary Barnard, July 6, 1940, collection of Yale University (see note 11).
11. Yale, YCAL MSS 75, Box 1. The correspondence is listed as a "Gift of J. J. Angleton, Nov. 1941," and includes letters from Forrest Anderson, Wystan Hugh Auden, Mary Barnard, John Peale Bishop, Kay Boyle, Cleanth Brooks, John Chamberlain, E. E. Cummings, John Drummond, Lawrence Durrell, Richard Eberhart, T. S. Eliot, William Empson, Robert A. Evans, Dudley Fitts, John Gould Fletcher, Charles Henri Ford, Horace Gregory, Lawrence Hart, Alfred Kreymborg, Christopher La Farge, James Laughlin, Wyndham Lewis, Archibald MacLeish, Louis MacNeice, Andre Maurois, Marianne Moore, B. Ortiz de Montellano, Kenneth Patchen, Silas H.

Perkins, William Lyon Phelps, Ezra Pound, John C. Powys, Paul Eaton Reeve, Ivor Armstrong Richards, Lynette Roberts, Selden Rodman, Theodore Spencer, Wallace Stevens, John L. Sweeney, Genevieve Taggard, Henry Treece, Parker Tyler, Peter Viereck, Andrews Wanning, Oscar Williams, William Carlos Williams, Marya Zaturenska, and Louis Zukovsky.

12. My translation.
13. Eliot, *Christianity and Culture*, 29.
14. Ibid., 33.
15. See Isaacson and Thomas, *The Wise Men*, 77.
16. Grose, *Gentleman Spy*, 17.
17. Abramson, *Spanning the Century*, 158–59.
18. Mangold, 34.
19. The contemporary poets included Frost, de La Mare, Mark Van Doren, E. A. Robinson, Amy Lowell, H.D., Ezra Pound, Robert Bridges, T. S. Eliot, Yeats, Cummings, Tate, and MacLeish.
20. An argument could be made that Western science itself derives from philology, as an inductive method.
21. Empson, *Seven Types of Ambiguity*, 1.
22. Ibid., 6–7.
23. Brooks and Warren, xiv–xv.
24. Ibid., ix.
25. Eliot does so in "Dante," a 1929 pamphlet dedicated to Charles Maurras. See Ackroyd, *T. S. Eliot*, 179. Harold Bloom sets forth his particular notion of "strong poets" in *The Anxiety of Influence* (1973).
26. Eliot, 36.
27. See William H. Epstein, "Counter-Intelligence," 79.
28. La Salle, "An Encounter with *Furioso*," 110.
29. Yale, YCAL MSS 75, Box 1.
30. Dupee and Stade, eds., *Selected Letters of E. E. Cummings*, 121.
31. JJA to E. E. Cummings, unsigned, undated, upper left corner torn off; envelope postmarked Milano 30.viii.39/NY September 21, 1939. Harvard, Houghton Library, bMS 1823 (35).
32. October 19, 1939, J. J. Angleton Esq., Milano, Corso Venezia 73.
33. See Meyer, *Facing Reality*, 2–3.
34. October 8, 1939.
35. Harvard, Houghton Library, bMS Am 1892 (31).
36. Holzman, "Cafe CIA Roma."
37. Yale, YCAL MSS 75, Box 1. Bishop, December 1, 1939.
38. Dupee and Stade, 157 (November 16, 1939).
39. Yale, YCAL MSS 75, Box 1. Empson, 1940 postmark.
40. "New Year Issue," *Furioso* 1, no. 2 (1940): 23.
41. Ibid., classified advertisement, inside back cover. It reads, "Will anyone with information concerning obscure 'works' or mss. of EZRA POUND, please help a frantic bibliographer. Communications to J. J. Angleton, 1456 Yale Station, New Haven, Conn."

42. Jane MacKillop thinks that the "Thomas" in question might be Dylan Thomas (personal communication).
43. Harvard, Houghton Library, bMS Am 1892 (31), typed letter, n.d., *Furioso* envelope postmarked March 19, 1940.
44. Yale, YCAL MSS 75, Richard Eberhart, May 25, 1940.
45. Yale, YCAL MSS 75, T. S. Eliot, June 6, 1940.
46. Yale, YCAL MSS 75, Empson, June 12 (1940 postmark).
47. Harvard, Houghton Library, bMS Am 1892, JJA to EEC, 19 Burns St., New Haven, August 4, 1940.
48. Yale, YCAL MSS 75, Marianne Moore, 260 Cumberland Street, Brooklyn, New York, September 16, 1940.
49. Robinson, *H.D.*, 262. Bryher adopted H.D.'s daughter Perdita in 1927.
50. For example, see Harvard University, Houghton Library: Cummings, bMS Am 1892 (668), Letter from NHP to eec, October 20, 1937, NHP letterhead, 147 Cottage Street; NHP editing the *Oxford Anthology of American Literature* with William Rose Benet.
51. There is a curious Yale/Colorado/CIA connection that might warrant some exploration.
52. Harvard, Houghton Library, bMS, Am 1823 (35), JJA to E. E. Cummings, *Furioso* letterhead n.d. (September 1940? [Houghton attribution]).
53. Yale, YCAL MSS 75, Richard Eberhart, October 2, 1940.
54. Mangold, 37.
55. Dupee and Stade, 158–59.
56. Harvard, Houghton Library, bMS, Am 1823 (35), JJA to E. E. Cummings, August 16, 1941 (date in JJA's ink).
57. Yale, Beinecke Rare Book and Manuscript Library, Pearson Papers, Letters, Box H, 1941, Draft, no date, no addressee, no signature, reverse of letterhead paper, The University of Chicago, Department of Surgery.
58. Yale, Beinecke Rare Book and Manuscript Library, Pearson Papers, Letters, Box H, postcard, postmark October 6, 1941, Boston.
59. Hugh Angleton had begun to spend time with the U.S. naval attaché Rome in around 1940. The attaché was, in effect, the representative of the Office of Naval Intelligence, and the elder Angleton became something of an unofficial agent. He remained in Rome until 1941, arriving at New York the day of the attack on Pearl Harbor. Thus he was available to the FBI as a contributor to their Pound dossier. Winks, 328–30; Mangold, 31–33.
60. "Report Made at Washington, D.C., Date When Made 1–13–43, Title Dr. Ezra Pound," Federal Bureau of Investigation, Archive, Ezra Pound; Freedom of Information Act Release of Documents Concerning Ezra Pound, 100–34099, Section 2, 61–179, pp. 6–7.
61. Harvard, Houghton Library, bMS Am 1892 (31), Handwritten letter, Cpl. James Angleton 31330179, Battle Creek, Mich., Aug. 26, 1943.
62. Mangold, 37.
63. Cicely Angleton, *A Cave of Overwhelming*, 25.
64. Mangold, 38, 37; Epstein, 98.

65. Harvard, Houghton Library, bMS Am 1892 (31), Handwritten letter signed, Cpl. James Angleton 31330179.
66. Harvard, Houghton Library, bMS Am 1892 (31).
67. "Professor F. S. C. Northrop credited his discussions of poetry with Angleton as having inspired the analysis of art that is at the heart of the professor's major book." Hood, "Angleton's World."

### 3. OSS

1. Philby, *My Silent War*, 78, 81–83.
2. Ibid., 88, 126.
3. Ibid., 50.
4. Ibid., 51.
5. Ibid., 52.
6. See Kent, *Strategic Intelligence for American World Policy*, 69.
7. Brown, *Wild Bill Donovan*, 185, quoting Muggeridge, "Book Review of a Very Limited Edition."
8. Knightley, *The Master Spy*, 91.
9. Edward Jay Epstein, *Deception*, 21.
10. Andrew and Gordievsky, *KGB*, 71–72. See also Epstein, *Deception*, 23–28.
11. "The United States managed by the early 1950s to completely infiltrate undercover agents into almost all the key positions in the Communist Party USA. The infiltration was so successful, according to one of the FBI counterespionage experts, that J. Edgar Hoover opposed congressional efforts to outlaw the Communist Party. Hoover maintained that since it was already an FBI-controlled organization, it could help identify and manipulate those who joined it. In this respect, it was not unlike the Trust." Epstein, *Deception*, 117.
12. "Until 1944, being a member of the Communist Party had not automatically excluded someone from secret work . . . But early in 1944 Churchill ordered a remorseless weeding out of every single known communist from all of Britain's secret services." Knightley, 123.
13. Winterbotham, *The ULTRA Secret*, 13.
14. Jeffreys-Jones, *The CIA and American Democracy*, 17.
15. Masterman, *The Double-Cross System in the War of 1939 to 1945*, 106.
16. Brown, 184.
17. Roosevelt, "The Overseas Targets," in *War Report of the OSS*, 2:5.
18. Records of the OSS Washington Director's Office, RG226, M1642, Roll 124, National Archives.
19. Costello, *Mask of Treachery*, 423–26.
20. Smith, *OSS*, 164.
21. Bryher, *The Days of Mars*, ix–x.
22. Ibid., 117.
23. Beinecke Rare Book and Manuscript Library, Za Pearson, Section 4, Wooden File Box 1, Row 1, OSS.
24. Beinecke Rare Book and Manuscript Library, H.D. Papers, Correspondence—Incoming, Schaffner, YCAL MSS 24, Box 15, Folder 510.

25. Beinecke Rare Book and Manuscript Library, Za Pearson, Section 4, Wooden File Box 2, Row 1, OSS.
26. Hood, "Angleton's World," 2.
27. Mangold, *Cold Warrior*, 38.
28. Corvo, *The O.S.S. in Italy, 1942–1945*, 14–15.
29. Thomas Powers, *The Man Who Kept the Secrets*, 23.
30. There were at least two OSS schools, one in New York City, the other in Maryland.
31. Martin, *Wilderness of Mirrors*, 13.
32. Burton Hersh, *The Old Boys*, 107–8.
33. Ibid., 106–8.
34. Pearson, "Foreword," in Masterman, *The Double-Cross System in the War of 1939 to 1945*, xiv.
35. And yet: "the essence of counterespionage is prevention . . . the most real successes of M.I.5 are represented by the fact that certain things never happened at all." Masterman, 87.
36. "B.1.A, which handled the counterespionage operations Masterman describes, was a section of M.I.5, the British internal security agency roughly equivalent to the American F.B.I." Pearson, ix.
37. Ibid., x; Masterman, 177.
38. Pearson, xiv.
39. Masterman, 69–70.
40. Ibid., 66–67.
41. Pearson, xv.
42. Ibid., xvi.
43. Masterman, 67.
44. Wright, *Spycatcher*, 38–39.
45. Martin, 15.
46. Kent, 140–41.
47. Darling, *The Central Intelligence Agency*, 18.
48. Mangold, 41.
49. Costello, 423–26.
50. Mangold, 41.
51. See Knightley, 118, and Hood, 6, for differing views of the Angleton-Philby relationship.
52. Martin, 13.
53. Bower, *The Perfect English Spy*, 47.
54. Naftali, "ARTIFICE," 224; Smith, 98. Citing "Memorandum of a meeting between Badoglio, Colonel C. C. Carter and Major J. H. Angleton, May 10, 1944, in the Goodfellow Papers, Hoover Institution, Stanford University." The role of Angleton's father in X-2 and its impact on James Angleton's career has not, to the best of my knowledge, been explored.
55. Winks, *Cloak and Gown*, 347.
56. Another, uncorroborated, glimpse of Angleton in London: "To judge for himself the importance of records MI5 held back, Angleton allegedly seduced the appropriate file clerk and availed himself of case reports [Al Ulmer]." Burton Hersh, 177–82.

57. Haffenden, *Selected Letters of William Empson*, 145.
58. Costello, 423–26.
59. Bower, 58–59.
60. The damage to the working class and Jewish East End was partially an effect of Double Cross, which succeeded in convincing the German rocket crews that their weapons were falling much further to the west than was actually the case.
61. Yale, Beinecke, Pearson Papers, Box I, Letterhead Mrs. Hubert H. D'Autremont, S. Arizona Bank, Tucson, Arizona, July 10, 1944.
62. Yale, Beinecke, Pearson Papers, Box I, Letterhead Mrs. Hubert H. D'Autremont, S. Arizona Bank, Tucson, Arizona, October 17, 1944.
63. Martin, 15.
64. Bower, 66.
65. Yale, Beinecke, H.D. Papers, Correspondence—Incoming, Schaffner, YCAL MSS 24, Series I, Box Number 15, folder 510.

### 4. ITALY: EAVESDROPPING ON THE POPE

1. Winks, *Cloak and Gown*, 350.
2. Milano and Brogan, *Soldiers, Spies, and the Rat Line*, 108.
3. Weinberg, *A World At Arms*, 726–27.
4. Corvo, *The O.S.S. in Italy, 1942–1945*, 146.
5. "By the time Angleton got to Italy, X-2 was in a bruising tussle with its British opposite numbers [for 'liaison hegemony']. Angleton won the fight in Italy." Hood, "Angleton's World," 8.
6. See Brown, *Wild Bill Donovan*, 505.
7. Riebling, *Wedge*, 116.
8. Corvo, 149.
9. In 1944, "OSS had already run afoul of the Communists. For months Arthur Goldberg's Labor Branch had been sending funds to the clandestine French Confederation of Labor. This underground union group included a socialist majority and a Communist minority, which began a campaign to seize control of the organization. Goldberg's money had been going to the Socialist leadership; the Communists insisted that the funds be divided between the two political factions. When OSS refused, the funding operation was publicly exposed in the Communist underground press, making Goldberg's activities known to the Gestapo." Smith, *OSS*, 182.
10. Naftali, "ARTIFICE," 218.
11. Corvo, 262.
12. Angleton received the Legion of Merit award at the end of the war. "The citation credited him for directing operations that enabled his special X-2 units to apprehend over a thousand enemy agents." He also received the Italian Order of the Crown of Italy (September 1945); Order of Malta—Cross of Malta (January 1947); and Italian War Cross for Merit (April 1947). Winks, 361.
13. "The CO in Rome was Lieutenant Colonel George Van der Hoef, a corpulent, ineffectual man who was an expert mainly in wielding knife and fork at the dinner table." Corvo, 230.
14. In March 1945, First Lieutenant Angleton, chief of X-2 for Italy (and the youngest

X-2 branch chief in OSS, cleared for ULTRA), had his office at 22 Via Sicilia, three blocks from the U.S. embassy. Mangold, *Cold Warrior*, 41.

15. Martin, *Wilderness of Mirrors*, 17.
16. Naftali, 220.
17. Ibid., 222–23.
18. As we shall see, there was another "superior source" available to Angleton in Washington in the 1950s: the so-called VENONA decrypts of 1940s KGB communications.
19. Leigh, *The Wilson Plot*, 16–19.
20. Martin, 18.
21. Brown, 499–502.
22. Ibid., 501.
23. Mangold, 42.
24. "Angleton's experience in Italy affirmed the principle that liaison is the most efficient way to expand the resources of a counterespionage service." Naftali, 223.
25. "An entirely separate Allied intelligence effort was conducted by the Jewish Agency Executive, whose Mideast agents performed some of the most suicidal Balkan missions of the war for OSS and SOE while cherishing their ultimate dream of a Zionist state in Palestine." Smith, 125.
26. Naftali, 223.
27. Ibid., 225–26.
28. Brown, 276–77, 283, 285.
29. Some sources indicate that Angleton dropped the issue with Washington, but continued working along these lines in Italy. See Grose, *Gentleman Spy*, 253.
30. For a summary of the VESSEL affair see Brown, 684–703.
31. Corvo, 189–90.
32. Ibid., 213, 226–27.
33. Brown, 683.
34. Ibid., 690.
35. Ibid., 696.
36. Ibid., 700.
37. Naftali, 233.
38. Loftus and Aarons, *The Secret War against the Jews*, 94, 99.
39. Naftali, 234.
40. Ted Pierce interview, National Public Radio, *All Things Considered*, May 5, 1995.
41. "In the cage" means "in the POW cage," in a standard phrase of World War II Italy under the U.S. occupation. Author interview with Frederick Burkhardt, April 28, 1995.
42. Pound, "Canto LXXIV," in *The Cantos of Ezra Pound*, The Pisan Cantos, 27.
43. Martin, 17.
44. The chief planners of Pound's defense were MacLeish, Dudley Fitts, James Laughlin, and Merrill Moore, all of Harvard and all published in *Furioso*. See Torrey, *The Roots of Treason*, 181. Pound arrived at St. Elizabeths on December 21, 1945. See Stock, *The Life of Ezra Pound*, 407.
45. Pound and Zinnes, *Ezra Pound and the Visual Arts*, 253.

46. See Holzman, "The Ideological Origins of American Studies at Yale."
47. During the Operation Sunrise negotiations, "James Angleton warned the Vatican that its codes had been compromised" and its messages were being read by Allied intelligence. Loftus and Aarons, 88.
48. Grose, 256. Among the many indications of a generousity of spirit otherwise unnoted in accounts of Angleton, we find this in his Top Secret testimony to the Church Committee: "When Mr. Dulles left the business, he was also a very close friend of my family, and he had a very difficult time to decompress. So I used to see him on the average of two or three times a week at his house." U.S. Senate, Assassination Transcripts of the Church Committee, CD-ROM, Assassination Archives and Research Center and History Matters, 2004, Angleton Testimony, February 6, 1976, 35. In those records of his conversations with Senators and their staff in the months following his forced retirement, Angleton hardly mentions a colleague without some term of praise. There are some exceptions, of course.
49. Hersh, *The Old Boys*, 177–82.
50. Guilbaut, *How New York Stole the Idea of Modern Art*, 105.
51. Richard Gid Powers, *Not without Honor*, 193–94.
52. Warner, *CIA Cold War Records*, 81.
53. Leigh, 3–4.
54. Powers, 215.
55. See ibid., 192.
56. Naftali, 221.
57. Ibid., 219.
58. Burton Hersh, 183; National Archives R.G. 226, entry 88, Box 638, SSU official dispatch, February 21, 1946, IN33127.
59. Simpson, *Blowback*, 197.
60. Naftali, 221.
61. Mangold, 43–44.
62. Harvard, Houghton Library, bMS, Am 1823, (34), Letter: Cicely Angleton to "Marion and Cummings," dated March 16, 1946, 4814 N. 33rd, Arlington, VA.
63. Houghton Library, bMS, Am 1892, (30), folder 1, Letterhead: Hubert H. D'Autremont, South Arizona Bank, Tucson, Arizona, typed.
64. Houghton Library, bMS, Am 1892.2, (21), Cicely Angleton to Marion Morehouse Cummings.
65. Houghton Library, bMS, Am 1892.2, (21), Cicely Angleton to Marion Cummings.
66. Houghton Library, bMS Am 1892, (30), folder 1, Letterhead: Mrs. Hubert H. D'Autremont, dated July 24, 1947.

### 5. COUP D'ÉTAT

1. Grose, *Gentleman Spy*, 308.
2. Naftali, "ARTIFICE," 229–30.
3. Filippelli, *American Labor and Postwar Italy, 1943–1953*, 71.
4. Ibid., 72.
5. Richard Gid Powers, *Not without Honor*, 123.
6. Ibid., 179–80.

7. Burton Hersh, *The Old Boys*, 239.
8. Max Corvo, *The O.S.S. in Italy, 1942—1945*, 268; Filippelli, 52. Irving Brown was director of the Labor and Management Division of the Foreign Economic Administration during World War II. Filippelli, 55.
9. Morgan, *A Covert Life*, 190.
10. Filippelli, 94.
11. Jeffreys-Jones, *The CIA and American Democracy*, 49–50.
12. Grose, 281.
13. George Kennan quoted in Burton Hersh, 222.
14. Kennan's role as godfather of the CIA's covert action tradition is emphasized in Tim Weiner's *Legacy of Ashes: The History of the CIA*.
15. Evangeline Monroe, private communication, citing U.S. Department of State, *Foreign Relations of the United States, 1948*, vol. 3, *Western Europe*, 727. (Hereafter cited as U.S. Department of State, *FRUS 1948*, vol. 3.)
16. Ibid., citing U.S. Department of State, *FRUS 1948*, vol. 3, 739.
17. Ibid., citing U.S. Department of State, *FRUS 1948*, vol. 3, 766, 767.
18. Miller, "Taking Off the Gloves," 43.
19. Ibid., 43.
20. Burton Hersh, 231–32.
21. Evangeline Monroe, private communication, citing U.S. Department of State, *FRUS 1948*, vol. 3, 754.
22. Houghton Library, bMS, Am 1823.2 (11), Cicely Angleton to Marion Cummings.
23. Houghton Library, bMS, Am 1892 (205), Letter: Ann W. D'Autremont to EEC; 11.20.47; 35 East 75th Street, New York, "Dear Marion & Cummings."
24. Houghton Library, bMS, Am 1892 (30), no date [1947?], Mrs. Hubert H. D'Autremont, c/o S. Arizona Bank, Tucson, Arizona.
25. Houghton Library, bMS, Am 1892.
26. See Jeffreys-Jones, 50–52; Filippelli, 112.
27. Simpson, *Blowback*, 91.
28. Trevor Barnes, "The Secret Cold War," 399.
29. Corson, *The Armies of Ignorance*, 298.
30. Ibid., 299.
31. Miller, 45.
32. Evangeline Monroe, private communication, citing U.S. Department of State, *FRUS 1948*, vol. 3, 766.
33. Central Intelligence Agency, "The Current Situation In Italy," ORE 47/1 (16 February 1948), in Warner, *CIA Cold War Records*, 183.
34. Simpson, 61.
35. Miller, 47.
36. Cline, *Secrets, Spies, and Scholars*, 102.
37. Miller, 48.
38. "Common Cause was a prototype of, and a sister organization to, the CIA-sponsored National Committee for a Free Europe." Simpson, 222.
39. Miller, 49.
40. Ibid., 51; private communication, Gerald Monroe.

41. Miller, 52; Grose, 284–85.
42. Miller, 52.
43. Simpson, 89.
44. Miller, 55.
45. O'Brien, "Interfering with Civil Society," 436.
46. Warner, *CIA Cold War Records*, 87–89.
47. Thomas Powers, *The Man Who Kept the Secrets*, 29.
48. On Staff C, see Burton Hersh, 188.
49. Corson, 286–88.
50. Memorandum from DCI Hillenkoetter for ADSO Galloway, March 22, 1948, "Additional functions of Office of Special Operations," March 22, 1948, in Warner, *CIA Cold War Records*, 191.
51. Philby, *My Silent War*, 190–93.
52. Burton Hersh, 293.
53. Victor Marchetti, "The CIA in Italy," 168.
54. Burton Hersh, 294.
55. Leigh, *The Wilson Plot*, 16–19.
56. Hood, "Angleton's World," 8–9.
57. Richelson, *A Century of Spies*, 217.
58. Edward Jay Epstein, *Deception*, 32–33.
59. It was significant that when Colby moved to fire Angleton in 1974, he first took away Angleton's responsibility for liaison with the Israelis.
60. Cicely Angleton to Marion Cummings, April 26, 1948, Houghton Library, bMS, Am 1892.2 (21).
61. Helen [Mrs. Hubert H.] D'Autremont to Marion Cummings, Tucson, May 19, 1948, Houghton Library, bMS, Am 1892.2 (181).
62. Marchetti and Marks, *The CIA and the Cult of Intelligence*, 110–11.
63. Houghton Library, bMS, Am 1892.2 (181), Helen [Mrs. Hubert H.] D'Autremont to Marion Cummings, Tucson, July 22, 1948.
64. Houghton Library, bMS, Am 1892.2 (181), Helen [Mrs. Hubert H.] D'Autremont to Marion Cummings, 320 London Road, Duluth 5, Minnesota, September 2, 1948.
65. Mangold, *Cold Warrior*, 45.
66. The d'Autremonts lived in a house set at the end of and far back from a curving, narrow road in a kind of desert nature preserve—private, fenced, and surprisingly isolated in the middle of Tucson.
67. In 1950 the Angletons bought a house in Arlington. James Angleton's salary was $10,750, at least equivalent to that of a Yale full professor at that time. Mangold, 49.
68. Houghton Library, bMS, Am 1823.2 (11), Cicely Angleton to Marion Cummings, November 22, 1949, Tucson.
69. Bradlee, *A Good Life*, 118–19.
70. See U.S. Senate, "Supplementary Detailed Staff Reports on Foreign and Military Intelligence," in *Final Report of the Select Committee to Study Governmental Operations with Respect to Intelligence Activities*, IV:43.
71. Guilbaut, *How New York Stole the Idea of Modern Art*, 4.

72. Angleton remained on the masthead of *Furioso* after the war, and he and his sister Carmen continued to be on its subscription list for some time after that.

6. FRIENDS, LOVERS, AND SPIES

1. Annan, *Our Age*, 179.
2. Ibid., 186.
3. Ibid., 180, 236.
4. Bower, *The Perfect English Spy*, 46.
5. Modin, *My Five Cambridge Friends*, 80–81.
6. Ibid., 88.
7. Annan, 118.
8. Modin, 43.
9. Ibid., 44–45.
10. George Orwell letter to Geoffrey Gorer (September 15, 1937), *An Age Like This*, 284.
11. Annan, 224.
12. Modin, 101.
13. Ibid., 118.
14. Ibid., 119.
15. Ibid., 90–91.
16. Ibid., 90.
17. Penrose and Freeman, *Conspiracy of Silence*, 251.
18. Modin, 93.
19. It will be observed that at this point that Burgess, whatever the ex post facto doubts of writers like Annan, was a recruiter for MI6.
20. Philby, *My Secret War*, 6–12.
21. Ibid., 19.
22. The Special Operations Executive was as thoroughly infiltrated by the German as was MI6 by the Soviet intelligence services.
23. Philby, 55.
24. Modin, 61.
25. Ibid., 107.
26. Another source gives a few more details: see Bower, 40.
27. Philby, 98.
28. Ibid., 114–25.
29. Costello, *Mask of Treachery*, 510; Leigh, *The Wilson Plot*, 16–19.
30. Not otherwise elucidated; Winks, *Cloak and Gown*, 377n.
31. Costello, 517.
32. Modin, 126–27.
33. Ibid., 130–31.
34. Ibid., 133.
35. Leigh, 11.
36. Finance Division to Executive, OPC [Wisner], "CIA Responsibility and Accountability for ECA Counterpart Funds Expended by OPC," 17 October 1949, in Warner, *CIA Cold War Records*, 321–22.

37. Burton Hersh, *The Old Boys*, 262.
38. Winks, 396.
39. Burton Hersh, 273–74.
40. Ibid., 263.
41. Phillip Knightley says that James McCarger was the American representative on the committee. Knightley, *The Master Spy*, 158–59. See also Burton Hersh, 264; Winks, 397.
42. Philby, 195.
43. Burton Hersh, 264.
44. Ibid., 273–74.
45. Winks, 398–400.
46. Knightley, 161.
47. Leigh, 16–19. The account of the Albanian affair in Weiner's *Legacy of Ashes* is quite at odds with that provided by others, placing the blame for Wisner's failures on Angleton. Given Angleton's bureaucratic position at the time, this seems quite improbable.
48. Gehlen, *The Service*, 103–4.
49. Ibid., 43.
50. Ibid., 103.
51. Ibid., 108.
52. Ibid., 141–43. The official chain of command ran through James Critchfield in Germany to Richard Helms in Washington; see Helms, *A Look Over My Shoulder*, 88ff.
53. Burton Hersh, 266, 269.
54. Gehlen, 145.
55. Ibid., 161.
56. Gehlen was not the only former high-ranking German playing this role. Kennan's particular favorite was the Soviet expert and former diplomat Gustav Hilgar. See his "Observations on the Communist 'Peace Offensive,'" January 21, 1949, in Warner, 243–44.
57. Simpson, *Blowback*, 281.
58. Burton Hersh, 267.
59. Simpson, 278.
60. Grose, *Gentleman Spy*, 300.
61. Andrew and Gordievsky, *KGB*, 316–21.
62. Thomas Powers, *The Man Who Kept the Secrets*, 47.
63. Edward Jay Epstein, *Deception*, 33–41.
64. Knightley, 149.
65. Modin, 185.
66. Lamphere and Shachtman, *The FBI–KGB War*, 127.
67. Knightley, 157–58.
68. Knightley, 158.
69. Philby, 190–93.
70. Edward Jay Epstein, *Deception*, 31, 35.
71. Knightley, 151.
72. Wright, *Spycatcher*, 185.

73. Benson and Warner, *Venona*, 315–17.
74. Ibid., xxiii, xxi.
75. Harvard, Houghton Library, bMS Am 1823.1 (15), E. E. Cummings to Cicely Angleton [carbon], March 8th [1950?].
76. Lamphere and Shachtman, 229.
77. Costello, 544–45.
78. It is perhaps of interest in this regard that years later, in Moscow, "Donald Maclean . . . was more open about his part in the passing of secrets on the atomic bomb," according to George Blake. See George Blake interview at *Red Files: Secret Victories of the KGB*, Public Broadcasting System, available at www.pbs.org/redfiles/kgb/deep/interv/k_int_george_blake.htm (accessed March 31, 2007).
79. U.S. Senate, Assassination Transcripts of the Church Committee, CD-ROM, Assassination Archives and Research Center and History Matters, 2004, Szulc Testimony, June 10, 1975, 42.
80. Benson and Warner, xxv.
81. "James Angleton noted in one memo that a drunken [Guy] Burgess had referred once to having had 'an interesting binge the night before at Joe Alsop's house'"; Angleton memo, 6/18/51, quoted in Martin, *Wilderness of Mirrors*, 55. On Alsop's homosexuality see Riebling, *Wedge*, 489.
82. Penrose and Freeman, 348. Recently released British documents are amusing to read on this point, depicting frantic attempts to locate Auden, or, for that matter, Ischia.
83. Ibid., 363.
84. Knightley, 180–81.
85. Burton Hersh, 321.
86. Knightley, 180.
87. See Edward Jay Epstein, *Deception*, 37–38.
88. Lamphere and Shachtman, 237–39.
89. Knightley, 157.
90. Ibid., 1.
91. Edward Jay Epstein, *Deception*, 42.
92. The CIA's Center for the Study of Intelligence helpfully provides monographs and a periodical, *Studies in Intelligence*. These disseminate the Agency's view of matters with which it is concerned. Its 2005 monograph *Directors of Central Intelligence as Leaders of the U.S. Intelligence Community* is a "redaction" of the Agency's internal histories, removing most warts. As with interviews with serving and retired CIA officials, CIA publications can be relied upon as accurate depictions of what the Agency wishes to be known and thought about its activities.
93. See Miranda Carter, *Anthony Blunt: His Lives* (2001).
94. T. S. Eliot, "The Waste Land" (1922).

### 7. THE BUSINESS OF COUNTERESPIONAGE

1. McGarvey, *C.I.A.*, 79–83.
2. Peter Wright, the eponymous British "spycatcher," gives an entertaining account of one of these occasions. There is no particular reason why it should be untrue. Wright, *Spycatcher*, 102–4.

3. Grose, *Gentleman Spy*, 415.
4. "Chrysoberyl," in Cicely Angleton, *A Cave of Overwhelming*.
5. Wise, *Molehunt*, following 184.
6. Grose, 307.
7. Ibid., 325.
8. Burton Hersh, *The Old Boys*, 316.
9. Wise, 30–32. As for Angleton's having "bugs all over town," this may have been a special case. The rooms in which Joan Braden slept were of interest to many in Washington.
10. Ibid., 36.
11. Grose, 336.
12. There are parallels with the Mary Meyer affair in the 1960s, described in a later chapter.
13. Corson, *The Armies of Ignorance*, 57.
14. See Jackson, *Allen Welsh Dulles as Director of Central Intelligence*, 1:73–77.
15. Grose, 326.
16. Knightley, *The Master Spy*, 192–95.
17. Ibid., 198.
18. Ibid., 211.
19. Penrose and Freeman, *Conspiracy of Silence*, 373.
20. Morgan, *A Covert Life*, 245–46.
21. Riebling, *Wedge*, 136; Ambrose, *Ike's Spies*, 188.
22. See Rebecca West, *The Meaning of Treason*, 224.
23. Edward Jay Epstein, *Deception*, 103.
24. Morgan, 250.
25. Johnson, William R., "Clandestinity and Current Intelligence," 183–84.
26. Masterman, *The Double-Cross System in the War of 1939 to 1945*, 188.
27. Ibid., 34–35.
28. Edward Jay Epstein, 107.
29. Ibid., 22.
30. Burton Hersh, 357–59.
31. Wise, 42–43.
32. See Marchetti and Marks, *The CIA and the Cult of Intelligence*, 213.
33. Wise, 37.
34. Jeffreys-Jones, *The CIA and American Democracy*, 106.
35. Federal Bureau of Investigation file, James Jesus Angleton, Freedom of Information Act request, collection of the author.
36. Riebling, 137–38.
37. Cicely Angleton, *A Cave of Overwhelming*, 4.
38. Edward Jay Epstein, 16–18.
39. Wise, 33–34.
40. Latham, *Orchids for Mother*, 3. One might ask what color socks Latham would have preferred Angleton to wear with a black suit and black shoes.
41. Riebling, 141.
42. Riebling, 140–41.

43. See Loch K. Johnson, *America's Secret Power*, 29–30.
44. Ibid., 30.
45. FBI memorandum, "Intelligence Activities within the United States by Foreign Governments," March 20, 1975, cited in Church Committee, *Final Report*, 1:164, quoted in Loch K. Johnson, *America's Secret Power*, 30.
46. Gramont, *The Secret War*, 199.
47. Burton Hersh, 318.

8. FOREIGN LIAISONS

1. Morgan, *A Covert Life*, 166.
2. Ibid., 168–69.
3. Ibid., 187.
4. Ibid., 198.
5. Ibid., 213.
6. Ibid., 225.
7. Ibid., 247.
8. Jackson, *Allen Welsh Dulles as Director of Central Intelligence*, 3:105.
9. Burton Hersh, *The Old Boys*, 317.
10. Morgan, 247–48.
11. Ibid., 246–47.
12. Ibid., 255.
13. Ibid., 263.
14. See ibid., 265, 271–72, 278–79.
15. Ibid., 259–60.
16. Prados, *Lost Crusader*, 59.
17. Burton Hersh, 294.
18. Colby and Forbath, *Honorable Men*, 120–21.
19. See Loch K. Johnson, *America's Secret Power*, 45.
20. McGarvey, *C.I.A.*, 58.
21. Colby and Forbath, 130–33.
22. Andrew and Gordievsky, *KGB*, 342.
23. Seymour M. Hersh, *The Samson Option*, 144–47.
24. According to one observer, Angleton's power derived from his Israeli account, which through Soviet émigrés gave some access to information from the denied area. Author interview with Burton Wides, February 9, 1998.
25. Blitzer, *Between Washington and Jerusalem*, 96.
26. Raviv and Melman, *Every Spy a Prince*, 77–78. The account of the history of Israeli intelligence presented here is drawn from the earlier pages of this book.
27. Raviv and Melman, 76–80.
28. Grose, *Gentleman Spy*, 422.
29. Mangold, *Cold Warrior*, 362n6.
30. Hood, "Angleton's World," 10.
31. Seymour M. Hersh, 146.
32. Ibid.
33. Ibid., 144–47.

34. Wise, *Molehunt*, 246.
35. Grose, 421–23.
36. Ibid., 423.
37. Raviv and Melman, 85–91. Others put in their own claims for priority. See Gehlen, *The Service*, 229.
38. Grose, 424.
39. "Popov passed along the first solid evidence of the contents of Khrushchev's secret speech." Murphy, Kondrashev, and Bailey, *Battleground Berlin*, 270. Togliatti, the Italian Communist Party leader, was in Moscow and received a copy of the speech the night before it was delivered. When he brought it back to Rome for discussion there was consternation in the upper ranks of the PCI. Personal communication, Evangeline Monroe.
40. Burton Hersh, 381–82.
41. Cline, *Secrets, Spies, and Scholars*, 163–64.
42. Edward Jay Epstein, *Deception*, 258.
43. Colby and Forbath, 133. See also Grose, 427.
44. Wolf, *Man Without a Face*, 84.
45. Murphy, Kondrashev, and Bailey, 238.
46. Winks, *Cloak and Gown*, 413. See also Ambrose, *Ike's Spies*.
47. Burton Hersh, 363.
48. "Working Notes from the Session of the CPSU CC Presidium on 31 October 1956."
49. Grose, 437.
50. Corson, *The Armies of Ignorance*, 366–71.
51. Morgan, 283–84.
52. Coleman, *The Liberal Conspiracy*, 134; as Coleman points out, the Congress for Cultural Freedom played a certain role in the endgame.
53. Ambrose, 237–39.
54. Evan Thomas, *The Very Best Men*, 375.
55. Corson, 366–71.
56. Cold War International History Project, Woodrow Wilson International Center for Scholars, no date, unpaginated.
57. Grose, 428.
58. Ibid., 434–35.
59. Ibid., 429, 433.
60. Jackson, 5:29.
61. Ibid., 5:35. Emphasis added.
62. Raviv and Melman, 85–91.
63. Jeffreys-Jones, *The CIA and American Democracy*, 108–9.
64. Burton Hersh, 396. Loftus and Aarons argue that Amory was right, that Angleton had been blackmailed early in his career by Israeli intelligence. Loftus and Aarons, *The Secret War Against the Jews*, 144ff.
65. Grose, 438.
66. Ambrose, 274.
67. Jeffreys-Jones, 108–9.
68. Maclean, *British Foreign Policy since Suez*, 63.

69. Wright, *Spycatcher*, 98.
70. See Seymour M. Hersh, 238.
71. Blitzer, 88–89.
72. Seymour M. Hersh, 35–43.
73. Cohen, *Israel and the Bomb*, 4.
74. Ibid., 81.
75. Ibid., 49.
76. Ibid., 53–54. It would not be out of the question that the Israelis at some point gave assurances to the Arab states that their arsenal was directed not at those neighbors, but at the Soviet Union.
77. Ibid., 55.
78. Seymour M. Hersh, 35–43.
79. Cohen, 82–83.
80. Ibid., 73, 75.
81. Ibid., 85.
82. Ibid., 88–89.
83. Seymour M. Hersh, 72.
84. Cohen, 84.
85. Seymour M. Hersh, 144–47.
86. U.S. Senate, Assassination Transcripts of the Church Committee, CD-ROM, Assassination Archives and Research Center and History Matters, 2004, Szulc Testimony, June 10, 1975, 39–40.
87. Ibid., 42.
88. Cohen, 214.
89. Ibid., 117.
90. Ibid., 231–32.
91. Ibid., 273–74.
92. Riebling, *Wedge*, 419.
93. Seymour M. Hersh, 5.
94. Ibid., 185n.
95. See Lamphere and Shachtman, *The FBI-KGB War*, 279–81.
96. But see Wise, 62.
97. See U.S. Senate, *Final Report of the Select Committee to Study Governmental Operations with Respect to Intelligence Activities Together with Additional Supplemental and Separate Views*, Book IV, *Supplementary Detailed Staff Reports on Foreign and Military Intelligence* (report no. 94–755 U.S.), 47.

### 9. ILLEGALITIES: INTERNATIONAL MAIL

1. Cicely Angleton to "Cummings & Marion," July 21, 1958, Houghton Library, bMS, Am 1823 (34).
2. Riebling, *Wedge*, 141–42.
3. Ibid., 149.
4. U.S. Senate, Assassination Transcripts of the Church Committee, CD-ROM, Assassination Archives and Research Center and History Matters, 2004, Angleton Testimony, September 17, 1975, 45.

5. Riebling, *Wedge*, 148.
6. Commission on CIA Activities within the United States, *Report to the President*, 103.
7. Ibid., 104–5.
8. Memorandum from James Angleton to Richard Helms, November 21, 1955, in U.S. Senate, *Hearings before the Select Committee to Study Governmental Operations with Respect to Intelligence Activities*, vol. 2, *Huston Plan*, 357–59.
9. Morgan, *A Covert Life*, 251–52.
10. Memorandum from James Angleton to Richard Helms, November 21, 1955, in U.S. Senate, *Hearings*, vol. 2, *Huston Plan*, 357–59.
11. Commission on CIA Activities within the United States, 105.
12. Riebling, 224.
13. U.S. Senate, *Final Report of the Select Committee to Study Governmental Operations with Respect to Intelligence Activities Together with Additional Supplemental and Separate Views*, Book II, *Intelligence Activities and the Rights of Americans*, 148, quoting a memorandum from deputy chief, CI Staff, to Director Office of Security, February 1, 1962.
14. Ibid., 69.
15. U.S. Senate, *Hearings*, vol. 5, *The National Security Agency and Fourth Amendment Rights*, 20–21.
16. Ibid., 24.
17. Ibid., 59–60.
18. In a Memorandum for the Record, Subject: HT/LINGUAL, April 8, 1969, from Angleton to DCI Helms, in U.S. Senate, *Hearings*, vol. 2, *Huston Plan*, 363–64.
19. U.S. Senate, *Final Report*, Book II, *Intelligence Activities and the Rights of Americans*, 12.
20. Gordon Stewart deposition, September 30, 1975, 32, quoted in U.S. Senate, *Final Report*, Book I, *Foreign and Military Intelligence*, 295 and 295n66.
21. Memorandum for the Record, Subject: DCI's Meeting Concerning HT/LINGUAL, May 19, 1971, in U.S. Senate, *Hearings*, vol. 2, *Huston Plan*, 365, 367.
22. U.S. Senate, Assassination Transcripts of the Church Committee, CD-ROM, Assassination Archives and Research Center and History Matters, 2004, Angleton Testimony, September 17, 1975, 35.
23. Memorandum for the Record, Subject: Meeting at DCI's Office Concerning HT/LINGUAL, June 3, 1971, ibid., 368–69.
24. U.S. Senate, *Final Report*, Book II, *Intelligence Activities and the Rights of Americans*, 203.
25. Commission on CIA Activities within the United States, 111–12.
26. U.S. Senate, *Final Report*, Book II, *Intelligence Activities and the Rights of Americans*, 209.
27. Ibid., 107–8, quoting a Routing Slip from J. Edgar Hoover to James Angleton, March 10, 1972.
28. Wise, *Molehunt*, 238–39.
29. Schorr, *Clearing the Air*, 183.
30. Loch K. Johnson, *A Season of Inquiry*, 33.

31. Talking Paper, Subject: Mail Intercept Program, James Angleton, February 14, 1973, in U.S. Senate, *Hearings*, vol. 2, *Huston Plan*, 373.
32. Ibid., 374–75.
33. Ibid., 375, 381, 386.
34. See "Report of the Department of Justice Concerning Its Investigation and Prosecutorial Decisions with Respect to Central Intelligence Agency Mail Opening Activities in the United States" [AG 202–739–2028]. See also Cord Meyer, *Facing Reality*, 162–63.
35. U.S. Senate, *Final Report*, Book II, *Intelligence Activities and the Rights of Americans*, 139.

### 10. CUBA, THE KENNEDYS, AND THE MOLEHUNT

1. Ambrose, *Ike's Spies*, 40, 41.
2. Ibid., 294, quoting U.S. Senate, *Alleged Assassination Plots Involving Foreign Leaders: An Interim Report of the Select Committee to Study Governmental Operations with Respect to Intelligence Activities* (1975), 51.
3. S. Herman Horton replaced Angleton as acting chief of the Counterintelligence Staff, and therefore handled the Eichmann matter in his stead after Mossad captured Eichmann in Argentina. See Naftali, "The CIA and Eichmann's Associates."
4. R. O. L'Allier to Mr. Belmont, FBI Memorandum, November 9, 1960. Freedom of Information Act request, in the possession of the author.
5. Morgan, *A Covert Life*, 328.
6. R. O. L'Allier to Mr. Belmont, FBI Memorandum, February 28, 1961. Freedom of Information Act request, in the possession of the author.
7. Thomas Powers, *The Man Who Kept the Secrets*, 328.
8. Postcard, n.d., postmarked July 12, 1961, red ink, addressed to Mr. and Mrs. E. E. Cummings, Houghton Library, bMS, Am 1892.2 (21).
9. Merry, *Taking on the World*, 367.
10. Evan Thomas, *The Very Best Men*, 205.
11. Morgan, 327–29.
12. Thomas Powers, 111.
13. Ibid., 124.
14. But see U.S. Department of State, *Foreign Relations of the United States, 1961–1963*, vol. 10, *Cuba, 1961–1962*, section 193, "Memorandum for the Record," Washington, May 1, 1961; editorial information includes "Source: Kennedy Library, National Security Files, Countries Series, Cuba, Subjects, Taylor Report. Secret; Eyes Only; Ultrasensitive. No drafter is indicated but it was probably Colonel Tarwater." (Hereafter, this volume is cited as U.S. Department of State, *FRUS 1961–1963*, vol. 10).
15. Thomas Powers, 109–110. This was possible because the CIA's system in Cuba had been penetrated. Kessler, *Inside the CIA*, 44.
16. Eisenhower was later to deny this, but the documentation is clear. See U.S. Department of State, *FRUS 1961–1963*, vol. 10, Editorial Preface.
17. Corson, *The Armies of Ignorance*, 30.
18. U.S. Department of State, *FRUS 1961–1963*, vol. 10, section 218, "Memorandum for

the Record," Washington, May 16, 1961; editorial information includes "Source: National Defense University, Taylor Papers, Box 12, Cuba, Paramilitary Study Group Correspondence. Secret. This record of the meeting is marked as a draft, which apparently means that it was not subsequently cleared with the White House. There is no drafting information to indicate who drafted the memorandum, but internal evidence suggests that it was drafted by General Taylor."

19. Houghton Library, bMS, Am 1892.2 (21).
20. U.S. Senate, Assassination Transcripts of the Church Committee, CD-ROM, Assassination Archives and Research Center and History Matters, 2004, Angleton Testimony, June 19, 1974, 84, 87.
21. U.S. Department of State, *FRUS 1961–1963*, vol. 10, section 337, "Memorandum for the Record," Washington, May 14, 1962; editorial information includes "Source: Central Intelligence Agency, DCI (McCone) Files: Job 80-B01285A, Box 11, DCI (Helms) Chrono, Jan-July 1967. Top Secret; Eyes Only. Prepared by Sheffield Edwards, CIA Director of Security."
22. A year later the effort to assassinate Castro became the responsibility of William King Harvey. See Wise, *The American Police State*, 215.
23. Ibid., 224–25.
24. U.S. Department of State, *FRUS 1961–1963*, vol. 10, section 337.
25. Was this done? Probably. What form did it take? How long did it last? Or is it, perhaps, still in existence?
26. U.S. Department of State, *FRUS 1961–1963*, vol. 10, section 223, "Paper Prepared in the Central Intelligence Agency," Washington, May 19, 1961.
27. Ibid., section 194, "Report Prepared by a Combined Working Group from the Bureau of Intelligence and Research of the Department of State and the Office of National Estimates of the Central Intelligence Agency," Washington, May 2, 1961.
28. Ibid., section 274, "Inter-Agency Staff Study," Washington, n.d.; editorial information includes "Source: Department of State, ARA/CCA Files: Lot 66 D 501, Inter-Agency Staff Study. Secret; Eyes Only."
29. Ibid., section 337.
30. Kennedy Library, Papers of Robert F. Kennedy, Attorney General Papers, Handwritten Notes, 11/7/61.
31. Ibid., section 270, "Editorial Note." Richard Helms says that there were six hundred CIA staff and between four and five thousand contract employees assigned to Mongoose. Helms, *A Look Over My Shoulder*, 202.
32. Wright, *Spycatcher*, 159–62.
33. See U.S. Department of State, *FRUS 1961–1963*, vol. 10, section 281, "Memorandum From the Chief of Operations, Operation Mongoose (Lansdale)," Washington, December 7, 1961; editorial information includes "Source: Central Intelligence Agency, DCI (McCone) Files: Job 80-B01285A, Box 5, DCI (McCone), Caribbean Survey Group. Top Secret; Eyes Only."
34. Ibid., section 371, "Editorial Note."
35. Senate Select Committee to Study Governmental Operations with Respect to Intelligence Activities, Assassination Transcripts of the Church Committee, Angleton, June 19, 1975, 84.

36. Schorr, *Clearing the Air*, 165–66. Richard Helms gives a different version of the AM/LASH matter; Helms, 231.
37. Beschloss, *Taking Charge*, 14. "The CIA had information [on November 23, 1963,] on foreign connections to the alleged assassin, Lee Harvey Oswald, which suggested to LBJ that Kennedy may have been murdered by an international conspiracy." Ibid., 22.
38. Edward Jay Epstein, *Legend*, 103, 168–69.
39. Schorr, 147.
40. Riebling, *Wedge*, 205.
41. Schorr, 171–72. Angleton was put in charge of the investigation because "Helms wanted to remove the Agency's Soviet Division, which Angleton believed was penetrated by the KGB, from any direct role in investigating possible KGB complicity in the president's death." Riebling, 203.
42. U.S. Senate, *Hearings before the Select Committee to Study Governmental Operations with Respect to Intelligence Activities*, vol. 6, *Federal Bureau of Investigation*, 182.
43. Riebling, 207–8.
44. Ibid.
45. Beschloss, 31n2.
46. Ibid., 46n3.
47. See Heuer, "Nosenko," 380–86.
48. U.S. House of Representatives, *Hearings, Select Committee on Assassinations: Investigation of the Assassination of President John F. Kennedy*, 12:509. See Wise, *Molehunt*, 137–38.
49. Powers thought that the Soviets had learned about the flying altitude of the U-2 from Oswald. Ambrose, 290. As if simply to complicate matters, the CIA was suspicious of Powers himself. Powers was eventually cleared, or at least left to return to civilian life. He eventually died in the crash of a traffic-reporting small plane in Los Angeles, history exercising its well-known propensity to follow tragedy with farce. Riebling, 159.
50. Heuer, 380.
51. Edward Jay Epstein, *Legend*, 4.
52. Heuer, 408.
53. Evan Thomas, 306.
54. Wise, *Molehunt*, 139.
55. Edward Jay Epstein, *Legend*, 43.
56. Turner, *Secrecy and Democracy*, 44–45.
57. Edward Jay Epstein, *Legend*, 45, 258.
58. Riebling, 217–18.
59. Hood, "Angleton's World," 11. Richard Helms also endorses this account of Angleton's position. Helms, 244.
60. Edward Jay Epstein, *Deception*, 93–94.
61. Thomas Powers, 71.
62. Richelson, *A Century of Spies*, 292.
63. Wise, *Molehunt*, 143–44. Helms discounts the severity of Nosenko's confinement. Helms, 243.

64. He was, in fact, subjected to most of "the principal coercive techniques of interrogation: arrest, detention, deprivation of sensory stimuli through solitary confinement or similar methods, threats and fear, debility, pain, heightened suggestibility and hypnosis, narcosis, and induced regression" (*KUBARK Counterintelligence Interrogation* manual; see n. 65 below). This last, "induced regression," was the goal of the process. Regressing, the subject of these procedures would become dependent on his captors and seek to please them by behaving as he thought they wished, telling them, in this case, that he had lied about the KGB and Oswald, if in fact that is what he had done.

65. The manual was released through an FOIA request by the *Baltimore Sun*. Copies are available at the National Security Archive, George Washington University, and at various sites on the Internet.

66. William R. Johnson, *Thwarting Enemies at Home and Abroad*, 38.

67. Much of Nosenko's information was confirmed. See Wise, *Molehunt*, 72.

68. Edward Jay Epstein, *Legend*, 47.

69. See Riebling, 219.

70. See ibid., 232.

71. Knightley, *The Master Spy*, 206.

72. The usual story is that in August 1962, Victor Rothschild, the éminence grise of British intelligence, met Flora Solomon at a party and she told him that Philby had been a Soviet secret agent since the 1930s. She had known, according to Peter Wright, because she and Philby had been lovers in the 1930s and Philby had tried to recruit her (*Spycatcher*, 172). This is very difficult to believe. Flora Solomon, nearly thirty years older than Philby, was a prominent British business executive who had started the employee benefits program of Marks and Spencer and during the Second World War set up the British Restaurants. To suppose that Solomon and Philby had been lovers and that he thought her a good recruit for the Comintern is rather imaginative.

73. George Blake thought Elliott had been sent to Beirut to warn Philby not to return to London.

74. Costello, *Mask of Treachery*, 584–85.

75. One story runs that Angleton instructed an agent to get the typewriter ribbon used for the confession, but the agent failed to do so. In the FBI files on Philby there is a reference to an unsuccessful attempt to read *two* typewriter ribbons from Philby's house.

76. Winks, *Cloak and Gown*, 405–6.

77. Wright, 164.

78. Ibid., 37.

79. Penrose and Freeman, *Conspiracy of Silence*, 415–16.

80. Ibid., 514.

81. Wright, 345.

82. Knightley, 226.

83. Burleigh, *A Very Private Woman*, 126.

84. See Thomas Powers, 328.

85. Andrew and Gordievsky, *KGB*, 379–81.

86. See Wright, 163.
87. Ibid., 308–9.
88. Wise, *Molehunt*, 22, citing Golitsyn, *New Lies for Old.*
89. Mangold, *Cold Warrior*, 71–74.
90. Martin, *Wilderness of Mirrors*, 107.
91. See Zubok, "Spy vs. Spy."
92. But see Winks, 548.
93. Riebling, 408.
94. Golitsyn, *New Lies for Old*, 70.
95. See also Wise, *Molehunt*, 74–76.
96. Zubok.
97. Ibid.
98. Wise, *Molehunt*, 161–62.
99. Senate Select Committee to Study Governmental Operations with Respect to Intelligence Activities, Assassination Transcripts of the Church Committee, Angleton, 9.17.75, 65.
100. Ibid., 9.
101. Ibid., 15–16.
102. Riebling, 220.
103. Wise, *Molehunt*, 95.
104. Ibid., 128.
105. Ibid., 285.
106. Ibid., 290.
107. Ibid., 25–26.
108. Riebling, 221.
109. Wise, *Molehunt*, 158–61.
110. Ibid., 162–66.
111. Murphy, Kondrashev, and Bailey, *Battleground Berlin*, 110–11.
112. Ibid., 246–48.
113. Wise, *Molehunt*, 225.
114. Private communication, Jim Rutman, July 2004.
115. Wise, *Molehunt*, 292.
116. Ibid., 206.
117. Ibid., 229–30.
118. Riebling, 196–97.
119. Edward Jay Epstein, *Deception*, 65–66.
120. Wise, Molehunt, 107.
121. Merry, 402.
122. Wise, *Molehunt*, 107.
123. Edward Jay Epstein, *Deception*, 78.
124. Riebling, 212, 224.
125. See Heuer, 390.
126. Ibid., 412–13.
127. Nigel West, *The Circus*, 162–63.
128. Riebling, 243–44.

129. See Heuer, 380–86.
130. Edward Jay Epstein, *Legend*, 32.
131. Costello, 606.
132. Edward Jay Epstein, *Legend*, 36–37.
133. Ibid., 20.
134. Ibid., 264.
135. Wise, *Nightmover*, 67.
136. Nigel West, 106. See also Wise, *Molehunt*, 153.
137. Leigh, *The Wilson Plot*, 63.
138. Ibid., 82.
139. Wright, 363.
140. Leigh, 156–57.
141. Wise, *Molehunt*, 99.
142. Ibid., 109, 112–14.
143. Author interview with Benjamin Bradlee, January 12, 1998.
144. Burleigh, 125–26.
145. Ibid., 179.
146. Ibid., 128.
147. Ibid., 161, quoting Noland.
148. Ibid., 18.
149. Ibid., 204.
150. Ibid., 221.
151. Ibid., 244–45.
152. Bradlee, *A Good Life*, 266–67.
153. Ibid., 267–71.
154. Ibid., 271.
155. Author interview with Benjamin Bradlee, January 12, 1998.
156. Burleigh, 245–48. See also "In Angleton's Custody," letter to the editor from Anne Truitt and Cicely Angleton, *New York Times Book Review*, November 5, 1995, 5.
157. Burleigh, 260.
158. Beschloss, 425.
159. Ibid., 450.
160. Ibid., 462.
161. Ibid., 518.
162. See Helms, 283ff.

11. ILLEGALITIES: CHAOS

1. Thomas Powers, *The Man Who Kept the Secrets*, 192.
2. U.S. Senate, *Final Report of the Select Committee to Study Governmental Operations with Respect to Intelligence Activities Together with Additional Supplemental and Separate Views*, Book IV, *Supplementary Detailed Staff Reports on Foreign and Military Intelligence*, 68.
3. Or "Bill Colby took the position that the United States had to work with Saigon and that therefore there could be no alternative. To the extent that Diem's regime had been infiltrated by Viet Cong informants, Americans simply had to understand

and work around *that* problem." (Emphases in original.) John Prados, *Lost Crusader*, 80.

4. Author interview with William Johnson.
5. Testimony of Richard Ober to the Rockefeller Commission (last week of January and February 2, 1975), 32, available at National Security Archive, George Washington University, Angus Mackenzie files (hereafter cited as Testimony of Richard Ober to the Rockefeller Commission).
6. See Richard Gid Powers, *Not without Honor*, 321.
7. Meyer, Angleton, and Richard Helms formed a Cold War triumvirate, of which some considered Angleton the dominant member. See Saunders, *Who Paid the Piper?*, 341–42.
8. MacKenzie, *Secrets*, 17.
9. MacKenzie, *Secrets*, 17.
10. U.S. Senate, *Final Report*, Book I, *Foreign and Military Intelligence*, 185n6.
11. Evan Thomas, *The Very Best Men*, 330.
12. Ibid., 44–45.
13. MacKenzie, 18–19.
14. U.S. Senate, *Final Report*, Book II, *Intelligence Activities and the Rights of Americans*, 69.
15. Ibid., 97, quoting "Central Intelligence Agency Operations in the United States," FBI-CIA Memorandum of Understanding, February 7, 1966. The report notes further that "As part of their handling of 'internal security factors,' CIA operatives were used after 1966 to report on domestic 'dissidents' for the FBI." Ibid.
16. MacKenzie, 16–17.
17. Evan Thomas, 408n33, citing Clandestine Services History 196, "The 1967 Crisis in Covert Action Operations" (CIA), 26, 33, 59.
18. Ibid. But see U.S. Senate, *Hearings before the Select Committee to Study Governmental Operations with Respect to Intelligence Activities*, vol. 3, *Internal Revenue Service*, 28.
19. Evan Thomas, 408n33, citing Clandestine Services History 196, "The 1967 Crisis in Covert Action Operations" (CIA), 26, 33, 59.
20. Morgan, *A Covert Life*, 338.
21. Ibid., 348. Pearson's successor also attracted the attention of the CIA; see Seymour M. Hersh, *The Price of Power*, 478.
22. "Problem of Expose of CIA Clandestine Youth and Student Activities," CIA, LBJ Library, Mandatory Review, case no. NLJ 96–185, Document 1.
23. MacKenzie, 20, 23.
24. Ibid., 21.
25. Inquiries spread from the National Student Association to other areas. For example, at Columbia University, a center of antiwar activity, there was much interest in the university's connections with the Agency. See North American Congress on Latin America, *Who Rules Columbia?*, 13–17.
26. MacKenzie, 20.
27. Ibid., 24.
28. Memorandum, March 7, 1969, item 374, file, Ramparts, vol. 3, box 4, National Security Archive, George Washington University.

29. Kessler, *Inside the CIA*, 76, citing CIA memo from James Angleton to the FBI director, September 20, 1967.
30. Churchill and Vander Wall, *The COINTELPRO Papers*, 50, quoting Wilkinson, *The Era of Libertarian Repression*.
31. See Goldstein, "An American Gulag? Summary Arrest and Emergency Detention of Political Dissidents in the United States," 562–63.
32. This has a bearing on the purpose of the lists recently found to have been made by George Orwell and given by him to the British secret intelligence services.
33. Most were sold after 1957. The camp at Allentown, Pennsylvania, became a federal prison. Goldstein, 564.
34. "Although the precise results of FBI efforts cannot be determined, between 1957 and 1959, what was left of the CP was virtually destroyed by factional infighting. Even as the CP collapsed into a tiny sect of a few thousand members, FBI COINTELPRO activities increased and expanded." Churchill and Vander Wall, 41. Yet, "By the mid-1950s, the Bureau believed that the Communist Party was no longer used for Soviet espionage; it represented only a 'potential' recruiting ground for spies." U.S. Senate, *Final Report*, Book II, *Intelligence Activities and the Rights of Americans*, 43.
35. Richard Gid Powers, 274.
36. U.S. Senate, *Final Report*, Book II, *Intelligence Activities and the Rights of Americans*, 54–56.
37. Churchill and Vander Wall, 179.
38. Ibid., 96.
39. U.S. Senate, *Final Report*, Book II, *Intelligence Activities and the Rights of Americans*, 215.
40. Ibid., 68.
41. Ibid., 72–73.
42. Churchill and Vander Wall, 303.
43. U.S. Senate, *Final Report*, Book II, *Intelligence Activities and the Rights of Americans*, 13.
44. Churchill and Vander Wall, 226.
45. The CIA had two other, smaller internal security programs at the time: "Project MERRIMACK (1967 to 1973) involved the infiltration by CIA agents of Washington-based peace groups and Black activist groups . . . Project RESISTANCE (1967 to 1973) was a broad effort to obtain general background information about radical groups across the country, particularly on campuses." U.S. Senate, *Final Report*, Book II, *Intelligence Activities and the Rights of Americans*, 103.
46. MacKenzie, 211.
47. Ramparts, Box 7, MH CHAOS chron file, National Security Archive, George Washington University.
48. MacKenzie, 27.
49. Testimony of Richard Ober to the Rockefeller Commission, 406.
50. U.S. Department of State, *Foreign Relations of the United States, 1945–1950, Emergence of the Intelligence Establishment*, 540, 547.
51. U.S. Senate, *Final Report*, Book II, *Intelligence Activities and the Rights of Americans*, 100.

52. Memorandum from Richard Helms to Deputy Directors for Plans and Intelligence, and Director of Security, September 26, 1967, in U.S. Senate, *Final Report*, Book III, *Supplementary Detailed Staff Reports on Intelligence Activities and the Rights of Americans*, 698.
53. MacKenzie, 28.
54. Testimony of Richard Ober to the Rockefeller Commission, 415.
55. Ibid., 570.
56. See Commission on CIA Activities within the United States, *Report to the President*. 145–46.
57. Testimony of Richard Ober to the Rockefeller Commission, 433.
58. "Chronology of Significant MHCHAOS Correspondence," Director, Domestic Contact Service, 31 May 1973, to Chief [ ], 7, National Security Archive, George Washington University, Angus Mackenzie files. Helms, Meyer, and Angleton were here linked in a way showing quite clearly their common responsibility for MHCHAOS, as with much else.
59. U.S. Senate, *Final Report*, Book II, *Intelligence Activities and the Rights of Americans*, 100. Interpolation in original.
60. See ibid., 101.
61. Churchill and Vander Wall, 176ff. In this way Lionel Trilling's university protected the liberal tradition.
62. Loch K. Johnson, *A Season of Inquiry*, 287n26; see also Wise, *The American Police State*, 200.
63. Riebling, *Wedge*, 268.
64. U.S. Senate, *Final Report*, Book III, *Supplementary Detailed Staff Reports on Intelligence Activities and the Rights of Americans*, 720.
65. Wise, *The American Police State*, 172n.
66. Riebling, 274.
67. Ibid., 272–73. There is a curious account of the "burrowing of CIA moles" posted on the Internet: Verne Lyon, "Domestic Surveillance: The History of Operation CHAOS," available at http://www.serendipity.li/cia/lyon.html (accessed May 9, 2007).
68. U.S. Senate, *Final Report*, Book II, *Intelligence Activities and the Rights of Americans*, 99.
69. As noted in a memorandum of June 9, 1970 (p. 9), from Richard Ober to James Angleton. Ibid., 98.
70. Ibid., 79–80.
71. Jeffreys-Jones, *The CIA and American Democracy*, 167–68.
72. As the Rockefeller Commission's report had it, "During six years, the Operation compiled some 13,000 different [personnel] files, including files on 7,200 American citizens. The documents in these files and related materials included the names of more than 300,000 persons and organizations, which were entered into a computerized index." Commission on CIA Activities within the United States, 130.
73. Testimony of Richard Ober to the Rockefeller Commission, 428.
74. U.S. Senate, *Final Report*, Book II, *Intelligence Activities and the Rights of Americans*, 98. Interpolation in original.

75. Ibid., 91–92.
76. Loch K. Johnson, *America's Secret Power*, 136, 701.
77. U.S. Senate, *Final Report*, Book III, *Supplementary Detailed Staff Reports on Intelligence Activities and the Rights of Americans*, 701–2.
78. Commission on CIA Activities within the United States, 139.
79. Testimony of Richard Ober to the Rockefeller Commission, 420–24.
80. Ibid., 448. We can find an account of this or a similar incident in the FBI's own files: Memorandum from Mr. W. C. Sullivan to Mr. C. D. DeLoach, March 6, 1970, in U.S. Senate, *Hearings*, vol. 2, *Huston Plan*, 346. One of many such on FBI/CIA problems.
81. Riebling, 235.
82. Ibid., 272.
83. Wise, *The American Police State*, 312.
84. Lowen, *Creating the Cold War University*.
85. U.S. Senate, *Hearings*, vol. 2, *Huston Plan*, 137–38.
86. U.S. Senate, *Final Report*, Book II, *Intelligence Activities and the Rights of Americans*, 76.
87. Ibid., 104. The report cites the FBI request as appearing in a March 10, 1972, memorandum from Hoover to Angleton.
88. Memorandum from W. C. Sullivan to C. D. DeLoach, April 14, 1970, in U.S. Senate, *Hearings*, vol. 2, *Huston Plan*, 357–58.
89. Richard Ober's testimony to the Rockefeller Commission, five years after Sullivan's meeting with Angleton, is difficult to understand except as a deliberate effort to obscure the CIA's work in the United States and its close relationship with the FBI. Testimony of Richard Ober to the Rockefeller Commission, 418.
90. Sullivan and Brown. *The Bureau*, 129.
91. Riebling, 273. The observation that Leary "did not wish to deal with the FBI" is from U.S. Senate, *Final Report*, Book III, *Supplementary Detailed Staff Reports on Intelligence Activities and the Rights of Americans*, 714, citing a Memorandum for the Record (October 21, 1970) by case officer Charles Marcules. Leary is not identified by name in the Senate report, but it is obviously him.
92. Richard Ober to the Rockefeller Commission, 446.
93. Meyer, *Facing Reality*, 215–16.
94. Commission on CIA Activities within the United States, 137.
95. Ibid., 138.
96. Ibid., 138–39.
97. Ibid., 140–41.
98. Personal recollection of the author.
99. Commission on CIA Activities within the United States, 141.
100. Testimony of Richard Ober to the Rockefeller Commission, 459–60.
101. See U.S. Senate, *Final Report*, Book III, *Supplementary Detailed Staff Reports on Intelligence Activities and the Rights of Americans*, 692.
102. Riebling, 266–67.
103. Jeffreys-Jones, 167–68.
104. Thomas Powers, 283–87.

105. U.S. Senate, *Final Report*, Book II, *Intelligence Activities and the Rights of Americans*, 181, citing a CIA report, "Definition and Assessment of Existing National Security Threat—Foreign," January 5, 1971, 3.
106. Ibid., 181 and 181n85, citing testimony of Richard Helms to the Rockefeller Commission, April 28, 1975 (2434–35), and January 13, 1975 (163–64).
107. Commission on CIA Activities within the United States, 149.
108. Evan Thomas, 322.
109. Bradlee, *A Good Life*, 287.
110. Paul Nitze remembered that "On October 21, [1967,] fifty thousand antiwar protesters marched on the Pentagon, where they confronted troops in battle gear . . . Three of my four children were among the demonstrators . . . Ten days after the march on the Pentagon, in a memorandum dated October 31, 1967, McNamara advised the President that an escalation of our role in Vietnam would produce continued but slow progress. But he questioned whether it would be possible in the current political climate to maintain our efforts for the time necessary to attain our objectives . . . [In November] McNamara decided his usefulness in the Johnson administration was over and accepted the President's offer to become president of the World Bank." Nitze, Smith, and Rearden. *From Hiroshima to Glasnost*, 269–70.
111. Similarly, "when Eagle Scouts from a troop he served as scoutmaster began dodging the draft, [Richard Helm's special assistant, Victor] Marchetti began to feel his CIA job was isolating him." MacKenzie, 43.
112. Burleigh, *A Very Private Woman*, 285.
113. Seymour M. Hersh, *The Price of Power*, 131.
114. Wise, *The American Police State*, 69.
115. Lasch, *The Agony of the American Left*, 30.
116. See Wise, *Molehunt*, 234–37.
117. Wright, *Spycatcher*, 308.
118. D. J. Brennan, Jr., to W. C. Sullivan, FBI Memorandum, September 12, 1968. FOIA FBI file on James Angleton in the possession of the author.
119. Morgan, 348. Morgan was given the FBI's Angleton files by the author, who obtained them through an FOIA request.
120. Grose, *Gentleman Spy*, 565.
121. "Services for the Honorable Allen Walsh Dulles, February 1, 1969, Georgetown Presbyterian Church—Tribute," Princeton University, Mudd Library, Allan Dulles Papers, Box 172, Re: Dulles, Allen W. Funeral 1969.
122. Author interview with Benjamin Bradlee, January 12, 1998.
123. S. J. Papich to D. J. Brennan, Jr., May 19, 1969, FOIA, FBI file on James Angleton in the possession of the author.
124. Wright, 347.
125. Haldeman, *The Ends of Power*.
126. Sullivan and Brown, 206–7.
127. Loch K. Johnson, 84–85.
128. Sullivan and Brown, 208.
129. Loch K. Johnson, 80.

130. U.S. Senate, *Final Report*, Book II, *Intelligence Activities and the Rights of Americans*, 112n538, citing a note written by Hoover on a letter from Helms to Hoover dated February 26, 1970.
131. Ibid., 112–13. The quoted passages are from a memorandum from Hoover to Helms dated March 31, 1970; a memorandum from Sullivan to DeLoach, March 30, 1970, is also cited.
132. Loch K. Johnson, 80–81.
133. U.S. Senate, *Hearings*, vol. 2, *Huston Plan*, 4.
134. The "working group" on the Huston Plan consisted of Sullivan and Brennan of the FBI, Angleton and Ober of the CIA, and their opposite numbers from NSA, DIA, Army, Navy, and Air Force intelligence. Ibid., 5.
135. See Loch K. Johnson, 140–41.
136. Ibid., 141.
137. U.S. Senate, *Final Report*, Book II, *Intelligence Activities and the Rights of Americans*, 113. Ober also prepared a study for the Interagency Committee on Intelligence (the "Huston Committee") in June 1970, "a long paper about this thick which was called 'Definition and Assessments of Existing Internal Security Threat by Foreign Groups, 15 June 1970.'" Testimony of Richard Ober to the Rockefeller Commission.
138. "Special Report: Interagency Committee on Intelligence," Chairman, J. Edgar Hoover, June 1970, in U.S. Senate, *Hearings*, vol. 2, *Huston Plan*, 151.
139. Ibid., 149, 159.
140. Huston testimony in executive session of the Church Committee, quoted in U.S. Senate, *Hearings*, vol. 2, *Huston Plan*, 45.
141. "The KGB's 1967 Annual Report, with Commentaries by Raymond Garthoff and Amy Knight," Andropov to Brezhnev, Cold War International History Project, Woodrow Wilson International Center for Scholars, Document Date: 6 May 1968.
142. Andrew and Gordievsky, *KGB*, 428.
143. Leigh, *The Wilson Plot*, 152.
144. Wright, 307–8.
145. Ibid., 346.
146. Ibid., 347.
147. Sullivan and Brown, 211.
148. Loch K. Johnson, 142.
149. See Wise, *The American Police State*, 154–56.
150. U.S. Senate, *Hearings*, vol. 2, *Huston Plan*, 20.
151. U.S. Senate, *Final Report*, Book IV, *Supplementary Detailed Staff Reports on Foreign and Military Intelligence*, 154.
152. Ibid., 168.
153. U.S. Senate, *Hearings*, vol. 2, *Huston Plan*, 21.
154. Wise, *The American Police State*, 154–56.
155. U.S. Senate, *Final Report*, Book IV, *Supplementary Detailed Staff Reports on Foreign and Military Intelligence*, 153–54.
156. U.S. Senate, *Final Report*, Book II, *Intelligence Activities and the Rights of Americans*, 115.
157. U.S. Senate, *Hearings*, vol. 2, *Huston Plan*, 9.

158. Ibid., 2. See the Interagency Committee's report concerning mail openings: "Special Report: Interagency Committee on Intelligence," Chairman, J. Edgar Hoover, June 1970, ibid. at 174, 176.
159. Loch K. Johnson, 155.
160. U.S. Senate, *Final Report,* Book II, *Intelligence Activities and the Rights of Americans,* 143.
161. U.S. Senate, *Hearings,* vol. 2, *Huston Plan,* 108. The memo referred to is found ibid., 255–57.
162. U.S. Senate, *Final Report,* Book II, *Intelligence Activities and the Rights of Americans,* 150.
163. Kutler, *Abuse of Power,* 3.
164. See Corson, *The Armies of Ignorance,* 417–18.
165. Sullivan and Brown, 217.
166. Mackenzie, 30. "Ober and FBI counterintelligence chief William Sullivan employed one special agent, Samuel Papich, just to carry thousands of daily reports by hand between FBI and CIA headquarters." Ibid., 33.
167. Ibid., 39–40.
168. U.S. Senate, *Hearings,* vol. 2, *Huston Plan,* 32.
169. U.S. Senate, *Final Report,* Book II, *Intelligence Activities and the Rights of Americans,* 126, quoting a memorandum from T. J. Smith to E. S. Miller, November 11, 1971.
170. Testimony of Richard Ober to the Rockefeller Commission, 431.
171. Commission on CIA Activities within the United States, 147.
172. Colby and Forbath, *Honorable Men,* 313–14.
173. Commission on CIA Activities within the United States, 147.
174. Churchill and Vander Wall, 228.
175. U.S. Senate, *Final Report,* Book III, *Supplementary Detailed Staff Reports on Intelligence Activities and the Rights of Americans,* 705–6.
176. Commission on CIA Activities within the United States, 148.
177. See Longaker, "Emergency Detention," and Allen, *Concentration Camps, U.S.A.*

### 12. ENDGAME

1. Thomas Powers, *The Man Who Kept the Secrets,* 324–25. Of course, this is exactly what did happen after the collapse of the Christian Democratic/Socialist governing class in the 1990s.
2. Colby and Forbath, *Honorable Men,* 243–45.
3. It was a vital position: "In the decade of the 1960's, paramilitary operations became the dominant CIA clandestine activity, surpassing covert psychological and political action in budgetary allocations by 1967." U.S. Senate, *Final Report of the Select Committee to Study Governmental Operations with Respect to Intelligence Activities together with Additional Supplemental and Separate Views,* Book IV, *Supplementary Detailed Staff Reports on Foreign and Military Intelligence,* 67.
4. Thomas Powers, 184.
5. Edward Jay Epstein, *Legend,* 329n4.
6. See Evan Thomas, *The Very Best Men,* 328–29.
7. Author interview with William Johnson. Other sources claimed that the French

national was neither Colby's mistress nor female. The latest version of this story is more damning. John Prados points to a French doctor (male) who was apprehended by the French security services in 1972 for passing documents to Soviet intelligence, and states that as a result of the investigation Angleton conducted an investigation of Colby himself. Prados, *Lost Crusader*, 80, 246–47.

8. Edward Jay Epstein, *Legend*, 272, 329.
9. Colby vigorously denied this in his autobiography. Colby and Forbath, 290.
10. Ibid., 297–98.
11. Wise, *Molehunt*, 211.
12. MacKenzie, *Secrets*, 48–49.
13. Edward Jay Epstein, *Deception*, 99.
14. See U.S. Senate, *Final Report*, Book II, *Intelligence Activities and the Rights of Americans*, 287–88.
15. Olmsted, *Challenging the Secret Government*, 30.
16. Meyer reported that "in his interview with me in October 1978, Schlesinger admitted that he had made a serious mistake in issuing a directive so sweeping in scope and so open-ended in time, and in retrospect he wished he had not done so . . . Colby had drafted the directive for his signature and . . . he had signed it as drafted." Meyer was clearly not one of Colby's admirers. Meyer, *Facing Reality* 160–62.
17. Jeffreys-Jones, *The CIA and American Democracy*, 190–91.
18. Colby and Forbath, 334.
19. Edward Jay Epstein, *Deception*, 100–101.
20. Riebling, 320.
21. Ibid., 321.
22. Wise, *Molehunt*, 239–40.
23. Morgan, *A Covert Life*, 349–50.
24. Riebling, 317.
25. U.S. Senate, *Final Report*, Book II, *Intelligence Activities and the Rights of Americans*, 6, 70.
26. Colby and Forbath, 334–35.
27. Riebling, 320–21.
28. Colby and Forbath, 364.
29. See Jeffreys-Jones, 206–7.
30. Colby and Forbath, 364–65.
31. Edward Jay Epstein, *Deception*, 100–101.
32. Colby and Forbath, 387–88.
33. Ibid.
34. Thomas Powers, 333.
35. Colby and Forbath, 396.
36. Riebling, 323.
37. Salisbury, *Without Fear or Favor*, 523. "Ultimately it transpired that instead of 10,000 dossiers on American citizens, as Hersh reported, the real total was 300,000." Ibid., 533n.
38. Seymour M. Hersh, "Huge C.I.A. Operation Reported in U.S. against Antiwar Forces," 26.

39. Ibid., 1.
40. Thomas Powers, 327.
41. Schorr, *Clearing the Air*, 135.
42. Ibid.
43. Ibid., 134–37. Angleton was no doubt actually referring to the "defenestration of Prague" incident, when a non-Communist minister of the Czech government fell, jumped, or was pushed from a window, clearing the way for the Communist takeover of the postwar Czech government.
44. Seymour M. Hersh, *The Samson Option*, 144n.
45. Edward Jay Epstein, *Deception*, 100–101.
46. Cram, *Of Moles and Molehunters*, 4.
47. See Corson, *The Armies of Ignorance*, 431.
48. Loftus and Aarons, *The Secret War against the Jews*, 320–21. Others agree with Loftus and Aarons: "CBS News reported . . . in 1975 that Angleton had lost his job in December 1974 because of policy disputes over Israel and not because of allegations of CIA domestic spying." Blitzer, *Between Washington and Jerusalem*, 89.
49. Jeffreys-Jones, 197.
50. Wise, *Molehunt*, 238.
51. Transcript, William E. Colby Oral History Interview II, June 2, 1981, by Ted Gittinger, LBJ Library, 26–27.
52. Morgan, 350. See also Holzman, "Was the Director of Central Intelligence a Soviet Agent?"
53. Meyer, 205–8.
54. Ibid.
55. Loch K. Johnson, *A Season of Inquiry* 71–72.
56. Riebling, 327.
57. Thomas Powers, 14.
58. Wolf and Melvoy, *Man without a Face*, 283.
59. See Wise, *The American Police State*, 192–93.
60. U.S. Senate, *Final Report*, Book I, *Foreign and Military Intelligence*, 2.
61. Ibid., 27.
62. Author interview with Frederick A. O. Schwarz, Jr., January 23, 1998.
63. Loch K. Johnson, *A Season of Inquiry*, 193.
64. Ibid., 82–83.
65. Olmsted, 148–49.
66. Author interview with Judge Harold Tyler, February 6, 1998. To the best of my knowledge, no other researchers spoke with Judge Tyler about his part in the effort to shield the CIA from the Church Committee investigations. Judge Tyler died in May 2005.
67. Author interview with Frederick A. O. Schwarz, Jr., January 23, 1998.
68. U.S. Senate, *Hearings before the Select Committee to Study Governmental Operations with Respect to Intelligence Activities*, vol. 2, *Huston Plan*, 52–53.
69. Ibid., 54.
70. Ibid., 57.
71. Ibid., 58–59. The use of the phrase "commander in chief" is troubling here and else-

where. The president is commander in chief of the armed forces of the United States, not of civilians like Angleton.

72. Olmsted, 142–43.
73. As quoted in U.S. Senate, *Final Report*, Book IV, *Supplementary Detailed Staff Reports on Foreign and Military Intelligence*, 148.
74. Ibid., 148–51.
75. U.S. Senate, *Hearings*, vol. 2, *Huston Plan*, 61.
76. Ibid., 61–62. Angleton was expressing his agreement with a similar statement by FBI Director Clarence M. Kelley.
77. U.S. Senate, *Hearings*, vol. 3, *Internal Revenue Service*, 14.
78. U.S. Senate, *Hearings*, vol. 2, *Huston Plan*, 74–75.
79. Ibid., 80–81.
80. Ibid., 71.
81. Ibid., 72.
82. Ibid., 72–73.
83. U.S. Senate, *Final Report*, Book IV, *Supplementary Detailed Staff Reports on Foreign and Military Intelligence*, 157–58.
84. U.S. Senate, *Oversight of U.S. Government Intelligence Functions: Hearings before the Committee on Government Operations, United States Senate, Ninety-fourth Congress, second session, January 21–February 6, 1976*, 33.
85. Loch K. Johnson, *A Season of Inquiry*, 129.
86. U.S. Senate, *Hearings*, vol. 2, *Huston Plan*, 117.
87. Olmsted, 146–47.
88. Wise, *The American Police State*, 256–57.
89. Loch K. Johnson, *A Season of Inquiry*, 108–9.
90. Ibid., 161–62.
91. Olmsted, 154–55.
92. Ibid., 182–84.
93. Loch K. Johnson, *A Season of Inquiry*, 176–77.
94. Ibid., 189.
95. Author interview with Judge Harold Tyler, February 6, 1998.
96. See Helms and Hood, *A Look Over My Shoulder*, 440ff, for Helms's account, including his belief that it was William Colby who instigated the perjury matter.
97. The Rockefeller "commission's final recommendations included modest reorganization proposals for the CIA, the creation of a joint oversight committee in Congress, and tighter executive oversight. But the commissioners did not recommend criminal sanctions—except in the case of employees who disclosed secret information." Olmsted, 85.
98. Author interview with Frederick A. O. Schwarz, Jr., January 23, 1998.
99. Author interview with Judge Harold Tyler, February 6, 1998.
100. Author interview with Senator Gary Hart, by telephone, April 21, 1998.
101. The ultimate fate of the HT/LINGUAL matter was curious. See Meyer, 162–63.
102. Edward Jay Epstein, *Deception*, 28.
103. Regarding the newsletter, see ibid., 102.
104. Cram, 6.

105. Envelope: J. A. Security and Intelligence Fund, Suite 500, 499 Capitol St., S.W., Washington, D.C. 20003, no date, postmark torn off. Lovestone files, Hoover Institution, Stanford.
106. Loftus and Aarons, 119–20, 373.
107. Turner, *Secrecy and Democracy*, 25.
108. Author interview with Burton Wides, by telephone, February 9, 1998.
109. Cram, 15–16, 27. Angleton subsequently referred Pincher to British counterintelligence's Arthur Martin and Christopher Phillpotts for further investigation.
110. Edward Jay Epstein, *Deception*, 272.
111. Cicely D'Autremont Angleton, "Two Cistercian Preaching Missions to the Languedoc in the Twelfth Century," iii.
112. Ibid., iv–v.
113. Morgan, *A Covert Life*, 367–68.
114. Mangold, *Cold Warrior*, 353.
115. U.S. Senate, *Final Report*, Book II, *Intelligence Activities and the Rights of Americans*, 144 and 144n31, citing testimony of William C. Sullivan, November 1, 1975.
116. U.S. House of Representatives Permanent Select Committee on Intelligence, *Report of Investigation: The Aldrich Ames Espionage Case*, 67.
117. Heuer, "Nosenko," 393.
118. See Riebling, 413–15.
119. Wolf and Melvoy, 285.
120. Riebling, 415.
121. Wise, *Nightmover*, 116.
122. Andrew, "His Face Radiated Kindness," 9.
123. Wolf and Melvoy, 175.
124. Chomsky, "Interview," 46.
125. William R. Johnson, *Thwarting Enemies at Home and Abroad*, 9.
126. Zinn, "The Politics of History in the Era of the Cold War," 40.
127. *Olmstead v. United States*, 277 U.S. 438 (1928), Justice Louis Brandeis, dissenting.

# Bibliography

ARCHIVES

Presidential Libraries: Gerald Ford Library, Ann Arbor, Michigan; Lyndon Baines Johnson Library, Austin, Texas; Franklin Roosevelt Library, Hyde Park, New York.

College and University Libraries: Beinecke Library and Yale University Archives, Yale University; Hoover Institution, Stanford University; Houghton Library, Harvard University; Mudd Library, Princeton University; National Security Archive, George Washington University; Vassar College Archives.

Government: Federal Bureau of Investigation; National Archives.

Other: New York Public Library.

FOIA DOCUMENTS

Federal Bureau of Investigation file, James Jesus Angleton, Freedom of Information Act request, collection of the author.

Federal Bureau of Investigation file, William Colby, Freedom of Information Act request, collection of the author.

Federal Bureau of Investigation, Archive, Ezra Pound, Freedom of Information Act Release of Documents Concerning Ezra Pound, 100–34099, Section 2, 61–179.

CENTRAL INTELLIGENCE AGENCY INTERNAL DOCUMENTS

Jackson, Wayne G. *Allen Welsh Dulles as Director of Central Intelligence, 26 February 1953–29 November 1961.* 5 vols. Washington, D.C.: Historical Staff, Central Intelligence Agency, [1973].

INTERVIEWS

Formal author interviews were held with Benjamin Bradlee, Frederick Burkhardt, Cleveland Cram, Senator Gary Hart, William Johnson, Cord Meyer, Frederick A. O. Schwarz Jr., Judge Harold Tyler, and Burton Wides.

ARTICLES AND BOOKS

Abramson, Rudy. *Spanning the Century: The Life of W. Averell Harriman, 1891–1986.* New York: William Morrow, 1992.

Ackroyd, Peter. *T. S. Eliot: A Life.* London: Hamish Hamilton, 1984.

Allen, Charles R. *Concentration Camps, U.S.A.* New York: Marzani and Munsell, 1966.

Ambrose, Stephen. *Ike's Spies: Eisenhower and the Espionage Establishment.* Garden City, N.Y.: Doubleday, 1981.

Andrew, Christopher. "His Face Radiated Kindness." *Times Literary Supplement,* May 17, 1996.

Andrew, Christopher, and Oleg Gordievsky. *KGB: The Inside Story.* London: Hodder & Stoughton, 1990.

Angleton, Cicely d'Autremont. *A Cave of Overwhelming: A Collection of Poems.* Cabin John, Md.: Britain Books, 1995.

———. "Two Cistercian Preaching Missions to the Languedoc in the Twelfth Century, 1145 and 1178." Ph.D. diss. Catholic University of America, 1984.

Angleton, James. "Golitsyn—'Indispensable Reading.'" *AFIO Periscope*, Spring 1984.

Angleton, James, and Charles J. V. Murray "On the Separation of Church and State." *American Cause*, Special Report, June 1976.

Annan, Noel. *Our Age: English Intellectuals between the World Wars—A Group Portrait.* New York: Random House, 1990.

Barnes, Trevor. "The Secret Cold War: The CIA and American Foreign Policy in Europe, 1946–1956." Part I, *Historical Journal* 24, no. 2 (1981): 399–415. Part II, *Historical Journal* 25, no. 3 (1982): 649–70.

Benson, Robert Louis, and Michael Warner, eds. *Venona: Soviet Espionage and the American Response, 1937–1957.* Washington, D.C.: National Security Agency/Central Intelligence Agency, 1996. Laguna Hills, Calif.: Aegean Park Press, 1996.

Bernstein, Carl, and Bob Woodward. *All the President's Men.* New York: Simon and Schuster, 1974.

Beschloss, Michael R., ed. *Taking Charge: The Johnson White House Tapes, 1963–1964.* New York: Simon and Schuster, 1997.

Betts, Richard K. *Soldiers, Statesmen, and Cold War Crises.* Cambridge: Harvard University Press, 1977.

Bissell, Richard M., Jr., with Jonathan E. Lewis and Frances T. Pudlo. *Reflections of a Cold Warrior: From Yalta to the Bay of Pigs.* New Haven: Yale University Press, 1996.

Blitzer, Wolf. *Between Washington and Jerusalem: A Reporter's Notebook.* New York: Oxford University Press, 1985.

Blum, William. *The CIA: A Forgotten History: US Global Interventions since World War 2.* London: Zed, 1986.

Bourdieu, Pierre. *The Field of Cultural Production: Essays on Art and Literature.* Edited and introduced by Randal Johnson. New York: Columbia University Press, 1993.

Bower, Tom. *The Perfect English Spy: Sir Dick White and the Secret War 1935–90.* London: Mandarin, 1995.

Braden, Tom. "I'm Glad the CIA Is 'Immoral.'" *Saturday Evening Post*, May 20, 1967, 10–14.

———. "What's Wrong with the CIA?" *Saturday Review*, April 5, 1975, 2.

Bradlee, Ben. *A Good Life: Newspapering and Other Adventures.* New York: Simon & Schuster, 1995.

Brightman, Carol. *Writing Dangerously: Mary McCarthy and Her World.* New York: Clarkson Potter, 1992.

———, ed. *Between Friends: The Correspondence of Hannah Arendt and Mary McCarthy, 1949–1975.* New York: Harcourt, 1995.

Brooks, Cleanth, Jr., and Robert Penn Warren. *Understanding Poetry: An Anthology for College Students.* New York: Henry Holt, 1938.

Brown, Anthony Cave. *Wild Bill Donovan: The Last Hero.* New York: Times Books, 1982.

Bryher. [Ellerman, Annie Winifred.] *The Days of Mars: A Memoir, 1940–46.* Harcourt Brace Jovanovich, 1972.

Buckley, William F., Jr. *God and Man at Yale: The Superstitions of "Academic Freedom."* Washington, D.C.: Regnery Gateway, 1986 [1951].

Burleigh, Nina. *A Very Private Woman: The Life and Unsolved Murder of Presidential Mistress Mary Meyer.* New York: Bantam, 1998.

Casillo, Robert. *The Genealogy of Demons: Anti-Semitism, Fascism, and the Myths of Ezra Pound.* Evanson, Ill.: Northwestern University Press, 1988.

Central Intelligence Retirees' Association. *CIRA Newsletter.*

Chang, Laurence, and Peter Kornbluh, eds. *The Cuban Missile Crisis, 1962: A National Security Archive Documents Reader.* New York: New Press, 1992.

Chomsky, Noam. "Interview." In *The Chomsky Reader*, edited by James Peck, 1–55. New York: Pantheon Books, 1987.

Churchill, Ward, and Jim Vander Wall. *The COINTELPRO Papers: Documents from the FBI's Secret Wars against Dissent in the United States.* Boston: South End Press, 1990.

Cline, Ray S. *Secrets, Spies, and Scholars: Blueprint of the Essential CIA.* Washington, D.C.: Acropolis, 1976.

Cohen, Avner. *Israel and the Bomb.* New York: Columbia University Press, 1998.

Colby, William, and Peter Forbath. *Honorable Men: My Life in the CIA.* New York: Simon and Schuster, 1978.

Cold War International History Project. "New Evidence on Soviet Intelligence: The KGB's 1967 Annual Report, with Commentaries by Raymond Garthoff and Amy Knight." *Cold War International History Project Bulletin* 10 (March 1998): 211–19.

Coleman, Peter. *The Liberal Conspiracy: The Congress for Cultural Freedom and the Struggle for the Mind of Postwar Europe.* New York: The Free Press, 1989.

Commission on CIA Activities within the United States. *Report to the President.* Washington, D.C.: U.S. GPO, 1975.

Cook, Blanche Wiesen. *The Declassified Eisenhower: A Divided Legacy of Peace and Political Warfare.* Garden City, N.Y.: Doubleday, 1981.

Corson, William R. *The Armies of Ignorance: The Rise of the American Intelligence Empire.* New York: Dial Press/James Wade Books, 1977.

Corvo, Max. *The O.S.S. in Italy, 1942–1945: A Personal Memoir.* New York: Praeger, 1990.

Costello, John. *Mask of Treachery.* New York: William Morrow, 1988.

Cram, Cleveland C. *Of Moles and Molehunters: A Review of Counterintelligence Literature, 1977–92.* [Washington, D.C.]: Center for the Study of Intelligence, 1993.

Darling, Arthur B. *The Central Intelligence Agency: An Instrument of Government, to 1950.* University Park: Pennsylvania State University Press, 1990.

Diamond, Sigmund. *Compromised Campus: The Collaboration of Universities with the Intelligence Community, 1945–1955.* New York: Oxford University Press, 1992.

Donner, Frank J. *The Age of Surveillance.* New York: Knopf, 1980.

Driberg, Tom. *Guy Burgess, A Portrait with Background.* London: Weidenfeld and Nicolson, 1956.

Dupee, F. W., and George Stade, eds. *Selected Letters of E. E. Cummings.* New York: Harcourt, Brace, 1969.

Eliot, T. S. *Christianity and Culture: The Idea of a Christian Society and Notes towards the Definition of Culture.* New York: Harcourt, Brace, 1949.

Empson, William. *Seven Types of Ambiguity.* New York: New Directions, 1947.

Epstein, Edward Jay. *Deception: The Invisible War between the KGB and the CIA*. New York: Simon and Schuster, 1989.

———. *Legend: The Secret World of Lee Harvey Oswald.* New York: McGraw-Hill, 1978.

Epstein, William H. "Counter-Intelligence: Cold-War Criticism and Eighteenth-Century Studies." *ELH* 57, no. 1 (Spring 1990): 63–99.

Eshed, Hagai. *One-Man Mossad: Reuven Shiloah, Father of Israeli Intelligence.* Tel Aviv: Edanim/Yediot Aharonot, 1988.

Ferris, John. "Coming in from the Cold War: The Historiography of American Intelligence, 1945–1990." *Diplomatic History* 19, no. 1 (Winter 1995): 87–115.

Filippelli, Ronald L. *American Labor and Postwar Italy, 1943–1953: A Study of Cold War Politics.* Stanford: Stanford University Press, 1989.

Freney, Denis. "Correspondent's Report" (Australian Broadcasting Corporation interview with James Angleton, June 12, 1977). In *The CIA's Australian Connection*, 75–80. Sydney: Denis Freney, 1977.

Gehlen, Reinhard. *The Service: The Memoirs of General Reinhard Gehlen.* Translated by David Irving. New York: World Publishing, 1972.

Godson, Roy, ed. *Intelligence Requirements for the 1980s: Counterintelligence.* Washington, D.C.: National Strategy Information Center, 1980.

Goldstein, Robert Justin. "An American Gulag? Summary Arrest and Emergency Detention of Political Dissidents in the United States." *Columbia Human Rights Law Review*, no. 10 (1978): 562–33.

Golitsyn, Anatoliy. *New Lies for Old: The Communist Strategy of Deception and Disinformation.* New York: Dodd, Mead, 1984.

Gramont, Sanche de. [Ted Morgan.] *The Secret War: The Story of International Espionage since World War II.* New York: G. P. Putnam's Sons, 1962.

Greenberg, Clement. "Avant-Garde and Kitsch." *Partisan Review* 6, no. 5 (Fall 1939): 34–49.

Grose, Peter. *Gentleman Spy: The Life of Allen Dulles.* London: Andre Deutsch, 1995.

Guilbaut, Serge. *How New York Stole the Idea of Modern Art: Abstract Expressionism, Freedom, and the Cold War.* Translated by Arthur Goldhammer. Chicago: University of Chicago Press, 1983.

Haffenden, John, ed. *Selected Letters of William Empson.* New York: Oxford University Press, 2006.

Haldeman, H. R. *The Ends of Power*. New York: Times Books, 1978.

———. *The Haldeman Diaries: Inside the Nixon White House.* New York: Putnam, 1994.

Halpern, Samuel, and Hayden Peake. "Did Angleton Jail Nosenko?" *International Journal of Intelligence and Counterintelligence* 3, no. 4 (Winter 1989): 451–64.

Helms, Richard, with William Hood. *A Look Over My Shoulder: A Life in the Central Intelligence Agency.* New York: Random House, 2003.

Hersh, Burton. *The Old Boys: The American Elite and the Origins of the CIA*. Charles Scribner's Sons, 1992.

Hersh, Seymour M. "The Angleton Story." *New York Times Magazine*, June 25, 1978, 13ff.

———. "Huge C.I.A. Operation Reported in U.S. Against Antiwar Forces, Other Dissidents in Nixon Years," *New York Times*, December 22, 1974.

———. *The Price of Power: Kissinger in the Nixon White House.* New York: Summit, 1983.

———. *The Samson Option: Israel, America and the Bomb.* New York: Random House, 1991.

Heuer, Richards J., Jr. "Nosenko: Five Paths to Judgment." [1987.] In *Inside CIA's Private World: Declassified Articles from the Agency's Internal Journal, 1955–1992,* edited by H. Bradford Westerfield, 379–414. New Haven: Yale University Press, 1995.

Hinsley, F. H. *British Intelligence in the Second World War.* Abridged ed. London: Cambridge University Press, 1993.

Holzman, Michael. "Cafe CIA Roma." *Prospects: An Annual Journal of American Cultural Studies* 26 (2001): 683–706.

———. "The Ideological Origins of American Studies at Yale." *American Studies* 40, no. 2 (Summer 1999): 71–91.

———. "Was the Director of Central Intelligence a Soviet Agent?" *Lobster* 51 (Summer 2006): 16–20.

Hood, William. "Angleton's World." In *Myths Surrounding James Angleton: Lessons for American Counterintelligence,* by William Hood, James Nolan, and Samuel Halpern. Washington, D.C.: Consortium for the Study of Intelligence, 1994.

———. *Mole: The True Story of the First Russian Spy to Become an American Counterspy.* Washington, D.C.: Brassey's, 1993 [1982].

Isaacson, Walter, and Evan Thomas. *The Wise Men: Six Friends and the World They Made.* New York: Simon and Schuster, 1986.

Jackson, Wayne G. *Allen Welsh Dulles as Director of Central Intelligence, 26 February 1953–29 November 1961.* 5 vols. Washington, D.C.: Historical Staff, Central Intelligence Agency, [1973].

Jacoby, Russell. *The Last Intellectuals: American Culture in the Age of Academe.* New York: Basic Books, 1987.

Jameson, Fredric. *Fables of Aggression: Wyndham Lewis, the Modernist as Fascist.* Berkeley: University of California Press, 1979.

Jeffreys-Jones, Rhodri. *The CIA and American Democracy.* New Haven: Yale University Press, 1989.

Johnson, Loch K. *America's Secret Power: The CIA in a Democratic Society.* New York: Oxford University Press, 1989.

———. *A Season of Inquiry: The Senate Intelligence Investigation.* Lexington: University Press of Kentucky, 1985.

Johnson, William R. "Clandestinity and Current Intelligence." In *Inside CIA's Private World: Declassified Articles from the Agency's Internal Journal, 1955–1992,* edited by H. Bradford Westerfield, 118–84. New Haven: Yale University Press, 1995.

———. *Thwarting Enemies at Home and Abroad: How to Be a Counterintelligence Officer.* Bethesda, Maryland: Stone Trail Press, 1987.

Judt, Tony. "Hero of His Times: The Twentieth-Century Saga of Manes Sperber" (review). *New Republic,* April 1, 1996.

Karlow, Serge Peter. *War Report of the OSS.* New York: Walker, 1976.

Kennedy, Richard S. *Dreams in the Mirror: A Biography of E. E. Cummings.* New York: Liveright, 1980.

Kent, Sherman. *Sherman Kent and the Board of National Estimates: Collected Essays.*

Edited by Donald P. Steury. Washington, D.C.: History Staff, Center for the Study of Intelligence, Central Intelligence Agency, 1994.
———. *Strategic Intelligence for American World Policy.* Princeton: Princeton University Press, 1949.
Kessler, Ronald. *Inside the CIA.* New York: Pocket Books, 1992.
Knightley, Phillip. *The Master Spy: The Story of Kim Philby.* New York: Alfred A. Knopf, 1989.
Kohler, Lotte, and Hans Saner, eds. *Hannah Arendt/Karl Jaspers: Correspondence, 1926–1969.* Translated by Robert and Rita Kimber. New York: Harcourt Brace, 1992.
Kutler, Stanley I. *Abuse of Power: The New Nixon Tapes.* New York: Free Press, 1997.
La Salle, Peter. "An Encounter with *Furioso.*" *Raritan* 12, no. 4 (Spring 1993): 109–19.
Lamphere, Robert J., and Tom Shachtman. *The FBI–KGB War: A Special Agent's Story.* New York: Random House, 1986.
Lasch, Christopher. *The Agony of the American Left.* New York: Alfred A. Knopf, 1969.
Latham, Aaron. *Orchids for Mother.* Boston: Little, Brown, 1977.
———. "Politics and the CIA—Was Angleton Spooked by State?" *New York Times,* March 10, 1975, 32–35.
Leigh, David. *The Wilson Plot: How the Spycatchers and Their American Allies Tried to Overthrow the British Government.* New York: Pantheon, 1988.
Lowen, Rebecca S. *Creating the Cold War University: The Transformation of Stanford.* Berkeley: University of California Press, 1997.
Loftus, John, and Mark Aarons. *The Secret War against the Jews: How Western Espionage Betrayed the Jewish People.* New York: St. Martin's, 1994.
Longaker, Richard. "Emergency Detention: The Generation Gap, 1950–1971." *Western Political Quarterly* 27, no. 3 (September 1974): 395–408.
MacKenzie, Angus. *Secrets: The CIA's War at Home.* Berkeley: University of California Press, 1997.
Maclean, Donald. *British Foreign Policy since Suez: 1956–1968.* London: Hodder and Stoughton, 1970.
Mangold, Tom. *Cold Warrior: James Jesus Angleton: The CIA's Master Spy Hunter.* New York: Simon & Schuster, 1991.
Marchetti, Victor. "The CIA in Italy: An Interview with Victor Marchetti." *Panorama.* Reprinted in Philip Agee and Louis Wolf, eds., *Dirty Work: The CIA in Western Europe.* Secaucus, N.J.: Lyle Stuart, 1978.
Marchetti, Victor, and John D. Marks. *The CIA and the Cult of Intelligence.* New York: Alfred A. Knopf, 1974.
Martin, David C. *Wilderness of Mirrors.* New York: Harper and Row, 1980.
Masterman, John C. *The Double-Cross System in the War of 1939 to 1945.* New Haven: Yale University Press, 1972.
McGarvey, Patrick J. *C.I.A.: The Myth and the Madness.* Baltimore: Penguin Books, 1973.
Merry, Robert W. *Taking on the World: Joseph and Stewart Alsop—Guardians of the American Century.* New York: Viking, 1996.
Meyer, Cord. *Facing Reality: From World Federalism to the CIA.* New York: Harper & Row, 1980.

Milano, James V., and Patrick Brogan. *Soldiers, Spies, and the Rat Line: America's Undeclared War against the Soviets.* Washington, D.C.: Brassey's, 1995.

Miller, James. "Taking Off the Gloves: The United States and the Italian Elections of 1948." *Diplomatic History* 7, no. 1 (Winter 1983): 35–55.

Modin, Yuri. *My Five Cambridge Friends: Burgess, Maclean, Philby, Blunt, and Cairncross—By Their KGB Controller.* With Jean-Charles Deniau and Aguieszka Ziarek. Translated by Anthony Roberts. New York: Farrar Straus Giroux, 1994.

Montague, Ludwell Lee. *General Walter Bedell Smith as Director of Central Intelligence: October 1950–February 1953.* University Park: Pennsylvania State University Press, 1992.

Morgan, Ted. *A Covert Life: Jay Lovestone, Communist, Anti-Communist, and Spymaster.* New York: Random House, 1999.

———. *The Secret War.* See Gramont, Sanche de.

Mosle, Ted. "Where Differences of Long Standing Begin." Undergraduate thesis, Yale University, 1987.

Muggeridge, Malcolm. "Book Review of a Very Limited Edition." *Esquire,* May 1966.

Murphy, David E., Sergei A. Kondrashev, and George Bailey. *Battleground Berlin: CIA vs. KGB in the Cold War.* New Haven: Yale University Press, 1997.

Naftali, Timothy J. "ARTIFICE: James Angleton and X-2 Operations in Italy." In *The Secrets War: The Office of Strategic Services in World War II,* edited by George C. Chalou. Washington, D.C.: National Archives and Records Administration, 1992.

———. "The CIA and Eichmann's Associates." In *U.S. Intelligence and the Nazis,* edited by Richard Breitman et al., 337–74. Washington, D.C.: National Archives Trust Fund Board for the Nazi War Crimes and Japanese Imperial Government Records Interagency Working Groups, 2004.

National Security Archive. *The U.S. Intelligence Community: Organization, Operations and Management, 1947–1989: Guide and Index.* Alexandria, Va.: Chadwyck-Healey, 1990.

Nitze, Paul, with Ann M. Smith and Steven L. Rearden. *From Hiroshima to Glasnost: At the Center of Decision—A Memoir.* New York: Grove Weidenfeld, 1989.

North American Congress on Latin America. *Who Rules Columbia? Original 1968 Strike Edition.* New York: NACLA, 1970. Also available online at http://www.utwatch.org/archives/whorulescolumbia.htmlusintel.

O'Brien, Kevin A. "Interfering with Civil Society: CIA and KGB Covert Political Action during the Cold War." *International Journal of Intelligence and Counterintelligence* 8, no. 4 (Winter 1995): 431–56.

O'Connor, William Van, and Stone, Edward, eds. *A Casebook on Ezra Pound.* New York: Thomas Crowell, 1959.

Olmsted, Kathryn S. *Challenging the Secret Government: The Post-Watergate Investigations of the CIA and FBI.* Chapel Hill: University of North Carolina Press, 1996.

Orgel, Stephen. In "The Status of Evidence: A Roundtable." *PMLA* 111, no. 1 (January 1996): 21–31.

Orwell, George. *An Age Like This, 1920–1940,* vol. 1 of *George Orwell: The Collected Essays,*

*Journalism & Letters*, edited by Sonia Orwell and Ian Angus. New York: Harcourt Brace Jovanovich, 1968; repr. Boston: David R. Godine, 2000.
Ostrovsky, Victor. *By Way of Deception.* New York: St. Martin's, 1990.
Pearson, Norman Holmes. *The Escape from Time: Poetry, Language and Symbol: Stein, Pound, Eliot.* Aquila Essays 11. Portree, Isle of Skye: Aquila, 1982.
———. "Foreword." In John C. Masterman, *The Double-Cross System in the War of 1939 to 1945.* New Haven: Yale University Press, 1972.
———. "The Nazi-Soviet Pact and the End of a Dream." In *America in Crisis*, edited by Daniel Aaron, 327–48. New York: Knopf, 1952.
Pelikan, Jaroslav. *The Idea of the University: A Reexamination.* New Haven: Yale University Press, 1992.
Penrose, Barrie, and Simon Freeman. *Conspiracy of Silence: The Secret Life of Anthony Blunt.* New York: Farrar, Straus and Giroux, 1987.
Philby, Kim (H. A. R.). *My Silent War.* New York: Grove Press, 1968.
Pierce, Ted. Interview, National Public Radio, "All Things Considered," May 5, 1995.
Pisani, Sallie. *The CIA and the Marshall Plan.* Lawrence: University Press of Kansas, 1991.
Pound, Ezra. *The Cantos of Ezra Pound.* New York: New Directions, 1948.
———. *Personae: Collected Shorter Poems.* New York: New Directions, 1971.
Powers, Richard Gid. *Not without Honor: The History of American Anticommunism.* New York: Free Press, 1995.
Powers, Thomas. *The Man Who Kept the Secrets: Richard Helms and the CIA.* New York: Alfred A. Knopf, 1979.
Prados, John. *Lost Crusader: The Secret Wars of CIA Director William Colby.* New York: Oxford University Press, 2003.
Procopius. *Secret History.* Translated by Richard Atwater. Ann Arbor: University of Michigan Press, 1963.
Radosh, Ronald. *American Labor and United States Foreign Policy: The Cold War in the Unions from Gompers to Lovestone.* New York: Vintage Books, 1970.
Ranelagh, John. *The Agency: The Rise and Decline of the CIA.* New York: Simon and Schuster, 1987.
Raviv, Dan, and Yossi Melman. *Every Spy a Prince: The Complete History of Israel's Intelligence Community.* Boston: Houghton Mifflin, 1990.
Redman, Tim. *Ezra Pound and Italian Fascism.* New York: Cambridge University Press, 1991.
Richelson, Jeffrey T. *A Century of Spies: Intelligence in the Twentieth Century.* New York: Oxford University Press, 1995.
Richelson, Jeffrey, and Desmond Ball. *The Ties That Bind: Intelligence Cooperation between the UKUSA Countries—the United Kingdom, the United States of America, Canada, Australia, and New Zealand.* Boston: Allen and Unwin, 1990.
Ricks, Christopher. *T. S. Eliot and Prejudice.* London: Faber and Faber, 1988.
Riebling, Mark. *Wedge: The Secret War between the FBI and the CIA.* New York: Alfred A. Knopf, 1994.
Robinson, Janice S. *H.D.: The Life and Work of an American Poet.* Boston: Houghton Mifflin, 1982.
Roosevelt, Kermit. *War Report of the OSS (Office of Strategic Services).* Prepared by

History Project, Strategic Services Unit, Office of the Assistant Secretary of War, War Department, Washington, D.C. 2 vols. New York: Walker and Company, 1976.
Salisbury, Harrison E. *Without Fear or Favor: An Uncompromising Look at the New York Times.* New York: Times Books, 1980.
Saunders, Frances Stonor. *Who Paid the Piper? The CIA and the Cultural Cold War.* London: Granta, 1999.
Schafner, Perdita. "Glass in My Typewriter." *East Hampton Star*, May 15, 1975.
Schorr, Daniel. *Clearing the Air.* Boston: Houghton Mifflin, 1977.
Simpson, Christopher. *Blowback: America's Recruitment of Nazis and Its Effects on the Cold War.* New York: Weidenfeld & Nicholson, 1988.
Smith, Richard Harris. *OSS: The Secret History of America's First Central Intelligence Agency.* Berkeley: University of California Press, 1972.
Stock, Noel. *The Life of Ezra Pound: An Expanded Edition.* San Francisco: North Point, 1982.
Sullivan, William C., with Bill Brown. *The Bureau: My Thirty Years in Hoover's FBI.* New York: W. W. Norton, 1979.
Thomas, Evan. *The Very Best Men: Four Who Dared: The Early Years of the CIA.* New York: Simon and Schuster, 1995.
Thomas, Hugh. *Suez.* New York: Harper and Row, 1966.
Thorne, C. Thomas, Jr., and David S. Patterson, eds. *Foreign Relations of the United States, 1945–1950: Emergence of the Intelligence Establishment.* Washington, D.C.: U.S. Government Printing Office, 1996.
Torrey, E. Fuller. *The Roots of Treason: Ezra Pound and the Secret of St. Elizabeths.* New York: McGraw-Hill, 1983.
Turner, Stansfield. *Secrecy and Democracy: The CIA in Transition.* Boston: Houghton Mifflin, 1985.
U.S. Central Intelligence Agency. "Israel: Foreign Intelligence and Security Services, 1979." In *Documents from the U.S. Espionage Den.* Tehran: Center for the Publication of the U.S. Espionage Den's Documents, 1982.
U.S. Department of State. *Foreign Relations of the United States, 1945–1950, Emergence of the Intelligence Establishment.* Washington, D.C.: U.S. Government Printing Office, 1996.
———. *Foreign Relations of the United States, 1948*, vol. 3, *Western Europe.* Washington, D.C.: U.S. Government Printing Office, 1974.
———. *Foreign Relations of the United States, 1961–1963*, vol. 10, *Cuba, 1961–1962.* Washington, D.C.: U.S. Government Printing Office, 1997.
U.S. House of Representatives. *Central Intelligence Agency Exemption in the Privacy Act of 1974: Hearings before the* House Committee on Government Operations, Subcommittee on Government Information and Individual Rights, *Ninety-fourth Congress, first session, March 5 and June 25, 1975.* Washington, D.C.: U.S. Government Printing Office, 1975.
———. *Hearings, Select Committee on Assassinations: Investigation of the Assassination of President John F. Kennedy.* Washington, D.C.: U.S. Government Printing Office, 1979.
———. Permanent Select Committee on Intelligence. *Report of Investigation: The Aldrich Ames Espionage Case.* Washington, D.C.: U.S. Government Printing Office, 1994.

U.S. Senate. Assassination Transcripts of the Church Committee. CD-ROM. Assassination Archives and Research Center and History Matters, 2004.
———. *Final Report of the Select Committee to Study Governmental Operations with Respect to Intelligence Activities Together with Additional Supplemental and Separate Views.* Washington, D.C.: U.S. Government Printing Office, 1976.
———. *Hearings before the Select Committee to Study Governmental Operations with Respect to Intelligence Activities.* Washington, D.C.: U.S. Government Printing Office, 1976.
———. *Oversight of U.S. Government Intelligence Functions: Hearings before the Committee on Government Operations, United States Senate, Ninety-fourth Congress, second session, January 21–February 6, 1976.* Washington, D.C.: U.S. Government Printing Office, 1976.
Viswanathan, Gauri. *Masks of Conquest: Literary Study and British Rule in India.* New York: Columbia University Press, 1989.
Warner, Michael. "Origins of the Congress for Cultural Freedom, 1949–50." *Studies in Intelligence* 38, no. 5 (1995): 89–98.
———, ed. *CIA Cold War Records: The CIA Under Harry Truman.* Washington, D.C.: History Staff, Center for the Study of Intelligence, Central Intelligence Agency, 1994.
Weinberg, Gerhard L. *A World At Arms: A Global History of World War II.* Cambridge: Cambridge University Press, 1994.
Weiner, Tim. *Legacy of Ashes: The History of the CIA.* New York: Doubleday, 2007.
West, Nigel. *The Circus: MI5 Operations 1945–1972.* New York: Stein and Day, 1983.
West, Rebecca [Cicily Isabel Fairfield]. *The Meaning of Treason.* London: Virago Press, 1982.
Westerfield, H. Bradford, ed. *Inside the CIA's Private World: Declassified Articles from the Agency's Internal Journal, 1955–1992.* New Haven: Yale University Press, 1995.
Whitfield, Stephen J. *The Culture of the Cold War.* Baltimore: Johns Hopkins University Press, 1991.
Wilkinson, Frank. *The Era of Libertarian Repression—1948 to 1973.* Akron: University of Akron Press, 1974.
Winks, Robin W. *Cloak and Gown: Scholars in the Secret War, 1939–1961.* New York: William Morrow, 1987.
Winterbotham, F. W. *The ULTRA Secret.* New York: Harper & Row, 1974.
Wise, David. *The American Police State: The Government against the People.* New York: Random House, 1976.
———. *Molehunt: The Secret Search for Traitors That Shattered the CIA.* New York: Random House, 1992.
———. *Nightmover: How Aldrich Ames Sold the CIA to the KGB for $4.6 Million.* New York: HarperCollins, 1995.
Wise, David, and Thomas B. Ross. *The Invisible Government.* New York: Random House, 1964.
Wolf, Markus, with Anne Melvoy. *Man without a Face: The Autobiography of Communism's Greatest Spymaster.* New York: Times Books, 1977.
Wolfe, Carey. The Limits of American Literary Ideology in Pound and Emerson. New York: Cambridge University Press, 1993.

"Working Notes from the Session of the CPSU CC Presidium on 31 October 1956." *Cold War International History Project Bulletin* 8–9 (Winter 1996): 393–94. Originally in TsKhSD, F. 3, Op. 12, D. 1006, ll. 15–18ob, compiled by V. N. Malin.
Wright, Peter. *Spycatcher.* New York: Viking Penguin, 1987.
Zinn, Howard. "The Politics of History in the Era of the Cold War: Repression and Resistance." In *The Cold War and the University: Toward an Intellectual History of the Postwar Years*, edited by Howard Zinn, 35–72. New York: New Press, 1997.
Zubok, Vladislav M. "Spy vs. Spy: The KGB vs. the CIA, 1960–1962." *Cold War International History Project Bulletin* 4 (Fall 1994): 22–33.

# Index